Striking a Chord

Other *For Better or For Worse*® Collections

Reality Check
With This Ring
Family Business
Graduation: A Time for Change
The Big 5-0
Sunshine and Shadow
Middle Age Spread
Growing Like a Weed
Love Just Screws Everything Up
Starting from Scratch
"There Goes My Baby!"
Things Are Looking Up . . .
What, Me Pregnant?
If This Is a Lecture, How Long Will It Be?
Pushing 40
It's All Downhill from Here
Keep the Home Fries Burning
The Last Straw
Just One More Hug
"It Must Be Nice to Be Little"
Is This "One of Those Days," Daddy?
I've Got the One-More-Washload Blues . . .

Retrospectives

Suddenly Silver: 25 Years of For Better or For Worse®
All About April
The Lives Behind the Lines: 20 Years of For Better or For Worse®
Remembering Farley: A Tribute to the Life of Our Favorite Cartoon Dog
It's the Thought That Counts . . . Fifteenth Anniversary Collection
A Look Inside . . . For Better or For Worse®: *The 10th Anniversary Collection*

Little Books

Isn't He Beautiful?
Isn't She Beautiful?
Wags and Kisses
A Perfect Christmas
Graduation: Just the Beginning!

With Andie Parton

Leaving Home
So You're Going to Be a Grandma!

Striking a Chord

A *For Better or For Worse*® Collection

by Lynn Johnston

Andrews McMeel
Publishing

Kansas City

05 06 07 08 09 BBG 10 9 8 7 6 5 4 3 2 1

ISBN: 0-7407-5315-0

Library of Congress Control Number: 2004116373

www.FBorFW.com

───── **ATTENTION: SCHOOLS AND BUSINESSES** ─────

Andrews McMeel books are available at quantity discounts with bulk purchase for educational, business, or sales promotional use. For information, please write to: Special Sales Department, Andrews McMeel Publishing, 4520 Main Street, Kansas City, Missouri 64111.

For my dad

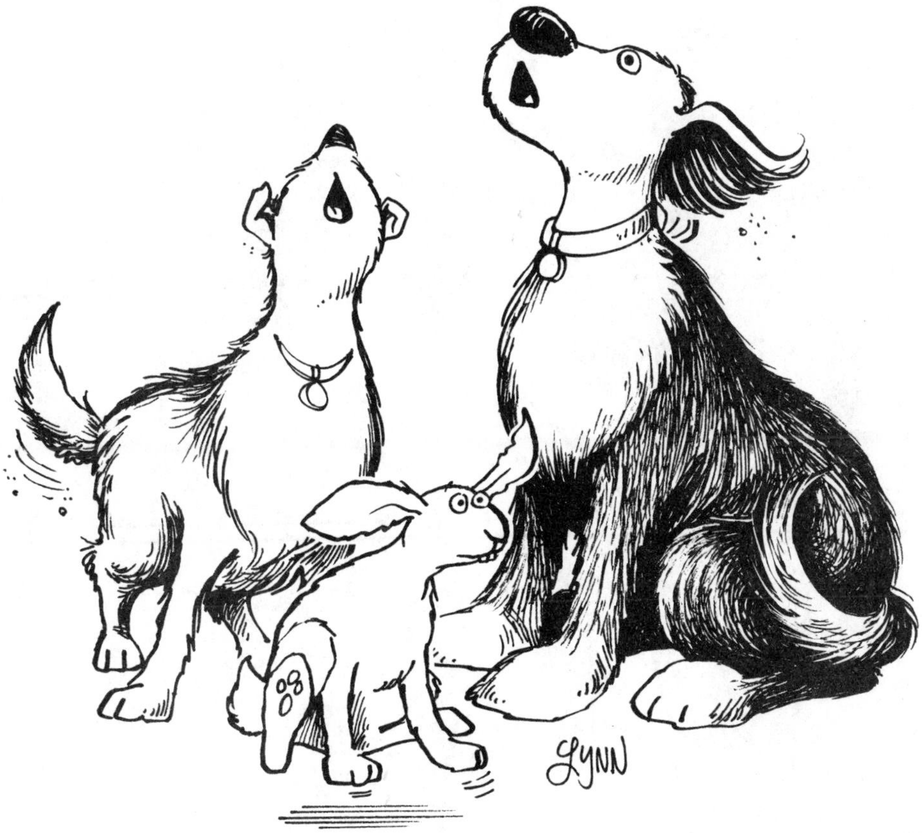
LYNN

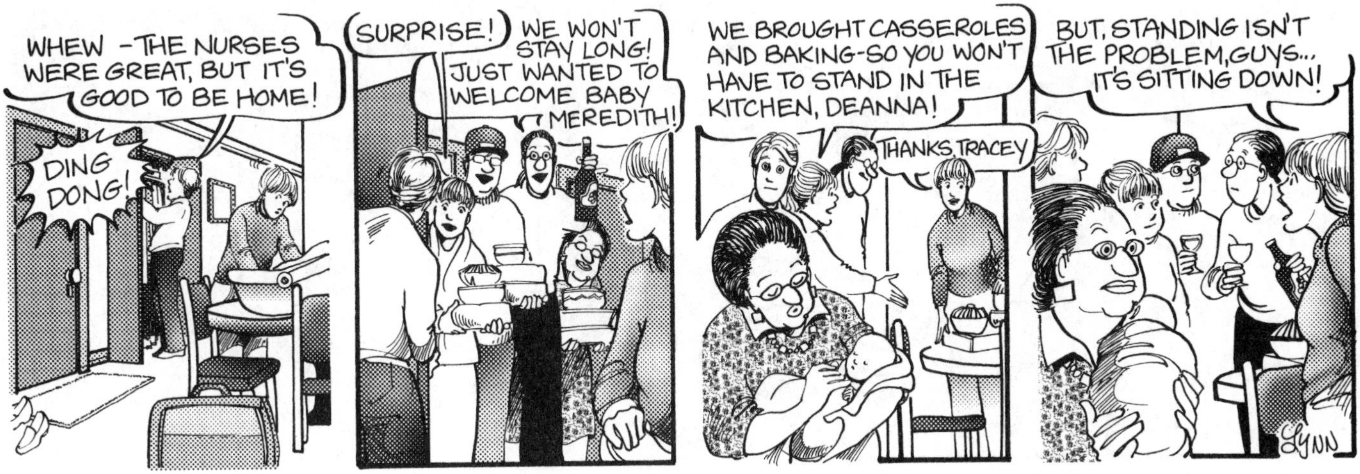
WHEW - THE NURSES WERE GREAT, BUT IT'S GOOD TO BE HOME!
DING DONG!
SURPRISE!
WE WON'T STAY LONG! JUST WANTED TO WELCOME BABY MEREDITH!
WE BROUGHT CASSEROLES AND BAKING-SO YOU WON'T HAVE TO STAND IN THE KITCHEN, DEANNA!
THANKS, TRACEY
BUT, STANDING ISN'T THE PROBLEM, GUYS... IT'S SITTING DOWN!
LYNN

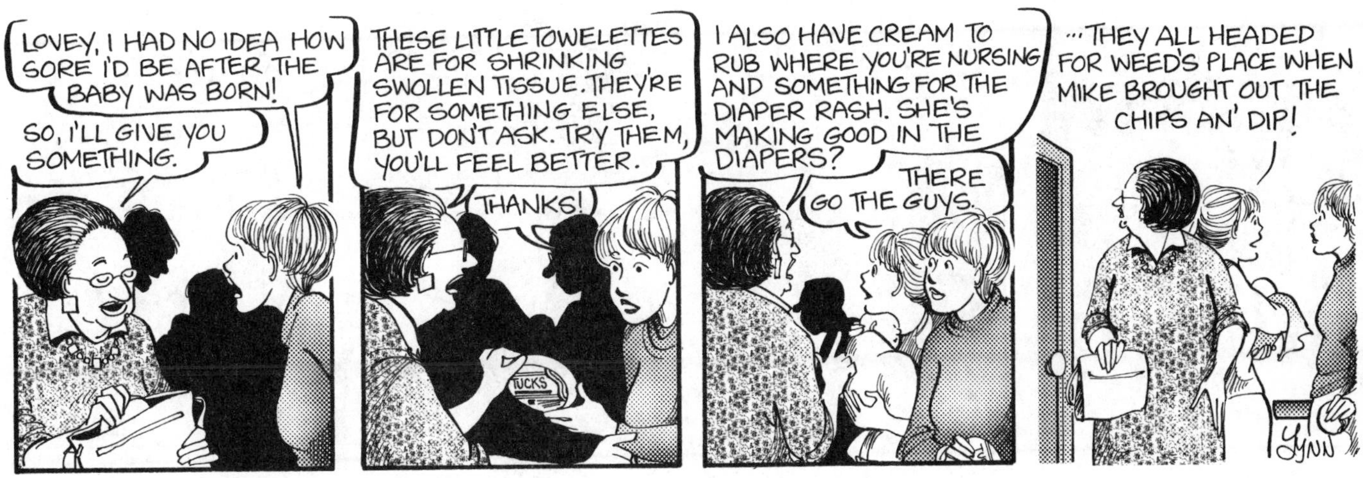
LOVEY, I HAD NO IDEA HOW SORE I'D BE AFTER THE BABY WAS BORN!
SO, I'LL GIVE YOU SOMETHING.
THESE LITTLE TOWELETTES ARE FOR SHRINKING SWOLLEN TISSUE. THEY'RE FOR SOMETHING ELSE, BUT DON'T ASK. TRY THEM, YOU'LL FEEL BETTER.
THANKS!
TUCKS
I ALSO HAVE CREAM TO RUB WHERE YOU'RE NURSING AND SOMETHING FOR THE DIAPER RASH. SHE'S MAKING GOOD IN THE DIAPERS?
THERE GO THE GUYS.
...THEY ALL HEADED FOR WEED'S PLACE WHEN MIKE BROUGHT OUT THE CHIPS AN' DIP!
LYNN

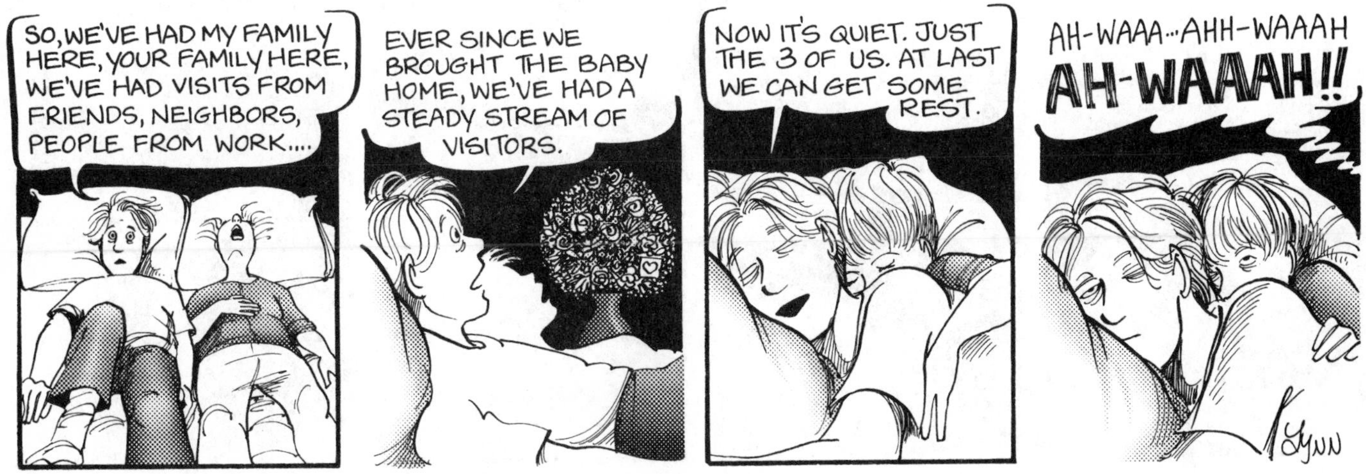
SO, WE'VE HAD MY FAMILY HERE, YOUR FAMILY HERE, WE'VE HAD VISITS FROM FRIENDS, NEIGHBORS, PEOPLE FROM WORK....
EVER SINCE WE BROUGHT THE BABY HOME, WE'VE HAD A STEADY STREAM OF VISITORS.
NOW IT'S QUIET. JUST THE 3 OF US. AT LAST WE CAN GET SOME REST.
AH-WAAA...AHH-WAAAH
AH-WAAAH!!
LYNN

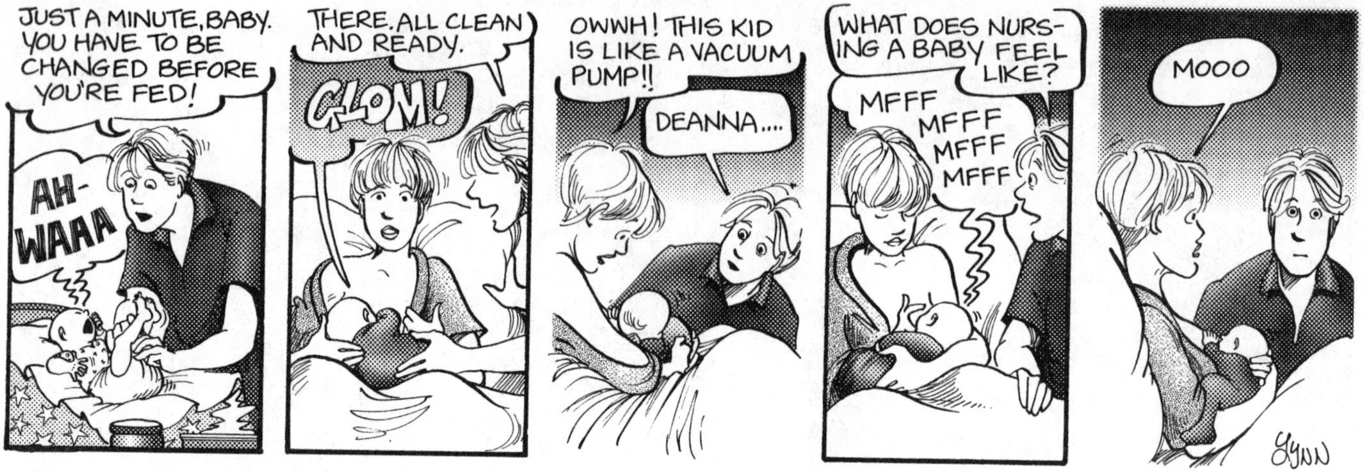
JUST A MINUTE, BABY. YOU HAVE TO BE CHANGED BEFORE YOU'RE FED!
AH-WAAA
THERE. ALL CLEAN AND READY.
GLOM!
OWWH! THIS KID IS LIKE A VACUUM PUMP!!
DEANNA....
WHAT DOES NURSING A BABY FEEL LIKE?
MFFF MFFF MFFF MFFF
MOOO
LYNN

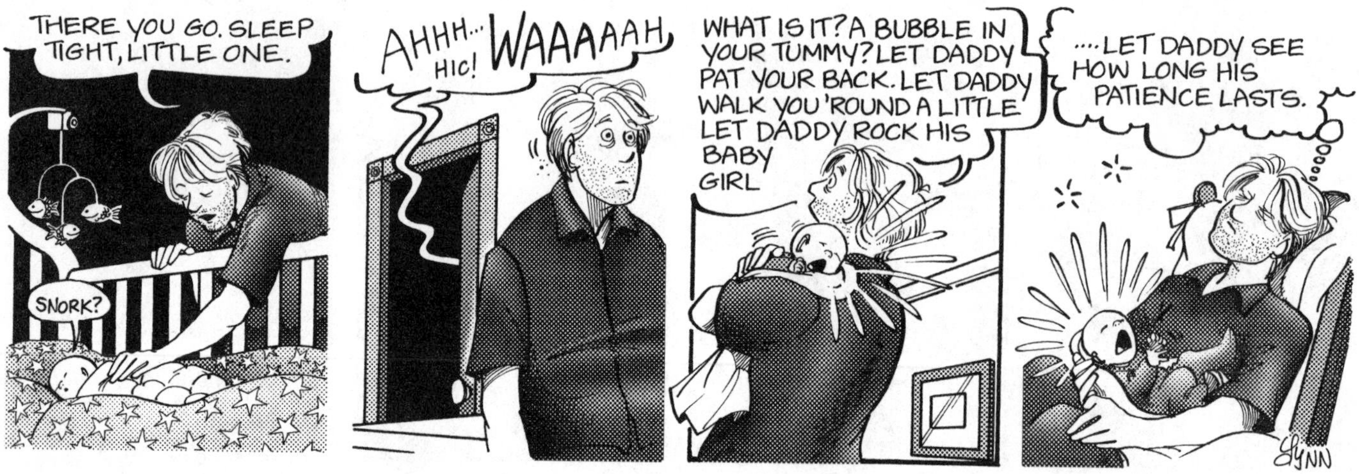
THERE YOU GO. SLEEP TIGHT, LITTLE ONE.
SNORK?
AHHH... HIC! WAAAAAH
WHAT IS IT? A BUBBLE IN YOUR TUMMY? LET DADDY PAT YOUR BACK. LET DADDY WALK YOU 'ROUND A LITTLE LET DADDY ROCK HIS BABY GIRL
....LET DADDY SEE HOW LONG HIS PATIENCE LASTS.
LYNN

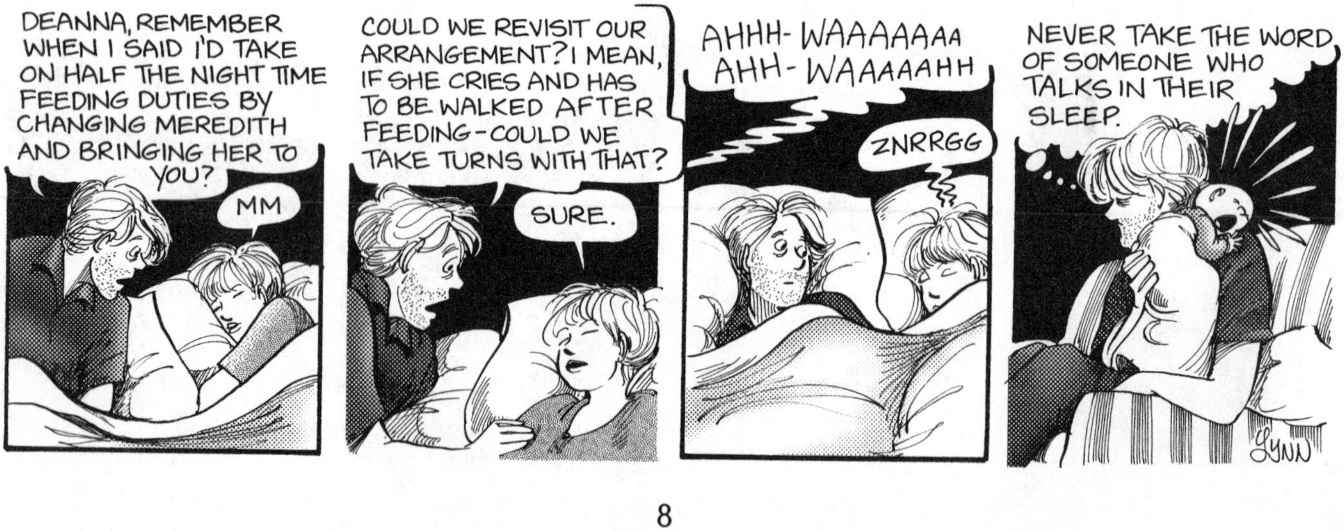
DEANNA, REMEMBER WHEN I SAID I'D TAKE ON HALF THE NIGHT TIME FEEDING DUTIES BY CHANGING MEREDITH AND BRINGING HER TO YOU?
MM
COULD WE REVISIT OUR ARRANGEMENT? I MEAN, IF SHE CRIES AND HAS TO BE WALKED AFTER FEEDING - COULD WE TAKE TURNS WITH THAT?
SURE.
AHHH- WAAAAAAA AHH- WAAAAAHH
ZNRRGG
NEVER TAKE THE WORD OF SOMEONE WHO TALKS IN THEIR SLEEP.
LYNN

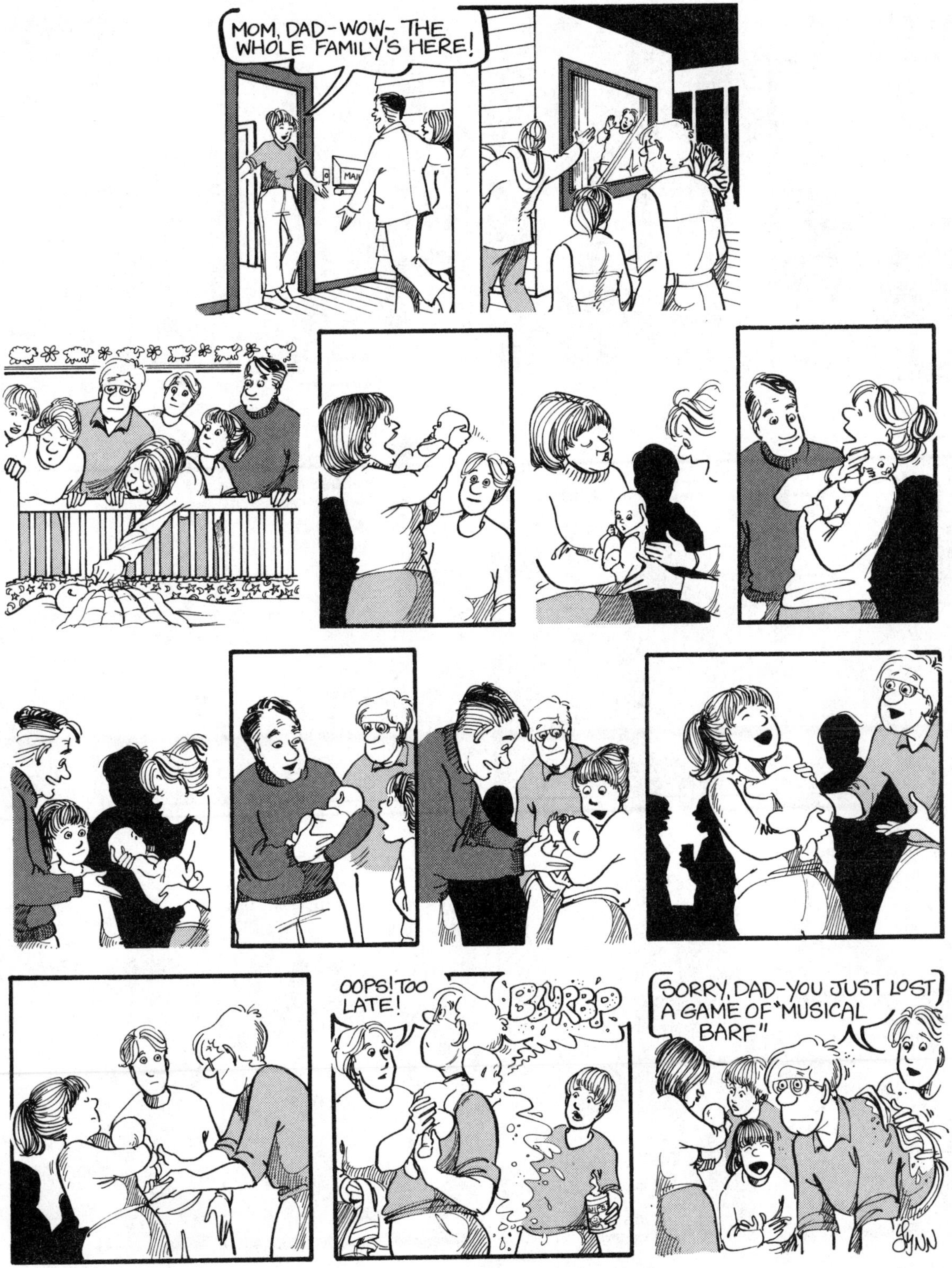
MOM, DAD-WOW- THE WHOLE FAMILY'S HERE!
OOPS! TOO LATE!
BLURBP
SORRY, DAD-YOU JUST LOST A GAME OF "MUSICAL BARF"
LYNN

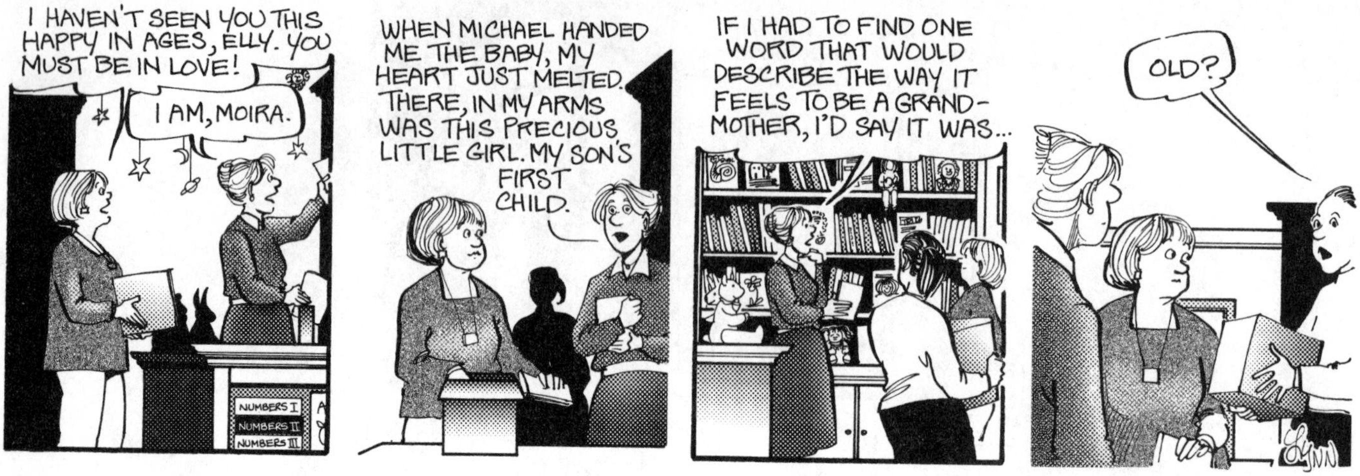
I HAVEN'T SEEN YOU THIS HAPPY IN AGES, ELLY. YOU MUST BE IN LOVE!
I AM, MOIRA.
NUMBERS I
NUMBERS II
NUMBERS III
WHEN MICHAEL HANDED ME THE BABY, MY HEART JUST MELTED. THERE, IN MY ARMS WAS THIS PRECIOUS LITTLE GIRL. MY SON'S FIRST CHILD.
IF I HAD TO FIND ONE WORD THAT WOULD DESCRIBE THE WAY IT FEELS TO BE A GRAND-MOTHER, I'D SAY IT WAS...
OLD?
LYNN

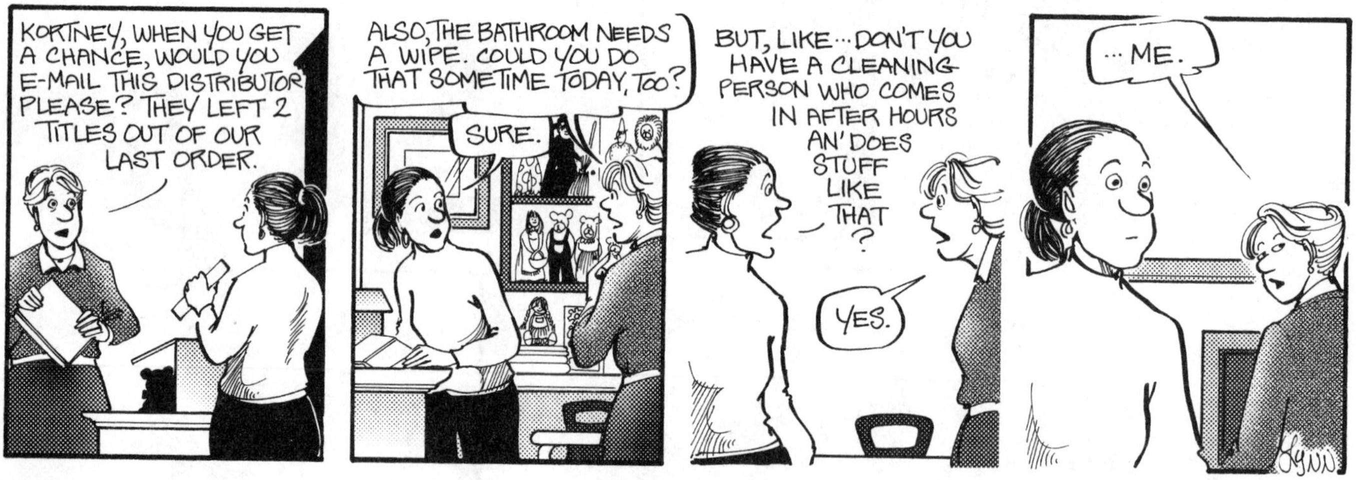
KORTNEY, WHEN YOU GET A CHANCE, WOULD YOU E-MAIL THIS DISTRIBUTOR PLEASE? THEY LEFT 2 TITLES OUT OF OUR LAST ORDER.
ALSO, THE BATHROOM NEEDS A WIPE. COULD YOU DO THAT SOMETIME TODAY, TOO?
SURE.
BUT, LIKE... DON'T YOU HAVE A CLEANING PERSON WHO COMES IN AFTER HOURS AN' DOES STUFF LIKE THAT?
YES.
... ME.
LYNN

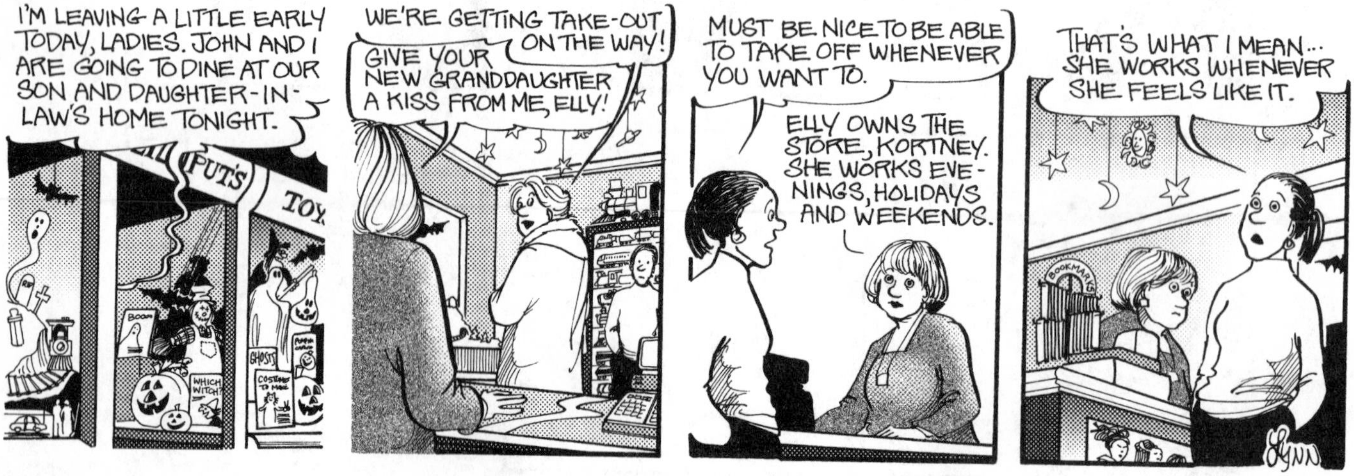
I'M LEAVING A LITTLE EARLY TODAY, LADIES. JOHN AND I ARE GOING TO DINE AT OUR SON AND DAUGHTER-IN-LAW'S HOME TONIGHT.
PUT'S
TOY
WE'RE GETTING TAKE-OUT ON THE WAY!
GIVE YOUR NEW GRANDDAUGHTER A KISS FROM ME, ELLY!
MUST BE NICE TO BE ABLE TO TAKE OFF WHENEVER YOU WANT TO.
ELLY OWNS THE STORE, KORTNEY. SHE WORKS EVE-NINGS, HOLIDAYS AND WEEKENDS.
THAT'S WHAT I MEAN... SHE WORKS WHENEVER SHE FEELS LIKE IT.
BOOKMARKS
LYNN

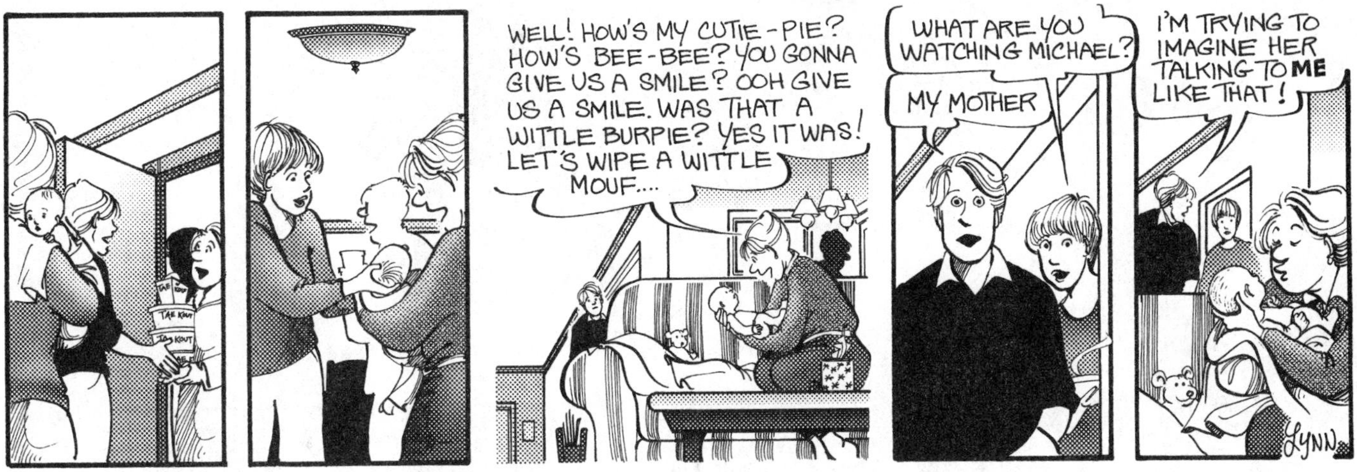
WELL! HOW'S MY CUTIE-PIE? HOW'S BEE-BEE? YOU GONNA GIVE US A SMILE? OOH GIVE US A SMILE. WAS THAT A WITTLE BURPIE? YES IT WAS! LET'S WIPE A WITTLE MOUF....
WHAT ARE YOU WATCHING MICHAEL?
MY MOTHER
I'M TRYING TO IMAGINE HER TALKING TO ME LIKE THAT!
LYNN

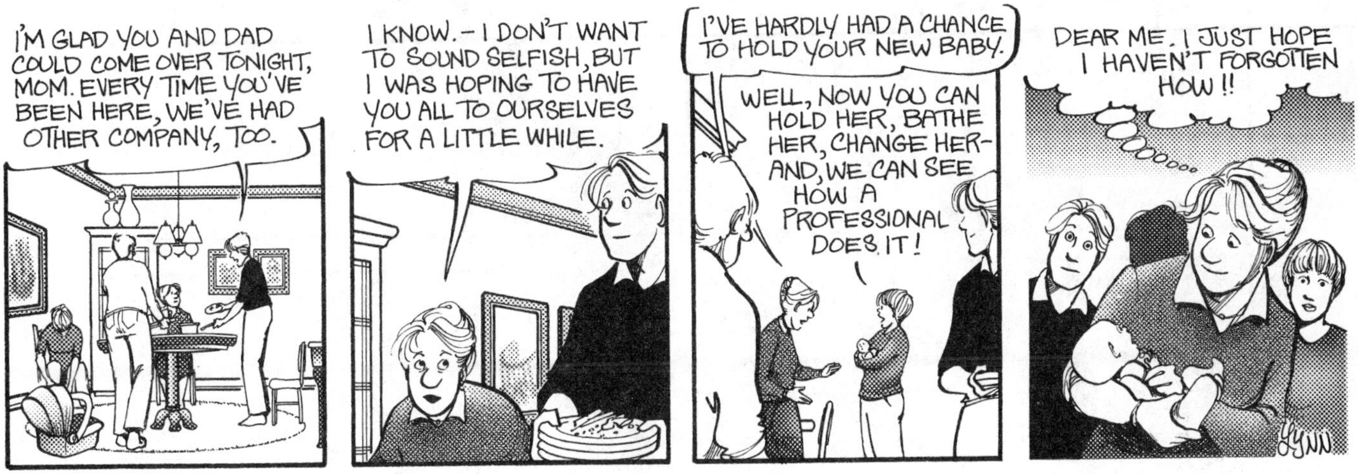
I'M GLAD YOU AND DAD COULD COME OVER TONIGHT, MOM. EVERY TIME YOU'VE BEEN HERE, WE'VE HAD OTHER COMPANY, TOO.
I KNOW. – I DON'T WANT TO SOUND SELFISH, BUT I WAS HOPING TO HAVE YOU ALL TO OURSELVES FOR A LITTLE WHILE.
I'VE HARDLY HAD A CHANCE TO HOLD YOUR NEW BABY.
WELL, NOW YOU CAN HOLD HER, BATHE HER, CHANGE HER-AND, WE CAN SEE HOW A PROFESSIONAL DOES IT!
DEAR ME. I JUST HOPE I HAVEN'T FORGOTTEN HOW!!
LYNN

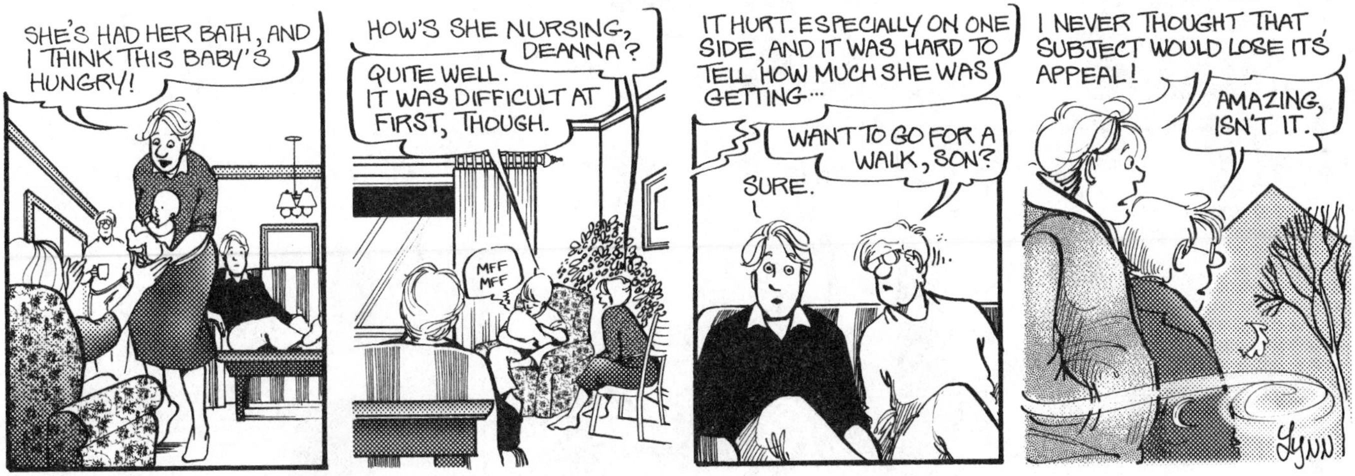
SHE'S HAD HER BATH, AND I THINK THIS BABY'S HUNGRY!
HOW'S SHE NURSING, DEANNA?
QUITE WELL. IT WAS DIFFICULT AT FIRST, THOUGH.
MFF MFF
IT HURT. ESPECIALLY ON ONE SIDE, AND IT WAS HARD TO TELL HOW MUCH SHE WAS GETTING...
WANT TO GO FOR A WALK, SON?
SURE.
I NEVER THOUGHT THAT SUBJECT WOULD LOSE ITS APPEAL!
AMAZING, ISN'T IT.
LYNN

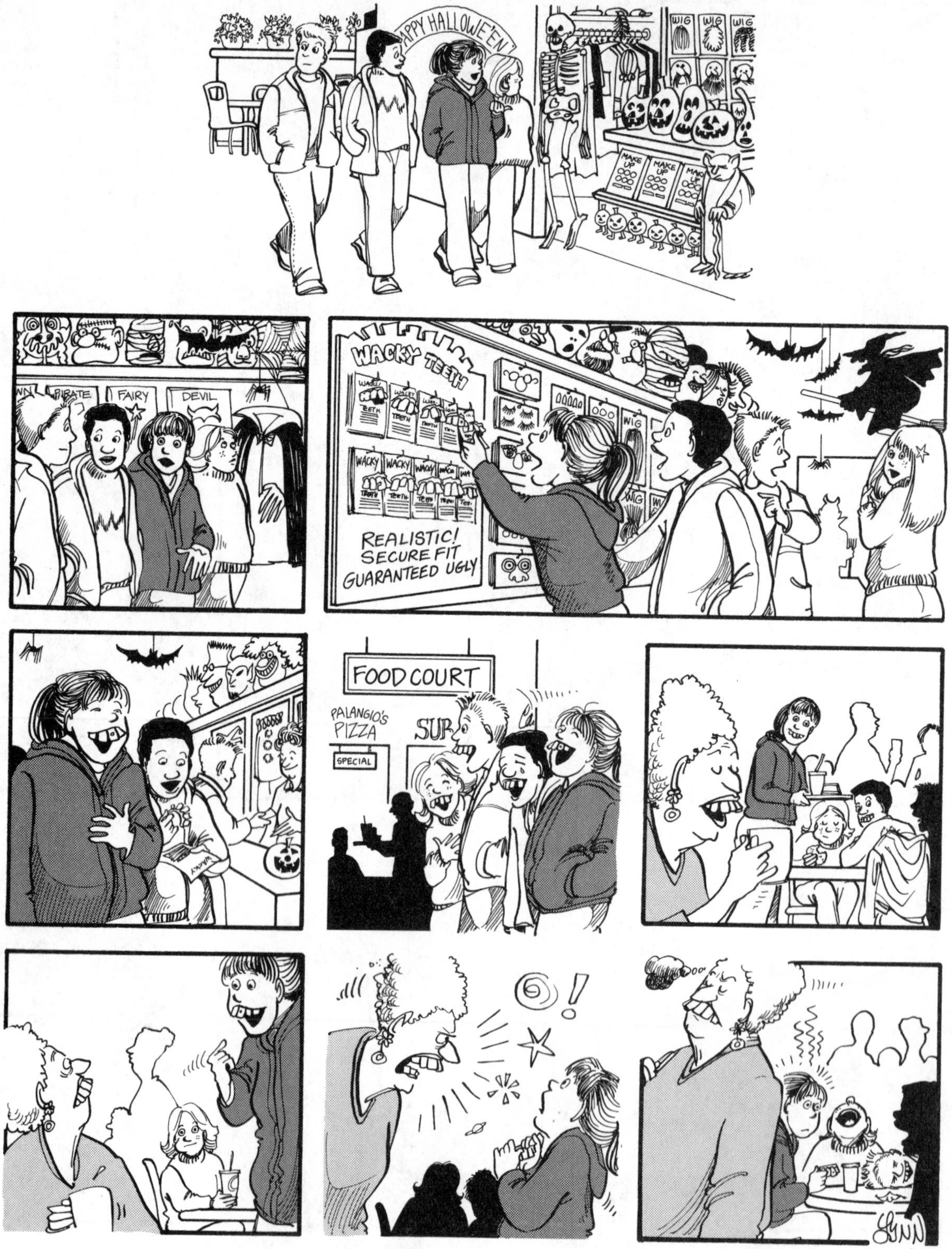
HAPPY HALLOWE'EN
WIG
WIG
WIG
MAKE UP
MAKE UP
MAKE UP
PIRATE
FAIRY
DEVIL
WACKY TEETH
REALISTIC!
SECURE FIT
GUARANTEED UGLY
FOOD COURT
PALANGIO'S PIZZA
SPECIAL
SUB
LYNN

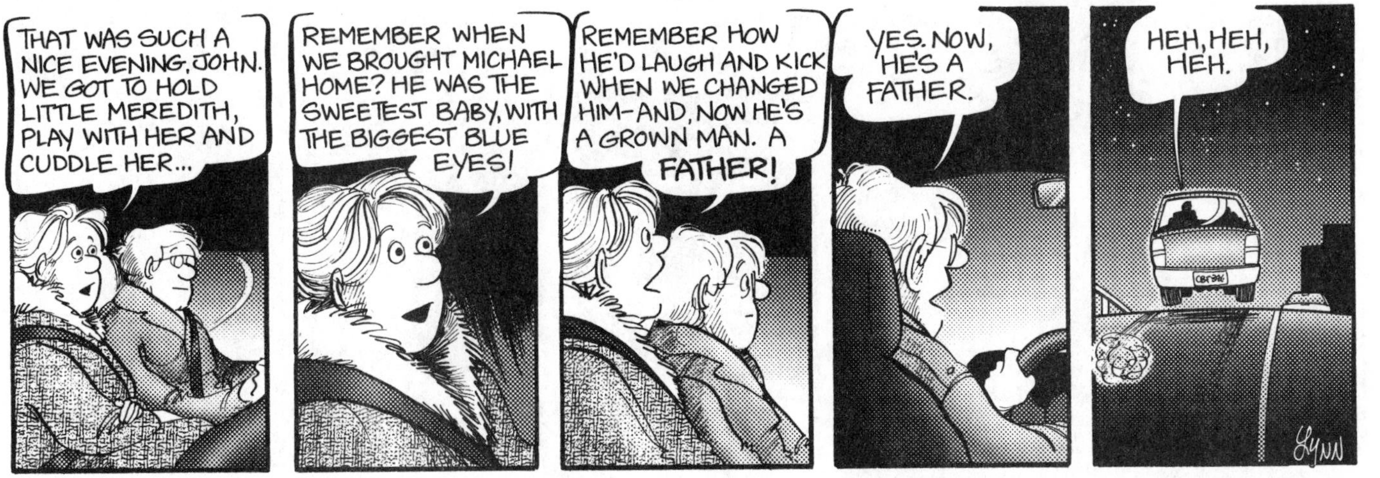
THAT WAS SUCH A NICE EVENING, JOHN. WE GOT TO HOLD LITTLE MEREDITH, PLAY WITH HER AND CUDDLE HER...
REMEMBER WHEN WE BROUGHT MICHAEL HOME? HE WAS THE SWEETEST BABY, WITH THE BIGGEST BLUE EYES!
REMEMBER HOW HE'D LAUGH AND KICK WHEN WE CHANGED HIM-AND, NOW HE'S A GROWN MAN. A FATHER!
YES. NOW, HE'S A FATHER.
HEH, HEH, HEH.
LYNN

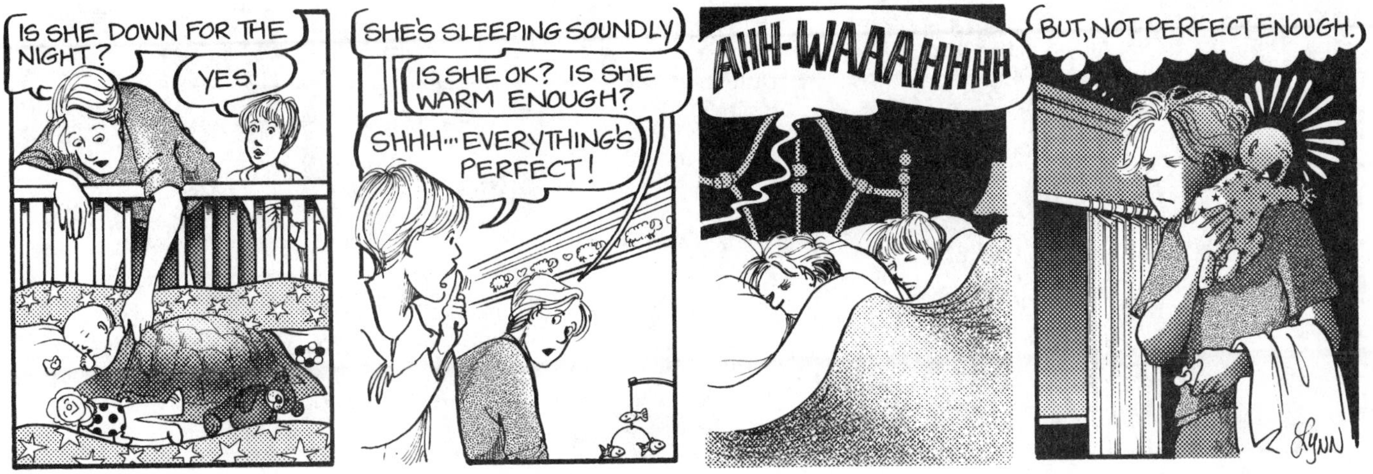
IS SHE DOWN FOR THE NIGHT?
YES!
SHE'S SLEEPING SOUNDLY
IS SHE OK? IS SHE WARM ENOUGH?
SHHH... EVERYTHING'S PERFECT!
AHH-WAAAHHHH
BUT, NOT PERFECT ENOUGH.
LYNN

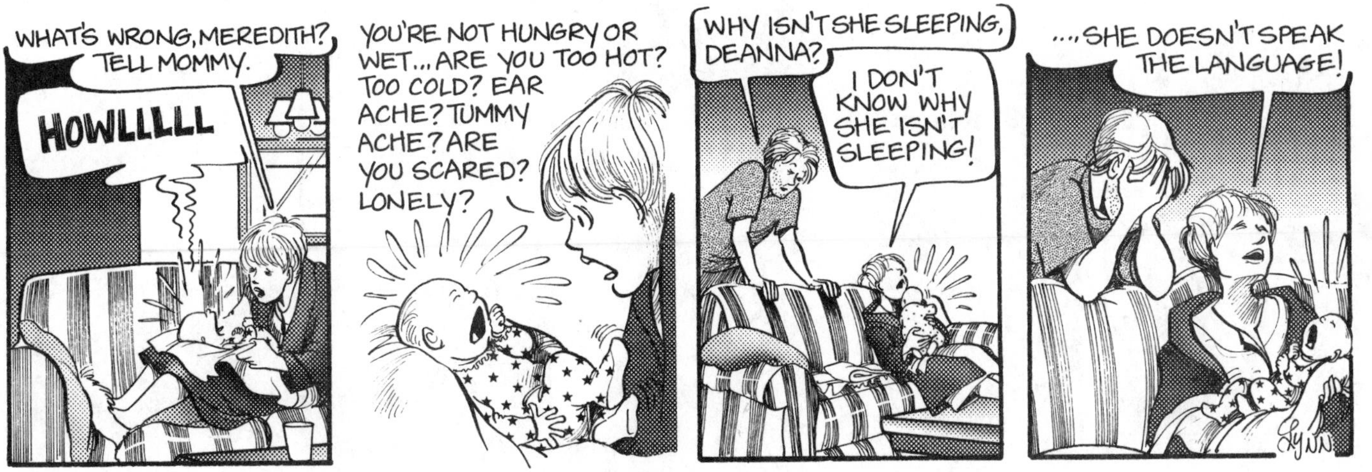
WHAT'S WRONG, MEREDITH? TELL MOMMY.
HOWLLLLL
YOU'RE NOT HUNGRY OR WET... ARE YOU TOO HOT? TOO COLD? EAR ACHE? TUMMY ACHE? ARE YOU SCARED? LONELY?
WHY ISN'T SHE SLEEPING, DEANNA?
I DON'T KNOW WHY SHE ISN'T SLEEPING!
..., SHE DOESN'T SPEAK THE LANGUAGE!
LYNN

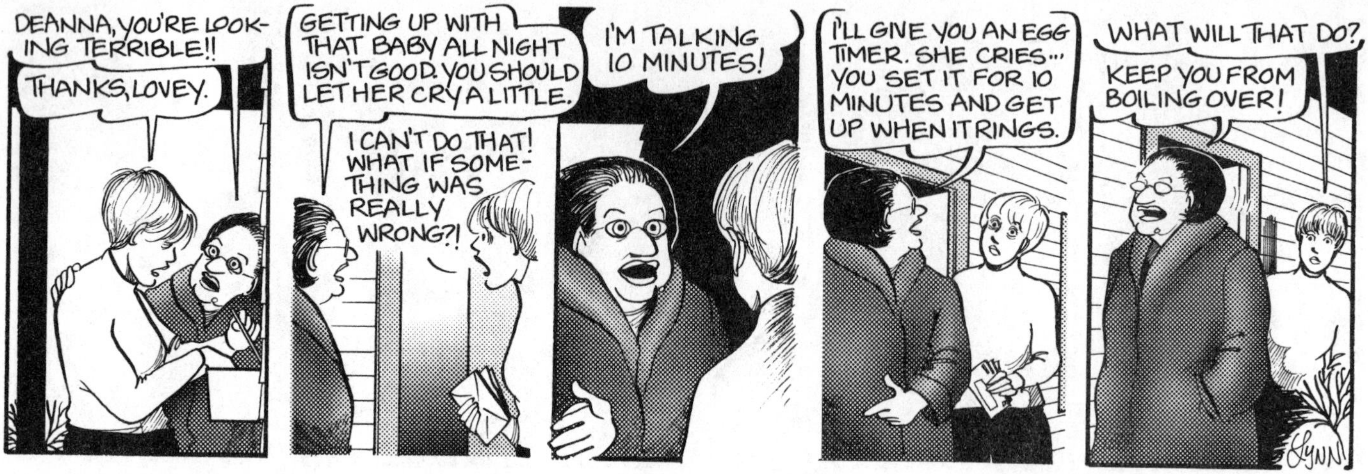
DEANNA, YOU'RE LOOKING TERRIBLE!!
THANKS, LOVEY.
GETTING UP WITH THAT BABY ALL NIGHT ISN'T GOOD. YOU SHOULD LET HER CRY A LITTLE.
I CAN'T DO THAT! WHAT IF SOMETHING WAS REALLY WRONG?!
I'M TALKING 10 MINUTES!
I'LL GIVE YOU AN EGG TIMER. SHE CRIES... YOU SET IT FOR 10 MINUTES AND GET UP WHEN IT RINGS.
WHAT WILL THAT DO?
KEEP YOU FROM BOILING OVER!
LYNN

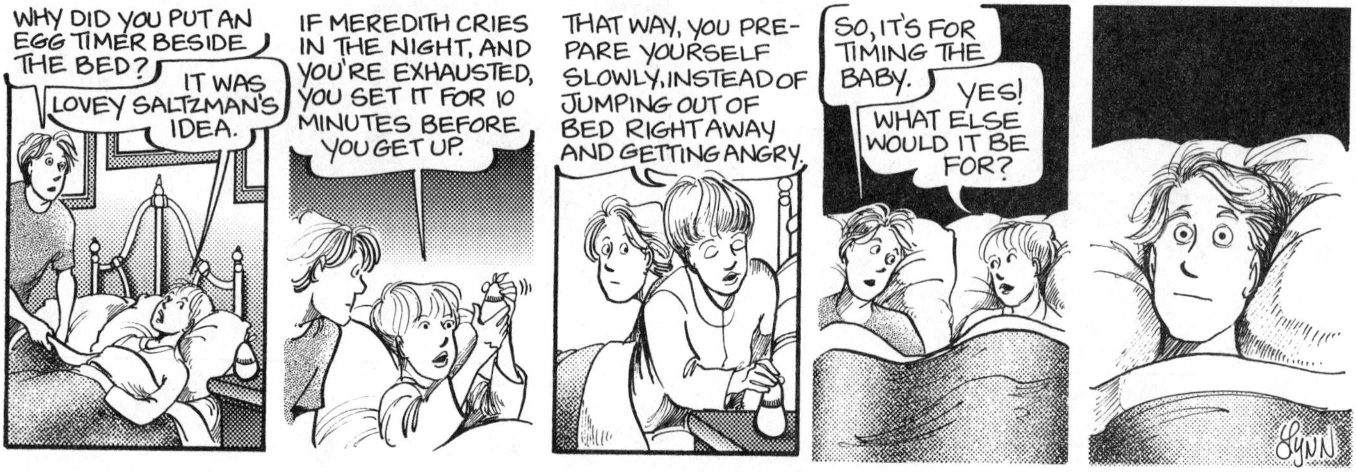
WHY DID YOU PUT AN EGG TIMER BESIDE THE BED?
IT WAS LOVEY SALTZMAN'S IDEA.
IF MEREDITH CRIES IN THE NIGHT, AND YOU'RE EXHAUSTED, YOU SET IT FOR 10 MINUTES BEFORE YOU GET UP.
THAT WAY, YOU PREPARE YOURSELF SLOWLY, INSTEAD OF JUMPING OUT OF BED RIGHT AWAY AND GETTING ANGRY.
SO, IT'S FOR TIMING THE BABY.
YES! WHAT ELSE WOULD IT BE FOR?
LYNN

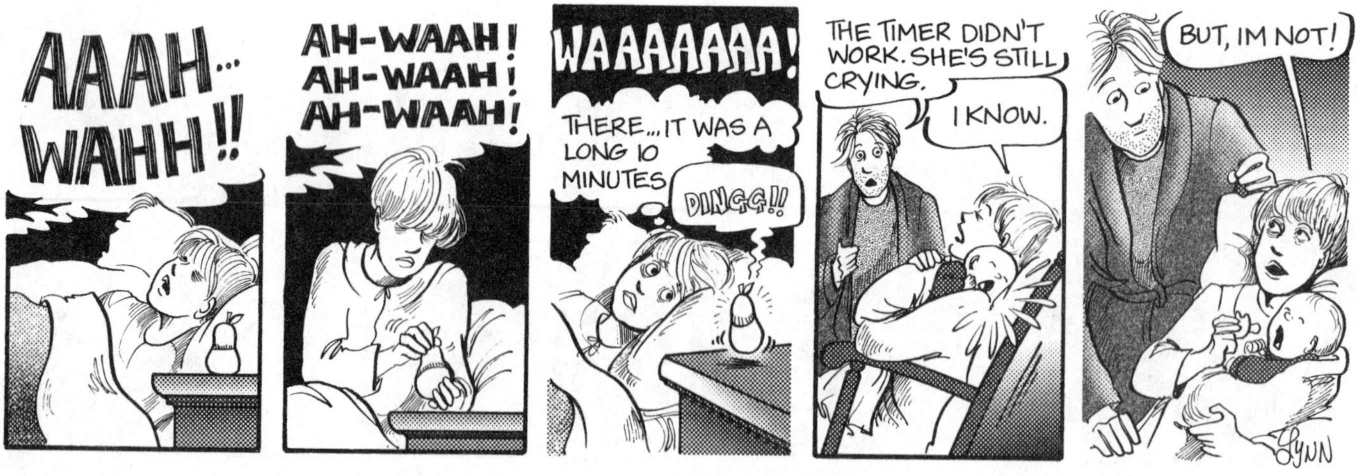
AAAH... WAHH!!
AH-WAAH! AH-WAAH! AH-WAAH!
WAAAAAAA!
THERE... IT WAS A LONG 10 MINUTES
DINGG!!
THE TIMER DIDN'T WORK. SHE'S STILL CRYING.
I KNOW.
BUT, IM NOT!
LYNN

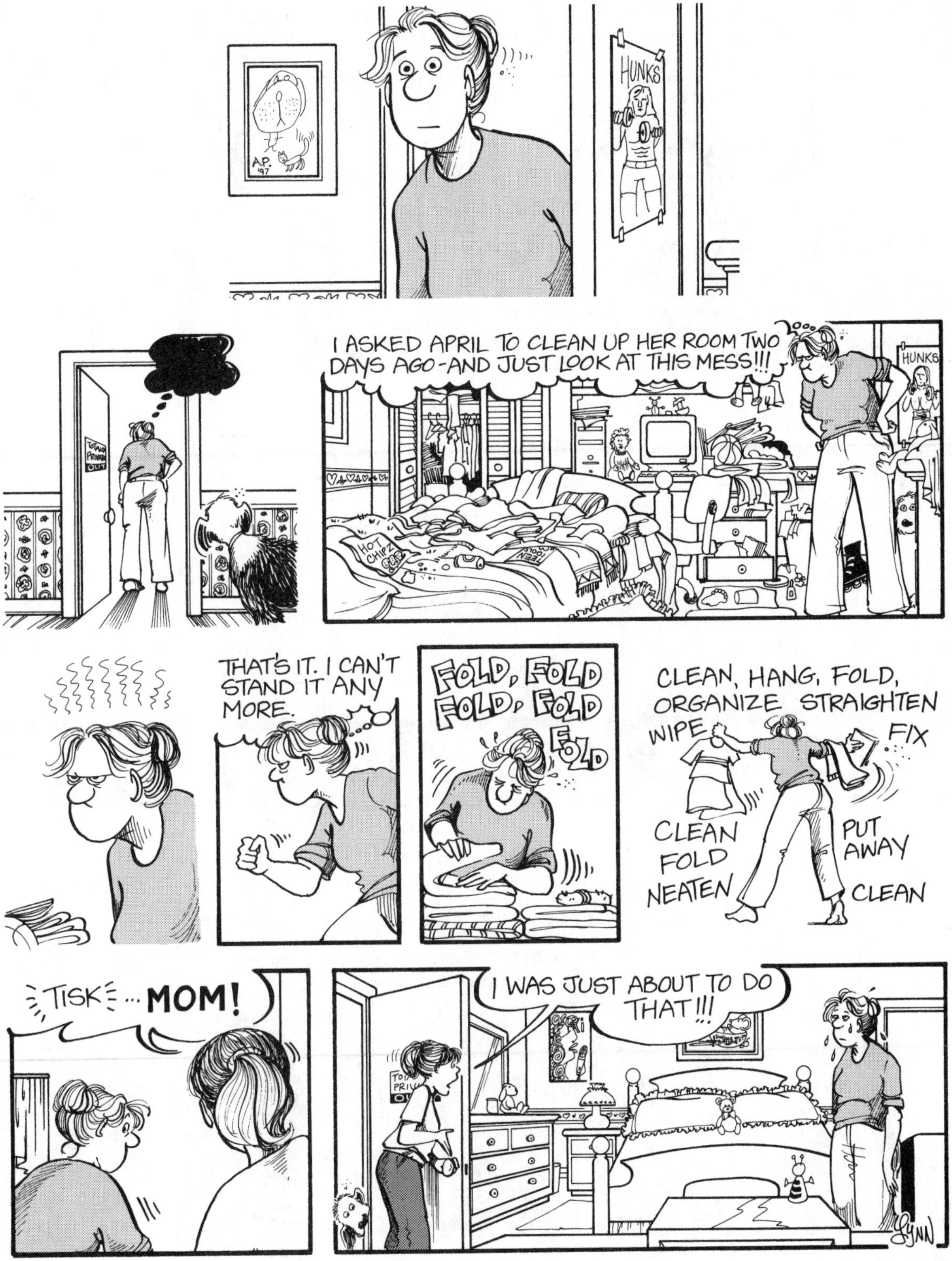
HUNKS
I ASKED APRIL TO CLEAN UP HER ROOM TWO DAYS AGO - AND JUST LOOK AT THIS MESS!!!
HUNKS
THAT'S IT. I CAN'T STAND IT ANY MORE.
FOLD, FOLD FOLD, FOLD FOLD
CLEAN, HANG, FOLD, ORGANIZE STRAIGHTEN
WIPE
FIX
CLEAN
FOLD
NEATEN
PUT AWAY
CLEAN
TISK ... MOM!
I WAS JUST ABOUT TO DO THAT!!!
LYNN

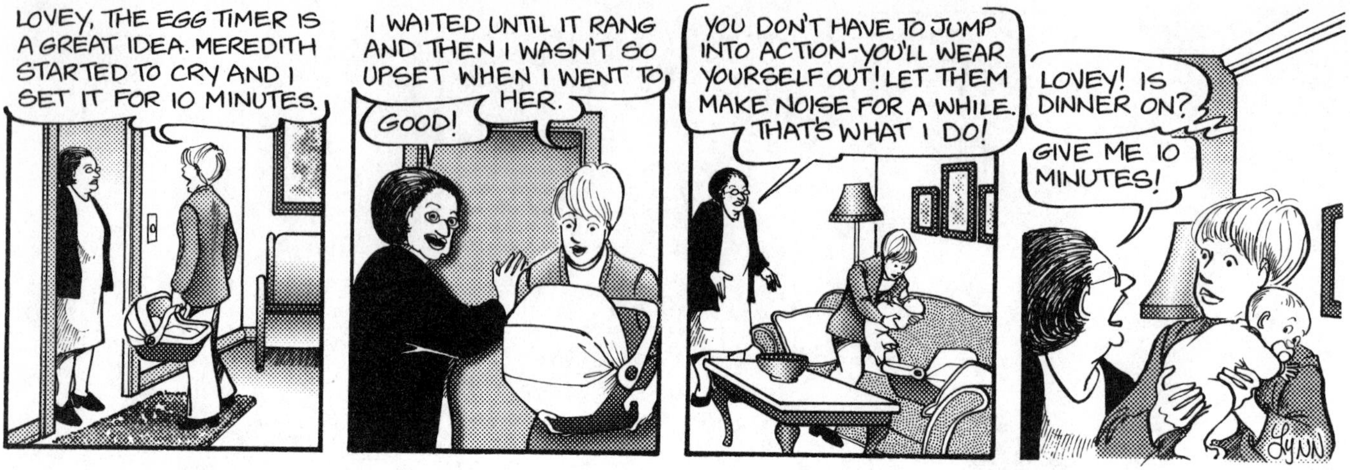
LOVEY, THE EGG TIMER IS A GREAT IDEA. MEREDITH STARTED TO CRY AND I SET IT FOR 10 MINUTES.
I WAITED UNTIL IT RANG AND THEN I WASN'T SO UPSET WHEN I WENT TO HER.
GOOD!
YOU DON'T HAVE TO JUMP INTO ACTION-YOU'LL WEAR YOURSELF OUT! LET THEM MAKE NOISE FOR A WHILE. THAT'S WHAT I DO!
LOVEY! IS DINNER ON?
GIVE ME 10 MINUTES!
LYNN

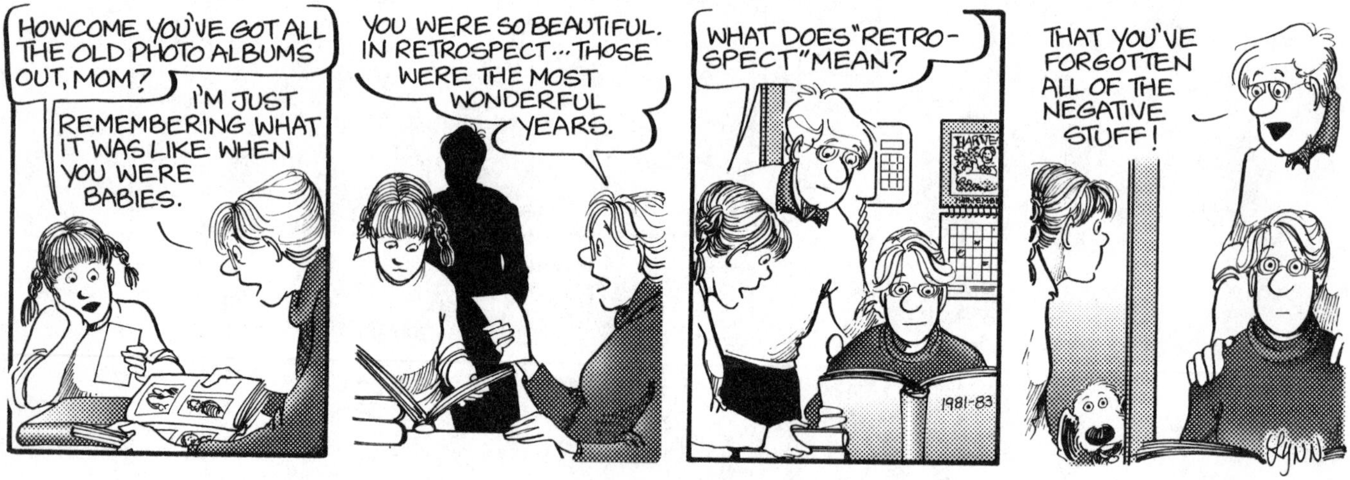
HOWCOME YOU'VE GOT ALL THE OLD PHOTO ALBUMS OUT, MOM?
I'M JUST REMEMBERING WHAT IT WAS LIKE WHEN YOU WERE BABIES.
YOU WERE SO BEAUTIFUL. IN RETROSPECT... THOSE WERE THE MOST WONDERFUL YEARS.
WHAT DOES "RETRO-SPECT" MEAN?
1981-83
THAT YOU'VE FORGOTTEN ALL OF THE NEGATIVE STUFF!
LYNN

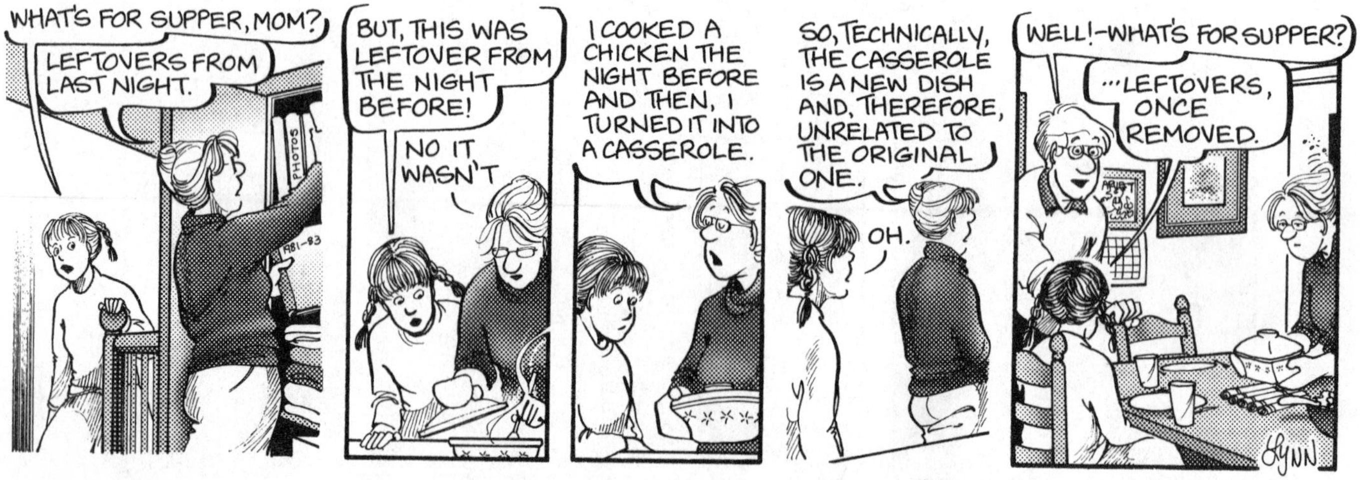
WHAT'S FOR SUPPER, MOM?
LEFTOVERS FROM LAST NIGHT.
PHOTOS
1981-83
BUT, THIS WAS LEFTOVER FROM THE NIGHT BEFORE!
NO IT WASN'T
I COOKED A CHICKEN THE NIGHT BEFORE AND THEN, I TURNED IT INTO A CASSEROLE.
SO, TECHNICALLY, THE CASSEROLE IS A NEW DISH AND, THEREFORE, UNRELATED TO THE ORIGINAL ONE.
OH.
WELL!-WHAT'S FOR SUPPER?
...LEFTOVERS, ONCE REMOVED.
LYNN

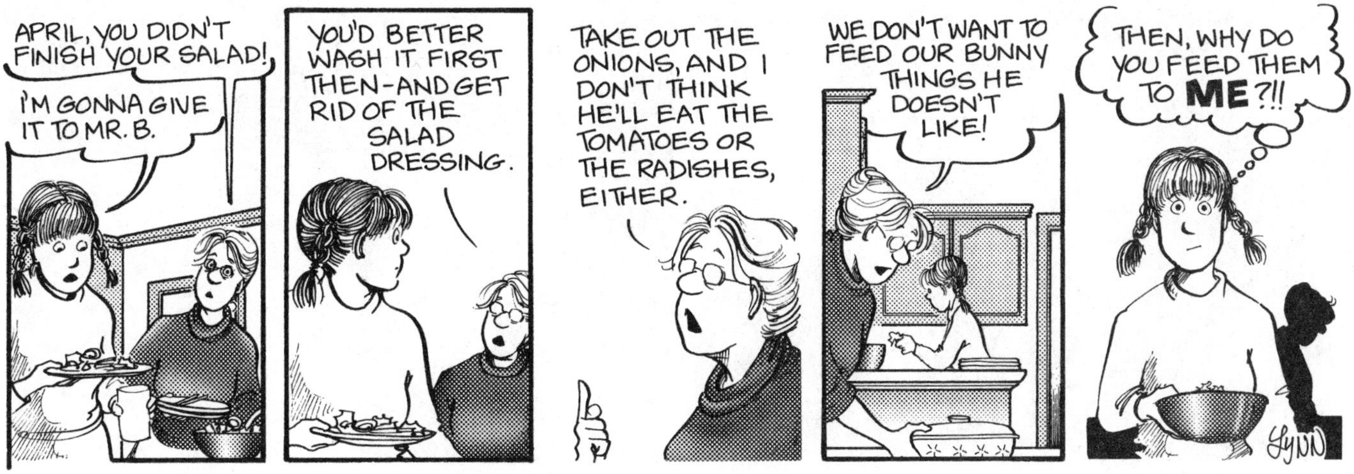
APRIL, YOU DIDN'T FINISH YOUR SALAD!
I'M GONNA GIVE IT TO MR. B.
YOU'D BETTER WASH IT FIRST THEN—AND GET RID OF THE SALAD DRESSING.
TAKE OUT THE ONIONS, AND I DON'T THINK HE'LL EAT THE TOMATOES OR THE RADISHES, EITHER.
WE DON'T WANT TO FEED OUR BUNNY THINGS HE DOESN'T LIKE!
THEN, WHY DO YOU FEED THEM TO **ME**?!!
LYNN

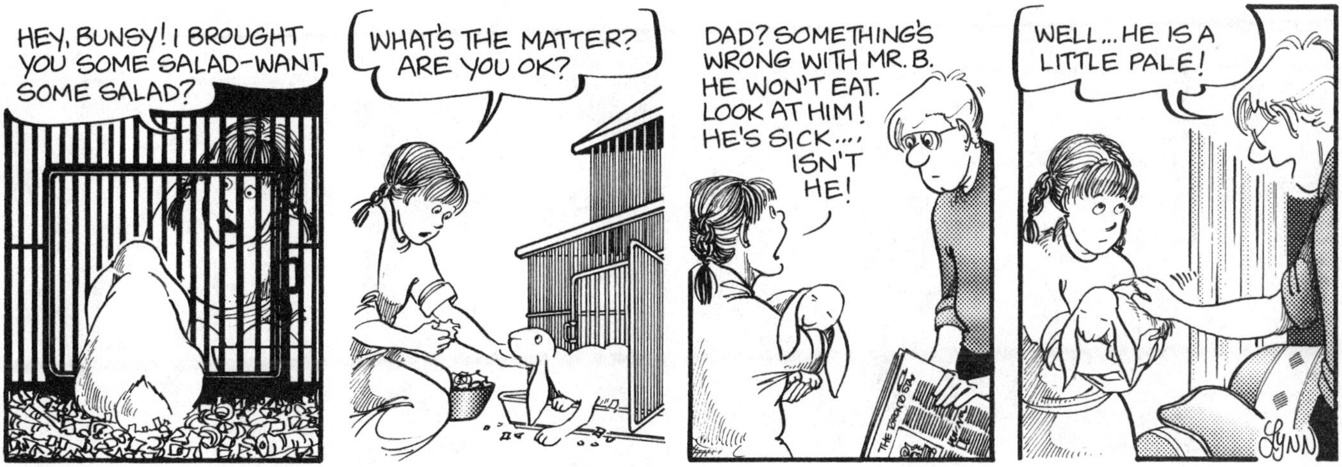
HEY, BUNSY! I BROUGHT YOU SOME SALAD—WANT SOME SALAD?
WHAT'S THE MATTER? ARE YOU OK?
DAD? SOMETHING'S WRONG WITH MR. B. HE WON'T EAT. LOOK AT HIM! HE'S SICK...., ISN'T HE!
WELL... HE IS A LITTLE PALE!
LYNN

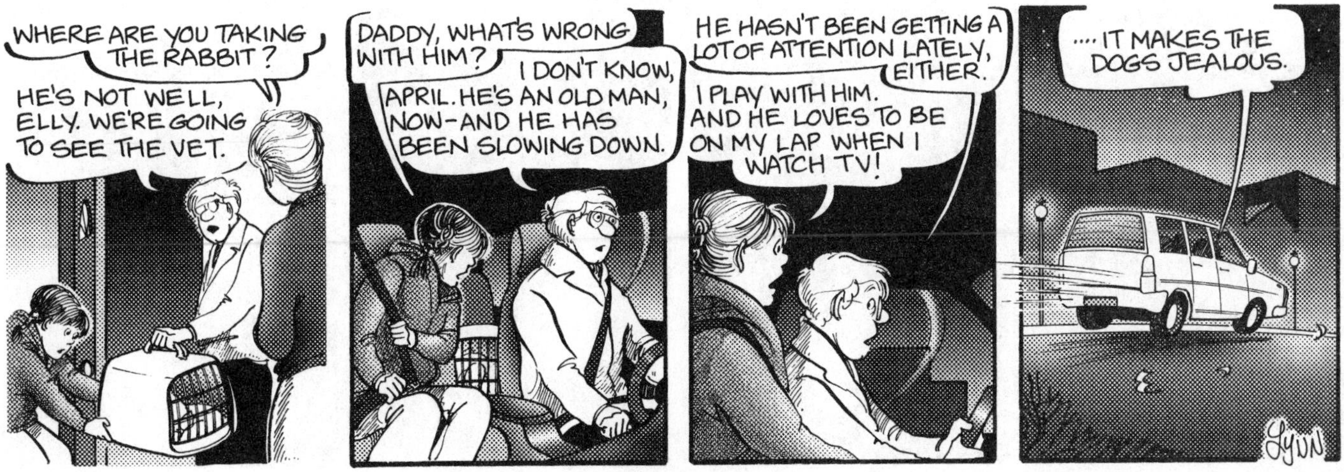
WHERE ARE YOU TAKING THE RABBIT?
HE'S NOT WELL, ELLY. WE'RE GOING TO SEE THE VET.
DADDY, WHAT'S WRONG WITH HIM?
I DON'T KNOW, APRIL. HE'S AN OLD MAN, NOW—AND HE HAS BEEN SLOWING DOWN.
HE HASN'T BEEN GETTING A LOT OF ATTENTION LATELY, EITHER.
I PLAY WITH HIM. AND HE LOVES TO BE ON MY LAP WHEN I WATCH TV!
.... IT MAKES THE DOGS JEALOUS.
LYNN

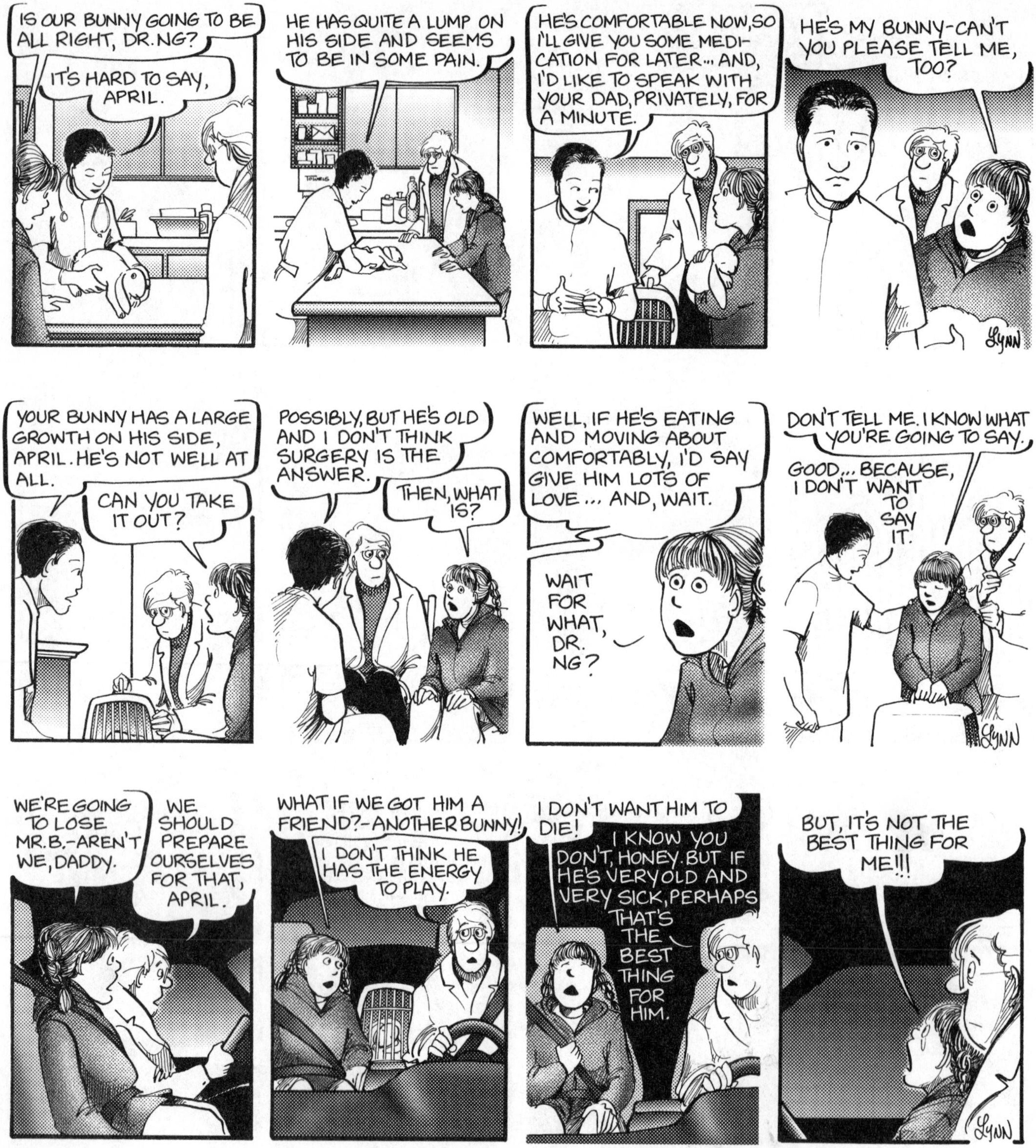
IS OUR BUNNY GOING TO BE ALL RIGHT, DR. NG?
IT'S HARD TO SAY, APRIL.
HE HAS QUITE A LUMP ON HIS SIDE AND SEEMS TO BE IN SOME PAIN.
HE'S COMFORTABLE NOW, SO I'LL GIVE YOU SOME MEDICATION FOR LATER... AND, I'D LIKE TO SPEAK WITH YOUR DAD, PRIVATELY, FOR A MINUTE.
HE'S MY BUNNY-CAN'T YOU PLEASE TELL ME, TOO?
LYNN
YOUR BUNNY HAS A LARGE GROWTH ON HIS SIDE, APRIL. HE'S NOT WELL AT ALL.
CAN YOU TAKE IT OUT?
POSSIBLY, BUT HE'S OLD AND I DON'T THINK SURGERY IS THE ANSWER.
THEN, WHAT IS?
WELL, IF HE'S EATING AND MOVING ABOUT COMFORTABLY, I'D SAY GIVE HIM LOTS OF LOVE... AND, WAIT.
WAIT FOR WHAT, DR. NG?
DON'T TELL ME. I KNOW WHAT YOU'RE GOING TO SAY.
GOOD... BECAUSE, I DON'T WANT TO SAY IT.
LYNN
WE'RE GOING TO LOSE MR. B.-AREN'T WE, DADDY.
WE SHOULD PREPARE OURSELVES FOR THAT, APRIL.
WHAT IF WE GOT HIM A FRIEND?-ANOTHER BUNNY!
I DON'T THINK HE HAS THE ENERGY TO PLAY.
I DON'T WANT HIM TO DIE!
I KNOW YOU DON'T, HONEY. BUT IF HE'S VERY OLD AND VERY SICK, PERHAPS THAT'S THE BEST THING FOR HIM.
BUT, IT'S NOT THE BEST THING FOR ME!!!
LYNN

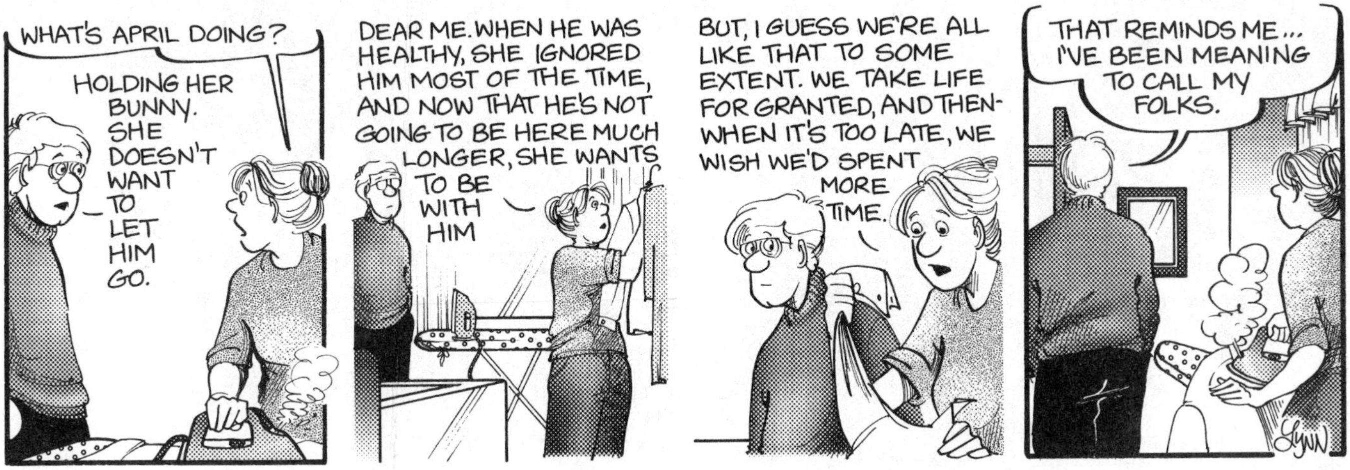
WHAT'S APRIL DOING?
HOLDING HER BUNNY. SHE DOESN'T WANT TO LET HIM GO.
DEAR ME. WHEN HE WAS HEALTHY, SHE IGNORED HIM MOST OF THE TIME, AND NOW THAT HE'S NOT GOING TO BE HERE MUCH LONGER, SHE WANTS TO BE WITH HIM
BUT, I GUESS WE'RE ALL LIKE THAT TO SOME EXTENT. WE TAKE LIFE FOR GRANTED, AND THEN- WHEN IT'S TOO LATE, WE WISH WE'D SPENT MORE TIME.
THAT REMINDS ME... I'VE BEEN MEANING TO CALL MY FOLKS.
LYNN

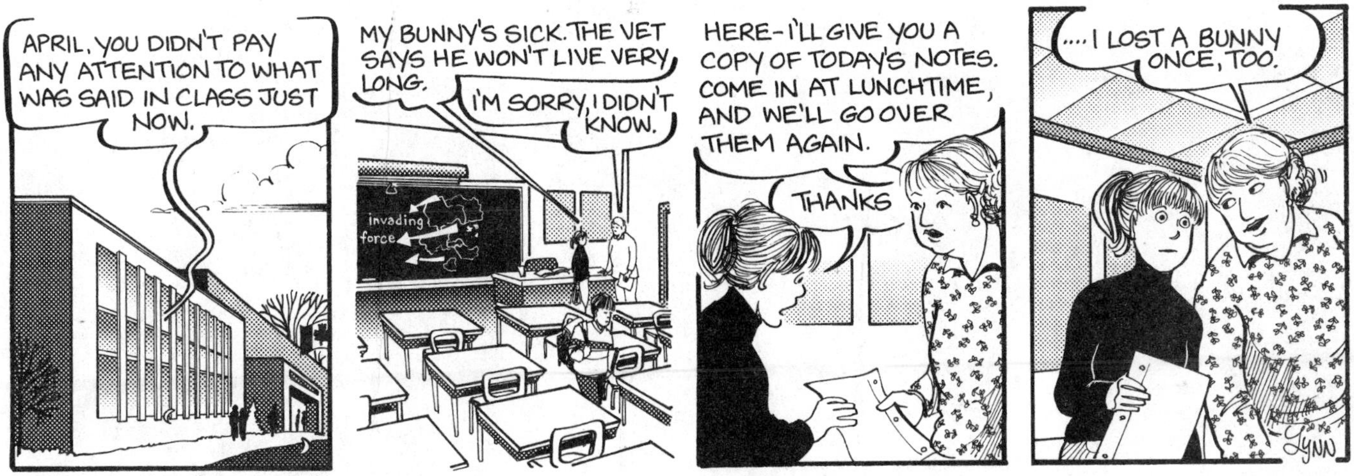
APRIL, YOU DIDN'T PAY ANY ATTENTION TO WHAT WAS SAID IN CLASS JUST NOW.
MY BUNNY'S SICK. THE VET SAYS HE WON'T LIVE VERY LONG.
I'M SORRY, I DIDN'T KNOW.
invading force
HERE- I'LL GIVE YOU A COPY OF TODAY'S NOTES. COME IN AT LUNCHTIME, AND WE'LL GO OVER THEM AGAIN.
THANKS
....I LOST A BUNNY ONCE, TOO.
LYNN

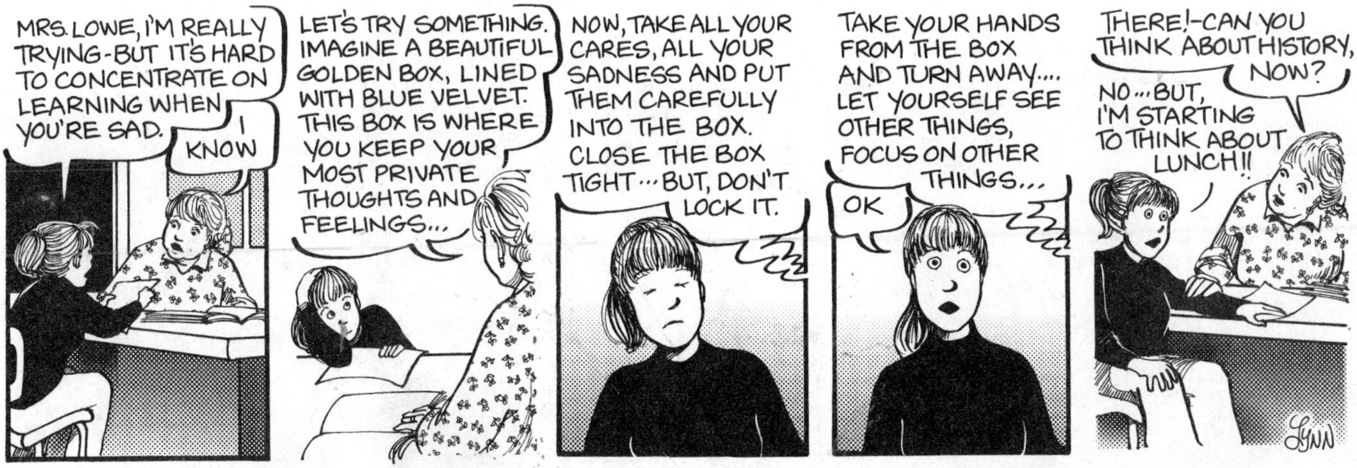
MRS. LOWE, I'M REALLY TRYING- BUT IT'S HARD TO CONCENTRATE ON LEARNING WHEN YOU'RE SAD.
I KNOW
LET'S TRY SOMETHING. IMAGINE A BEAUTIFUL GOLDEN BOX, LINED WITH BLUE VELVET. THIS BOX IS WHERE YOU KEEP YOUR MOST PRIVATE THOUGHTS AND FEELINGS...
NOW, TAKE ALL YOUR CARES, ALL YOUR SADNESS AND PUT THEM CAREFULLY INTO THE BOX. CLOSE THE BOX TIGHT... BUT, DON'T LOCK IT.
TAKE YOUR HANDS FROM THE BOX AND TURN AWAY.... LET YOURSELF SEE OTHER THINGS, FOCUS ON OTHER THINGS...
OK
THERE!- CAN YOU THINK ABOUT HISTORY, NOW?
NO... BUT, I'M STARTING TO THINK ABOUT LUNCH!!
LYNN

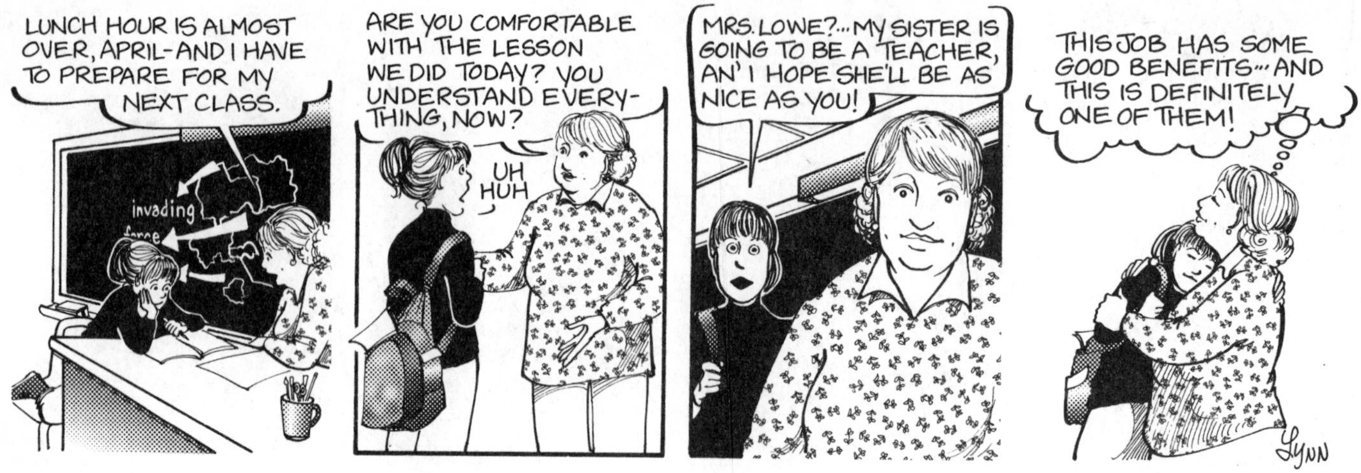
LUNCH HOUR IS ALMOST OVER, APRIL–AND I HAVE TO PREPARE FOR MY NEXT CLASS.
invading
ARE YOU COMFORTABLE WITH THE LESSON WE DID TODAY? YOU UNDERSTAND EVERYTHING, NOW?
UH HUH
MRS. LOWE?... MY SISTER IS GOING TO BE A TEACHER, AN' I HOPE SHE'LL BE AS NICE AS YOU!
THIS JOB HAS SOME GOOD BENEFITS... AND THIS IS DEFINITELY ONE OF THEM!
LYNN

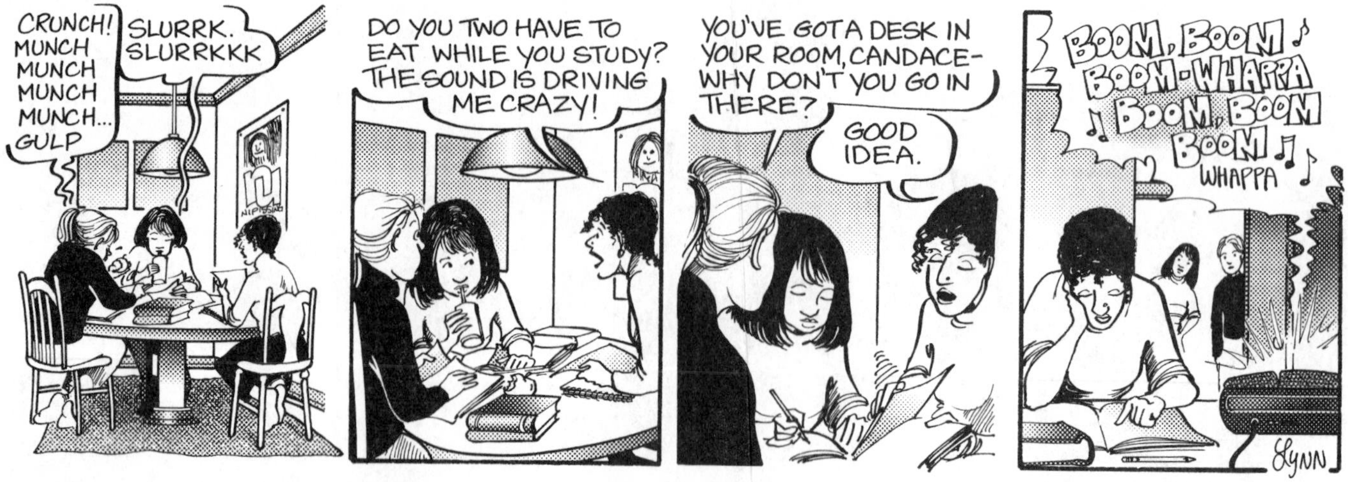
CRUNCH! MUNCH MUNCH MUNCH MUNCH... GULP
SLURRK. SLURRKKK
DO YOU TWO HAVE TO EAT WHILE YOU STUDY? THE SOUND IS DRIVING ME CRAZY!
YOU'VE GOT A DESK IN YOUR ROOM, CANDACE–WHY DON'T YOU GO IN THERE?
GOOD IDEA.
BOOM, BOOM BOOM-WHAPPA BOOM, BOOM BOOM
WHAPPA
LYNN

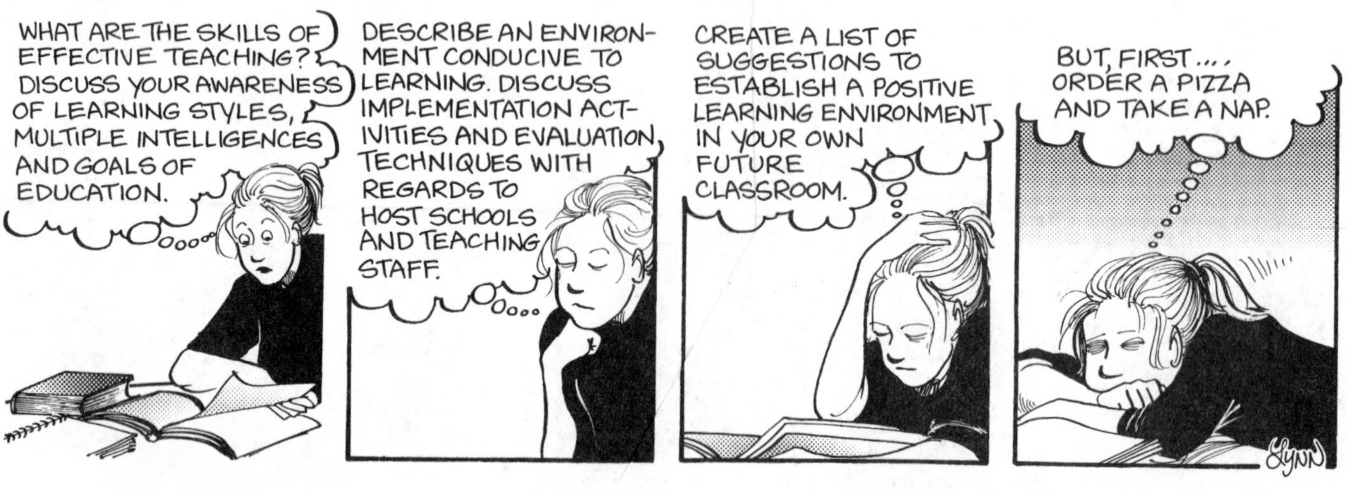
WHAT ARE THE SKILLS OF EFFECTIVE TEACHING? DISCUSS YOUR AWARENESS OF LEARNING STYLES, MULTIPLE INTELLIGENCES AND GOALS OF EDUCATION.
DESCRIBE AN ENVIRONMENT CONDUCIVE TO LEARNING. DISCUSS IMPLEMENTATION ACTIVITIES AND EVALUATION TECHNIQUES WITH REGARDS TO HOST SCHOOLS AND TEACHING STAFF.
CREATE A LIST OF SUGGESTIONS TO ESTABLISH A POSITIVE LEARNING ENVIRONMENT IN YOUR OWN FUTURE CLASSROOM.
BUT, FIRST..., ORDER A PIZZA AND TAKE A NAP.
LYNN

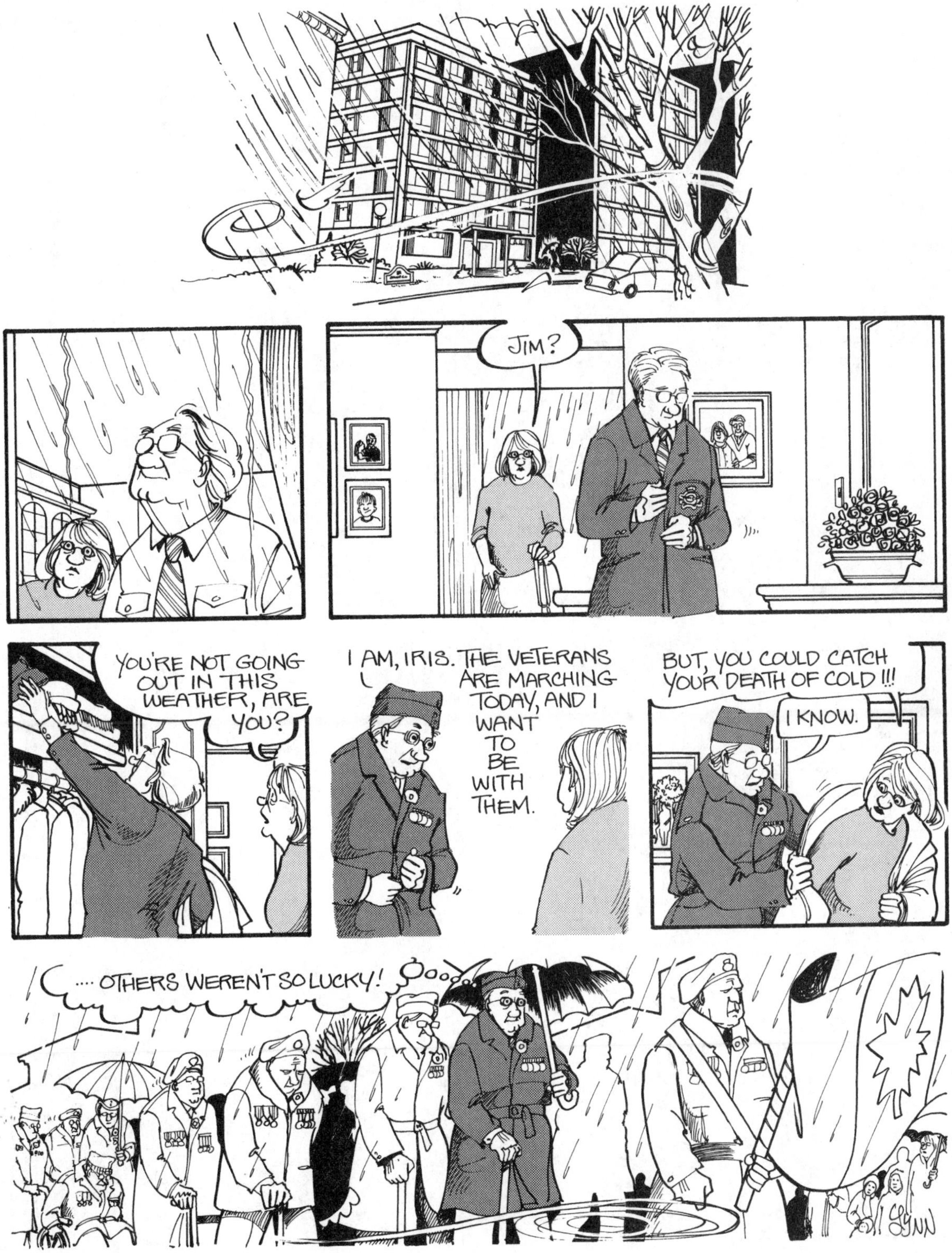
JIM?
YOU'RE NOT GOING OUT IN THIS WEATHER, ARE YOU?
I AM, IRIS. THE VETERANS ARE MARCHING TODAY, AND I WANT TO BE WITH THEM.
BUT, YOU COULD CATCH YOUR DEATH OF COLD!!!
I KNOW.
.... OTHERS WEREN'T SO LUCKY!
LYNN

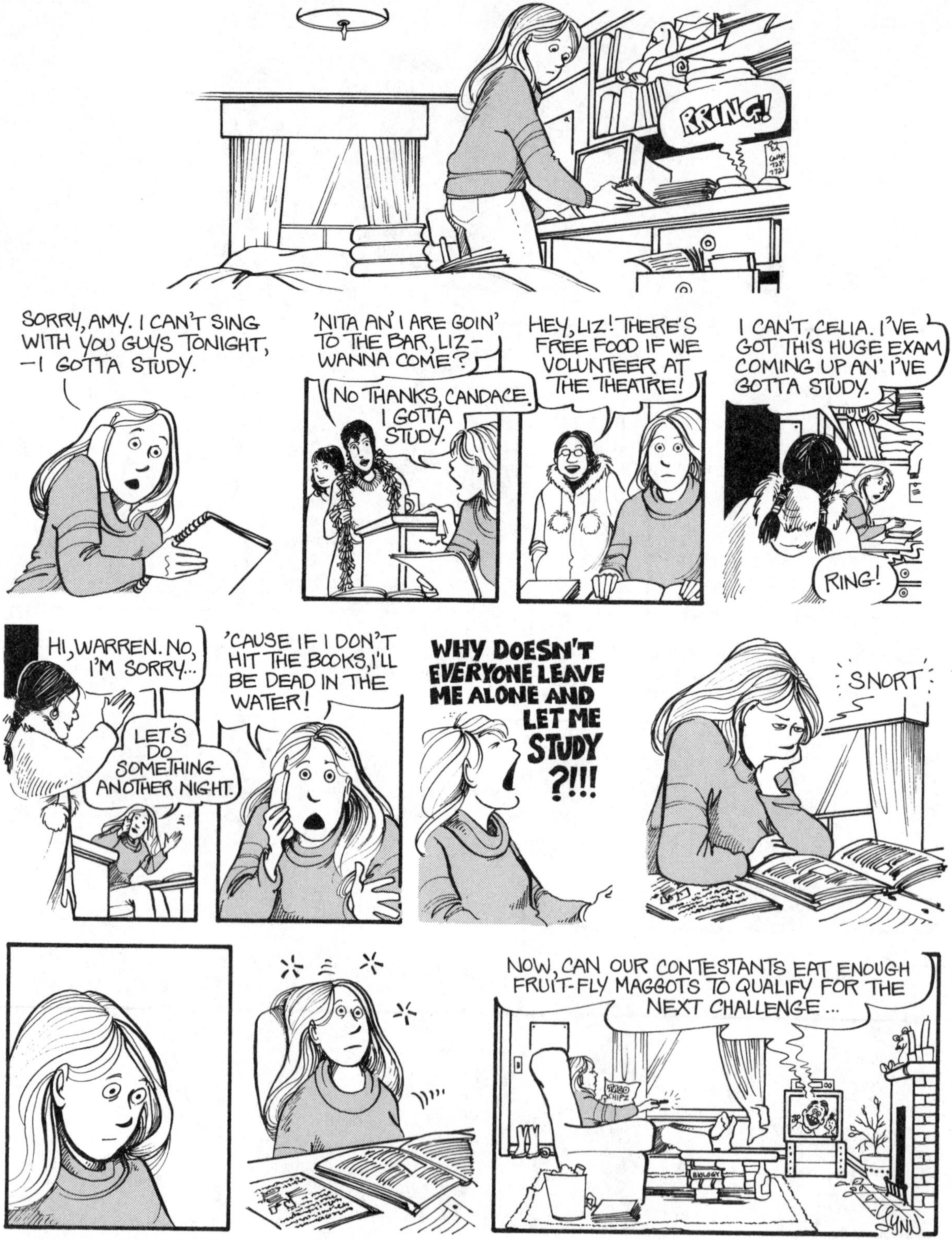
RRING!
CALL 723-7721
SORRY, AMY. I CAN'T SING WITH YOU GUYS TONIGHT, —I GOTTA STUDY.
'NITA AN' I ARE GOIN' TO THE BAR, LIZ—WANNA COME?
NO THANKS, CANDACE. I GOTTA STUDY.
HEY, LIZ! THERE'S FREE FOOD IF WE VOLUNTEER AT THE THEATRE!
I CAN'T, CELIA. I'VE GOT THIS HUGE EXAM COMING UP AN' I'VE GOTTA STUDY.
RING!
HI, WARREN. NO, I'M SORRY...
LET'S DO SOMETHING ANOTHER NIGHT.
'CAUSE IF I DON'T HIT THE BOOKS, I'LL BE DEAD IN THE WATER!
WHY DOESN'T EVERYONE LEAVE ME ALONE AND LET ME STUDY?!!!
SNORT
NOW, CAN OUR CONTESTANTS EAT ENOUGH FRUIT-FLY MAGGOTS TO QUALIFY FOR THE NEXT CHALLENGE...
TACO CHIPZ
BIOLOGY
LYNN

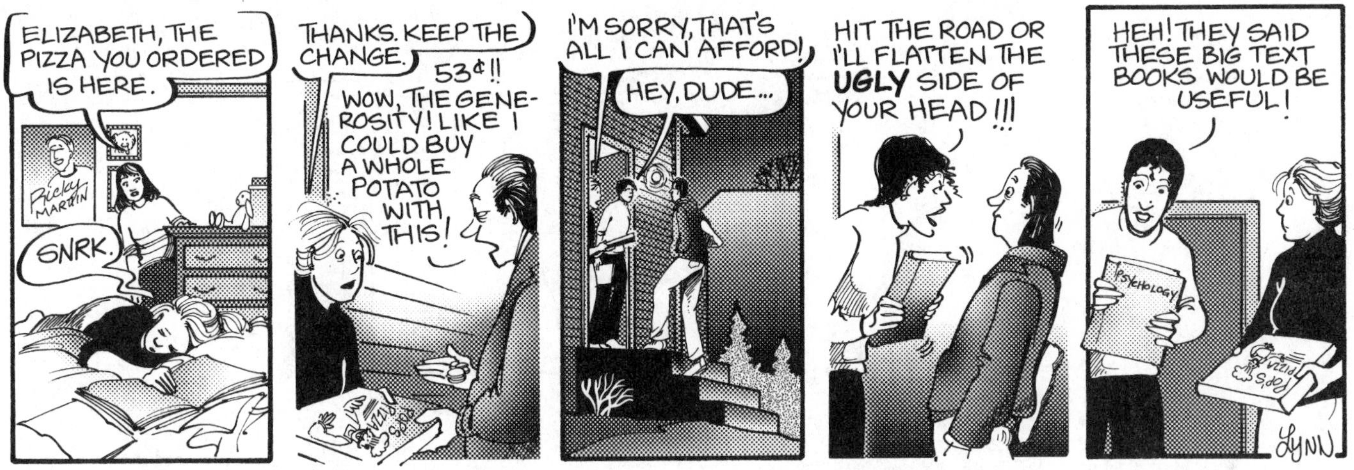
ELIZABETH, THE PIZZA YOU ORDERED IS HERE.
Ricky MARTIN
SNRK.
THANKS. KEEP THE CHANGE.
53¢!! WOW, THE GENEROSITY! LIKE I COULD BUY A WHOLE POTATO WITH THIS!
I'M SORRY, THAT'S ALL I CAN AFFORD!
HEY, DUDE...
HIT THE ROAD OR I'LL FLATTEN THE **UGLY** SIDE OF YOUR HEAD!!!
HEH! THEY SAID THESE BIG TEXT BOOKS WOULD BE USEFUL!
PSYCHOLOGY
LYNN

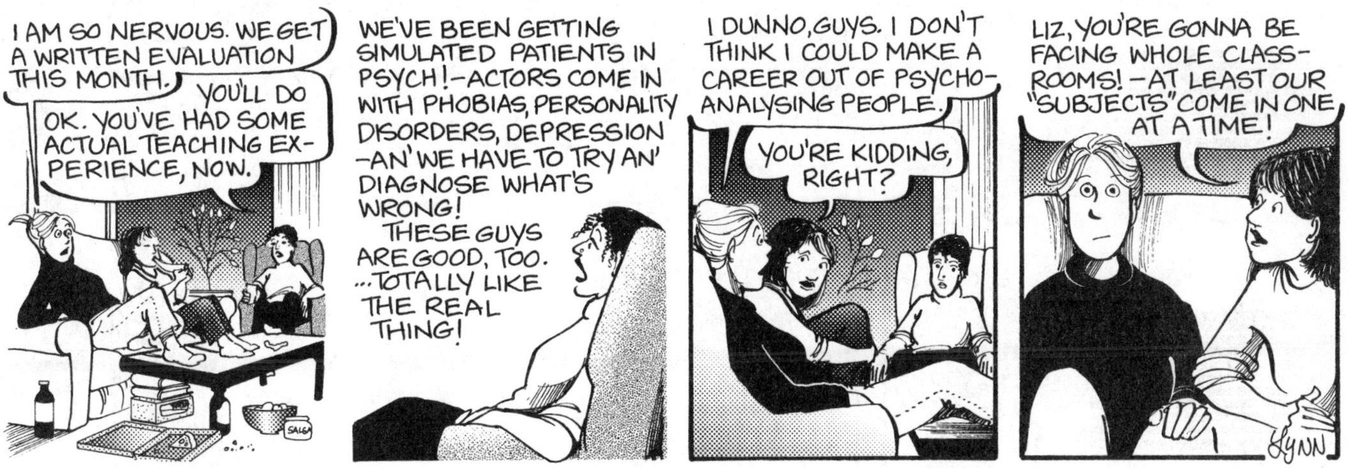
I AM SO NERVOUS. WE GET A WRITTEN EVALUATION THIS MONTH.
YOU'LL DO OK. YOU'VE HAD SOME ACTUAL TEACHING EXPERIENCE, NOW.
SALSA
WE'VE BEEN GETTING SIMULATED PATIENTS IN PSYCH! –ACTORS COME IN WITH PHOBIAS, PERSONALITY DISORDERS, DEPRESSION –AN' WE HAVE TO TRY AN' DIAGNOSE WHAT'S WRONG!
THESE GUYS ARE GOOD, TOO. ...TOTALLY LIKE THE REAL THING!
I DUNNO, GUYS. I DON'T THINK I COULD MAKE A CAREER OUT OF PSYCHO-ANALYSING PEOPLE.
YOU'RE KIDDING, RIGHT?
LIZ, YOU'RE GONNA BE FACING WHOLE CLASS-ROOMS! –AT LEAST OUR "SUBJECTS" COME IN ONE AT A TIME!
LYNN

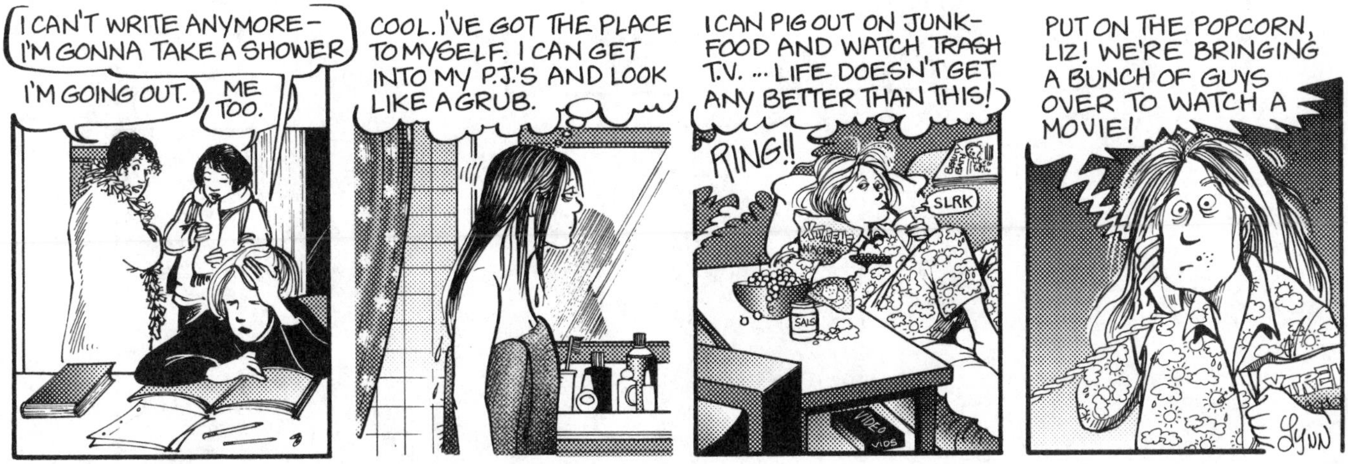
I CAN'T WRITE ANYMORE – I'M GONNA TAKE A SHOWER
I'M GOING OUT.
ME TOO.
COOL. I'VE GOT THE PLACE TO MYSELF. I CAN GET INTO MY P.J.'S AND LOOK LIKE A GRUB.
I CAN PIG OUT ON JUNK-FOOD AND WATCH TRASH T.V. ... LIFE DOESN'T GET ANY BETTER THAN THIS!
RING!!
SLRK
VIDEO
PUT ON THE POPCORN, LIZ! WE'RE BRINGING A BUNCH OF GUYS OVER TO WATCH A MOVIE!
LYNN

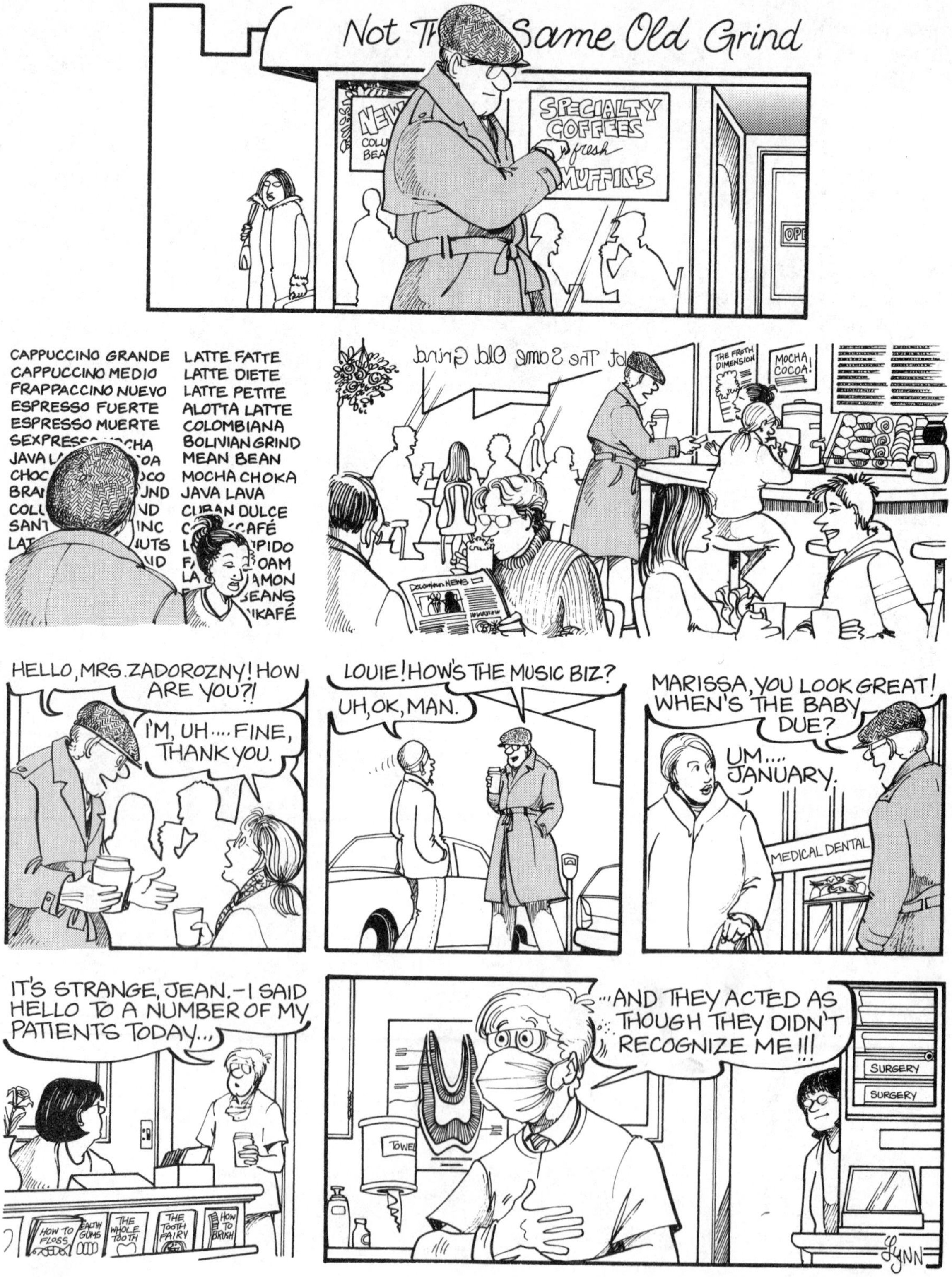

Not Th
Same Old Grind
SPECIALTY COFFEES fresh MUFFINS
CAPPUCCINO GRANDE
CAPPUCCINO MEDIO
FRAPPACCINO NUEVO
ESPRESSO FUERTE
ESPRESSO MUERTE
LATTE FATTE
LATTE DIETE
LATTE PETITE
ALOTTA LATTE
COLOMBIANA
BOLIVIAN GRIND
MEAN BEAN
MOCHA CHOKA
JAVA LAVA
CUBAN DULCE
THE FROTH DIMENSION
MOCHA COCOA!
HELLO, MRS. ZADOROZNY! HOW ARE YOU?!
I'M, UH.... FINE, THANK YOU.
LOUIE! HOW'S THE MUSIC BIZ?
UH, OK, MAN.
MARISSA, YOU LOOK GREAT! WHEN'S THE BABY DUE?
UM.... JANUARY.
MEDICAL DENTAL
IT'S STRANGE, JEAN. – I SAID HELLO TO A NUMBER OF MY PATIENTS TODAY...,
HOW TO FLOSS
THE WHOLE TOOTH
THE TOOTH FAIRY
HOW TO BRUSH
...AND THEY ACTED AS THOUGH THEY DIDN'T RECOGNIZE ME!!!
SURGERY
SURGERY
Lynn

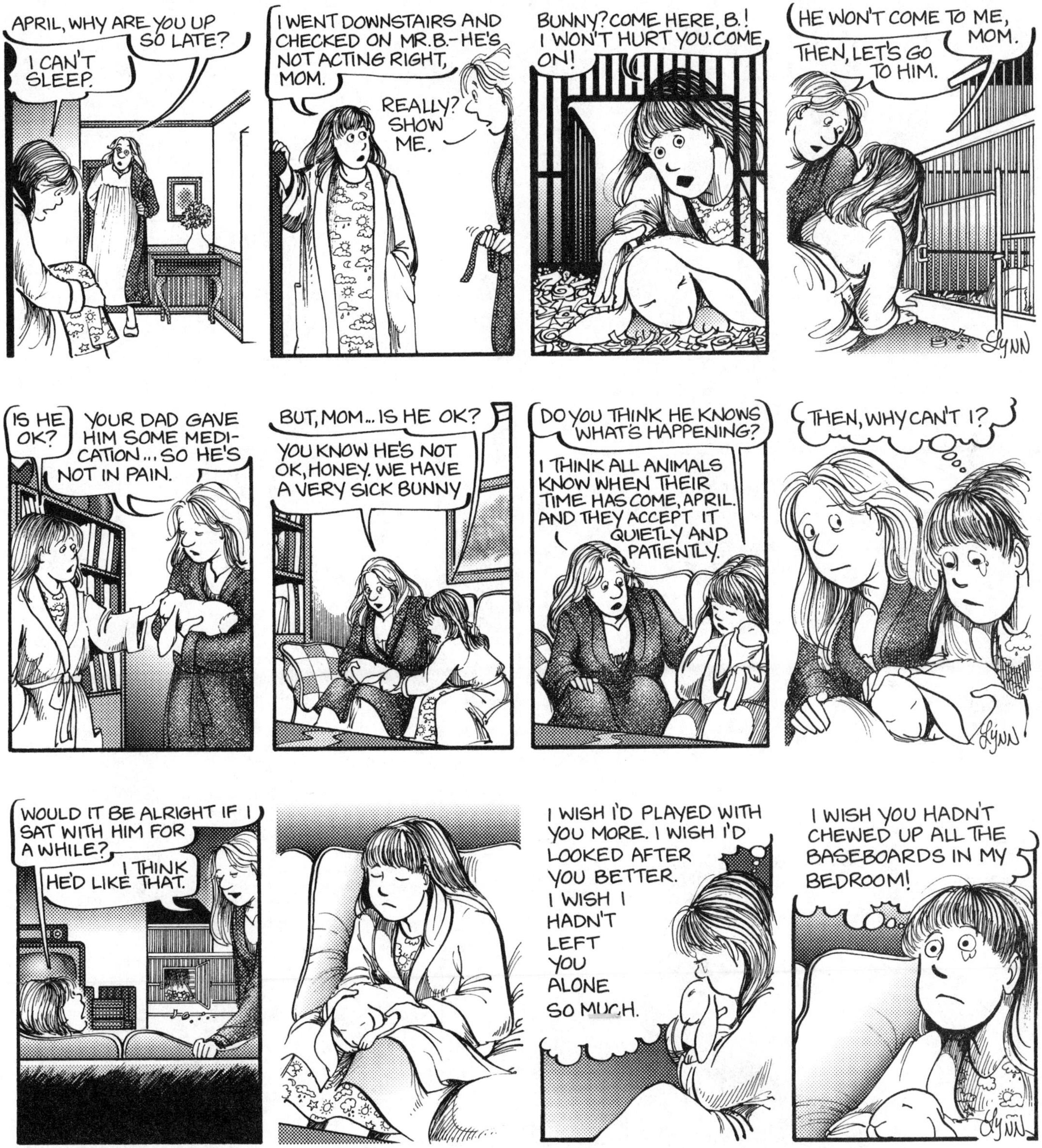
APRIL, WHY ARE YOU UP SO LATE?
I CAN'T SLEEP.
I WENT DOWNSTAIRS AND CHECKED ON MR. B.- HE'S NOT ACTING RIGHT, MOM.
REALLY? SHOW ME.
BUNNY? COME HERE, B.! I WON'T HURT YOU. COME ON!
HE WON'T COME TO ME, MOM.
THEN, LET'S GO TO HIM.
LYNN
IS HE OK?
YOUR DAD GAVE HIM SOME MEDICATION... SO HE'S NOT IN PAIN.
BUT, MOM... IS HE OK?
YOU KNOW HE'S NOT OK, HONEY. WE HAVE A VERY SICK BUNNY.
DO YOU THINK HE KNOWS WHAT'S HAPPENING?
I THINK ALL ANIMALS KNOW WHEN THEIR TIME HAS COME, APRIL. AND THEY ACCEPT IT QUIETLY AND PATIENTLY.
THEN, WHY CAN'T I?
LYNN
WOULD IT BE ALRIGHT IF I SAT WITH HIM FOR A WHILE?
I THINK HE'D LIKE THAT.
I WISH I'D PLAYED WITH YOU MORE. I WISH I'D LOOKED AFTER YOU BETTER. I WISH I HADN'T LEFT YOU ALONE SO MUCH.
I WISH YOU HADN'T CHEWED UP ALL THE BASEBOARDS IN MY BEDROOM!
LYNN

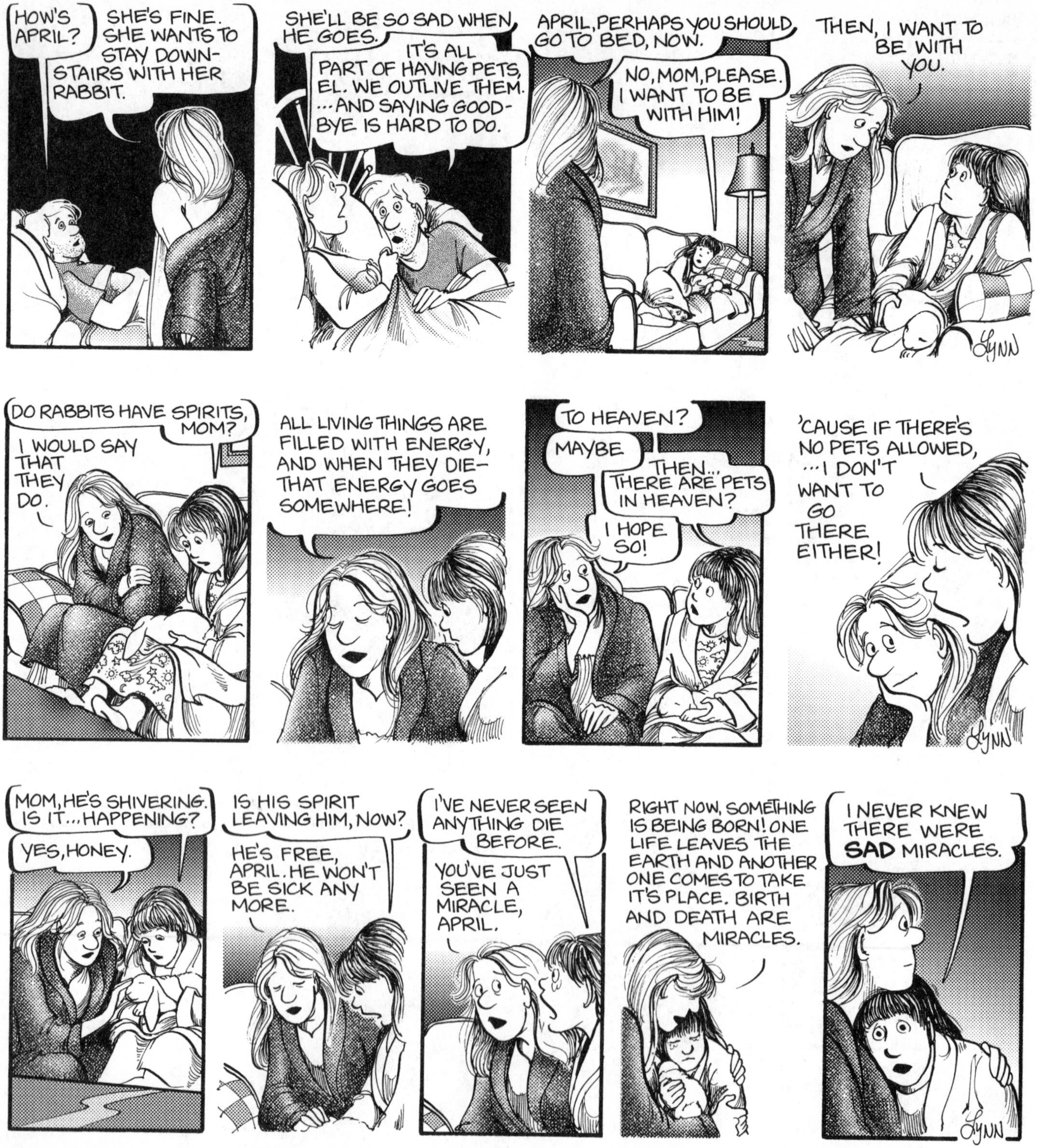
HOW'S APRIL?
SHE'S FINE. SHE WANTS TO STAY DOWN-STAIRS WITH HER RABBIT.
SHE'LL BE SO SAD WHEN HE GOES.
IT'S ALL PART OF HAVING PETS, EL. WE OUTLIVE THEM. ...AND SAYING GOOD-BYE IS HARD TO DO.
APRIL, PERHAPS YOU SHOULD GO TO BED, NOW.
NO, MOM, PLEASE. I WANT TO BE WITH HIM!
THEN, I WANT TO BE WITH YOU.
LYNN
DO RABBITS HAVE SPIRITS, MOM?
I WOULD SAY THAT THEY DO.
ALL LIVING THINGS ARE FILLED WITH ENERGY, AND WHEN THEY DIE-THAT ENERGY GOES SOMEWHERE!
TO HEAVEN?
MAYBE
THEN... THERE ARE PETS IN HEAVEN?
I HOPE SO!
'CAUSE IF THERE'S NO PETS ALLOWED, ...I DON'T WANT TO GO THERE EITHER!
LYNN
MOM, HE'S SHIVERING. IS IT... HAPPENING?
YES, HONEY.
IS HIS SPIRIT LEAVING HIM, NOW?
HE'S FREE, APRIL. HE WON'T BE SICK ANY MORE.
I'VE NEVER SEEN ANYTHING DIE BEFORE.
YOU'VE JUST SEEN A MIRACLE, APRIL.
RIGHT NOW, SOMETHING IS BEING BORN! ONE LIFE LEAVES THE EARTH AND ANOTHER ONE COMES TO TAKE IT'S PLACE. BIRTH AND DEATH ARE MIRACLES.
I NEVER KNEW THERE WERE **SAD** MIRACLES.
LYNN

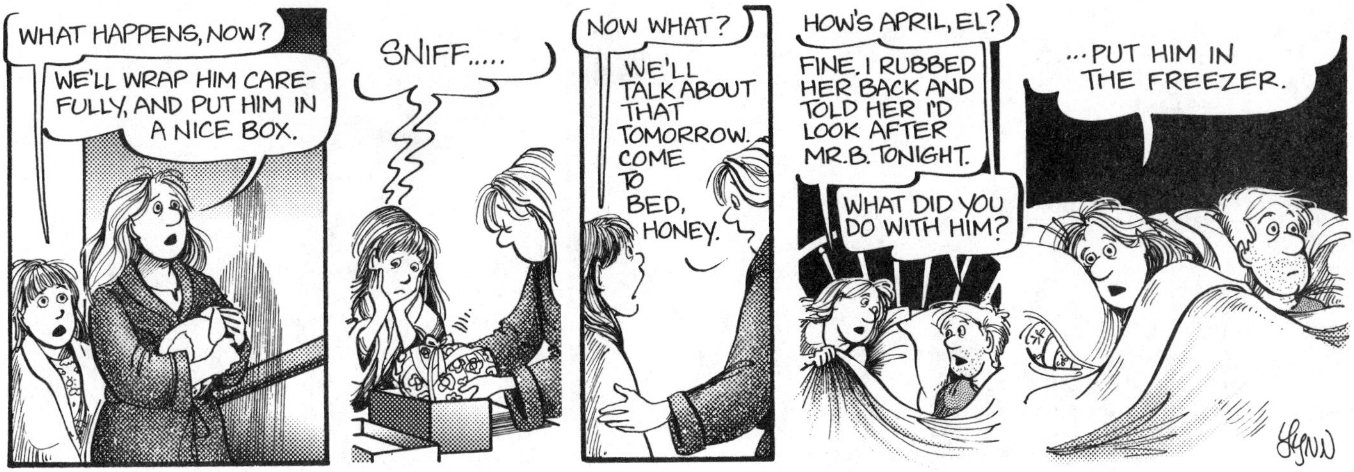
WHAT HAPPENS, NOW?
WE'LL WRAP HIM CAREFULLY, AND PUT HIM IN A NICE BOX.
SNIFF.....
NOW WHAT?
WE'LL TALK ABOUT THAT TOMORROW. COME TO BED, HONEY.
HOW'S APRIL, EL?
FINE. I RUBBED HER BACK AND TOLD HER I'D LOOK AFTER MR.B. TONIGHT.
WHAT DID YOU DO WITH HIM?
...PUT HIM IN THE FREEZER.
LYNN

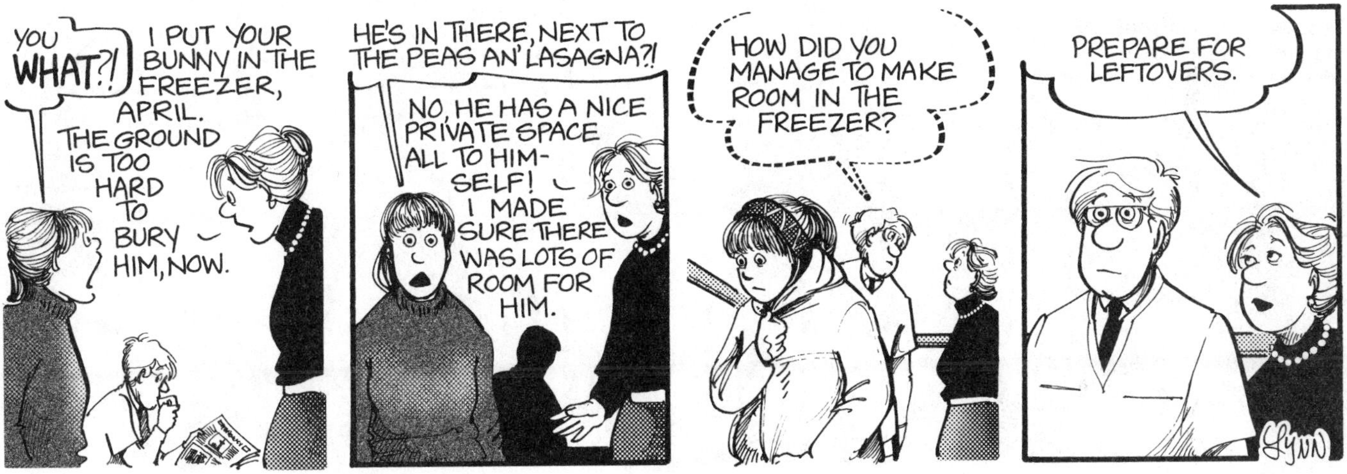
YOU WHAT?!
I PUT YOUR BUNNY IN THE FREEZER, APRIL. THE GROUND IS TOO HARD TO BURY HIM, NOW.
HE'S IN THERE, NEXT TO THE PEAS AN' LASAGNA?!
NO, HE HAS A NICE PRIVATE SPACE ALL TO HIMSELF! I MADE SURE THERE WAS LOTS OF ROOM FOR HIM.
HOW DID YOU MANAGE TO MAKE ROOM IN THE FREEZER?
PREPARE FOR LEFTOVERS.
LYNN

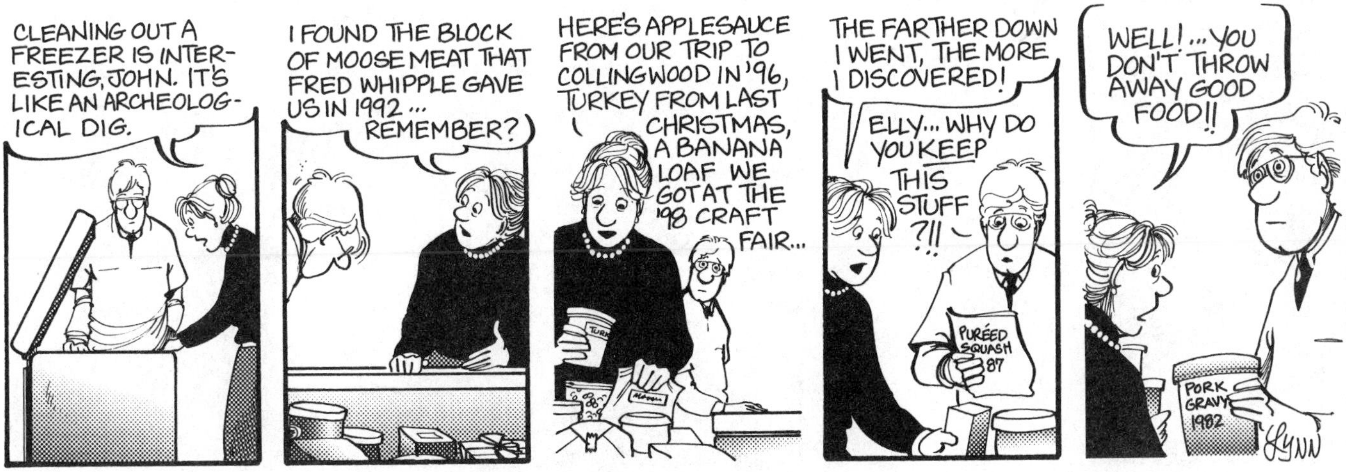
CLEANING OUT A FREEZER IS INTERESTING, JOHN. IT'S LIKE AN ARCHEOLOGICAL DIG.
I FOUND THE BLOCK OF MOOSE MEAT THAT FRED WHIPPLE GAVE US IN 1992... REMEMBER?
HERE'S APPLESAUCE FROM OUR TRIP TO COLLINGWOOD IN '96, TURKEY FROM LAST CHRISTMAS, A BANANA LOAF WE GOT AT THE '98 CRAFT FAIR...
THE FARTHER DOWN I WENT, THE MORE I DISCOVERED!
ELLY... WHY DO YOU KEEP THIS STUFF ?!!
PURÉED SQUASH 87
WELL! ...YOU DON'T THROW AWAY GOOD FOOD!!
PORK GRAVY 1982
LYNN

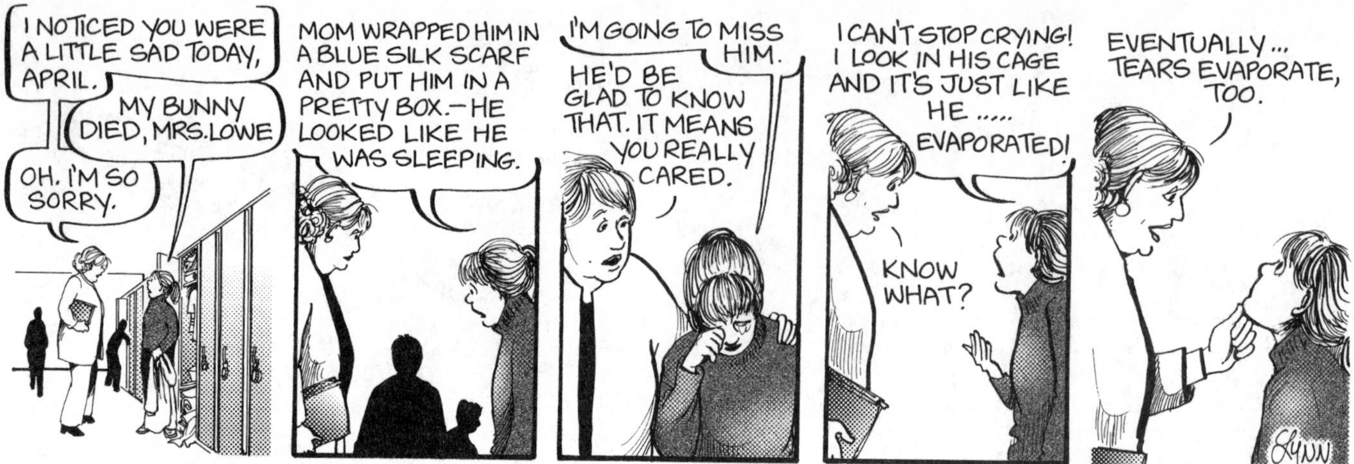
I NOTICED YOU WERE A LITTLE SAD TODAY, APRIL.
MY BUNNY DIED, MRS. LOWE
OH. I'M SO SORRY.
MOM WRAPPED HIM IN A BLUE SILK SCARF AND PUT HIM IN A PRETTY BOX.—HE LOOKED LIKE HE WAS SLEEPING.
I'M GOING TO MISS HIM.
HE'D BE GLAD TO KNOW THAT. IT MEANS YOU REALLY CARED.
I CAN'T STOP CRYING! I LOOK IN HIS CAGE AND IT'S JUST LIKE HE ..... EVAPORATED!
KNOW WHAT?
EVENTUALLY... TEARS EVAPORATE, TOO.
LYNN

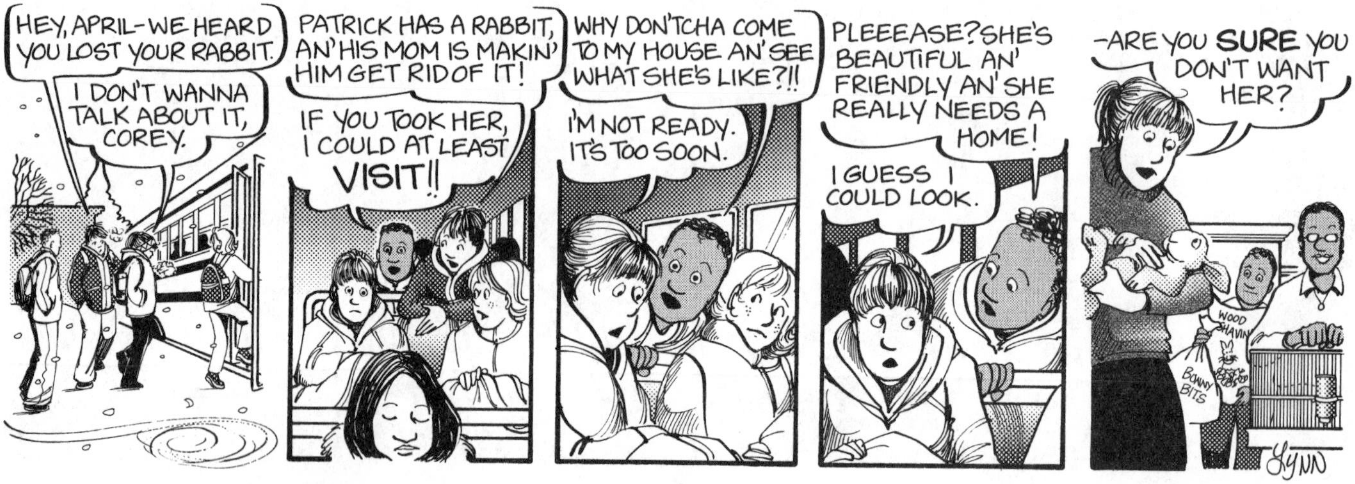
HEY, APRIL-WE HEARD YOU LOST YOUR RABBIT.
I DON'T WANNA TALK ABOUT IT, COREY.
PATRICK HAS A RABBIT, AN' HIS MOM IS MAKIN' HIM GET RID OF IT!
IF YOU TOOK HER, I COULD AT LEAST VISIT!!
WHY DON'TCHA COME TO MY HOUSE AN' SEE WHAT SHE'S LIKE?!!
I'M NOT READY. IT'S TOO SOON.
PLEEEASE? SHE'S BEAUTIFUL AN' FRIENDLY AN' SHE REALLY NEEDS A HOME!
I GUESS I COULD LOOK.
-ARE YOU SURE YOU DON'T WANT HER?
WOOD SHAVIN
BUNNY BITS
LYNN

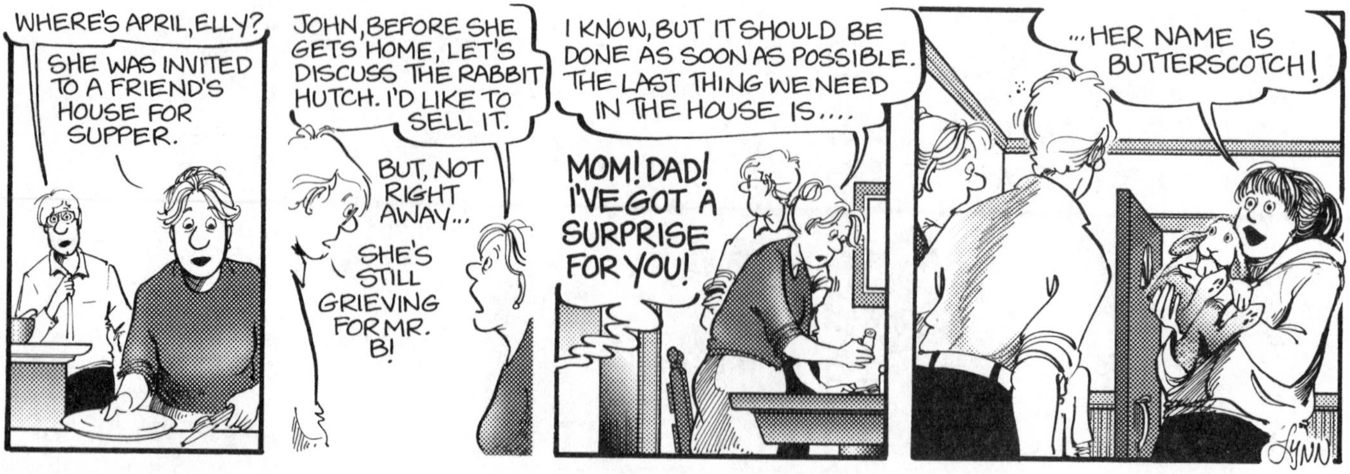
WHERE'S APRIL, ELLY?
SHE WAS INVITED TO A FRIEND'S HOUSE FOR SUPPER.
JOHN, BEFORE SHE GETS HOME, LET'S DISCUSS THE RABBIT HUTCH. I'D LIKE TO SELL IT.
BUT, NOT RIGHT AWAY...
SHE'S STILL GRIEVING FOR MR. B!
I KNOW, BUT IT SHOULD BE DONE AS SOON AS POSSIBLE. THE LAST THING WE NEED IN THE HOUSE IS....
MOM! DAD! I'VE GOT A SURPRISE FOR YOU!
...HER NAME IS BUTTERSCOTCH!
LYNN

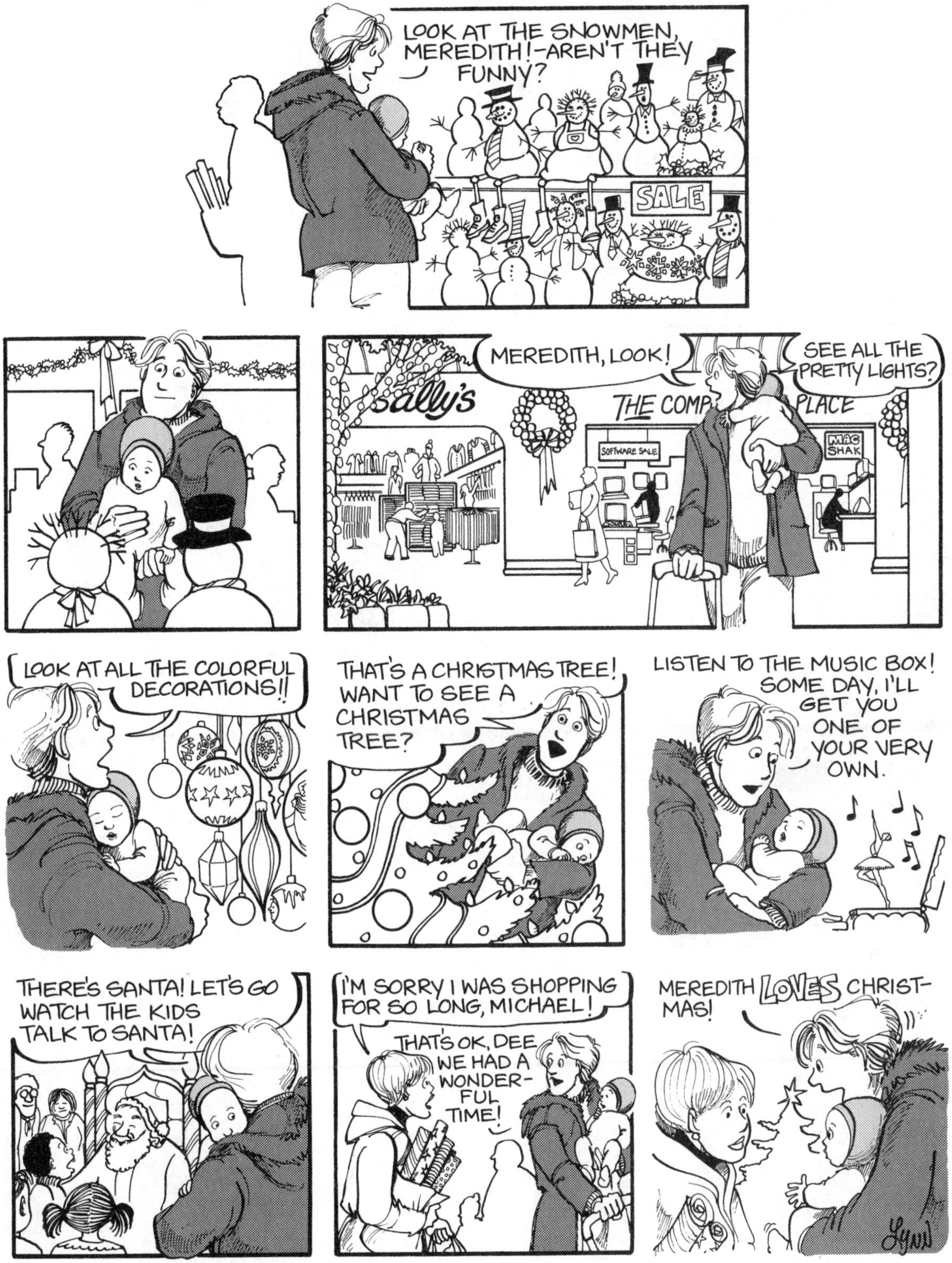
LOOK AT THE SNOWMEN, MEREDITH!-AREN'T THEY FUNNY?
SALE
MEREDITH, LOOK!
SEE ALL THE PRETTY LIGHTS?
sally's
THE COMP PLACE
SOFTWARE SALE
MAC SHAK
LOOK AT ALL THE COLORFUL DECORATIONS!!
THAT'S A CHRISTMAS TREE! WANT TO SEE A CHRISTMAS TREE?
LISTEN TO THE MUSIC BOX! SOME DAY, I'LL GET YOU ONE OF YOUR VERY OWN.
THERE'S SANTA! LET'S GO WATCH THE KIDS TALK TO SANTA!
I'M SORRY I WAS SHOPPING FOR SO LONG, MICHAEL!
THAT'S OK, DEE WE HAD A WONDERFUL TIME!
MEREDITH LOVES CHRISTMAS!
Lynn

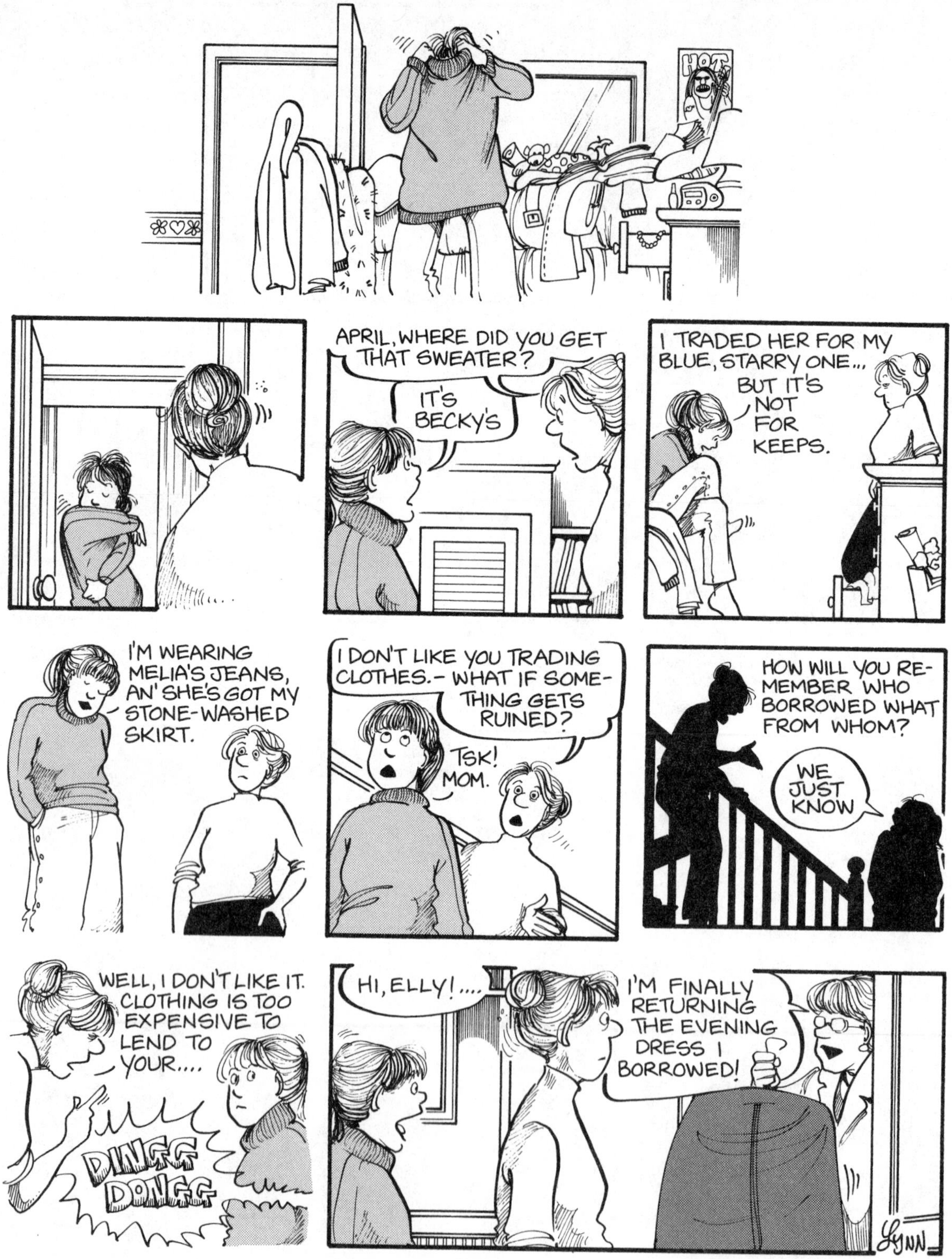
HOT
APRIL, WHERE DID YOU GET THAT SWEATER?
IT'S BECKY'S
I TRADED HER FOR MY BLUE, STARRY ONE...,
BUT IT'S NOT FOR KEEPS.
I'M WEARING MELIA'S JEANS, AN' SHE'S GOT MY STONE-WASHED SKIRT.
I DON'T LIKE YOU TRADING CLOTHES.- WHAT IF SOMETHING GETS RUINED?
TSK! MOM.
HOW WILL YOU REMEMBER WHO BORROWED WHAT FROM WHOM?
WE JUST KNOW
WELL, I DON'T LIKE IT. CLOTHING IS TOO EXPENSIVE TO LEND TO YOUR....
DINGG DONGG
HI, ELLY!....
I'M FINALLY RETURNING THE EVENING DRESS I BORROWED!
Lynn

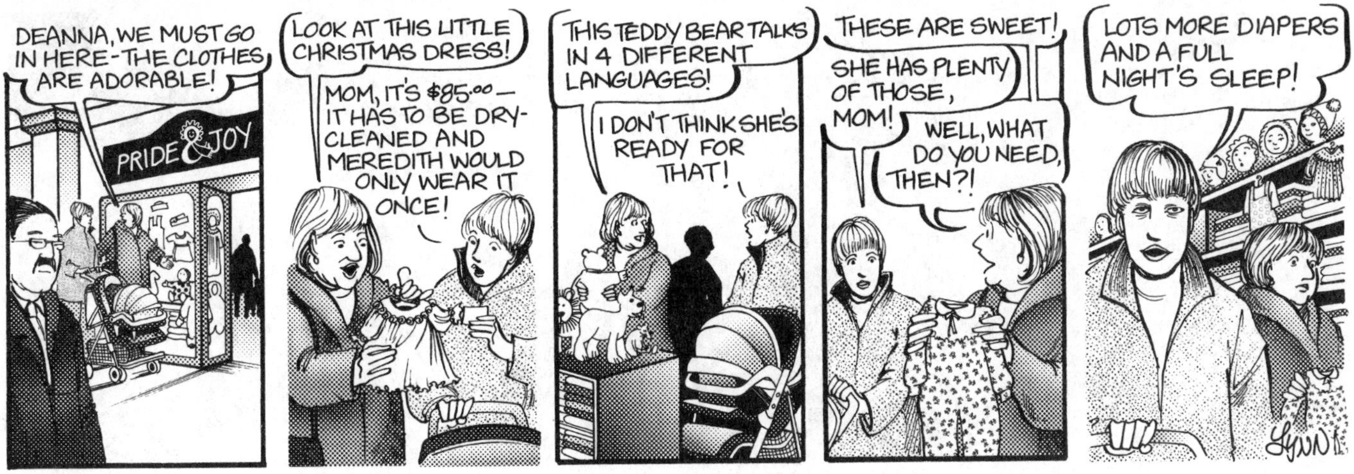
DEANNA, WE MUST GO IN HERE-THE CLOTHES ARE ADORABLE!
PRIDE & JOY
LOOK AT THIS LITTLE CHRISTMAS DRESS!
MOM, IT'S $85.00— IT HAS TO BE DRY-CLEANED AND MEREDITH WOULD ONLY WEAR IT ONCE!
THIS TEDDY BEAR TALKS IN 4 DIFFERENT LANGUAGES!
I DON'T THINK SHE'S READY FOR THAT!
THESE ARE SWEET!
SHE HAS PLENTY OF THOSE, MOM!
WELL, WHAT DO YOU NEED, THEN?!
LOTS MORE DIAPERS AND A FULL NIGHT'S SLEEP!
LYNN

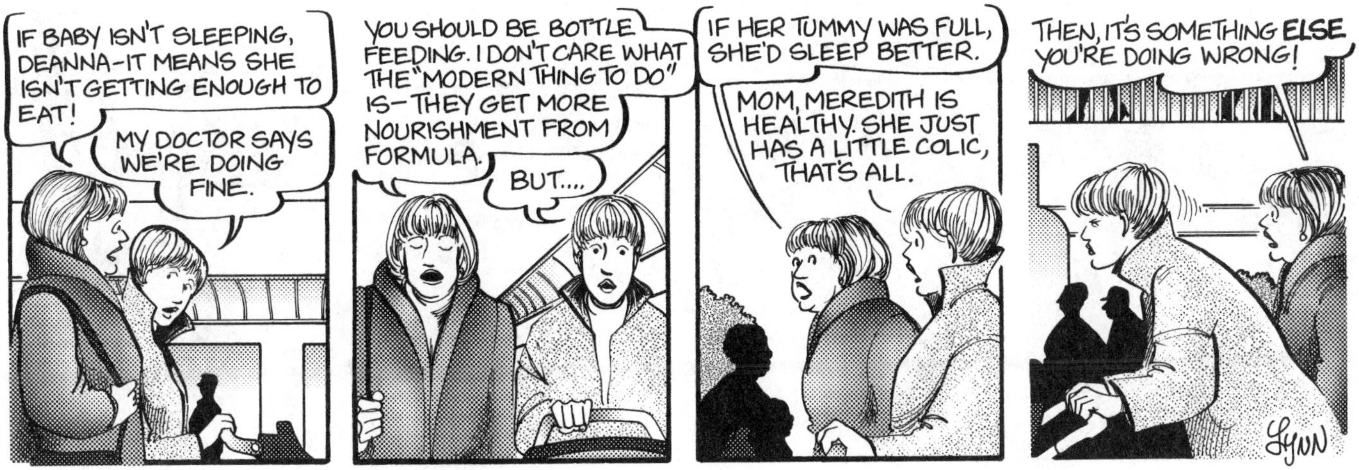
IF BABY ISN'T SLEEPING, DEANNA-IT MEANS SHE ISN'T GETTING ENOUGH TO EAT!
MY DOCTOR SAYS WE'RE DOING FINE.
YOU SHOULD BE BOTTLE FEEDING. I DON'T CARE WHAT THE "MODERN THING TO DO" IS- THEY GET MORE NOURISHMENT FROM FORMULA.
BUT....
IF HER TUMMY WAS FULL, SHE'D SLEEP BETTER.
MOM, MEREDITH IS HEALTHY. SHE JUST HAS A LITTLE COLIC, THAT'S ALL.
THEN, IT'S SOMETHING **ELSE** YOU'RE DOING WRONG!
LYNN

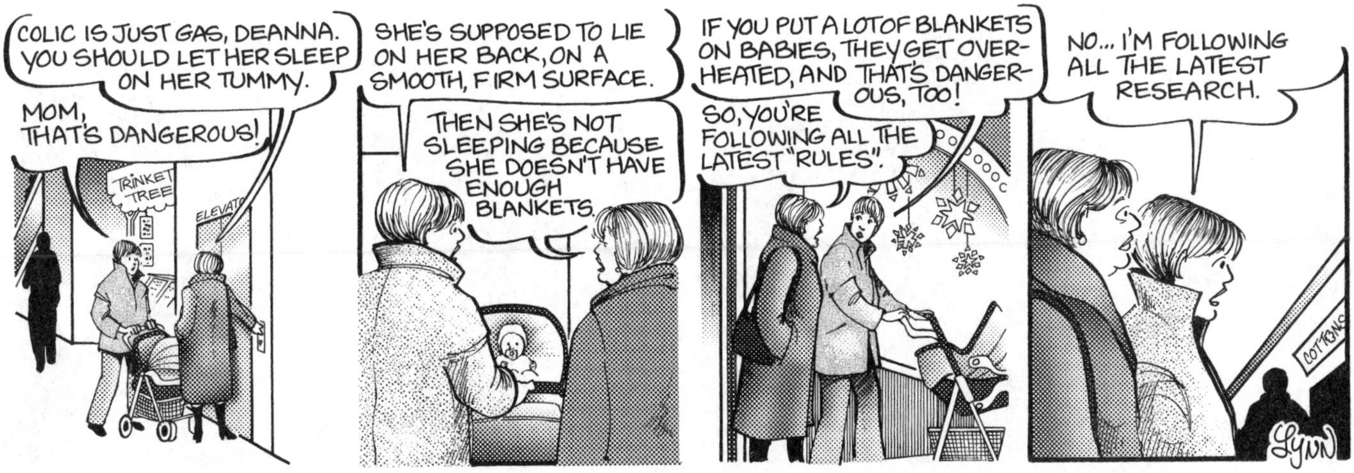
COLIC IS JUST GAS, DEANNA. YOU SHOULD LET HER SLEEP ON HER TUMMY.
MOM, THAT'S DANGEROUS!
TRINKET TREE
SHE'S SUPPOSED TO LIE ON HER BACK, ON A SMOOTH, FIRM SURFACE.
THEN SHE'S NOT SLEEPING BECAUSE SHE DOESN'T HAVE ENOUGH BLANKETS.
IF YOU PUT A LOT OF BLANKETS ON BABIES, THEY GET OVER-HEATED, AND THAT'S DANGER-OUS, TOO!
SO, YOU'RE FOLLOWING ALL THE LATEST "RULES".
NO... I'M FOLLOWING ALL THE LATEST RESEARCH.
LYNN

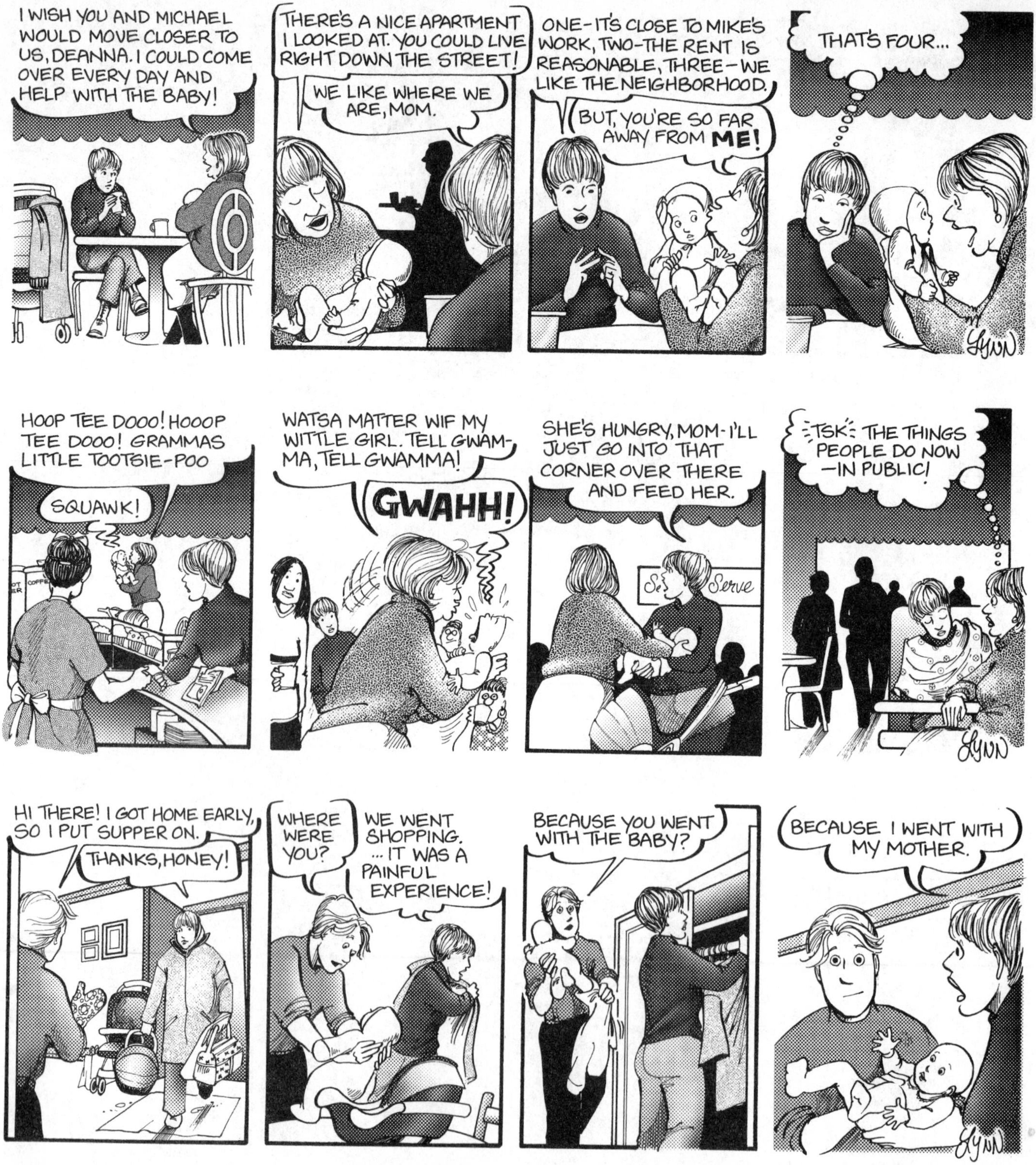
I WISH YOU AND MICHAEL WOULD MOVE CLOSER TO US, DEANNA. I COULD COME OVER EVERY DAY AND HELP WITH THE BABY!
THERE'S A NICE APARTMENT I LOOKED AT. YOU COULD LIVE RIGHT DOWN THE STREET!
WE LIKE WHERE WE ARE, MOM.
ONE-IT'S CLOSE TO MIKE'S WORK, TWO-THE RENT IS REASONABLE, THREE-WE LIKE THE NEIGHBORHOOD.
BUT, YOU'RE SO FAR AWAY FROM ME!
THAT'S FOUR...
LYNN
HOOP TEE DOOO! HOOOP TEE DOOO! GRAMMAS LITTLE TOOTSIE-POO
SQUAWK!
WATSA MATTER WIF MY WITTLE GIRL. TELL GWAMMA, TELL GWAMMA!
GWAHH!
SHE'S HUNGRY, MOM-I'LL JUST GO INTO THAT CORNER OVER THERE AND FEED HER.
TSK THE THINGS PEOPLE DO NOW —IN PUBLIC!
LYNN
HI THERE! I GOT HOME EARLY, SO I PUT SUPPER ON.
THANKS, HONEY!
WHERE WERE YOU?
WE WENT SHOPPING. ...IT WAS A PAINFUL EXPERIENCE!
BECAUSE YOU WENT WITH THE BABY?
BECAUSE I WENT WITH MY MOTHER.
LYNN

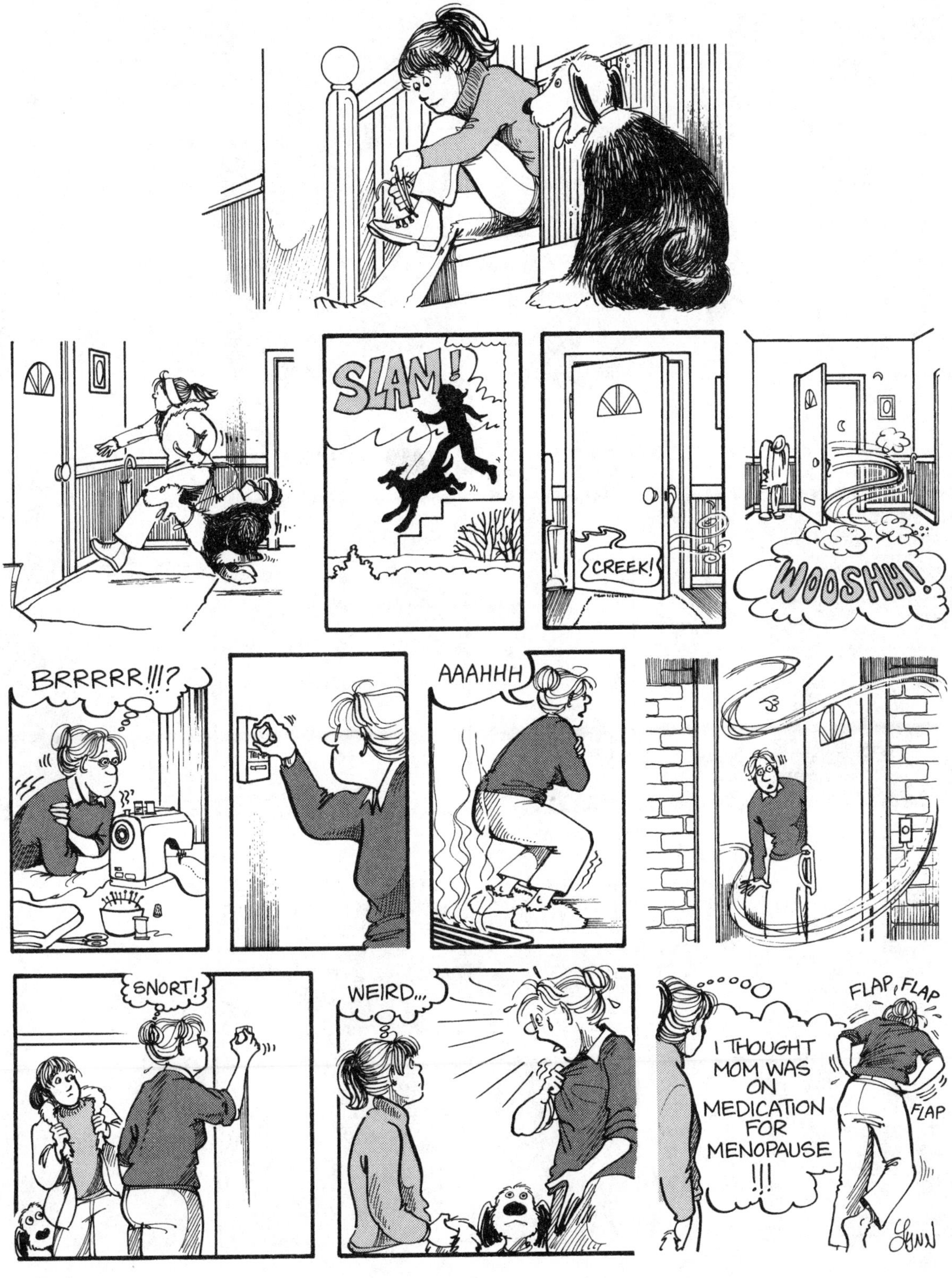
SLAM!
CREEK!
WOOSHH!
BRRRRR!!!?
TEMP
AAAHHH
SNORT!
WEIRD...
I THOUGHT MOM WAS ON MEDICATION FOR MENOPAUSE !!!
FLAP, FLAP
FLAP
LYNN

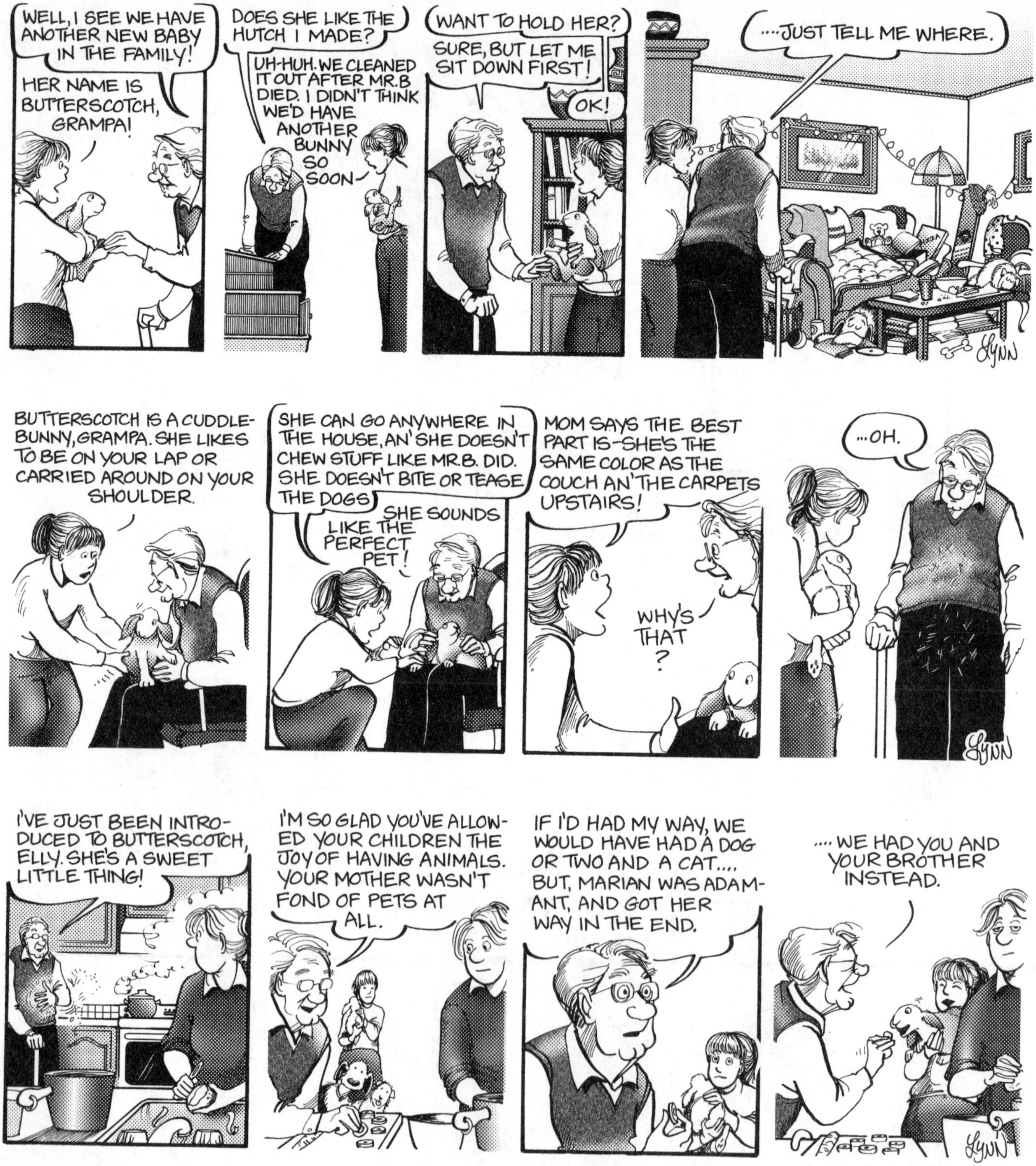
WELL, I SEE WE HAVE ANOTHER NEW BABY IN THE FAMILY!
HER NAME IS BUTTERSCOTCH, GRAMPA!
DOES SHE LIKE THE HUTCH I MADE?
UH-HUH. WE CLEANED IT OUT AFTER MR. B DIED. I DIDN'T THINK WE'D HAVE ANOTHER BUNNY SO SOON.
WANT TO HOLD HER?
SURE, BUT LET ME SIT DOWN FIRST!
OK!
....JUST TELL ME WHERE.
Lynn
BUTTERSCOTCH IS A CUDDLE-BUNNY, GRAMPA. SHE LIKES TO BE ON YOUR LAP OR CARRIED AROUND ON YOUR SHOULDER.
SHE CAN GO ANYWHERE IN THE HOUSE, AN' SHE DOESN'T CHEW STUFF LIKE MR. B. DID. SHE DOESN'T BITE OR TEASE THE DOGS.
SHE SOUNDS LIKE THE PERFECT PET!
MOM SAYS THE BEST PART IS–SHE'S THE SAME COLOR AS THE COUCH AN' THE CARPETS UPSTAIRS!
WHY'S THAT?
...OH.
Lynn
I'VE JUST BEEN INTRODUCED TO BUTTERSCOTCH, ELLY. SHE'S A SWEET LITTLE THING!
I'M SO GLAD YOU'VE ALLOWED YOUR CHILDREN THE JOY OF HAVING ANIMALS. YOUR MOTHER WASN'T FOND OF PETS AT ALL.
IF I'D HAD MY WAY, WE WOULD HAVE HAD A DOG OR TWO AND A CAT.... BUT, MARIAN WAS ADAMANT, AND GOT HER WAY IN THE END.
....WE HAD YOU AND YOUR BROTHER INSTEAD.
Lynn

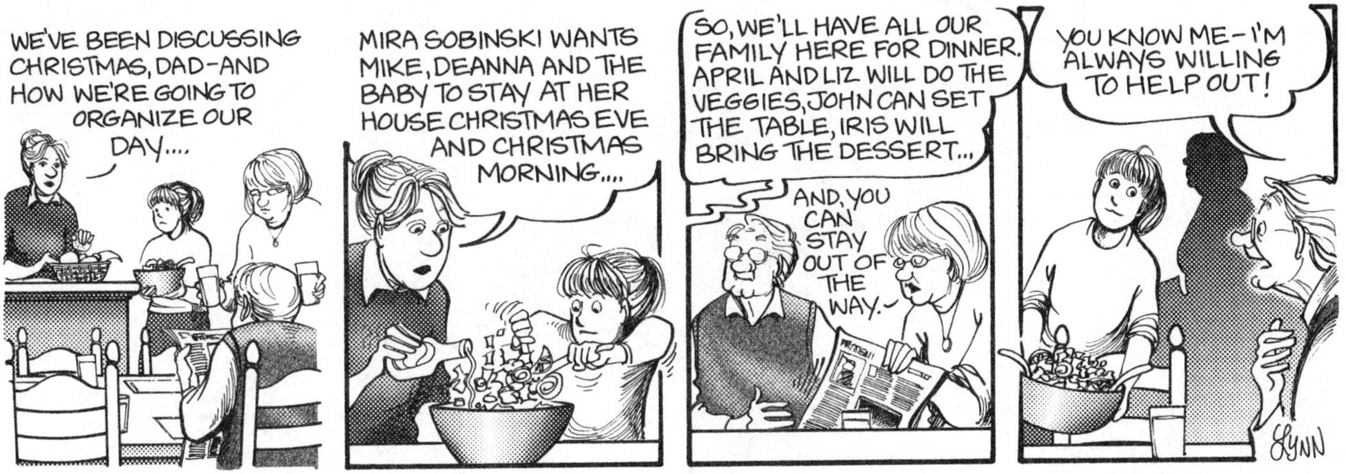
WE'VE BEEN DISCUSSING CHRISTMAS, DAD-AND HOW WE'RE GOING TO ORGANIZE OUR DAY....
MIRA SOBINSKI WANTS MIKE, DEANNA AND THE BABY TO STAY AT HER HOUSE CHRISTMAS EVE AND CHRISTMAS MORNING....
SO, WE'LL HAVE ALL OUR FAMILY HERE FOR DINNER. APRIL AND LIZ WILL DO THE VEGGIES, JOHN CAN SET THE TABLE, IRIS WILL BRING THE DESSERT...
AND, YOU CAN STAY OUT OF THE WAY.
YOU KNOW ME - I'M ALWAYS WILLING TO HELP OUT!
LYNN

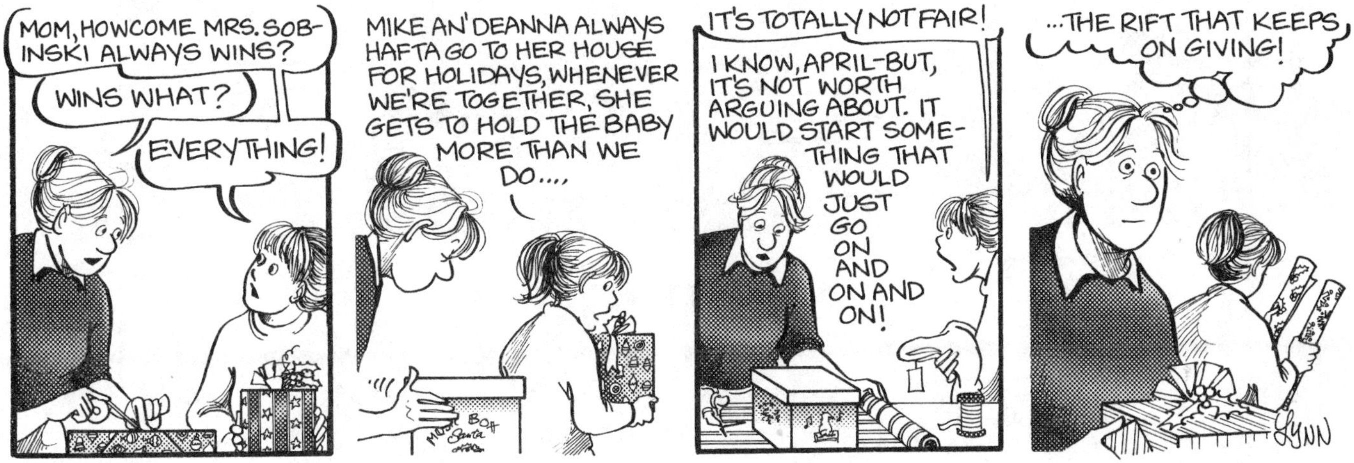
MOM, HOWCOME MRS. SOBINSKI ALWAYS WINS?
WINS WHAT?
EVERYTHING!
MIKE AN' DEANNA ALWAYS HAFTA GO TO HER HOUSE FOR HOLIDAYS, WHENEVER WE'RE TOGETHER, SHE GETS TO HOLD THE BABY MORE THAN WE DO....
IT'S TOTALLY NOT FAIR!
I KNOW, APRIL-BUT, IT'S NOT WORTH ARGUING ABOUT. IT WOULD START SOMETHING THAT WOULD JUST GO ON AND ON AND ON!
...THE RIFT THAT KEEPS ON GIVING!
LYNN

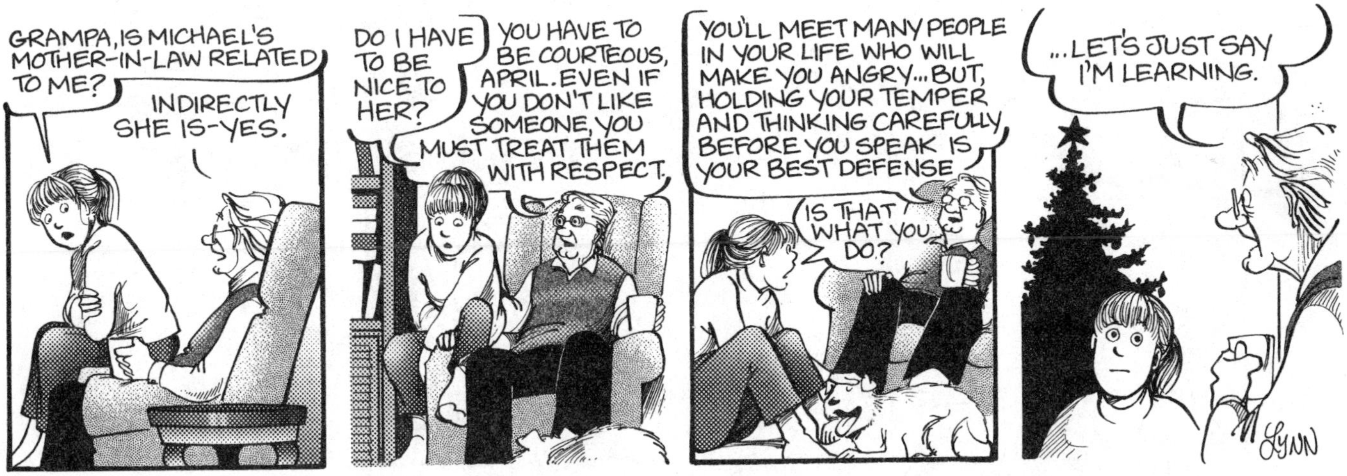
GRAMPA, IS MICHAEL'S MOTHER-IN-LAW RELATED TO ME?
INDIRECTLY SHE IS-YES.
DO I HAVE TO BE NICE TO HER?
YOU HAVE TO BE COURTEOUS, APRIL. EVEN IF YOU DON'T LIKE SOMEONE, YOU MUST TREAT THEM WITH RESPECT.
YOU'LL MEET MANY PEOPLE IN YOUR LIFE WHO WILL MAKE YOU ANGRY... BUT, HOLDING YOUR TEMPER AND THINKING CAREFULLY BEFORE YOU SPEAK IS YOUR BEST DEFENSE
IS THAT WHAT YOU DO?
...LET'S JUST SAY I'M LEARNING.
LYNN

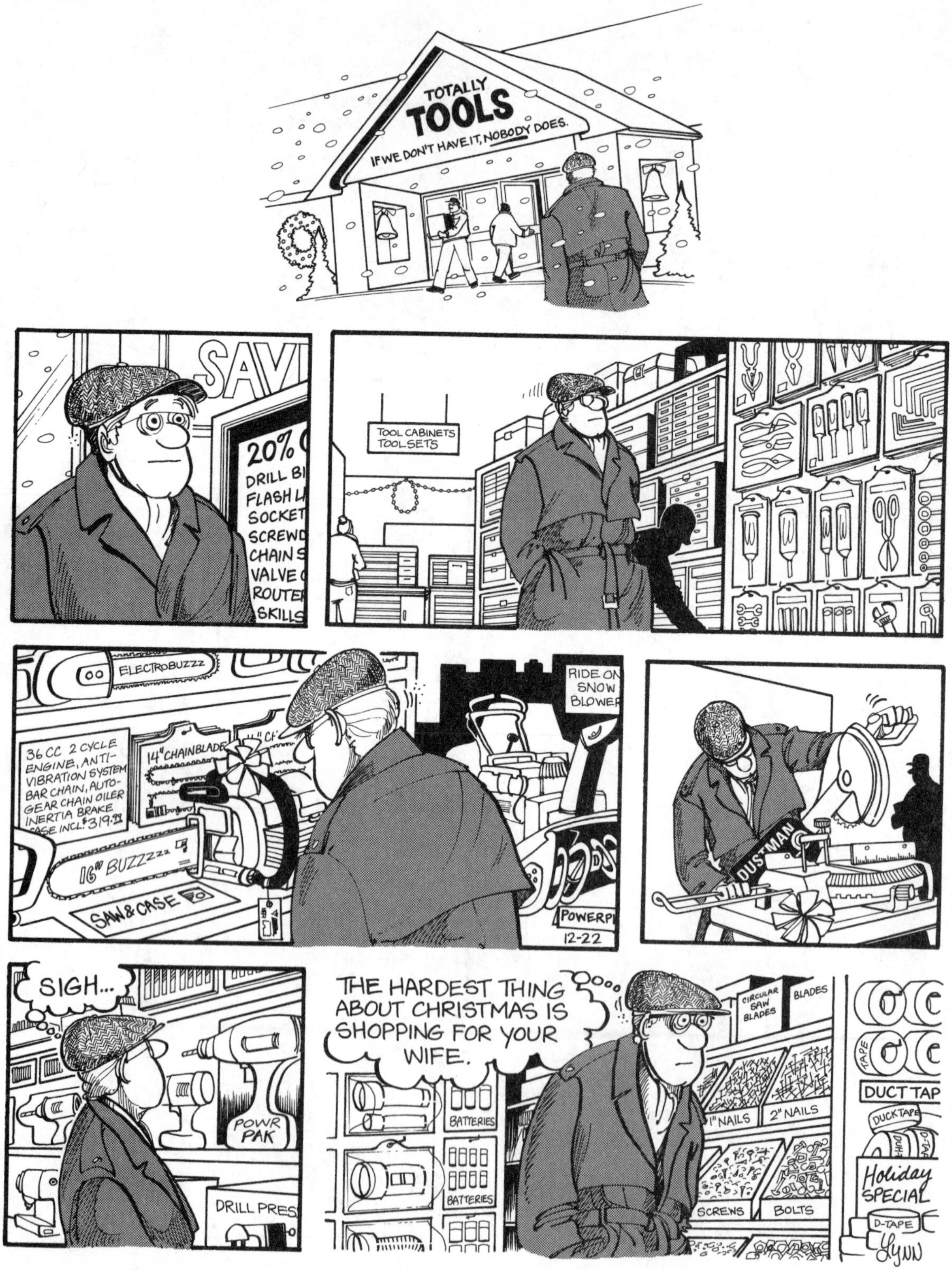
TOTALLY TOOLS
IF WE DON'T HAVE IT, NOBODY DOES.
TOOL CABINETS TOOL SETS
ELECTROBUZZZ
36 CC 2 CYCLE ENGINE, ANTI-VIBRATION SYSTEM BAR CHAIN, AUTO-GEAR CHAIN OILER INERTIA BRAKE CASE INCL. $319.99
14" CHAINBLADE
16" BUZZZZZ
SAW & CASE
RIDE ON SNOW BLOWER
12-22
DUSTMAN
SIGH...
POWR PAK
DRILL PRES
THE HARDEST THING ABOUT CHRISTMAS IS SHOPPING FOR YOUR WIFE.
CIRCULAR SAW BLADES
BLADES
BATTERIES
BATTERIES
1" NAILS
2" NAILS
DUCK TAPE
SCREWS
BOLTS
Holiday SPECIAL
D-TAPE
Lynn

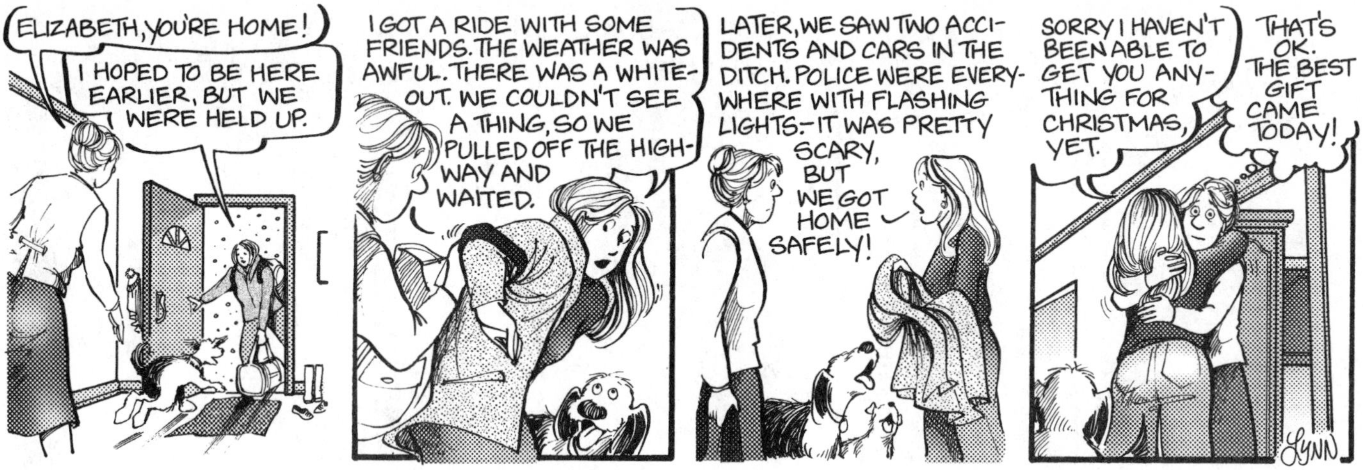
ELIZABETH, YOU'RE HOME!
I HOPED TO BE HERE EARLIER, BUT WE WERE HELD UP.
I GOT A RIDE WITH SOME FRIENDS. THE WEATHER WAS AWFUL. THERE WAS A WHITE-OUT. WE COULDN'T SEE A THING, SO WE PULLED OFF THE HIGHWAY AND WAITED.
LATER, WE SAW TWO ACCIDENTS AND CARS IN THE DITCH. POLICE WERE EVERYWHERE WITH FLASHING LIGHTS.-IT WAS PRETTY SCARY, BUT WE GOT HOME SAFELY!
SORRY I HAVEN'T BEEN ABLE TO GET YOU ANYTHING FOR CHRISTMAS, YET.
THAT'S OK. THE BEST GIFT CAME TODAY!
LYNN

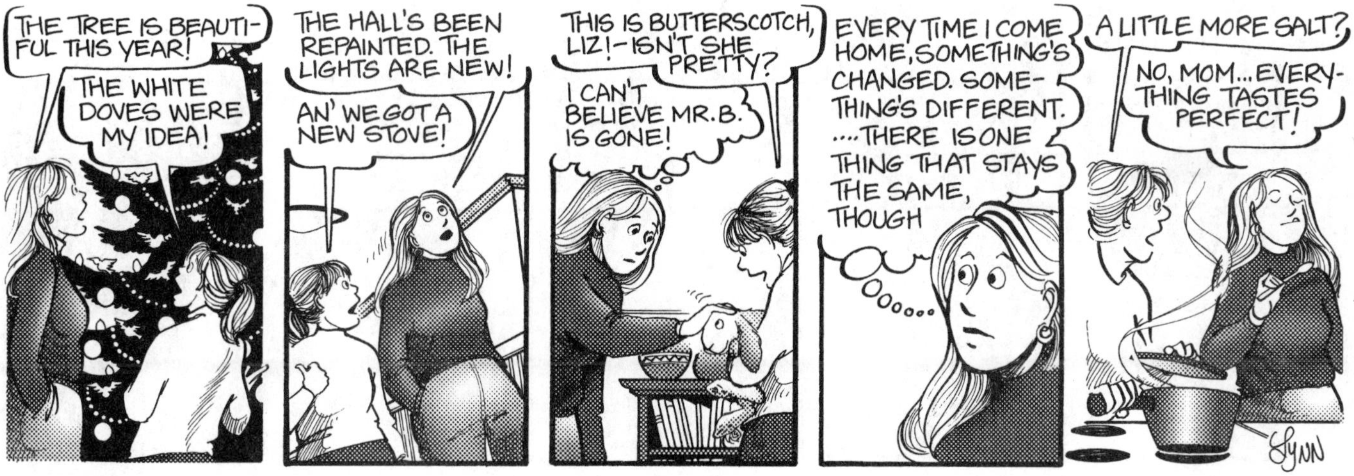
THE TREE IS BEAUTIFUL THIS YEAR!
THE WHITE DOVES WERE MY IDEA!
THE HALL'S BEEN REPAINTED. THE LIGHTS ARE NEW!
AN' WE GOT A NEW STOVE!
THIS IS BUTTERSCOTCH, LIZ!-ISN'T SHE PRETTY?
I CAN'T BELIEVE MR. B. IS GONE!
EVERY TIME I COME HOME, SOMETHING'S CHANGED. SOMETHING'S DIFFERENT. ....THERE IS ONE THING THAT STAYS THE SAME, THOUGH
A LITTLE MORE SALT?
NO, MOM... EVERYTHING TASTES PERFECT!
LYNN

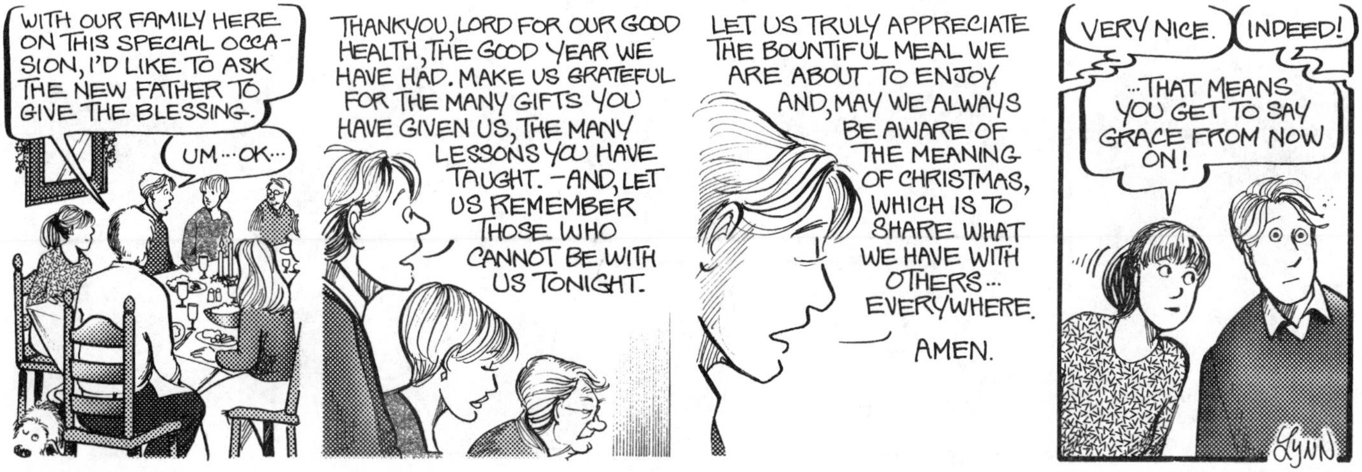
WITH OUR FAMILY HERE ON THIS SPECIAL OCCASION, I'D LIKE TO ASK THE NEW FATHER TO GIVE THE BLESSING.
UM... OK...
THANKYOU, LORD FOR OUR GOOD HEALTH, THE GOOD YEAR WE HAVE HAD. MAKE US GRATEFUL FOR THE MANY GIFTS YOU HAVE GIVEN US, THE MANY LESSONS YOU HAVE TAUGHT. -AND, LET US REMEMBER THOSE WHO CANNOT BE WITH US TONIGHT.
LET US TRULY APPRECIATE THE BOUNTIFUL MEAL WE ARE ABOUT TO ENJOY AND, MAY WE ALWAYS BE AWARE OF THE MEANING OF CHRISTMAS, WHICH IS TO SHARE WHAT WE HAVE WITH OTHERS... EVERYWHERE.
AMEN.
VERY NICE.
INDEED!
...THAT MEANS YOU GET TO SAY GRACE FROM NOW ON!
LYNN

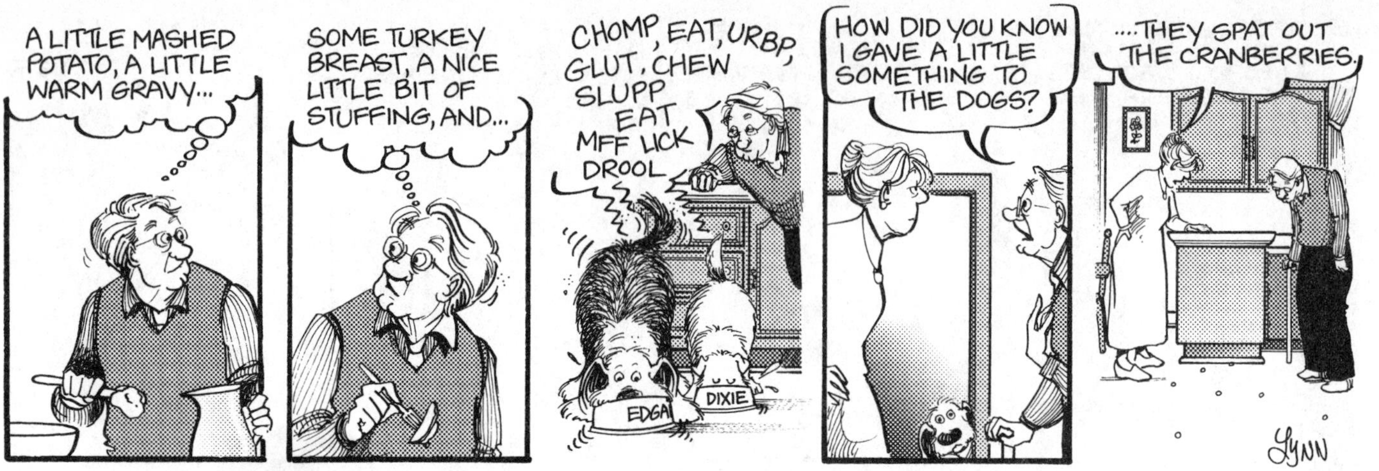
A LITTLE MASHED POTATO, A LITTLE WARM GRAVY...
SOME TURKEY BREAST, A NICE LITTLE BIT OF STUFFING, AND...
CHOMP, EAT, URBP, GLUT, CHEW
SLUPP
EAT
MFF LICK
DROOL
EDGA
DIXIE
HOW DID YOU KNOW I GAVE A LITTLE SOMETHING TO THE DOGS?
....THEY SPAT OUT THE CRANBERRIES.
Lynn

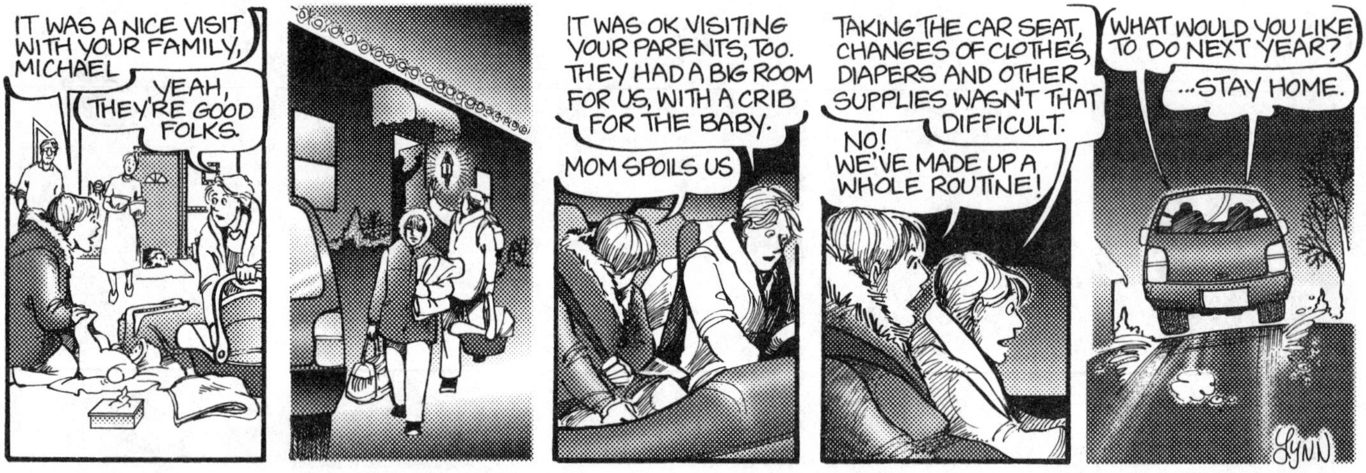
IT WAS A NICE VISIT WITH YOUR FAMILY, MICHAEL
YEAH, THEY'RE GOOD FOLKS.
IT WAS OK VISITING YOUR PARENTS, TOO. THEY HAD A BIG ROOM FOR US, WITH A CRIB FOR THE BABY.
MOM SPOILS US
TAKING THE CAR SEAT, CHANGES OF CLOTHES, DIAPERS AND OTHER SUPPLIES WASN'T THAT DIFFICULT.
NO! WE'VE MADE UP A WHOLE ROUTINE!
WHAT WOULD YOU LIKE TO DO NEXT YEAR?
...STAY HOME.
Lynn

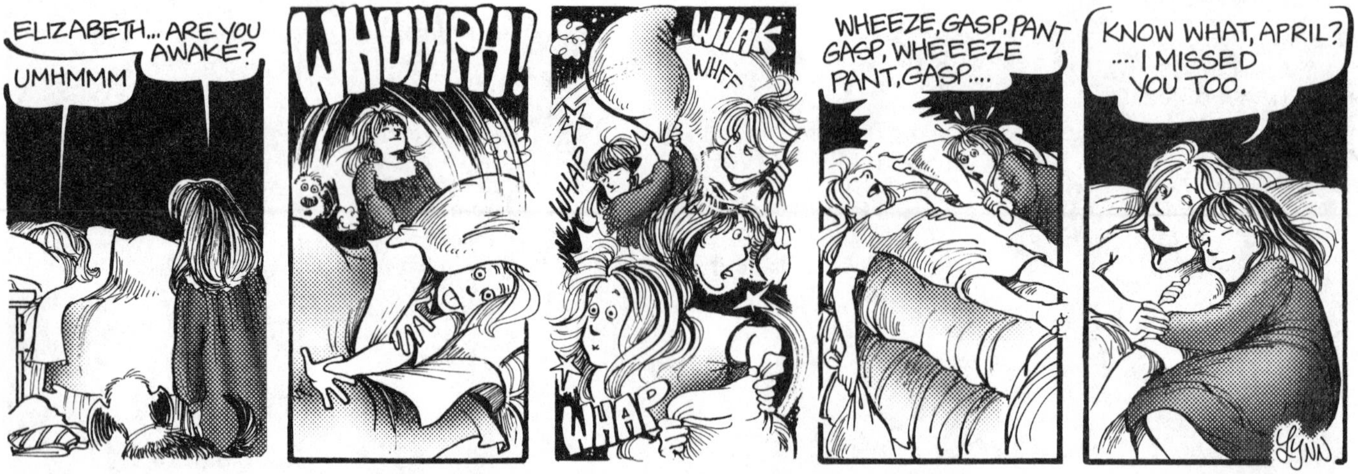
ELIZABETH... ARE YOU AWAKE?
UMHMMM
WHUMPH!
WHAK
WHFF
WHAP
WHAP
WHEEZE, GASP, PANT GASP, WHEEEZE PANT, GASP....
KNOW WHAT, APRIL? .... I MISSED YOU TOO.
Lynn

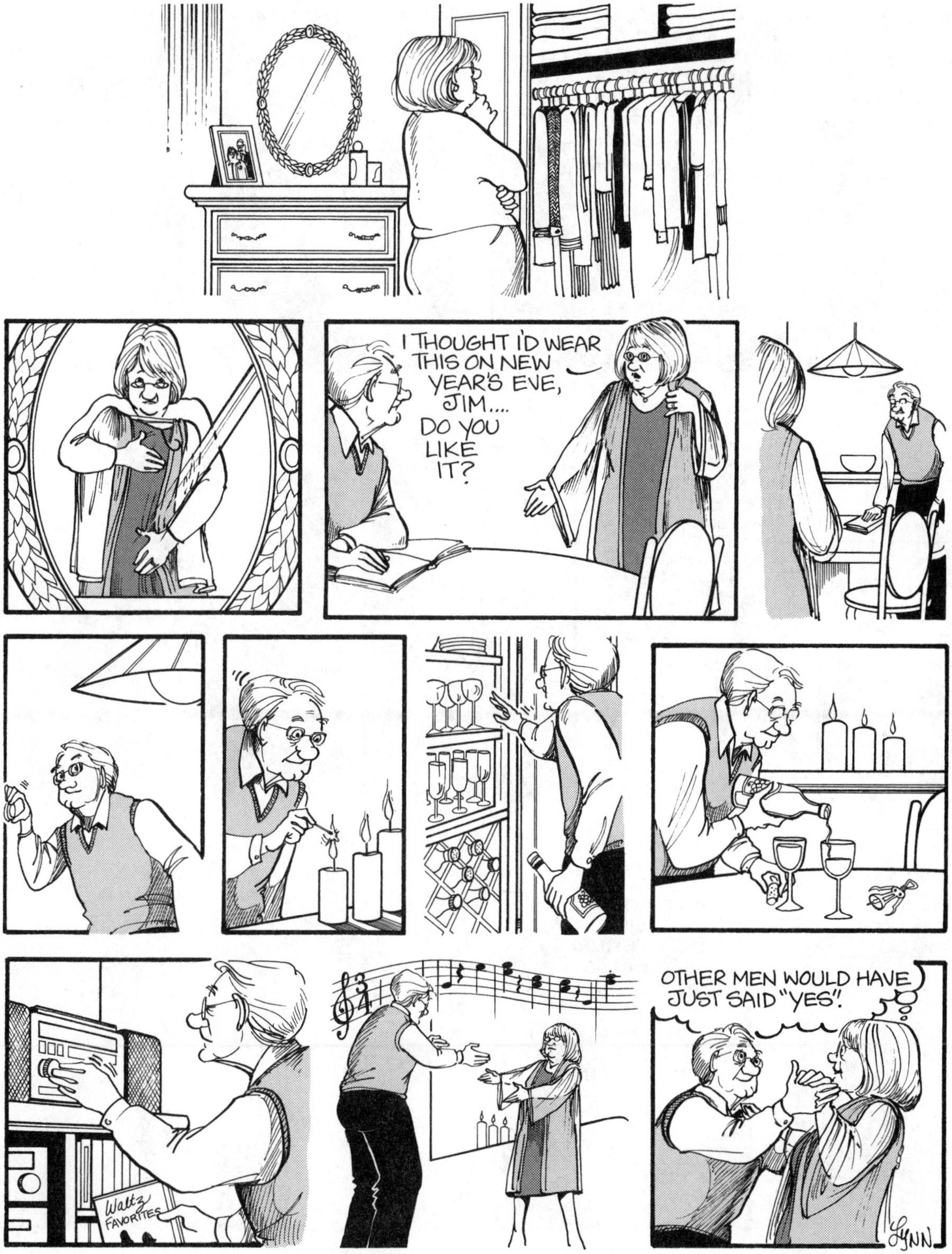
I THOUGHT I'D WEAR THIS ON NEW YEAR'S EVE, JIM.... DO YOU LIKE IT?
Waltz FAVORITES
OTHER MEN WOULD HAVE JUST SAID "YES".
LYNN

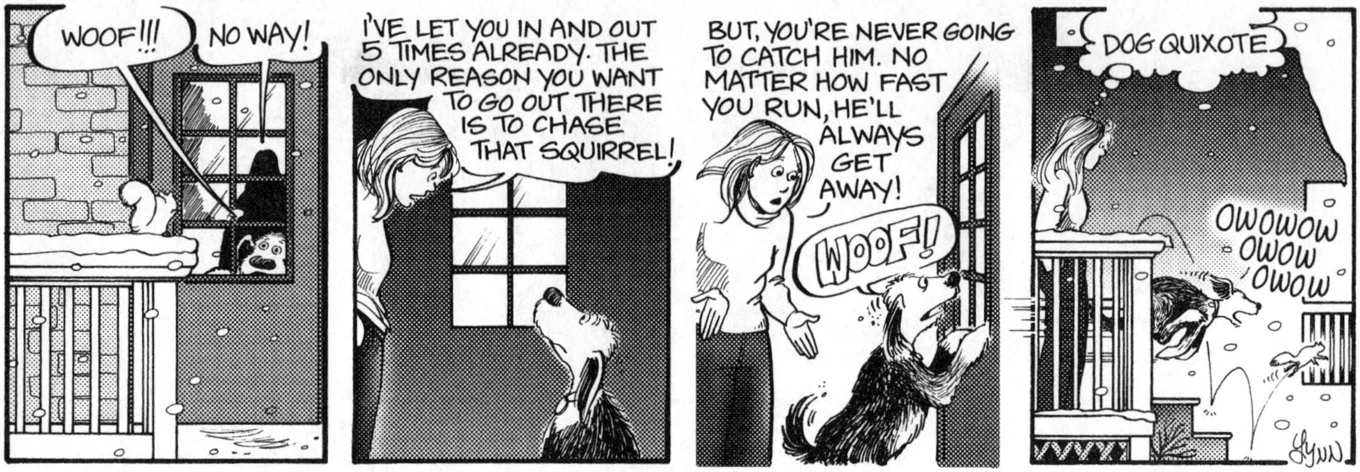
WOOF!!!
NO WAY!
I'VE LET YOU IN AND OUT 5 TIMES ALREADY. THE ONLY REASON YOU WANT TO GO OUT THERE IS TO CHASE THAT SQUIRREL!
BUT, YOU'RE NEVER GOING TO CATCH HIM. NO MATTER HOW FAST YOU RUN, HE'LL ALWAYS GET AWAY!
WOOF!
DOG QUIXOTE
OWOWOW OWOW OWOW
LYNN

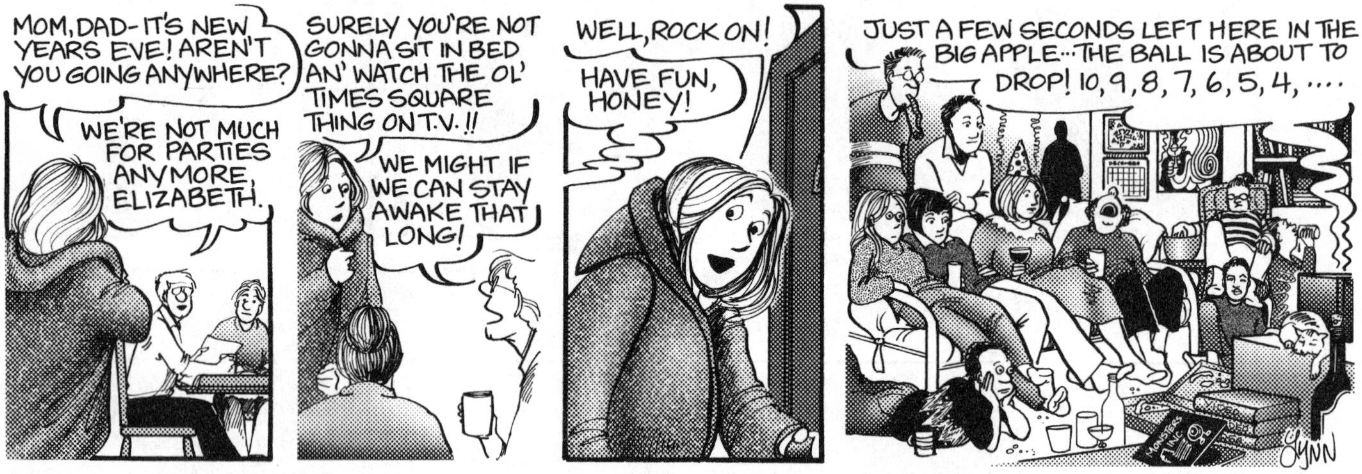
MOM, DAD- IT'S NEW YEARS EVE! AREN'T YOU GOING ANYWHERE?
WE'RE NOT MUCH FOR PARTIES ANYMORE, ELIZABETH.
SURELY YOU'RE NOT GONNA SIT IN BED AN' WATCH THE OL' TIMES SQUARE THING ON T.V. !!
WE MIGHT IF WE CAN STAY AWAKE THAT LONG!
WELL, ROCK ON!
HAVE FUN, HONEY!
JUST A FEW SECONDS LEFT HERE IN THE BIG APPLE... THE BALL IS ABOUT TO DROP! 10, 9, 8, 7, 6, 5, 4, ...
LYNN

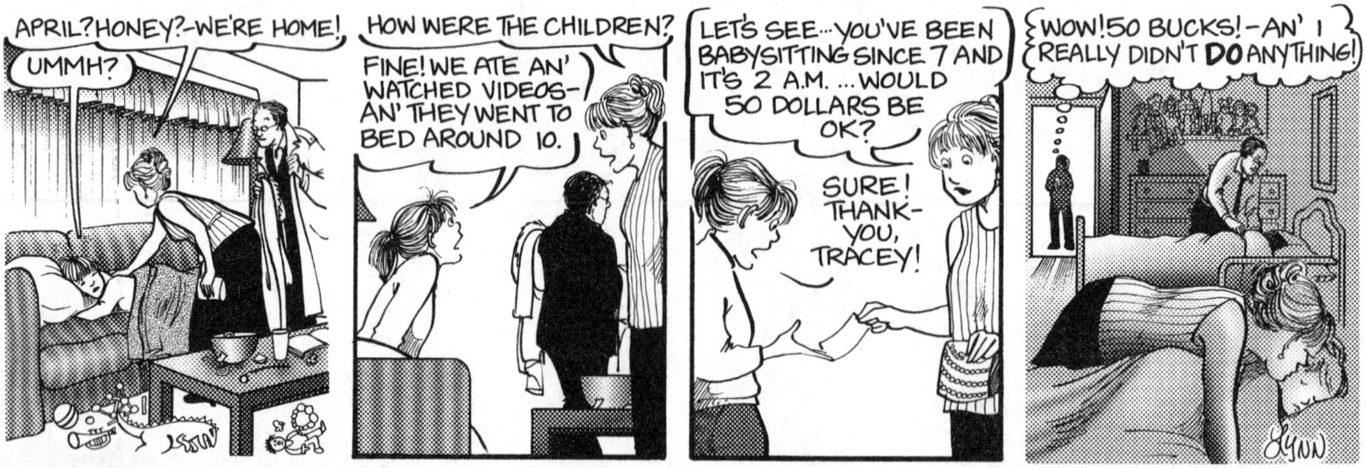
APRIL? HONEY?-WE'RE HOME!
UMMH?
HOW WERE THE CHILDREN?
FINE! WE ATE AN' WATCHED VIDEOS- AN' THEY WENT TO BED AROUND 10.
LET'S SEE... YOU'VE BEEN BABYSITTING SINCE 7 AND IT'S 2 A.M. ... WOULD 50 DOLLARS BE OK?
SURE! THANK-YOU, TRACEY!
WOW! 50 BUCKS! - AN' I REALLY DIDN'T **DO** ANYTHING!
LYNN

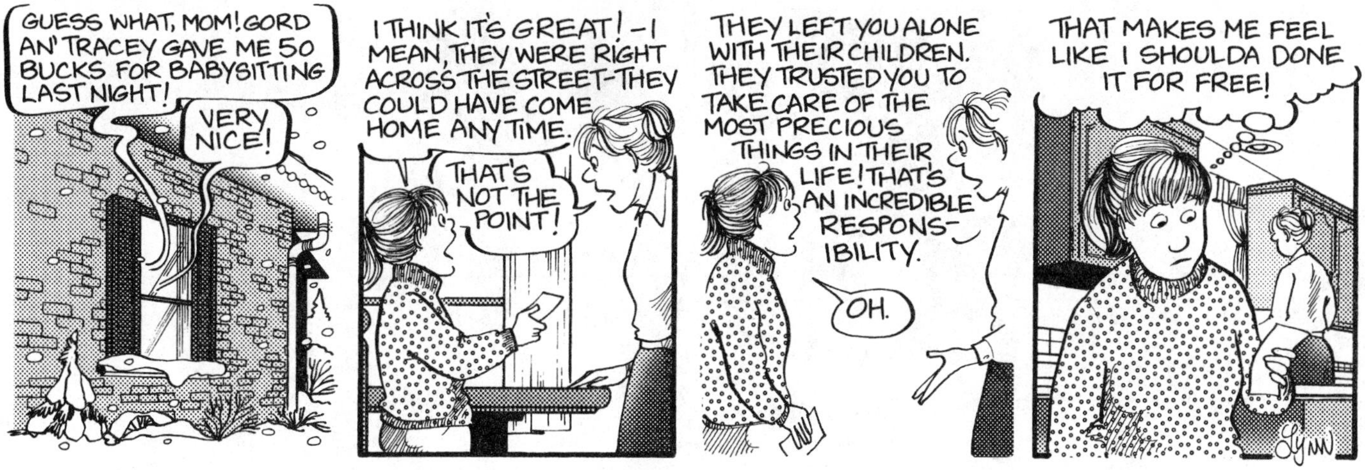
GUESS WHAT, MOM! GORD AN' TRACEY GAVE ME 50 BUCKS FOR BABYSITTING LAST NIGHT!
VERY NICE!
I THINK IT'S GREAT! -I MEAN, THEY WERE RIGHT ACROSS THE STREET-THEY COULD HAVE COME HOME ANY TIME.
THAT'S NOT THE POINT!
THEY LEFT YOU ALONE WITH THEIR CHILDREN. THEY TRUSTED YOU TO TAKE CARE OF THE MOST PRECIOUS THINGS IN THEIR LIFE! THAT'S AN INCREDIBLE RESPONS-IBILITY.
OH.
THAT MAKES ME FEEL LIKE I SHOULDA DONE IT FOR FREE!
LYNN

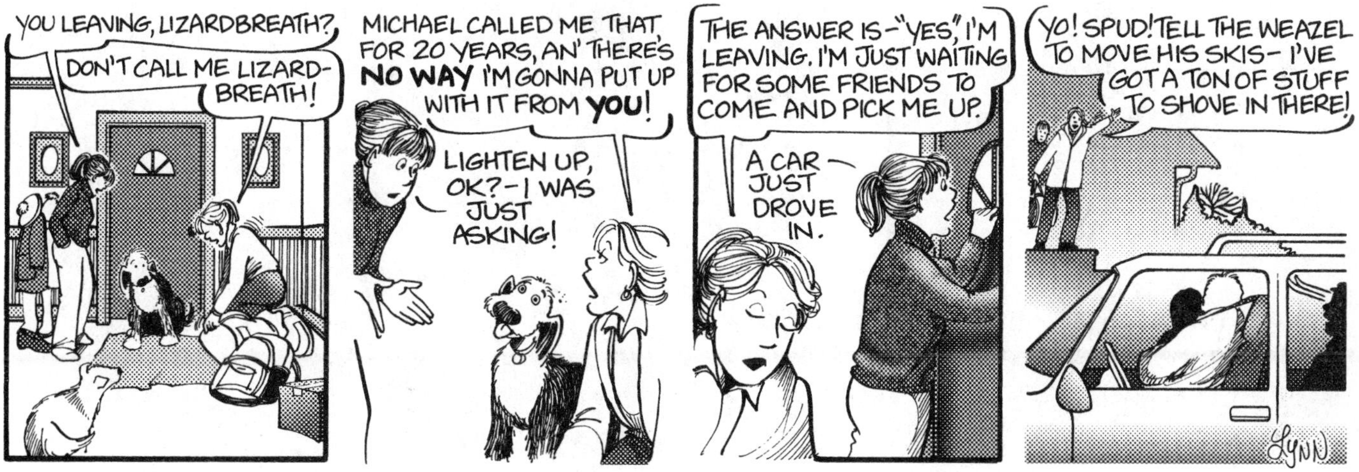
YOU LEAVING, LIZARDBREATH?
DON'T CALL ME LIZARD-BREATH!
MICHAEL CALLED ME THAT FOR 20 YEARS, AN' THERE'S NO WAY I'M GONNA PUT UP WITH IT FROM YOU!
LIGHTEN UP, OK?-I WAS JUST ASKING!
THE ANSWER IS-"YES," I'M LEAVING. I'M JUST WAITING FOR SOME FRIENDS TO COME AND PICK ME UP.
A CAR JUST DROVE IN.
YO! SPUD! TELL THE WEAZEL TO MOVE HIS SKIS- I'VE GOT A TON OF STUFF TO SHOVE IN THERE!
LYNN

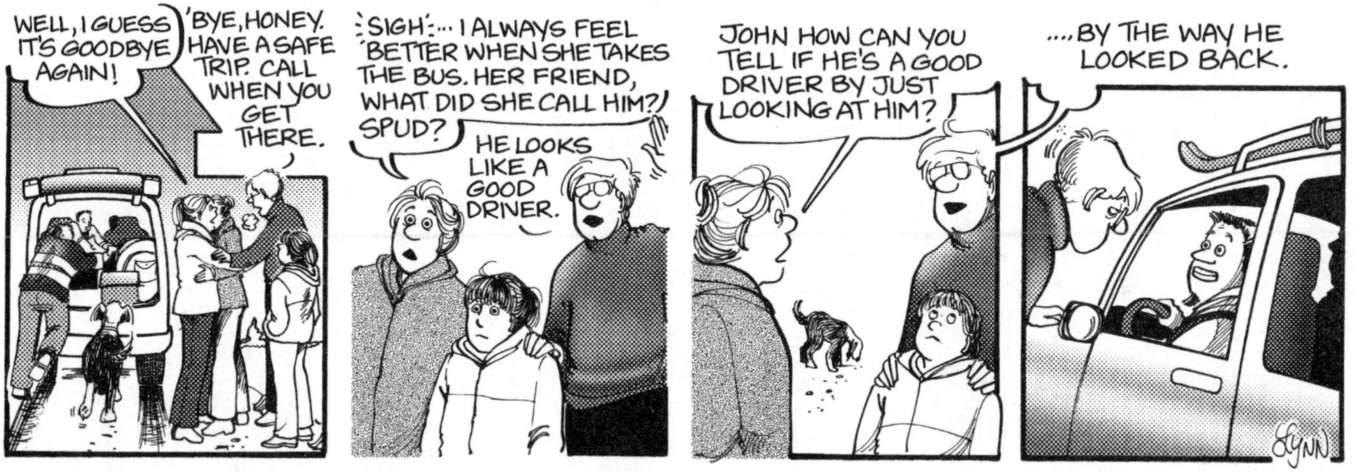
WELL, I GUESS IT'S GOODBYE AGAIN!
'BYE, HONEY. HAVE A SAFE TRIP. CALL WHEN YOU GET THERE.
SIGH... I ALWAYS FEEL BETTER WHEN SHE TAKES THE BUS. HER FRIEND, WHAT DID SHE CALL HIM? SPUD?
HE LOOKS LIKE A GOOD DRIVER.
JOHN HOW CAN YOU TELL IF HE'S A GOOD DRIVER BY JUST LOOKING AT HIM?
....BY THE WAY HE LOOKED BACK.
LYNN

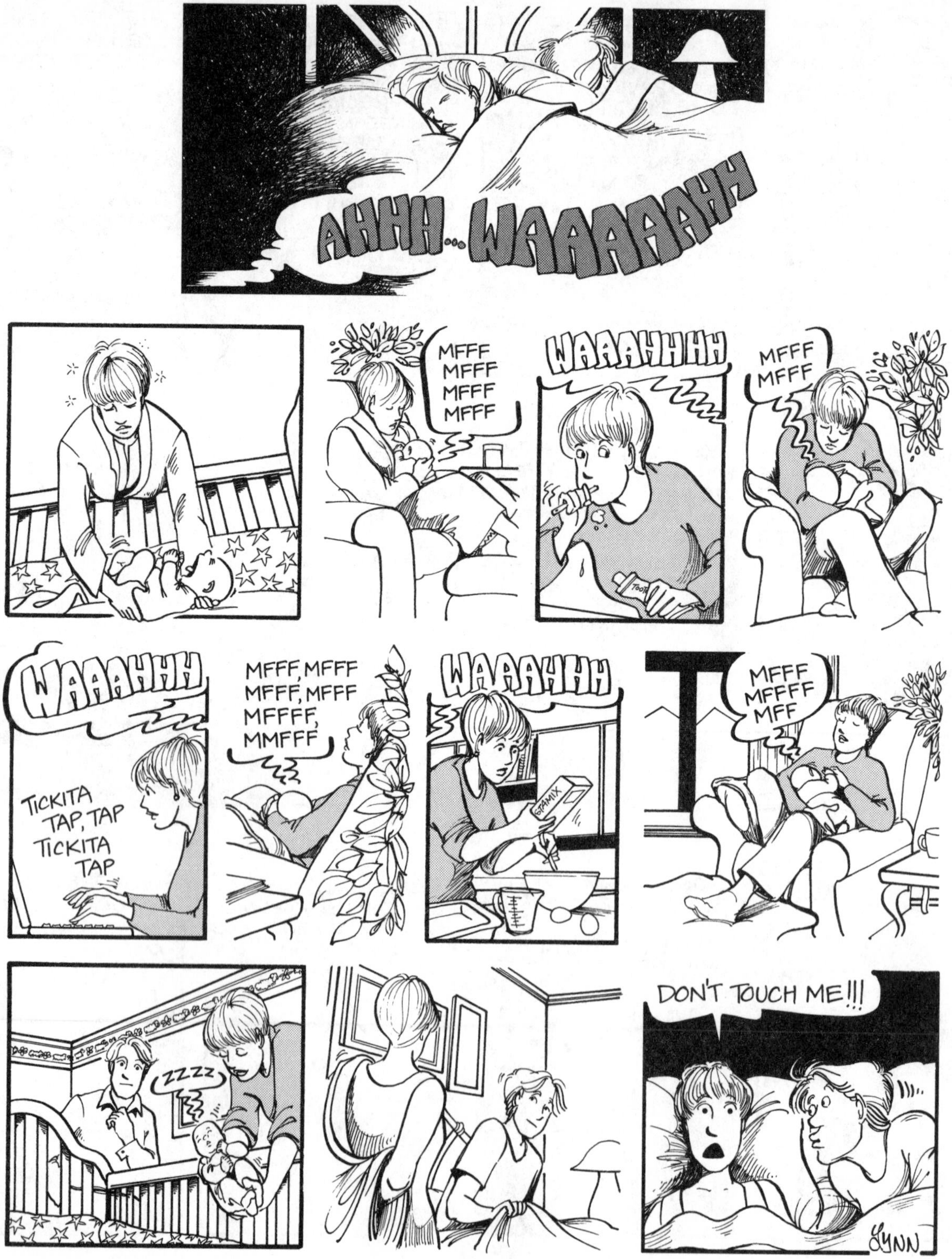
AHHH...WAAAAAHH
MFFF MFFF MFFF MFFF
WAAAHHHH
MFFF MFFF
WAAAHHH
TICKITA TAP, TAP TICKITA TAP
MFFF, MFFF MFFF, MFFF MFFFF, MMFFF
WAAAHHH
STAMIX
MFFF MFFFF MFF
ZZZZ
DON'T TOUCH ME!!!
LYNN

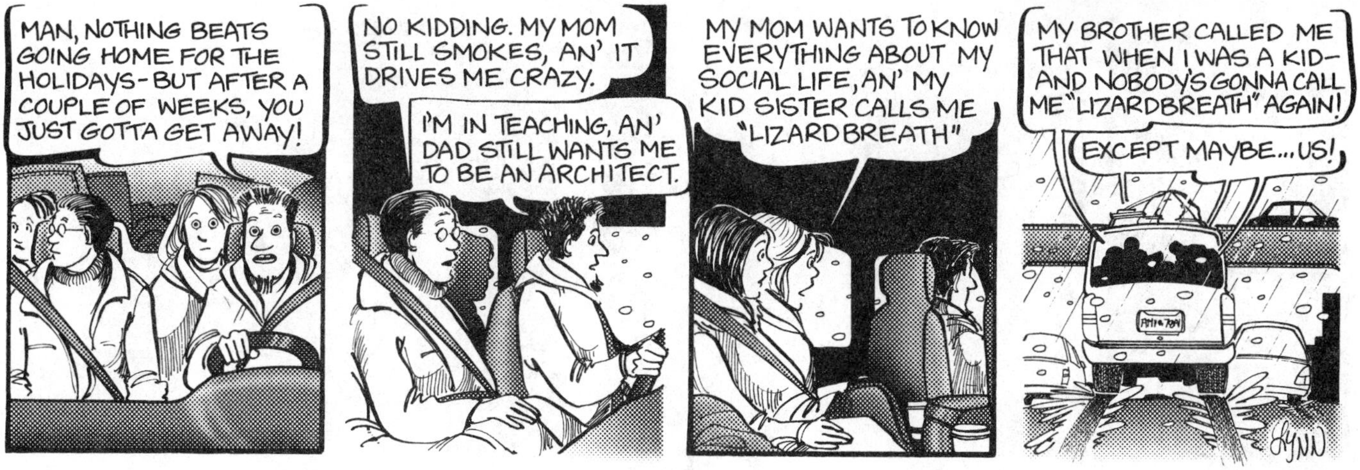
MAN, NOTHING BEATS GOING HOME FOR THE HOLIDAYS- BUT AFTER A COUPLE OF WEEKS, YOU JUST GOTTA GET AWAY!
NO KIDDING. MY MOM STILL SMOKES, AN' IT DRIVES ME CRAZY.
I'M IN TEACHING, AN' DAD STILL WANTS ME TO BE AN ARCHITECT.
MY MOM WANTS TO KNOW EVERYTHING ABOUT MY SOCIAL LIFE, AN' MY KID SISTER CALLS ME "LIZARDBREATH"
MY BROTHER CALLED ME THAT WHEN I WAS A KID- AND NOBODY'S GONNA CALL ME "LIZARDBREATH" AGAIN!
EXCEPT MAYBE... US!
LYNN

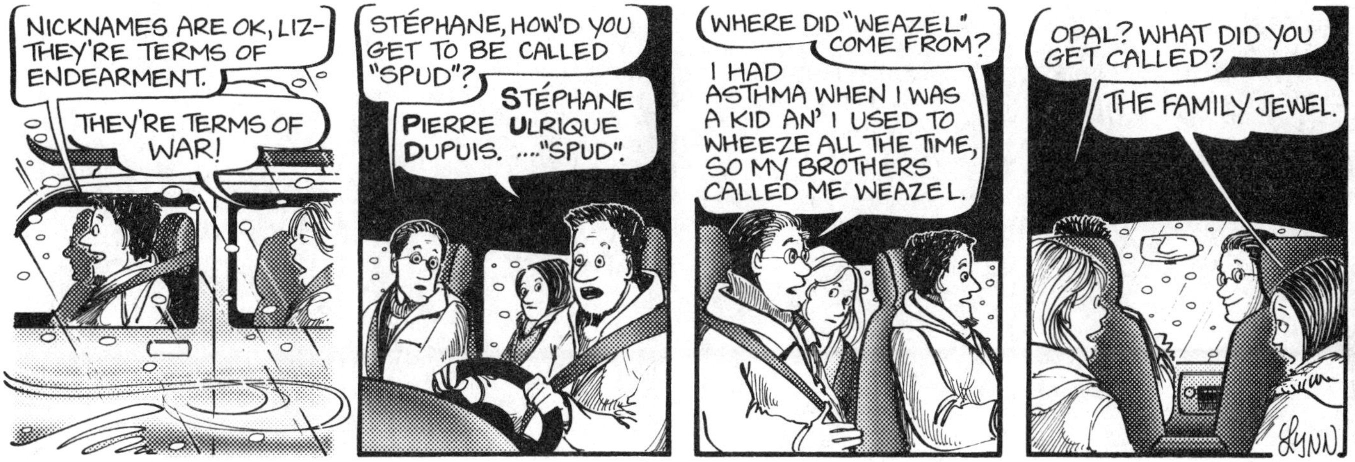
NICKNAMES ARE OK, LIZ- THEY'RE TERMS OF ENDEARMENT.
THEY'RE TERMS OF WAR!
STÉPHANE, HOW'D YOU GET TO BE CALLED "SPUD"?
STÉPHANE PIERRE ULRIQUE DUPUIS. ...."SPUD".
WHERE DID "WEAZEL" COME FROM?
I HAD ASTHMA WHEN I WAS A KID AN' I USED TO WHEEZE ALL THE TIME, SO MY BROTHERS CALLED ME WEAZEL.
OPAL? WHAT DID YOU GET CALLED?
THE FAMILY JEWEL.
LYNN

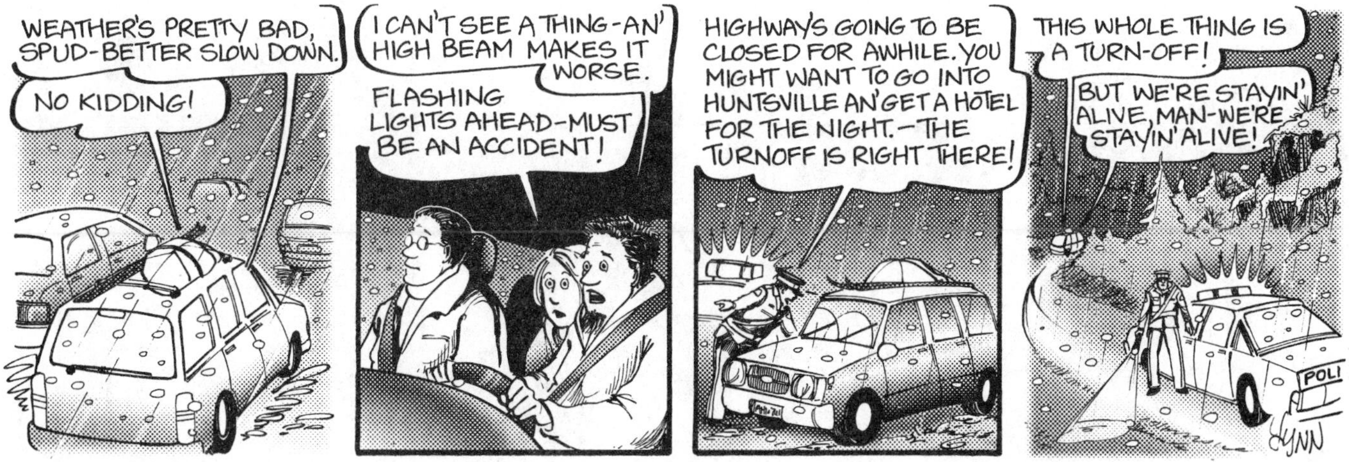
WEATHER'S PRETTY BAD, SPUD- BETTER SLOW DOWN.
NO KIDDING!
I CAN'T SEE A THING- AN' HIGH BEAM MAKES IT WORSE.
FLASHING LIGHTS AHEAD- MUST BE AN ACCIDENT!
HIGHWAY'S GOING TO BE CLOSED FOR AWHILE. YOU MIGHT WANT TO GO INTO HUNTSVILLE AN' GET A HOTEL FOR THE NIGHT. - THE TURNOFF IS RIGHT THERE!
THIS WHOLE THING IS A TURN-OFF!
BUT WE'RE STAYIN' ALIVE, MAN- WE'RE STAYIN' ALIVE!
POLI
LYNN

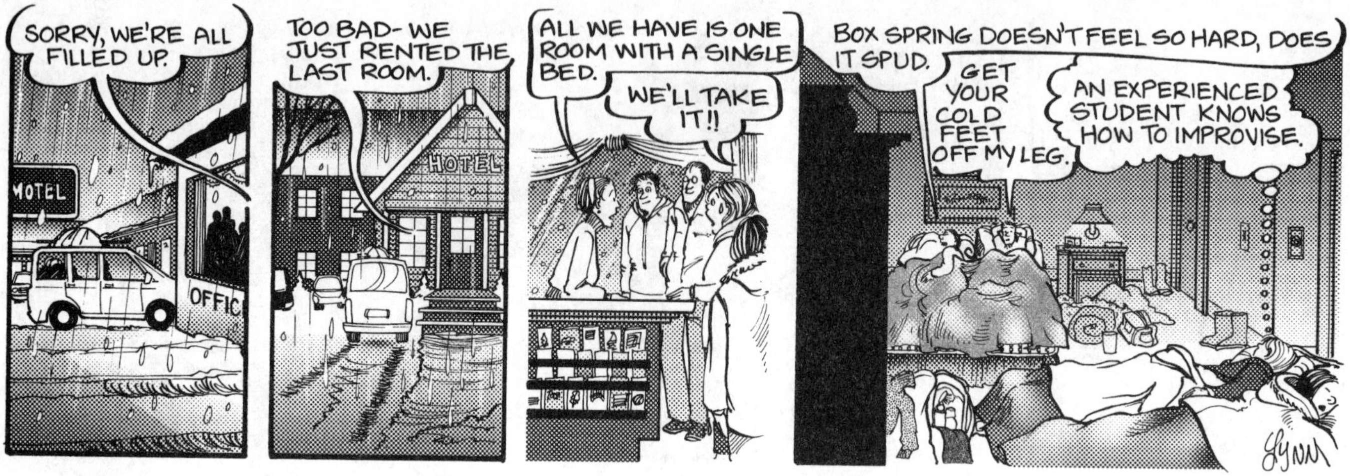
SORRY, WE'RE ALL FILLED UP.
MOTEL
OFFIC
TOO BAD- WE JUST RENTED THE LAST ROOM.
HOTEL
ALL WE HAVE IS ONE ROOM WITH A SINGLE BED.
WE'LL TAKE IT!!
BOX SPRING DOESN'T FEEL SO HARD, DOES IT SPUD.
GET YOUR COLD FEET OFF MY LEG.
AN EXPERIENCED STUDENT KNOWS HOW TO IMPROVISE.
LYNN

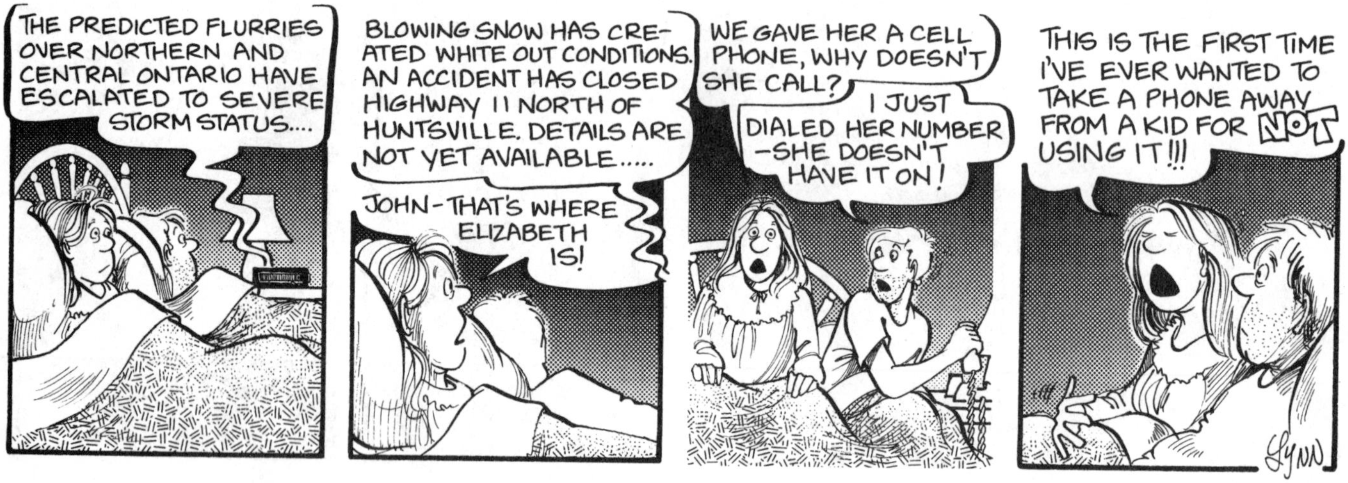
THE PREDICTED FLURRIES OVER NORTHERN AND CENTRAL ONTARIO HAVE ESCALATED TO SEVERE STORM STATUS....
BLOWING SNOW HAS CREATED WHITE OUT CONDITIONS. AN ACCIDENT HAS CLOSED HIGHWAY 11 NORTH OF HUNTSVILLE. DETAILS ARE NOT YET AVAILABLE.....
JOHN- THAT'S WHERE ELIZABETH IS!
WE GAVE HER A CELL PHONE, WHY DOESN'T SHE CALL?
I JUST DIALED HER NUMBER -SHE DOESN'T HAVE IT ON!
THIS IS THE FIRST TIME I'VE EVER WANTED TO TAKE A PHONE AWAY FROM A KID FOR NOT USING IT!!!
LYNN

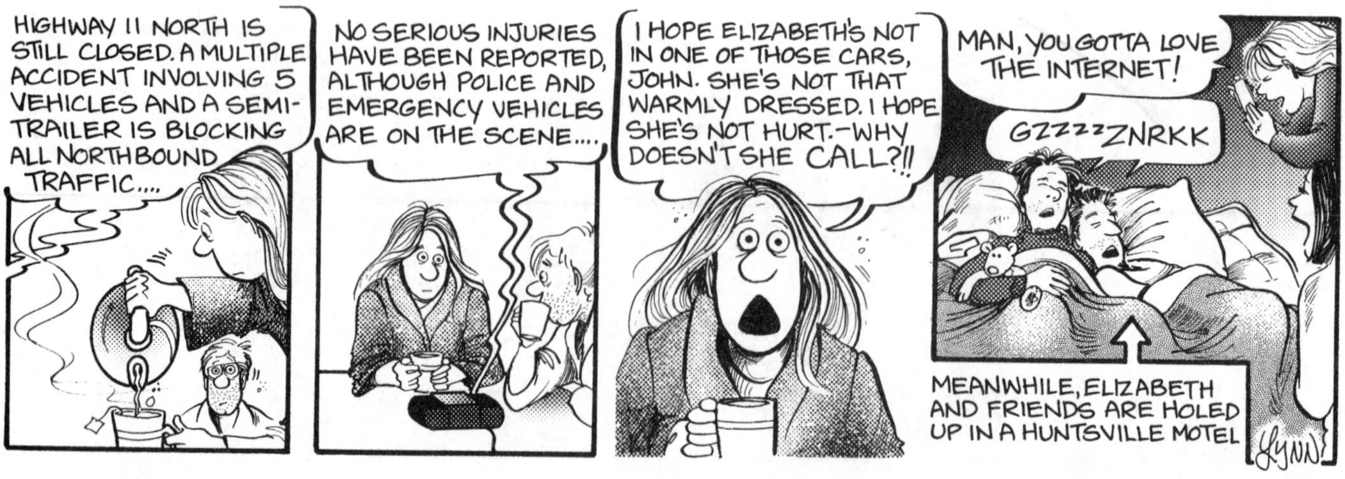
HIGHWAY 11 NORTH IS STILL CLOSED. A MULTIPLE ACCIDENT INVOLVING 5 VEHICLES AND A SEMI-TRAILER IS BLOCKING ALL NORTHBOUND TRAFFIC....
NO SERIOUS INJURIES HAVE BEEN REPORTED, ALTHOUGH POLICE AND EMERGENCY VEHICLES ARE ON THE SCENE....
I HOPE ELIZABETH'S NOT IN ONE OF THOSE CARS, JOHN. SHE'S NOT THAT WARMLY DRESSED. I HOPE SHE'S NOT HURT.-WHY DOESN'T SHE CALL?!!
MAN, YOU GOTTA LOVE THE INTERNET!
GZZZZZNRKK
MEANWHILE, ELIZABETH AND FRIENDS ARE HOLED UP IN A HUNTSVILLE MOTEL
LYNN

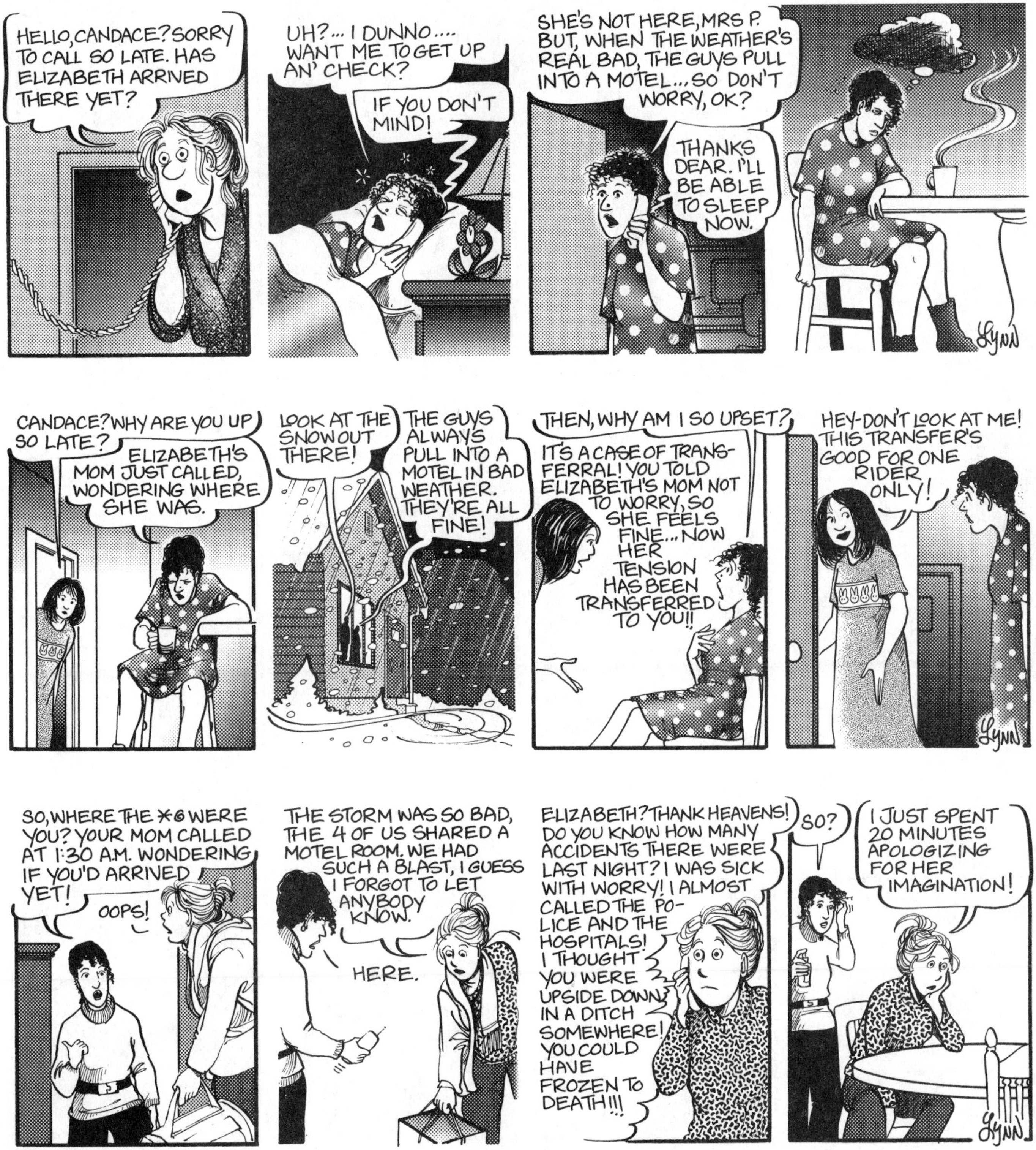
HELLO, CANDACE? SORRY TO CALL SO LATE. HAS ELIZABETH ARRIVED THERE YET?
UH?... I DUNNO.... WANT ME TO GET UP AN' CHECK?
IF YOU DON'T MIND!
SHE'S NOT HERE, MRS P. BUT, WHEN THE WEATHER'S REAL BAD, THE GUYS PULL INTO A MOTEL... SO DON'T WORRY, OK?
THANKS DEAR. I'LL BE ABLE TO SLEEP NOW.
LYNN
CANDACE? WHY ARE YOU UP SO LATE?
ELIZABETH'S MOM JUST CALLED, WONDERING WHERE SHE WAS.
LOOK AT THE SNOW OUT THERE!
THE GUYS ALWAYS PULL INTO A MOTEL IN BAD WEATHER. THEY'RE ALL FINE!
THEN, WHY AM I SO UPSET?
IT'S A CASE OF TRANS-FERRAL! YOU TOLD ELIZABETH'S MOM NOT TO WORRY, SO SHE FEELS FINE... NOW HER TENSION HAS BEEN TRANSFERRED TO YOU!!
HEY-DON'T LOOK AT ME! THIS TRANSFER'S GOOD FOR ONE RIDER ONLY!
LYNN
SO, WHERE THE *@ WERE YOU? YOUR MOM CALLED AT 1:30 A.M. WONDERING IF YOU'D ARRIVED YET!
OOPS!
THE STORM WAS SO BAD, THE 4 OF US SHARED A MOTEL ROOM. WE HAD SUCH A BLAST, I GUESS I FORGOT TO LET ANYBODY KNOW.
HERE.
ELIZABETH? THANK HEAVENS! DO YOU KNOW HOW MANY ACCIDENTS THERE WERE LAST NIGHT? I WAS SICK WITH WORRY! I ALMOST CALLED THE PO-LICE AND THE HOSPITALS! I THOUGHT YOU WERE UPSIDE DOWN IN A DITCH SOMEWHERE! YOU COULD HAVE FROZEN TO DEATH!!!
SO?
I JUST SPENT 20 MINUTES APOLOGIZING FOR HER IMAGINATION!
LYNN

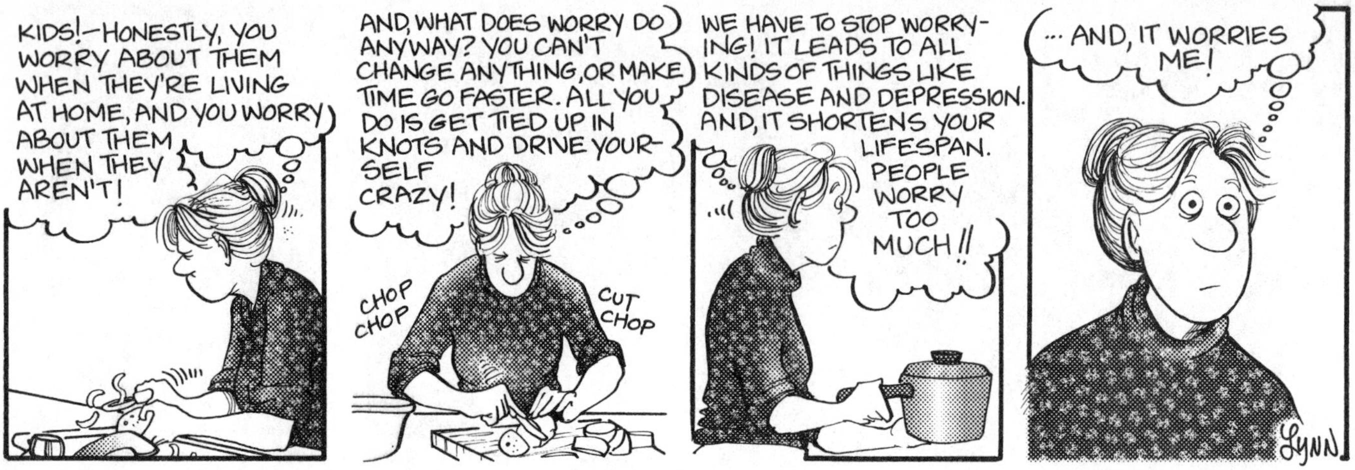
KIDS!—HONESTLY, YOU WORRY ABOUT THEM WHEN THEY'RE LIVING AT HOME, AND YOU WORRY ABOUT THEM WHEN THEY AREN'T!
AND, WHAT DOES WORRY DO ANYWAY? YOU CAN'T CHANGE ANYTHING, OR MAKE TIME GO FASTER. ALL YOU DO IS GET TIED UP IN KNOTS AND DRIVE YOURSELF CRAZY!
CHOP CHOP
CUT CHOP
WE HAVE TO STOP WORRYING! IT LEADS TO ALL KINDS OF THINGS LIKE DISEASE AND DEPRESSION. AND, IT SHORTENS YOUR LIFESPAN. PEOPLE WORRY TOO MUCH!!
... AND, IT WORRIES ME!
LYNN

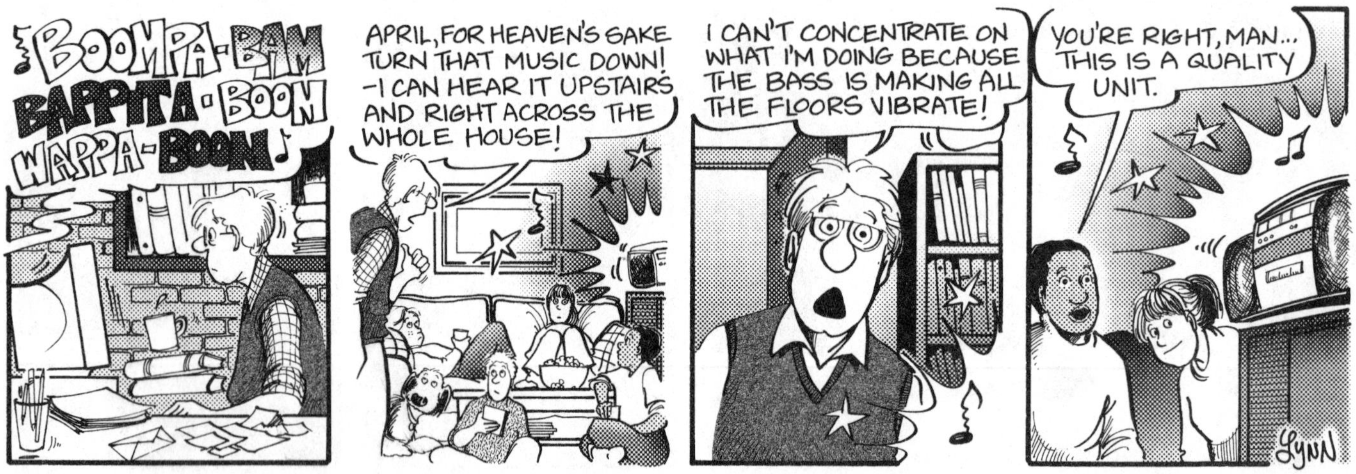
BOOMPA-BAM BAPPITA-BOOM WAPPA-BOOM
APRIL, FOR HEAVEN'S SAKE TURN THAT MUSIC DOWN! -I CAN HEAR IT UPSTAIRS AND RIGHT ACROSS THE WHOLE HOUSE!
I CAN'T CONCENTRATE ON WHAT I'M DOING BECAUSE THE BASS IS MAKING ALL THE FLOORS VIBRATE!
YOU'RE RIGHT, MAN... THIS IS A QUALITY UNIT.
LYNN

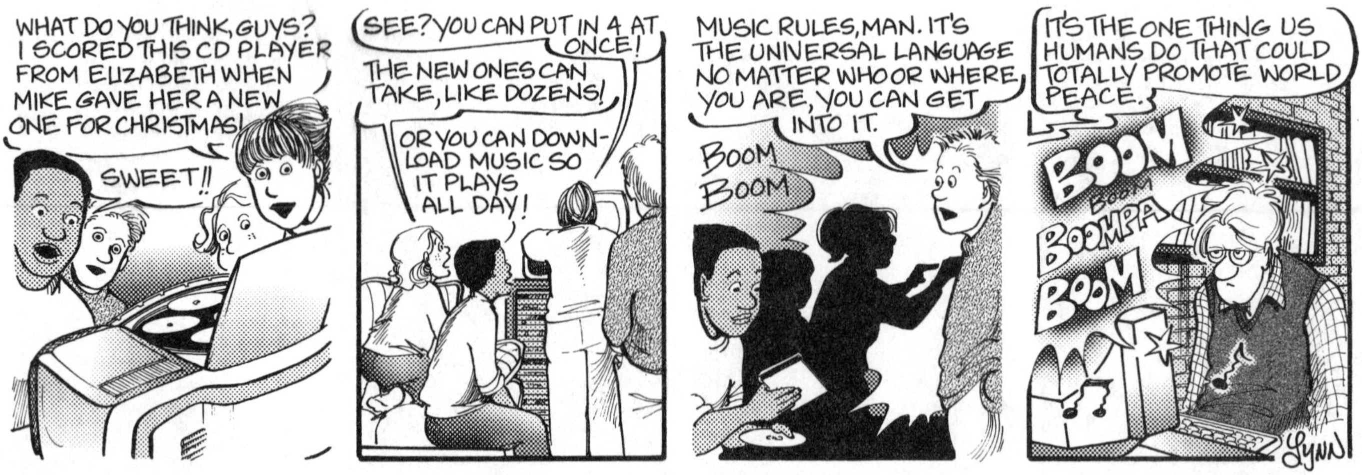
WHAT DO YOU THINK, GUYS? I SCORED THIS CD PLAYER FROM ELIZABETH WHEN MIKE GAVE HER A NEW ONE FOR CHRISTMAS!
SWEET!!
SEE? YOU CAN PUT IN 4 AT ONCE!
THE NEW ONES CAN TAKE, LIKE DOZENS!
OR YOU CAN DOWNLOAD MUSIC SO IT PLAYS ALL DAY!
MUSIC RULES, MAN. IT'S THE UNIVERSAL LANGUAGE NO MATTER WHO OR WHERE YOU ARE, YOU CAN GET INTO IT.
BOOM BOOM
IT'S THE ONE THING US HUMANS DO THAT COULD TOTALLY PROMOTE WORLD PEACE.
BOOM BOOM BOOMPA BOOM
LYNN

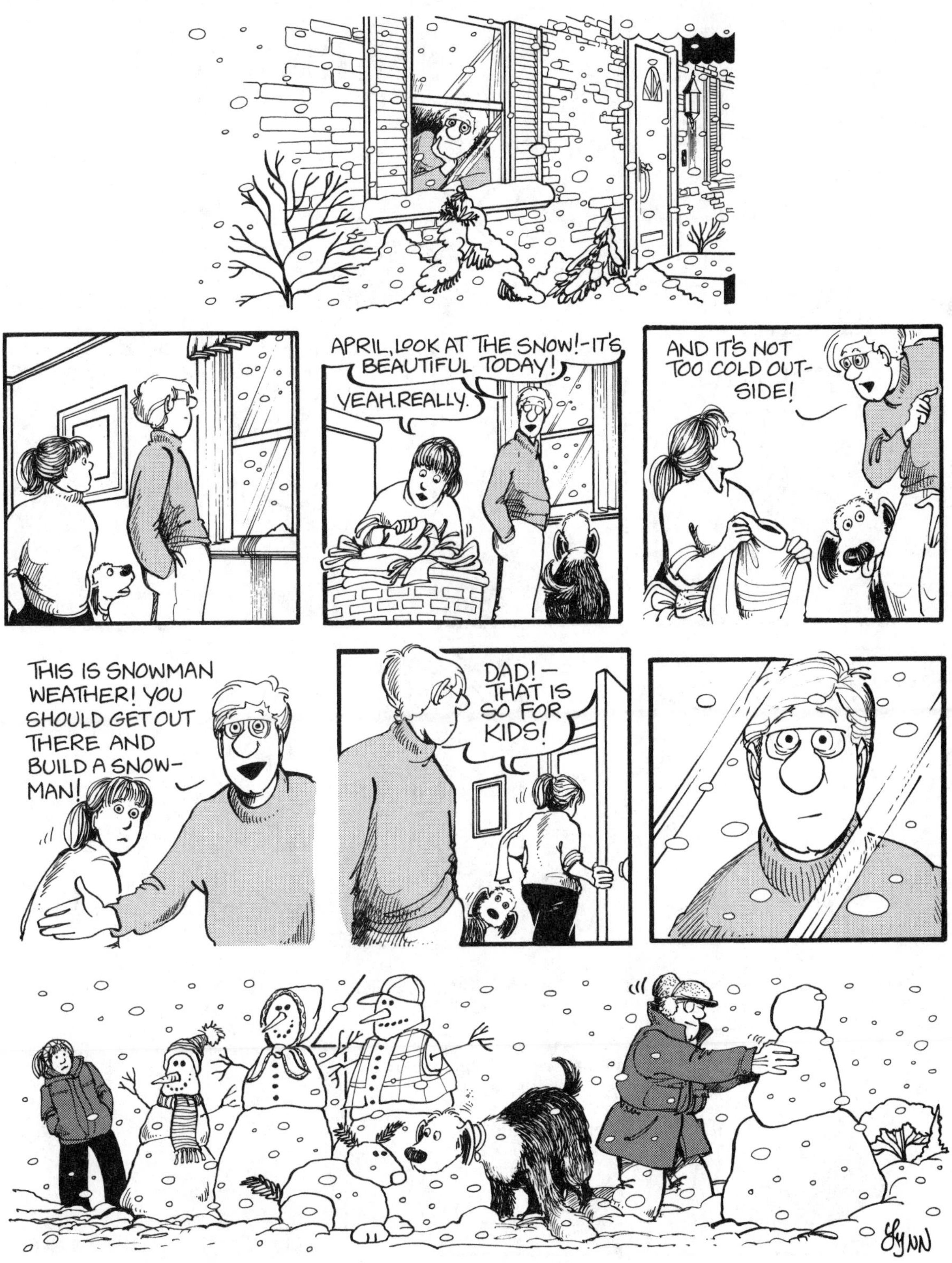
APRIL, LOOK AT THE SNOW! - IT'S BEAUTIFUL TODAY!
YEAH. REALLY.
AND IT'S NOT TOO COLD OUT-SIDE!
THIS IS SNOWMAN WEATHER! YOU SHOULD GET OUT THERE AND BUILD A SNOW-MAN!
DAD! - THAT IS SO FOR KIDS!
Lynn

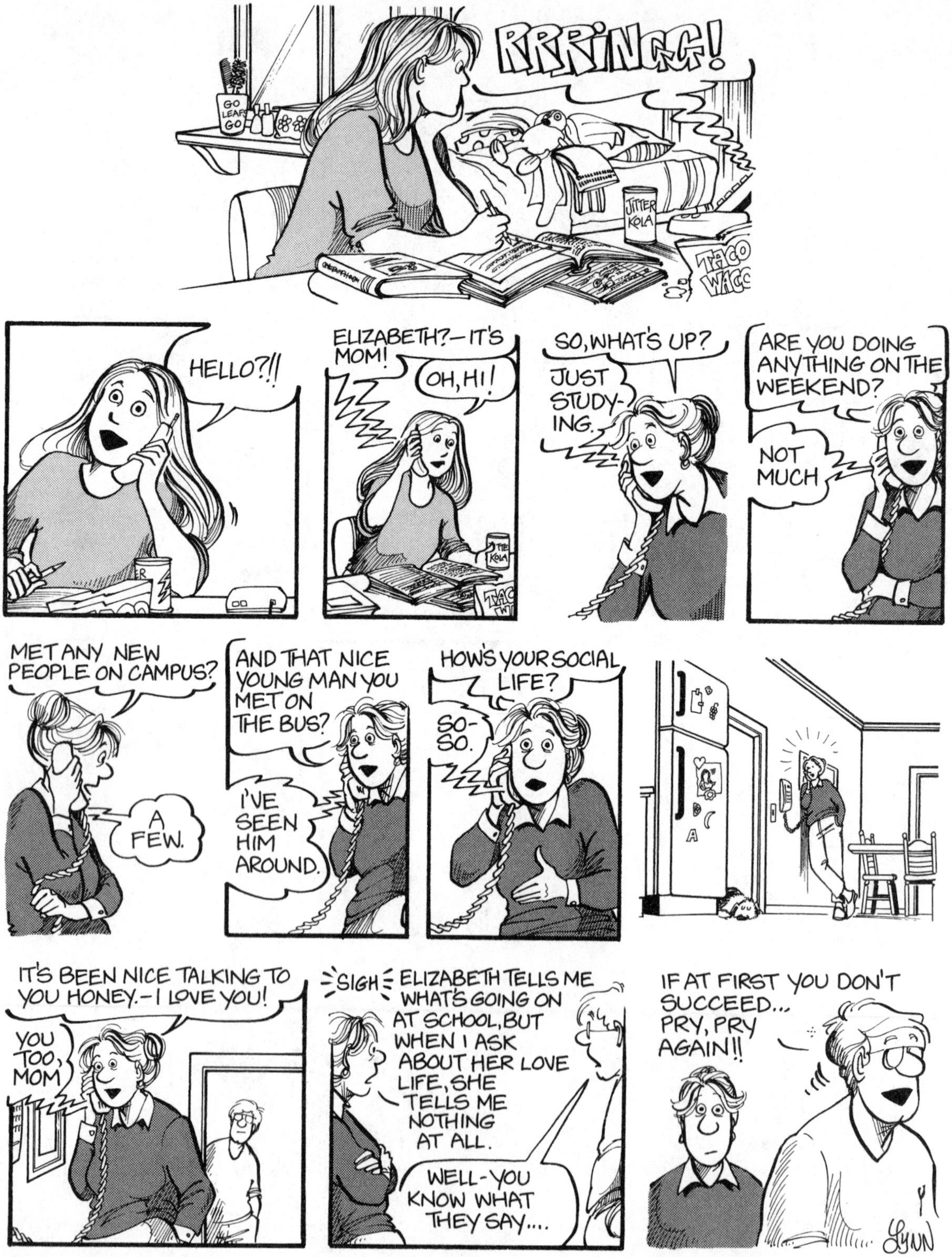
RRRINGG!
GO LEAFS GO
JITTER KOLA
TACO WACO
HELLO?!!
ELIZABETH?—IT'S MOM!
OH, HI!
SO, WHAT'S UP?
JUST STUDYING.
ARE YOU DOING ANYTHING ON THE WEEKEND?
NOT MUCH
MET ANY NEW PEOPLE ON CAMPUS?
A FEW.
AND THAT NICE YOUNG MAN YOU MET ON THE BUS?
I'VE SEEN HIM AROUND.
HOW'S YOUR SOCIAL LIFE?
SO-SO.
IT'S BEEN NICE TALKING TO YOU HONEY.—I LOVE YOU!
YOU TOO, MOM
SIGH
ELIZABETH TELLS ME WHAT'S GOING ON AT SCHOOL, BUT WHEN I ASK ABOUT HER LOVE LIFE, SHE TELLS ME NOTHING AT ALL.
WELL-YOU KNOW WHAT THEY SAY....
IF AT FIRST YOU DON'T SUCCEED... PRY, PRY AGAIN!!
LYNN

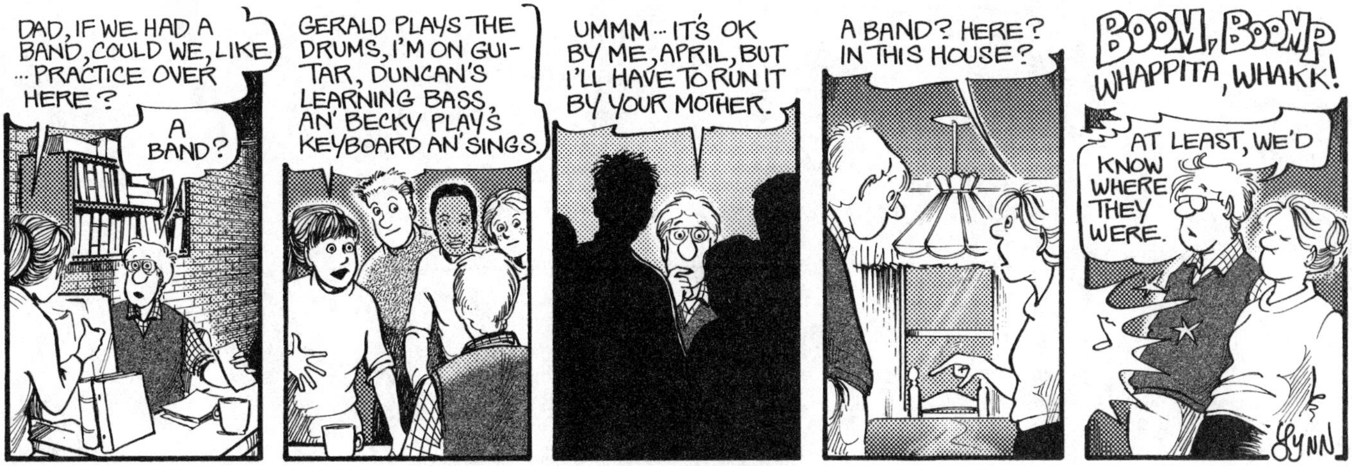
DAD, IF WE HAD A BAND, COULD WE, LIKE ... PRACTICE OVER HERE?
A BAND?
GERALD PLAYS THE DRUMS, I'M ON GUITAR, DUNCAN'S LEARNING BASS, AN' BECKY PLAYS KEYBOARD AN' SINGS.
UMMM ... IT'S OK BY ME, APRIL, BUT I'LL HAVE TO RUN IT BY YOUR MOTHER.
A BAND? HERE? IN THIS HOUSE?
BOOM, BOOMP
WHAPPITA, WHAKK!
AT LEAST, WE'D KNOW WHERE THEY WERE.
LYNN

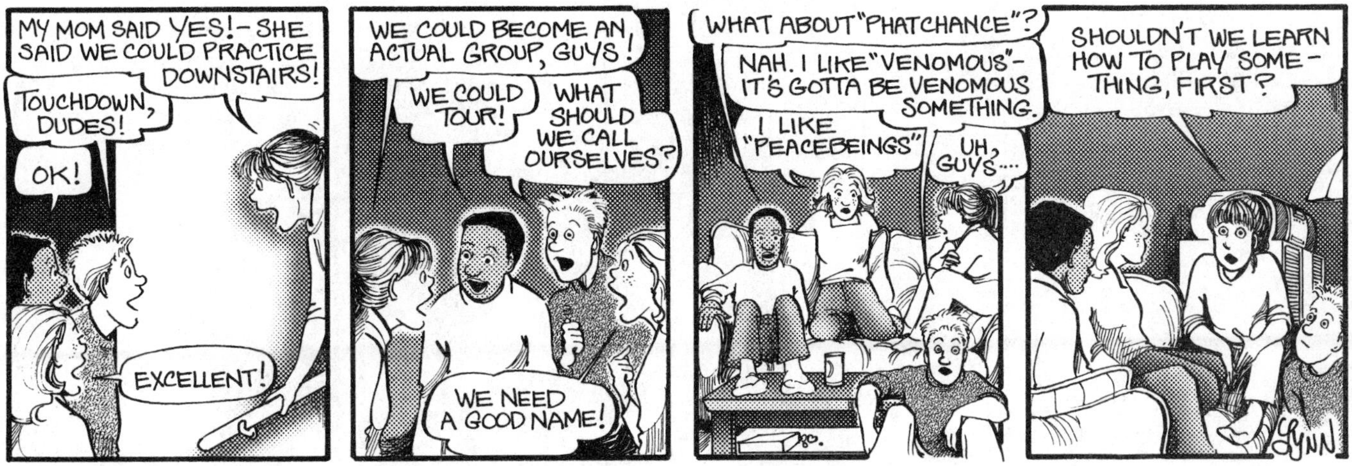
MY MOM SAID YES! - SHE SAID WE COULD PRACTICE DOWNSTAIRS!
TOUCHDOWN, DUDES!
OK!
EXCELLENT!
WE COULD BECOME AN ACTUAL GROUP, GUYS!
WE COULD TOUR!
WHAT SHOULD WE CALL OURSELVES?
WE NEED A GOOD NAME!
WHAT ABOUT "PHATCHANCE"?
NAH. I LIKE "VENOMOUS" - IT'S GOTTA BE VENOMOUS SOMETHING.
I LIKE "PEACEBEINGS"
UH, GUYS....
SHOULDN'T WE LEARN HOW TO PLAY SOMETHING, FIRST?
LYNN

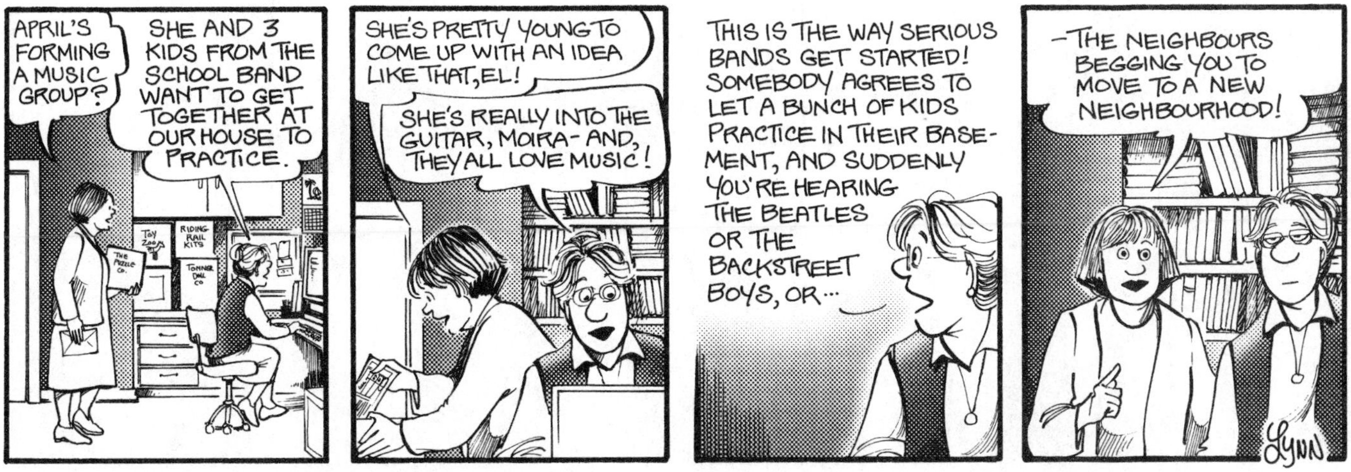
APRIL'S FORMING A MUSIC GROUP?
SHE AND 3 KIDS FROM THE SCHOOL BAND WANT TO GET TOGETHER AT OUR HOUSE TO PRACTICE.
TOY ZOO
RIDING RAIL KITS
THE PUZZLE CO.
TONNER DOLL CO
SHE'S PRETTY YOUNG TO COME UP WITH AN IDEA LIKE THAT, EL!
SHE'S REALLY INTO THE GUITAR, MOIRA - AND, THEY ALL LOVE MUSIC!
THIS IS THE WAY SERIOUS BANDS GET STARTED! SOMEBODY AGREES TO LET A BUNCH OF KIDS PRACTICE IN THEIR BASEMENT, AND SUDDENLY YOU'RE HEARING THE BEATLES OR THE BACKSTREET BOYS, OR ...
- THE NEIGHBOURS BEGGING YOU TO MOVE TO A NEW NEIGHBOURHOOD!
LYNN

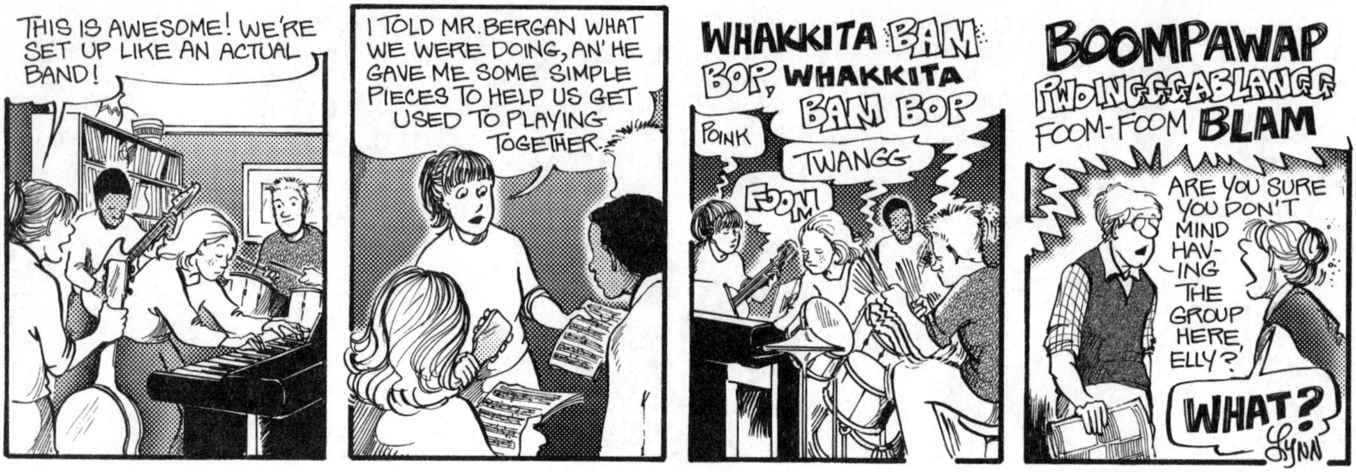
THIS IS AWESOME! WE'RE SET UP LIKE AN ACTUAL BAND!
I TOLD MR. BERGAN WHAT WE WERE DOING, AN' HE GAVE ME SOME SIMPLE PIECES TO HELP US GET USED TO PLAYING TOGETHER.
WHAKKITA BAM BOP, WHAKKITA BAM BOP
POINK
TWANGG
FOOM
BOOMPAWAP
PWDINGGGABLANGG
FOOM-FOOM BLAM
ARE YOU SURE YOU DON'T MIND HAV-ING THE GROUP HERE, ELLY?
WHAT?
LYNN

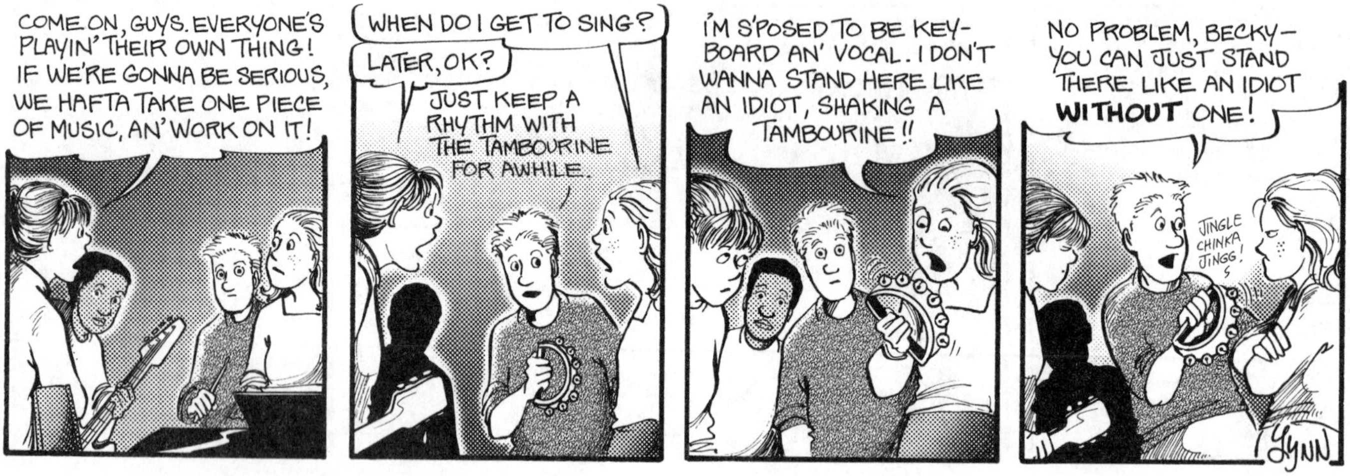
COME ON, GUYS. EVERYONE'S PLAYIN' THEIR OWN THING! IF WE'RE GONNA BE SERIOUS, WE HAFTA TAKE ONE PIECE OF MUSIC, AN' WORK ON IT!
WHEN DO I GET TO SING?
LATER, OK?
JUST KEEP A RHYTHM WITH THE TAMBOURINE FOR AWHILE.
I'M S'POSED TO BE KEY-BOARD AN' VOCAL. I DON'T WANNA STAND HERE LIKE AN IDIOT, SHAKING A TAMBOURINE!!
NO PROBLEM, BECKY– YOU CAN JUST STAND THERE LIKE AN IDIOT WITHOUT ONE!
JINGLE CHINKA JINGG!
LYNN

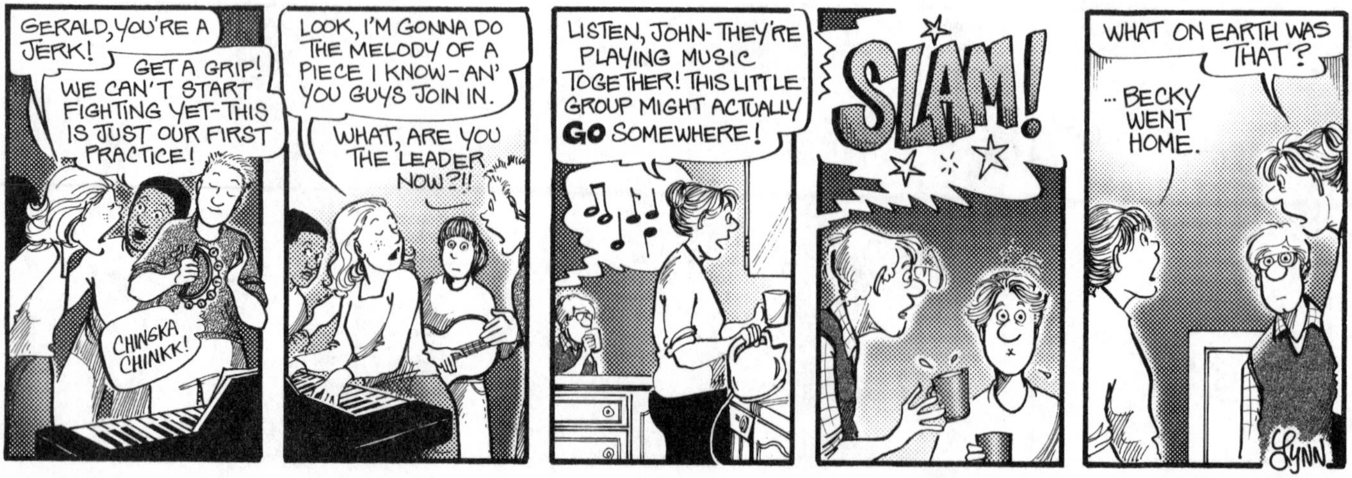
GERALD, YOU'RE A JERK!
GET A GRIP! WE CAN'T START FIGHTING YET–THIS IS JUST OUR FIRST PRACTICE!
CHINGKA CHINKK!
LOOK, I'M GONNA DO THE MELODY OF A PIECE I KNOW–AN' YOU GUYS JOIN IN.
WHAT, ARE YOU THE LEADER NOW?!!
LISTEN, JOHN–THEY'RE PLAYING MUSIC TOGETHER! THIS LITTLE GROUP MIGHT ACTUALLY GO SOMEWHERE!
SLAM!
WHAT ON EARTH WAS THAT?
...BECKY WENT HOME.
LYNN

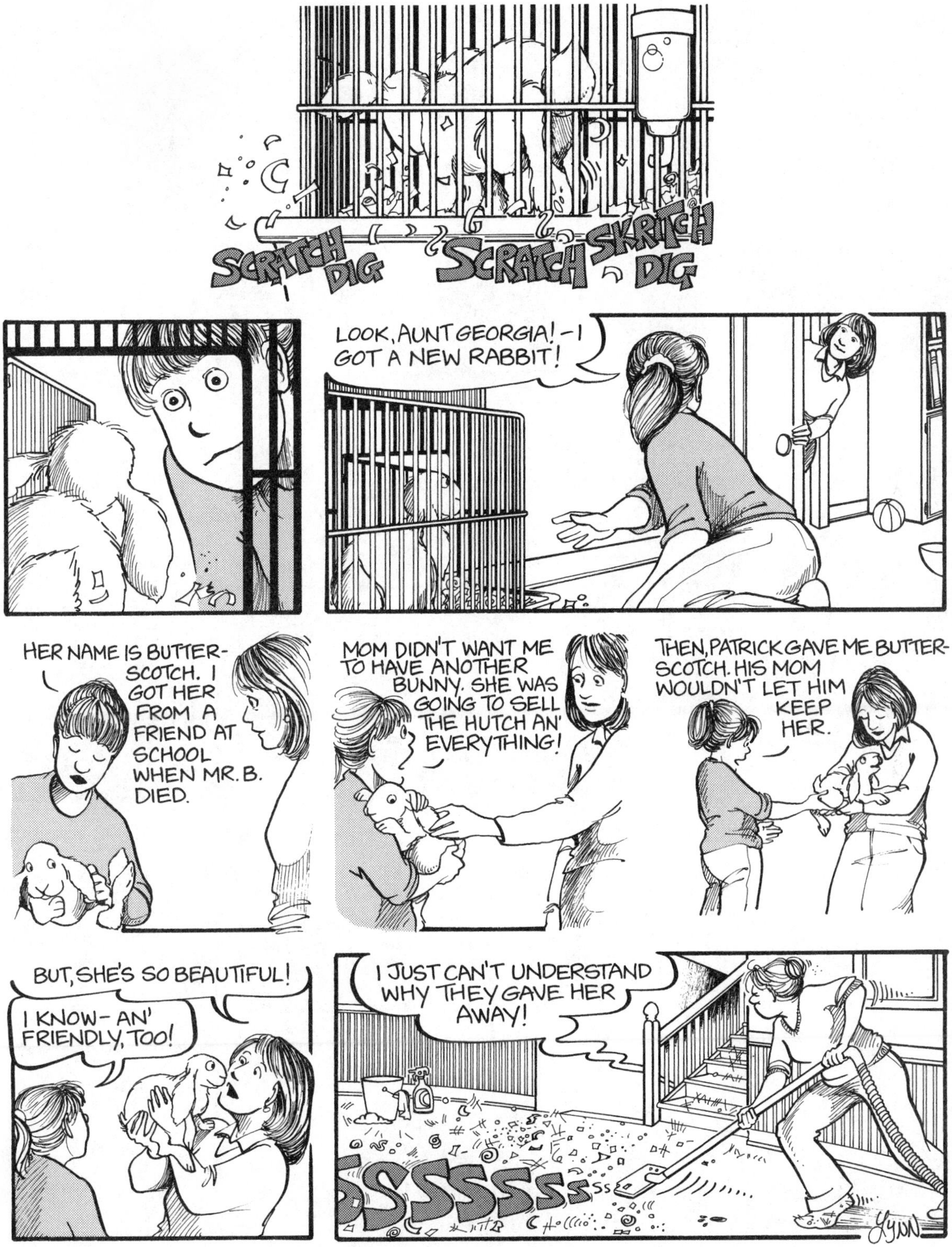
SCRATCH DIG
SCRATCH
SKRITCH DIG
LOOK, AUNT GEORGIA! - I GOT A NEW RABBIT!
HER NAME IS BUTTER-SCOTCH. I GOT HER FROM A FRIEND AT SCHOOL WHEN MR. B. DIED.
MOM DIDN'T WANT ME TO HAVE ANOTHER BUNNY. SHE WAS GOING TO SELL THE HUTCH AN' EVERYTHING!
THEN, PATRICK GAVE ME BUTTER-SCOTCH. HIS MOM WOULDN'T LET HIM KEEP HER.
BUT, SHE'S SO BEAUTIFUL!
I KNOW- AN' FRIENDLY, TOO!
I JUST CAN'T UNDERSTAND WHY THEY GAVE HER AWAY!
SSSSSSsss
Lynn

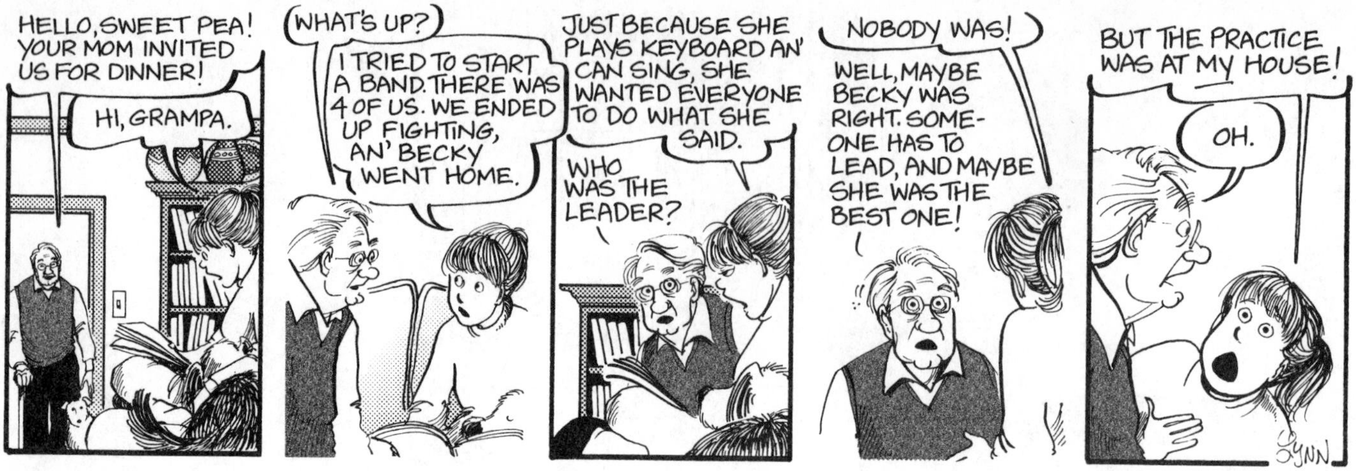
HELLO, SWEET PEA! YOUR MOM INVITED US FOR DINNER!
HI, GRAMPA.
WHAT'S UP?
I TRIED TO START A BAND. THERE WAS 4 OF US. WE ENDED UP FIGHTING, AN' BECKY WENT HOME.
JUST BECAUSE SHE PLAYS KEYBOARD AN' CAN SING, SHE WANTED EVERYONE TO DO WHAT SHE SAID.
WHO WAS THE LEADER?
NOBODY WAS!
WELL, MAYBE BECKY WAS RIGHT. SOME-ONE HAS TO LEAD, AND MAYBE SHE WAS THE BEST ONE!
BUT THE PRACTICE WAS AT MY HOUSE!
OH.
LYNN

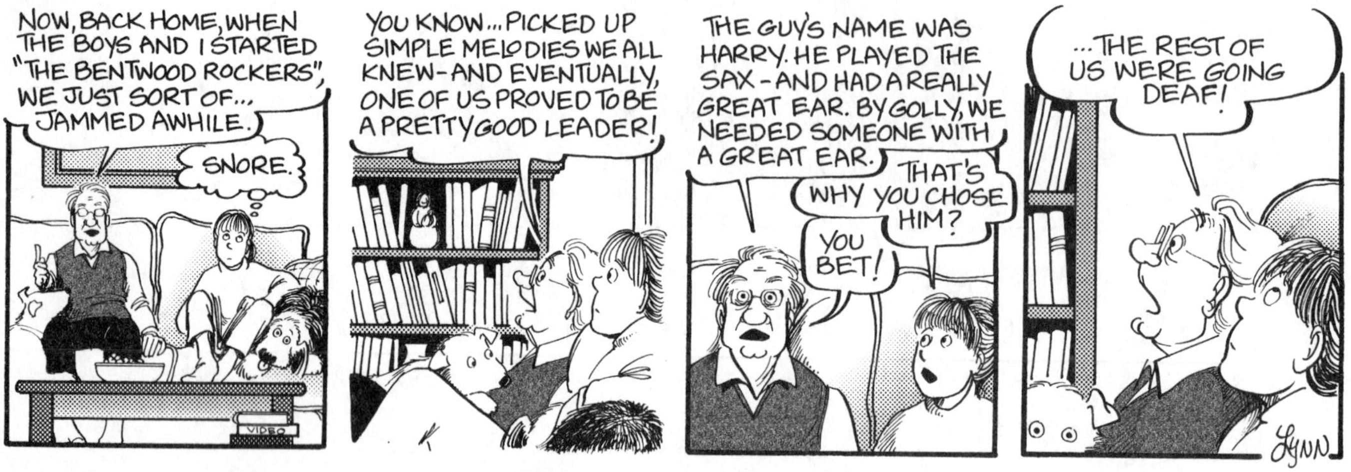
NOW, BACK HOME, WHEN THE BOYS AND I STARTED "THE BENTWOOD ROCKERS", WE JUST SORT OF... JAMMED AWHILE.
SNORE.
VIDEO
YOU KNOW... PICKED UP SIMPLE MELODIES WE ALL KNEW - AND EVENTUALLY, ONE OF US PROVED TO BE A PRETTY GOOD LEADER!
THE GUY'S NAME WAS HARRY. HE PLAYED THE SAX - AND HAD A REALLY GREAT EAR. BY GOLLY, WE NEEDED SOMEONE WITH A GREAT EAR.
THAT'S WHY YOU CHOSE HIM?
YOU BET!
...THE REST OF US WERE GOING DEAF!
LYNN

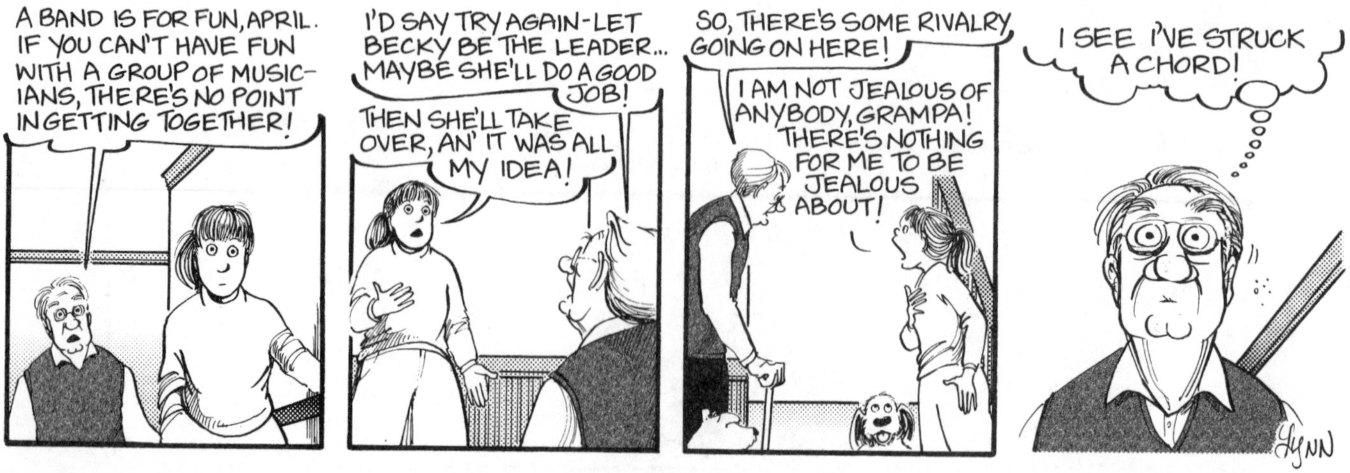
A BAND IS FOR FUN, APRIL. IF YOU CAN'T HAVE FUN WITH A GROUP OF MUSIC-IANS, THERE'S NO POINT IN GETTING TOGETHER!
I'D SAY TRY AGAIN - LET BECKY BE THE LEADER... MAYBE SHE'LL DO A GOOD JOB!
THEN SHE'LL TAKE OVER, AN' IT WAS ALL MY IDEA!
SO, THERE'S SOME RIVALRY GOING ON HERE!
I AM NOT JEALOUS OF ANYBODY, GRAMPA! THERE'S NOTHING FOR ME TO BE JEALOUS ABOUT!
I SEE I'VE STRUCK A CHORD!
LYNN

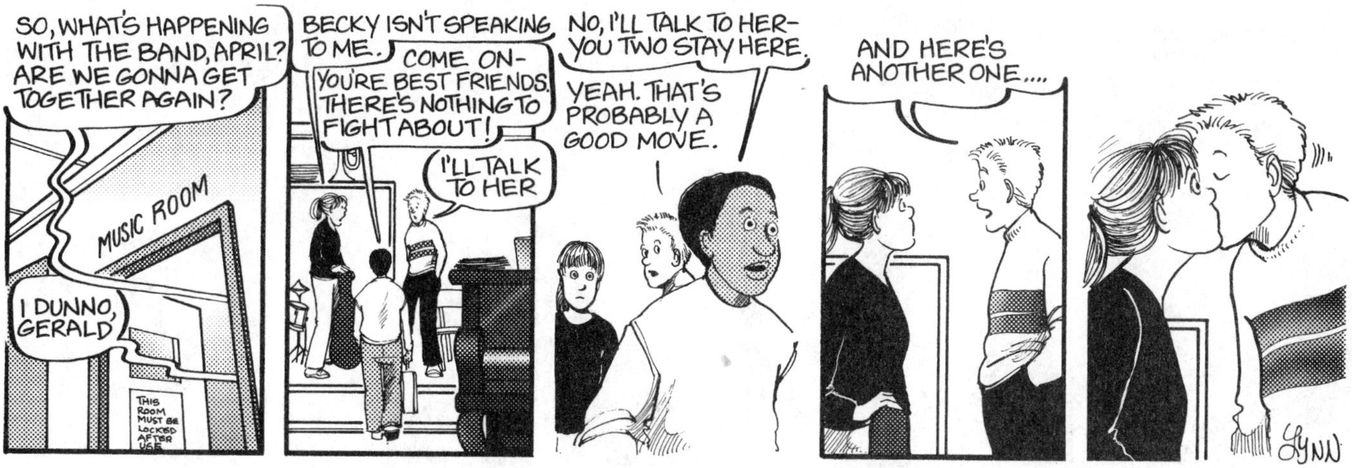
SO, WHAT'S HAPPENING WITH THE BAND, APRIL? ARE WE GONNA GET TOGETHER AGAIN?
MUSIC ROOM
I DUNNO, GERALD
THIS ROOM MUST BE LOCKED AFTER USE
BECKY ISN'T SPEAKING TO ME.
COME ON- YOU'RE BEST FRIENDS. THERE'S NOTHING TO FIGHT ABOUT!
I'LL TALK TO HER
NO, I'LL TALK TO HER- YOU TWO STAY HERE.
YEAH. THAT'S PROBABLY A GOOD MOVE.
AND HERE'S ANOTHER ONE....
LYNN

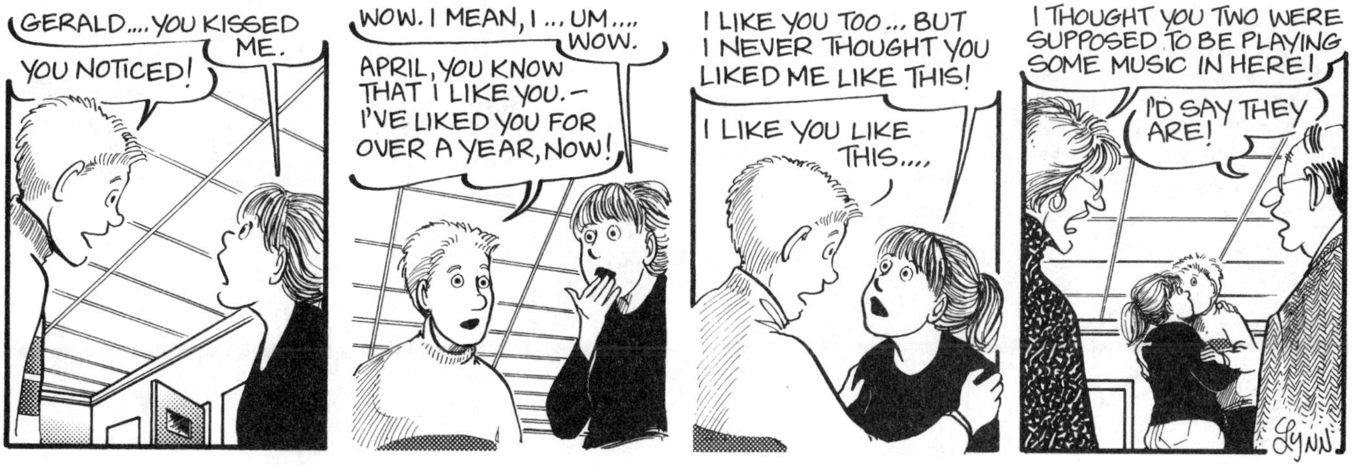
GERALD.... YOU KISSED ME.
YOU NOTICED!
WOW. I MEAN, I ... UM.... WOW.
APRIL, YOU KNOW THAT I LIKE YOU.- I'VE LIKED YOU FOR OVER A YEAR, NOW!
I LIKE YOU TOO... BUT I NEVER THOUGHT YOU LIKED ME LIKE THIS!
I LIKE YOU LIKE THIS....
I THOUGHT YOU TWO WERE SUPPOSED TO BE PLAYING SOME MUSIC IN HERE!
I'D SAY THEY ARE!
LYNN

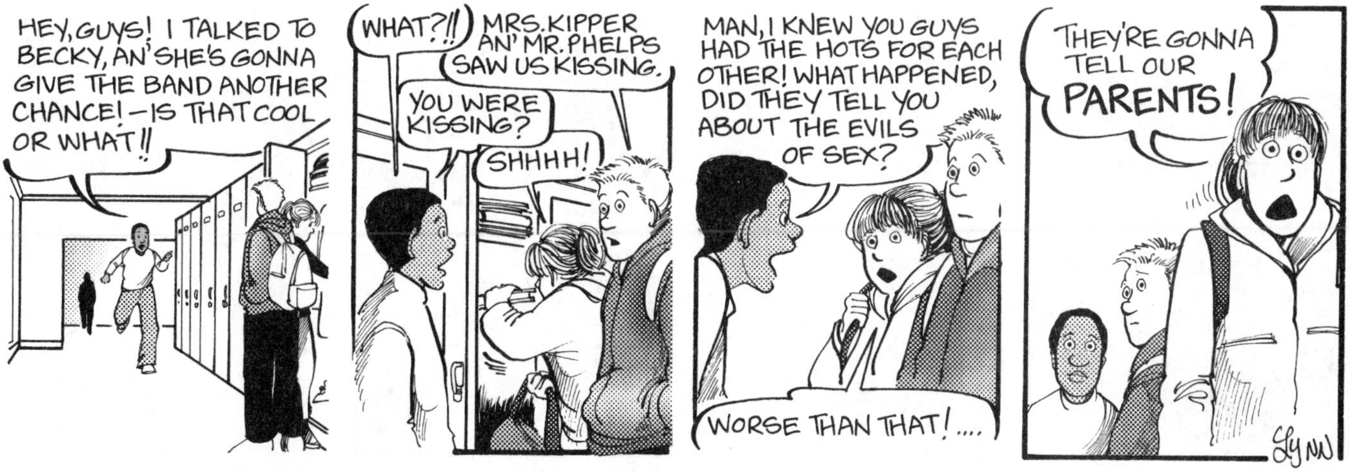
HEY, GUYS! I TALKED TO BECKY, AN' SHE'S GONNA GIVE THE BAND ANOTHER CHANCE! -IS THAT COOL OR WHAT!!
WHAT?!!
MRS. KIPPER AN' MR. PHELPS SAW US KISSING.
YOU WERE KISSING?
SHHHH!
MAN, I KNEW YOU GUYS HAD THE HOTS FOR EACH OTHER! WHAT HAPPENED, DID THEY TELL YOU ABOUT THE EVILS OF SEX?
WORSE THAN THAT!....
THEY'RE GONNA TELL OUR PARENTS!
LYNN

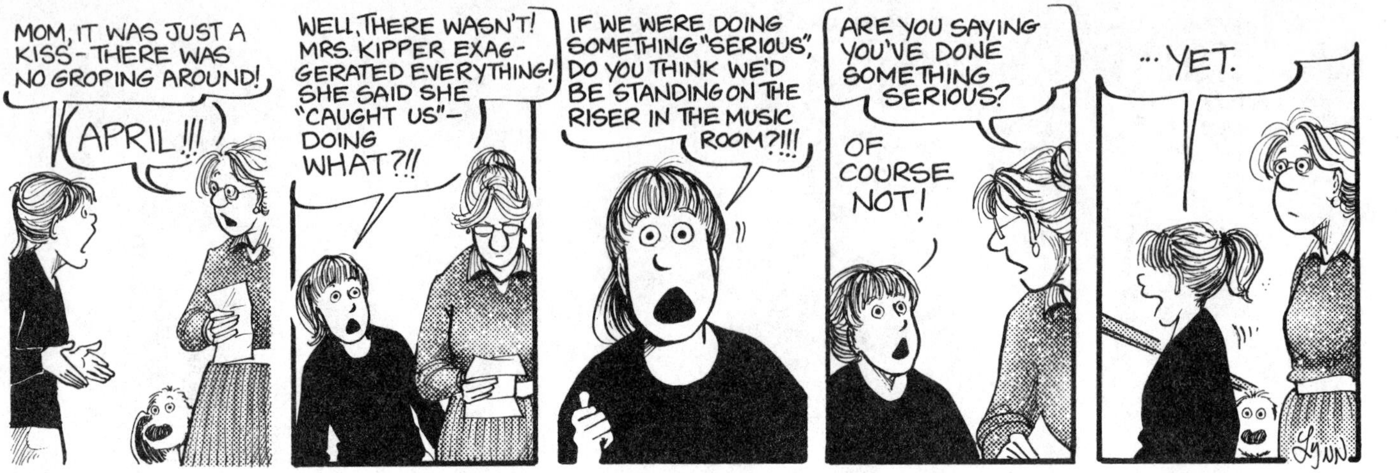
MOM, IT WAS JUST A KISS - THERE WAS NO GROPING AROUND!
APRIL!!!
WELL, THERE WASN'T! MRS. KIPPER EXAGGERATED EVERYTHING! SHE SAID SHE "CAUGHT US"- DOING WHAT?!!
IF WE WERE DOING SOMETHING "SERIOUS", DO YOU THINK WE'D BE STANDING ON THE RISER IN THE MUSIC ROOM?!!!
ARE YOU SAYING YOU'VE DONE SOMETHING SERIOUS?
OF COURSE NOT!
... YET.
Lynn

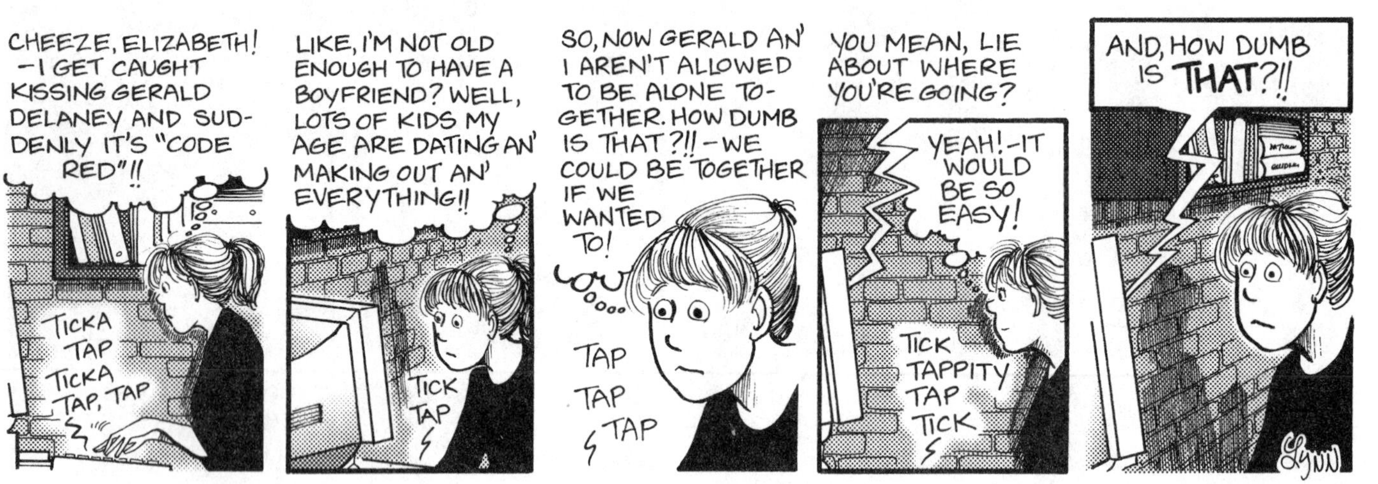
CHEEZE, ELIZABETH! -I GET CAUGHT KISSING GERALD DELANEY AND SUDDENLY IT'S "CODE RED"!!
TICKA TAP TICKA TAP, TAP
LIKE, I'M NOT OLD ENOUGH TO HAVE A BOYFRIEND? WELL, LOTS OF KIDS MY AGE ARE DATING AN' MAKING OUT AN' EVERYTHING!!
TICK TAP
SO, NOW GERALD AN' I AREN'T ALLOWED TO BE ALONE TOGETHER. HOW DUMB IS THAT?!! - WE COULD BE TOGETHER IF WE WANTED TO!
TAP TAP TAP
YOU MEAN, LIE ABOUT WHERE YOU'RE GOING?
YEAH! - IT WOULD BE SO EASY!
TICK TAPPITY TAP TICK
AND, HOW DUMB IS THAT?!!
Lynn

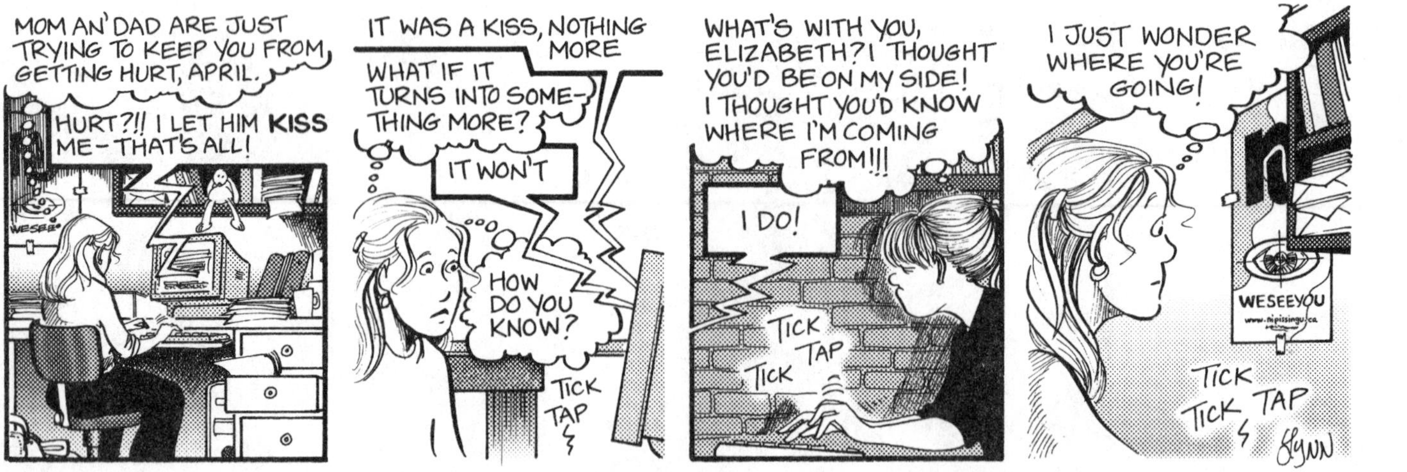
MOM AN' DAD ARE JUST TRYING TO KEEP YOU FROM GETTING HURT, APRIL.
HURT?!! I LET HIM KISS ME - THAT'S ALL!
WESEE
IT WAS A KISS, NOTHING MORE
WHAT IF IT TURNS INTO SOMETHING MORE?
IT WON'T
HOW DO YOU KNOW?
TICK TAP
WHAT'S WITH YOU, ELIZABETH?! I THOUGHT YOU'D BE ON MY SIDE! I THOUGHT YOU'D KNOW WHERE I'M COMING FROM!!!
I DO!
TICK TAP TICK
I JUST WONDER WHERE YOU'RE GOING!
WESEEYOU
www.nipissingu.ca
TICK TICK TAP
Lynn

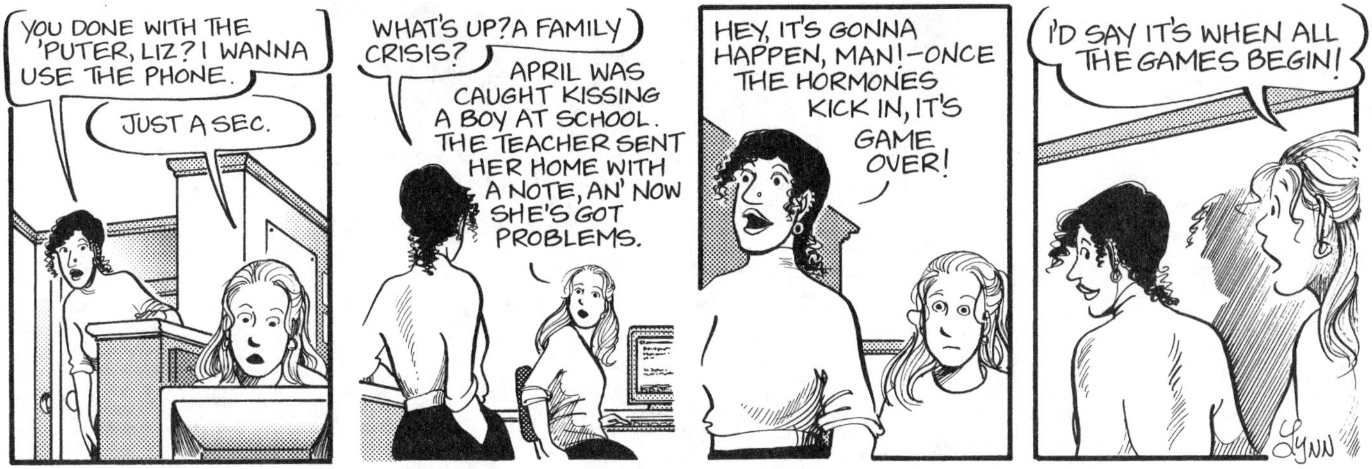
YOU DONE WITH THE 'PUTER, LIZ? I WANNA USE THE PHONE.
JUST A SEC.
WHAT'S UP? A FAMILY CRISIS?
APRIL WAS CAUGHT KISSING A BOY AT SCHOOL. THE TEACHER SENT HER HOME WITH A NOTE, AN' NOW SHE'S GOT PROBLEMS.
HEY, IT'S GONNA HAPPEN, MAN! -ONCE THE HORMONES KICK IN, IT'S GAME OVER!
I'D SAY IT'S WHEN ALL THE GAMES BEGIN!
LYNN

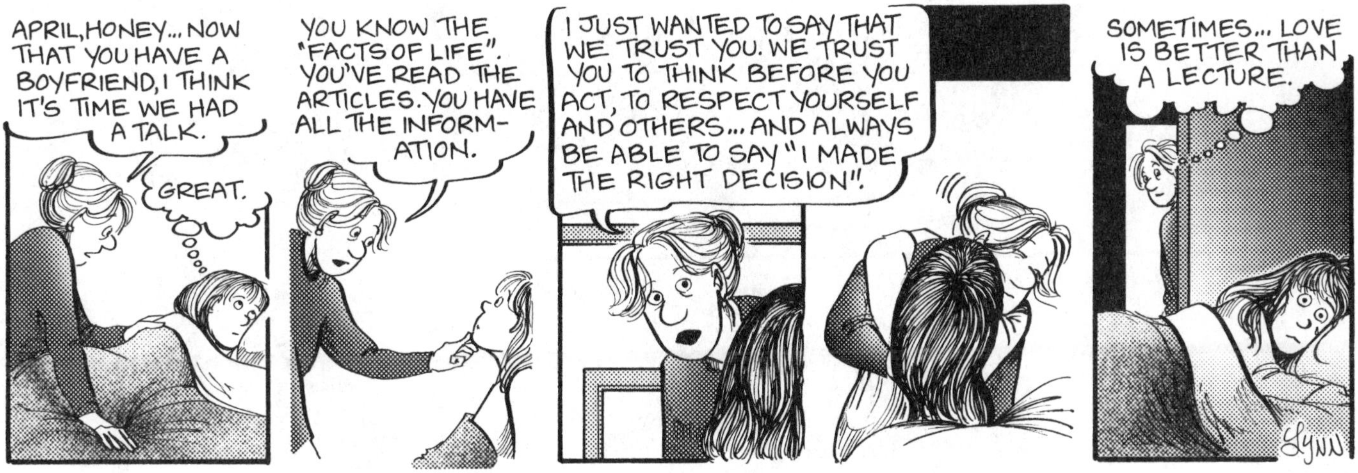
APRIL, HONEY... NOW THAT YOU HAVE A BOYFRIEND, I THINK IT'S TIME WE HAD A TALK.
GREAT.
YOU KNOW THE "FACTS OF LIFE". YOU'VE READ THE ARTICLES. YOU HAVE ALL THE INFORM-ATION.
I JUST WANTED TO SAY THAT WE TRUST YOU. WE TRUST YOU TO THINK BEFORE YOU ACT, TO RESPECT YOURSELF AND OTHERS... AND ALWAYS BE ABLE TO SAY "I MADE THE RIGHT DECISION".
SOMETIMES... LOVE IS BETTER THAN A LECTURE.
LYNN

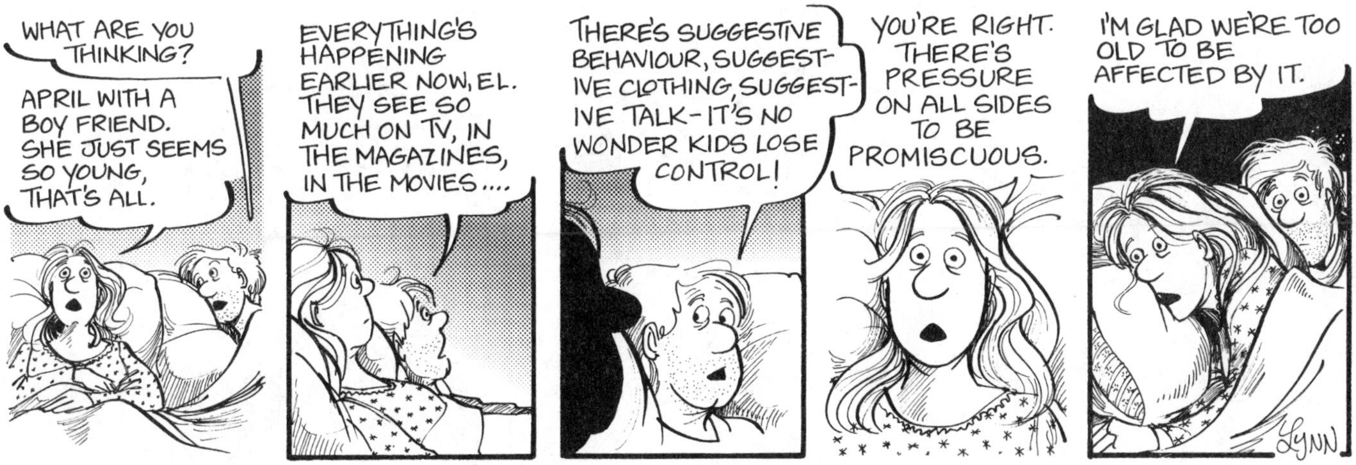
WHAT ARE YOU THINKING?
APRIL WITH A BOY FRIEND. SHE JUST SEEMS SO YOUNG, THAT'S ALL.
EVERYTHING'S HAPPENING EARLIER NOW, EL. THEY SEE SO MUCH ON TV, IN THE MAGAZINES, IN THE MOVIES....
THERE'S SUGGESTIVE BEHAVIOUR, SUGGEST-IVE CLOTHING, SUGGEST-IVE TALK- IT'S NO WONDER KIDS LOSE CONTROL!
YOU'RE RIGHT. THERE'S PRESSURE ON ALL SIDES TO BE PROMISCUOUS.
I'M GLAD WE'RE TOO OLD TO BE AFFECTED BY IT.
LYNN

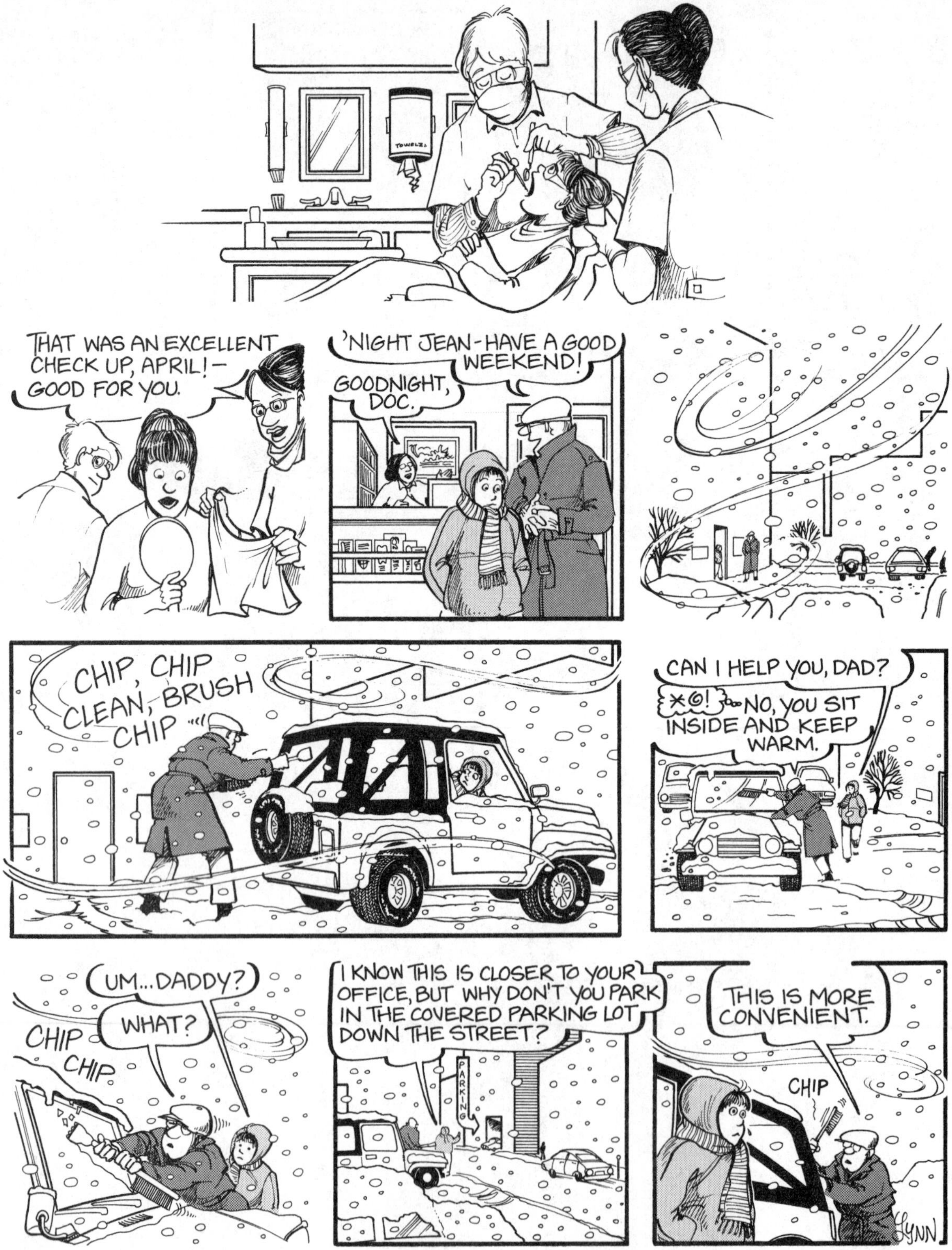
THAT WAS AN EXCELLENT CHECK UP, APRIL! – GOOD FOR YOU.
'NIGHT JEAN - HAVE A GOOD WEEKEND!
GOODNIGHT, DOC.
CHIP, CHIP CLEAN, BRUSH CHIP
CAN I HELP YOU, DAD?
*@!
NO, YOU SIT INSIDE AND KEEP WARM.
UM... DADDY?
WHAT?
CHIP CHIP
I KNOW THIS IS CLOSER TO YOUR OFFICE, BUT WHY DON'T YOU PARK IN THE COVERED PARKING LOT DOWN THE STREET?
PARKING
THIS IS MORE CONVENIENT.
CHIP
LYNN

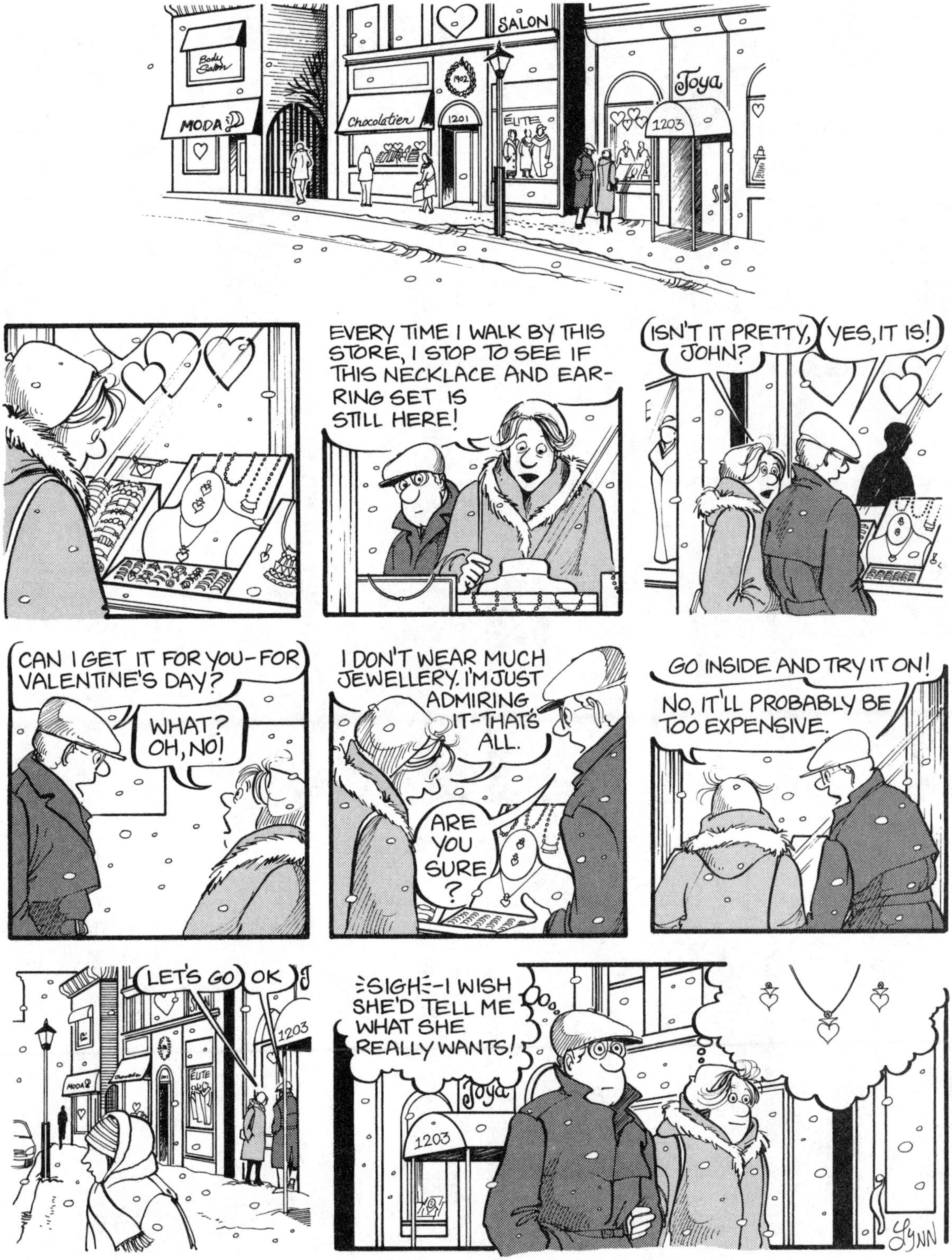

MODA
Chocolatier
1201
SALON
ÉLITE
Joya
1203
EVERY TIME I WALK BY THIS STORE, I STOP TO SEE IF THIS NECKLACE AND EAR-RING SET IS STILL HERE!
ISN'T IT PRETTY, JOHN?
YES, IT IS!
CAN I GET IT FOR YOU—FOR VALENTINE'S DAY?
WHAT? OH, NO!
I DON'T WEAR MUCH JEWELLERY. I'M JUST ADMIRING IT—THAT'S ALL.
ARE YOU SURE?
GO INSIDE AND TRY IT ON!
NO, IT'LL PROBABLY BE TOO EXPENSIVE.
LET'S GO
OK
SIGH—I WISH SHE'D TELL ME WHAT SHE REALLY WANTS!
LYNN

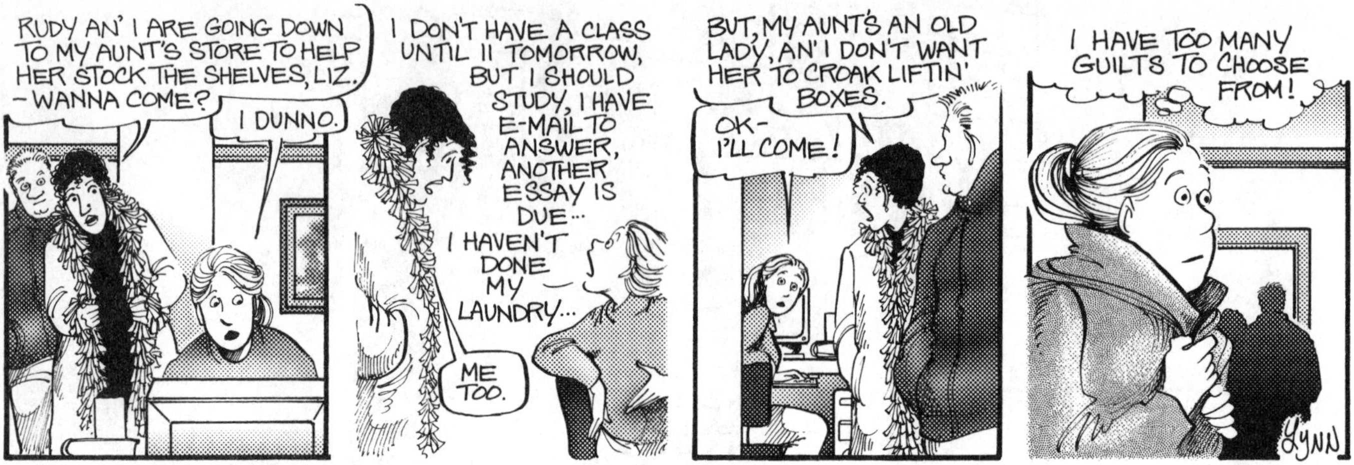
RUDY AN' I ARE GOING DOWN TO MY AUNT'S STORE TO HELP HER STOCK THE SHELVES, LIZ. -WANNA COME?
I DUNNO.
I DON'T HAVE A CLASS UNTIL 11 TOMORROW, BUT I SHOULD STUDY, I HAVE E-MAIL TO ANSWER, ANOTHER ESSAY IS DUE... I HAVEN'T DONE MY LAUNDRY...
ME TOO.
BUT, MY AUNT'S AN OLD LADY, AN' I DON'T WANT HER TO CROAK LIFTIN' BOXES.
OK- I'LL COME!
I HAVE TOO MANY GUILTS TO CHOOSE FROM!
LYNN

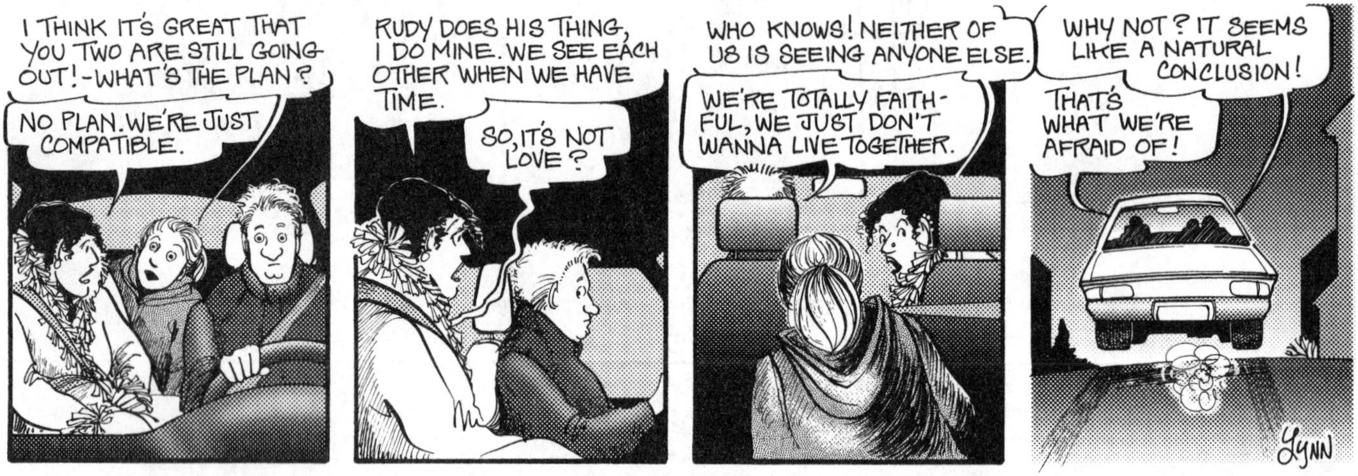
I THINK IT'S GREAT THAT YOU TWO ARE STILL GOING OUT! -WHAT'S THE PLAN?
NO PLAN. WE'RE JUST COMPATIBLE.
RUDY DOES HIS THING, I DO MINE. WE SEE EACH OTHER WHEN WE HAVE TIME.
SO, IT'S NOT LOVE?
WHO KNOWS! NEITHER OF US IS SEEING ANYONE ELSE.
WE'RE TOTALLY FAITHFUL, WE JUST DON'T WANNA LIVE TOGETHER.
WHY NOT? IT SEEMS LIKE A NATURAL CONCLUSION!
THAT'S WHAT WE'RE AFRAID OF!
LYNN

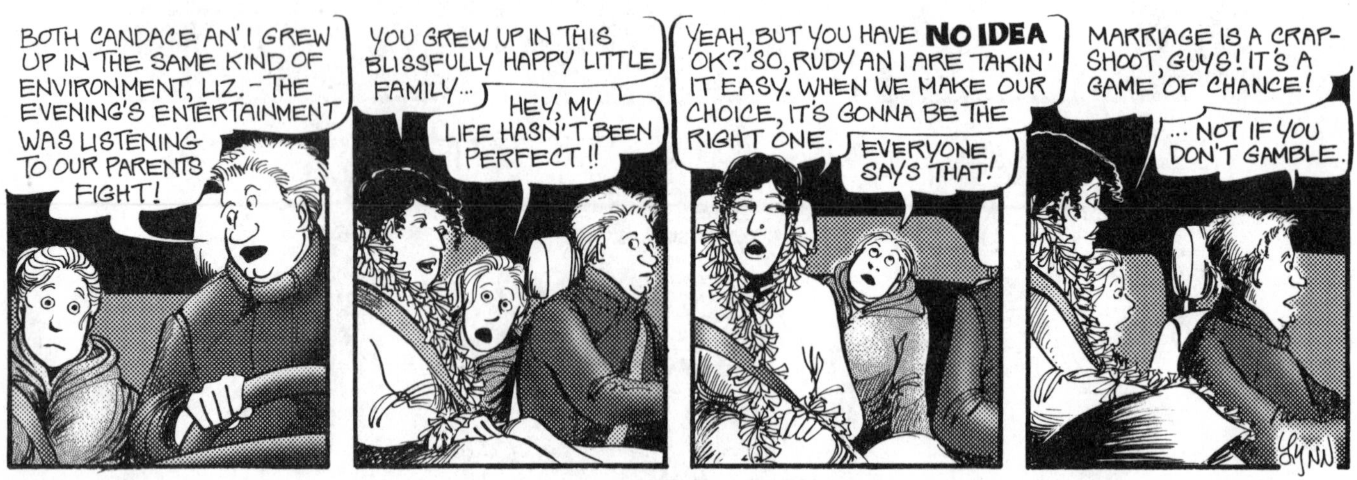
BOTH CANDACE AN' I GREW UP IN THE SAME KIND OF ENVIRONMENT, LIZ. -THE EVENING'S ENTERTAINMENT WAS LISTENING TO OUR PARENTS FIGHT!
YOU GREW UP IN THIS BLISSFULLY HAPPY LITTLE FAMILY...
HEY, MY LIFE HASN'T BEEN PERFECT!!
YEAH, BUT YOU HAVE NO IDEA OK? SO, RUDY AN I ARE TAKIN' IT EASY. WHEN WE MAKE OUR CHOICE, IT'S GONNA BE THE RIGHT ONE.
EVERYONE SAYS THAT!
MARRIAGE IS A CRAP-SHOOT, GUYS! IT'S A GAME OF CHANCE!
... NOT IF YOU DON'T GAMBLE.
LYNN

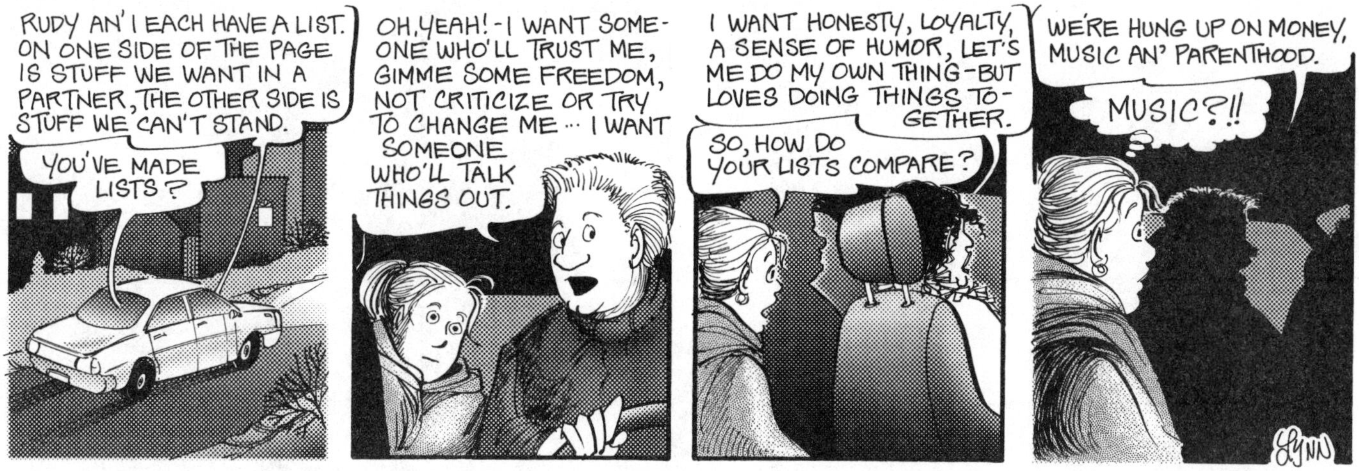
RUDY AN' I EACH HAVE A LIST. ON ONE SIDE OF THE PAGE IS STUFF WE WANT IN A PARTNER, THE OTHER SIDE IS STUFF WE CAN'T STAND.
YOU'VE MADE LISTS?
OH, YEAH! - I WANT SOMEONE WHO'LL TRUST ME, GIMME SOME FREEDOM, NOT CRITICIZE OR TRY TO CHANGE ME ... I WANT SOMEONE WHO'LL TALK THINGS OUT.
I WANT HONESTY, LOYALTY, A SENSE OF HUMOR, LET'S ME DO MY OWN THING - BUT LOVES DOING THINGS TOGETHER.
SO, HOW DO YOUR LISTS COMPARE?
WE'RE HUNG UP ON MONEY, MUSIC AN' PARENTHOOD.
MUSIC?!!
LYNN

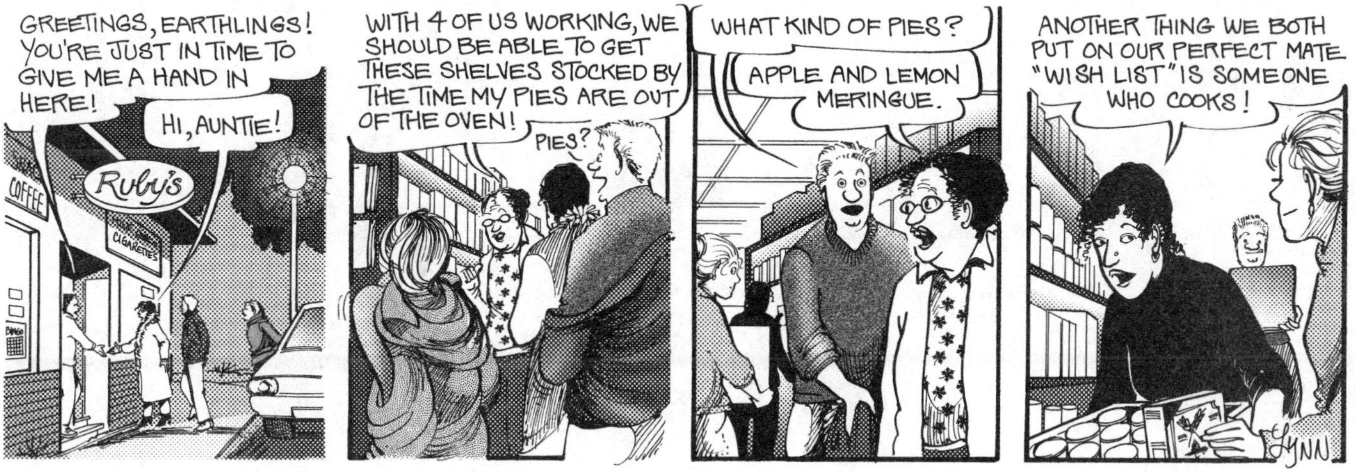
GREETINGS, EARTHLINGS! YOU'RE JUST IN TIME TO GIVE ME A HAND IN HERE!
HI, AUNTIE!
Ruby's
COFFEE
CIGARETTES
WITH 4 OF US WORKING, WE SHOULD BE ABLE TO GET THESE SHELVES STOCKED BY THE TIME MY PIES ARE OUT OF THE OVEN!
PIES?
WHAT KIND OF PIES?
APPLE AND LEMON MERINGUE.
ANOTHER THING WE BOTH PUT ON OUR PERFECT MATE "WISH LIST" IS SOMEONE WHO COOKS!
LYNN

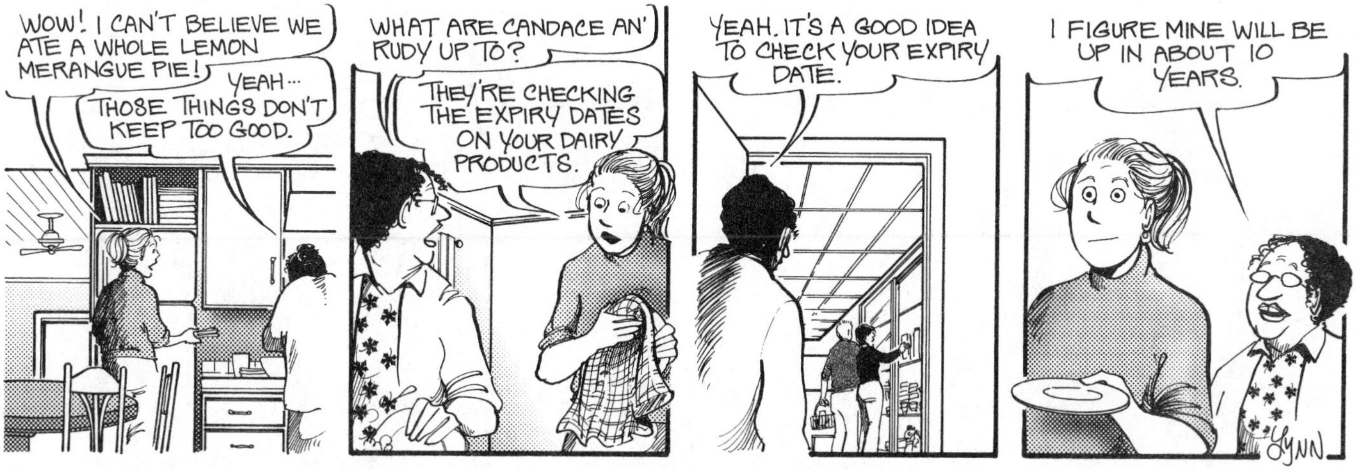
WOW! I CAN'T BELIEVE WE ATE A WHOLE LEMON MERANGUE PIE!
YEAH... THOSE THINGS DON'T KEEP TOO GOOD.
WHAT ARE CANDACE AN' RUDY UP TO?
THEY'RE CHECKING THE EXPIRY DATES ON YOUR DAIRY PRODUCTS.
YEAH. IT'S A GOOD IDEA TO CHECK YOUR EXPIRY DATE.
I FIGURE MINE WILL BE UP IN ABOUT 10 YEARS.
LYNN

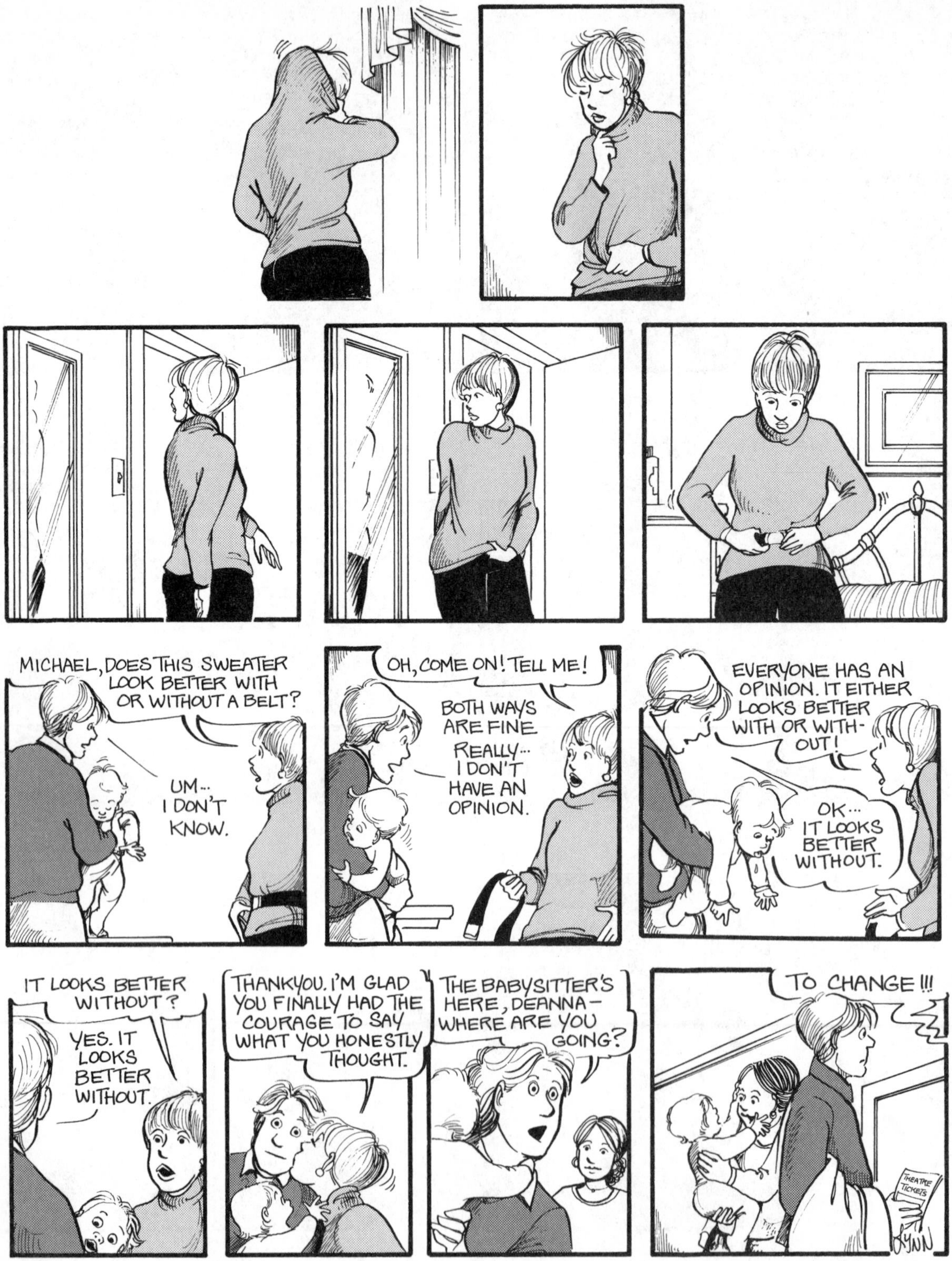

MICHAEL, DOES THIS SWEATER LOOK BETTER WITH OR WITHOUT A BELT?
UM... I DON'T KNOW.
OH, COME ON! TELL ME!
BOTH WAYS ARE FINE
REALLY... I DON'T HAVE AN OPINION.
EVERYONE HAS AN OPINION. IT EITHER LOOKS BETTER WITH OR WITH-OUT!
OK... IT LOOKS BETTER WITHOUT.
IT LOOKS BETTER WITHOUT?
YES. IT LOOKS BETTER WITHOUT.
THANKYOU. I'M GLAD YOU FINALLY HAD THE COURAGE TO SAY WHAT YOU HONESTLY THOUGHT.
THE BABYSITTER'S HERE, DEANNA—WHERE ARE YOU GOING?
TO CHANGE!!!
THEATRE TICKETS
LYNN

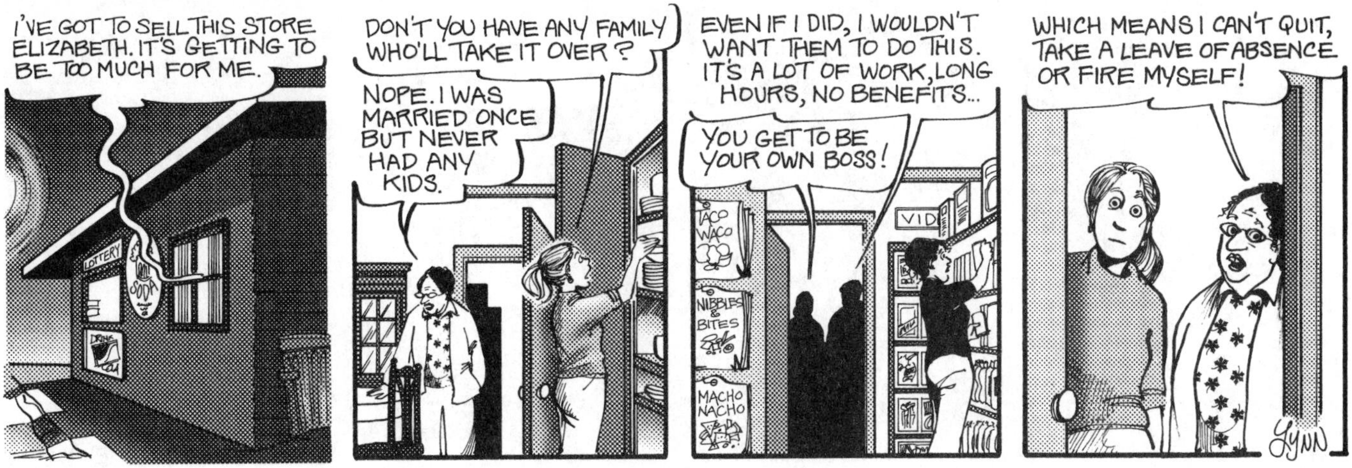
I'VE GOT TO SELL THIS STORE ELIZABETH. IT'S GETTING TO BE TOO MUCH FOR ME.
LOTTERY
SODA
DON'T YOU HAVE ANY FAMILY WHO'LL TAKE IT OVER?
NOPE. I WAS MARRIED ONCE BUT NEVER HAD ANY KIDS.
EVEN IF I DID, I WOULDN'T WANT THEM TO DO THIS. IT'S A LOT OF WORK, LONG HOURS, NO BENEFITS...
YOU GET TO BE YOUR OWN BOSS!
TACO WACO
NIBBLES & BITES
MACHO NACHO
VID
WHICH MEANS I CAN'T QUIT, TAKE A LEAVE OF ABSENCE OR FIRE MYSELF!
LYNN

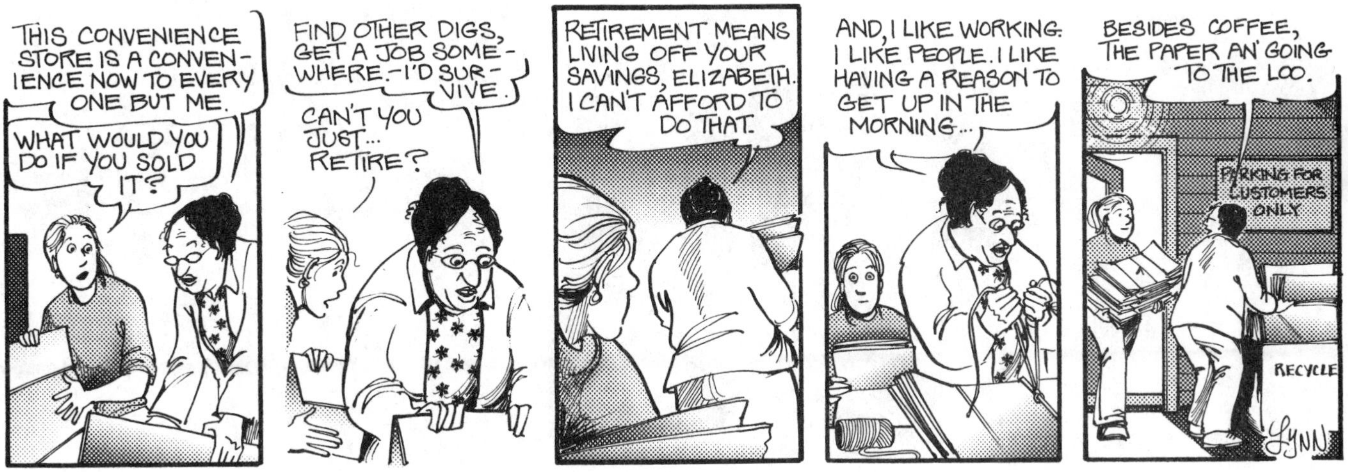
THIS CONVENIENCE STORE IS A CONVENIENCE NOW TO EVERY ONE BUT ME.
WHAT WOULD YOU DO IF YOU SOLD IT?
FIND OTHER DIGS, GET A JOB SOMEWHERE. – I'D SURVIVE.
CAN'T YOU JUST... RETIRE?
RETIREMENT MEANS LIVING OFF YOUR SAVINGS, ELIZABETH. I CAN'T AFFORD TO DO THAT.
AND, I LIKE WORKING. I LIKE PEOPLE. I LIKE HAVING A REASON TO GET UP IN THE MORNING...
BESIDES COFFEE, THE PAPER AN' GOING TO THE LOO.
PARKING FOR CUSTOMERS ONLY
RECYCLE
LYNN

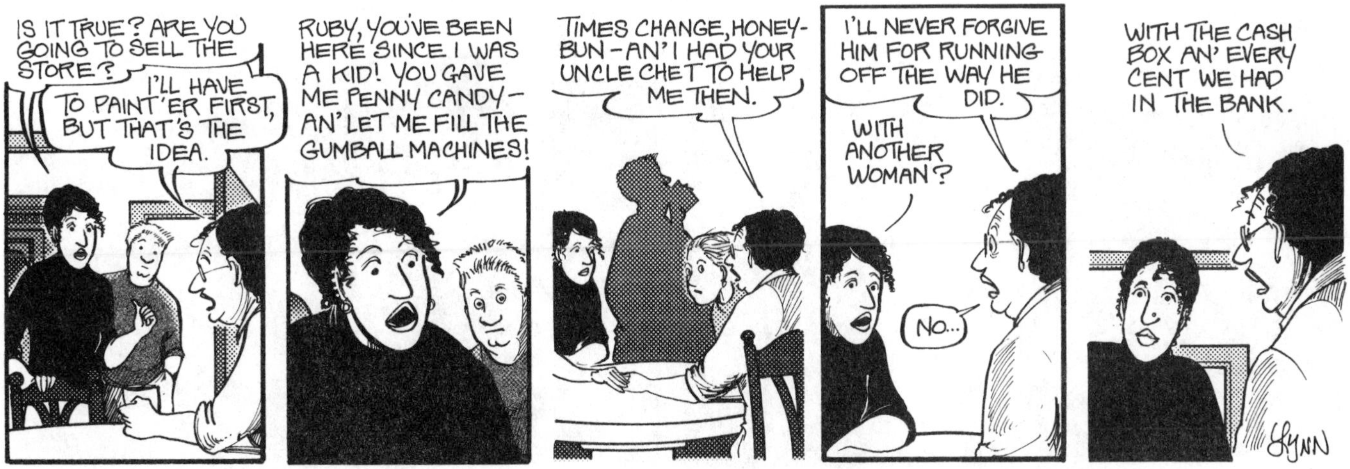
IS IT TRUE? ARE YOU GOING TO SELL THE STORE?
I'LL HAVE TO PAINT 'ER FIRST, BUT THAT'S THE IDEA.
RUBY, YOU'VE BEEN HERE SINCE I WAS A KID! YOU GAVE ME PENNY CANDY – AN' LET ME FILL THE GUMBALL MACHINES!
TIMES CHANGE, HONEY-BUN – AN' I HAD YOUR UNCLE CHET TO HELP ME THEN.
I'LL NEVER FORGIVE HIM FOR RUNNING OFF THE WAY HE DID.
WITH ANOTHER WOMAN?
NO...
WITH THE CASH BOX AN' EVERY CENT WE HAD IN THE BANK.
LYNN

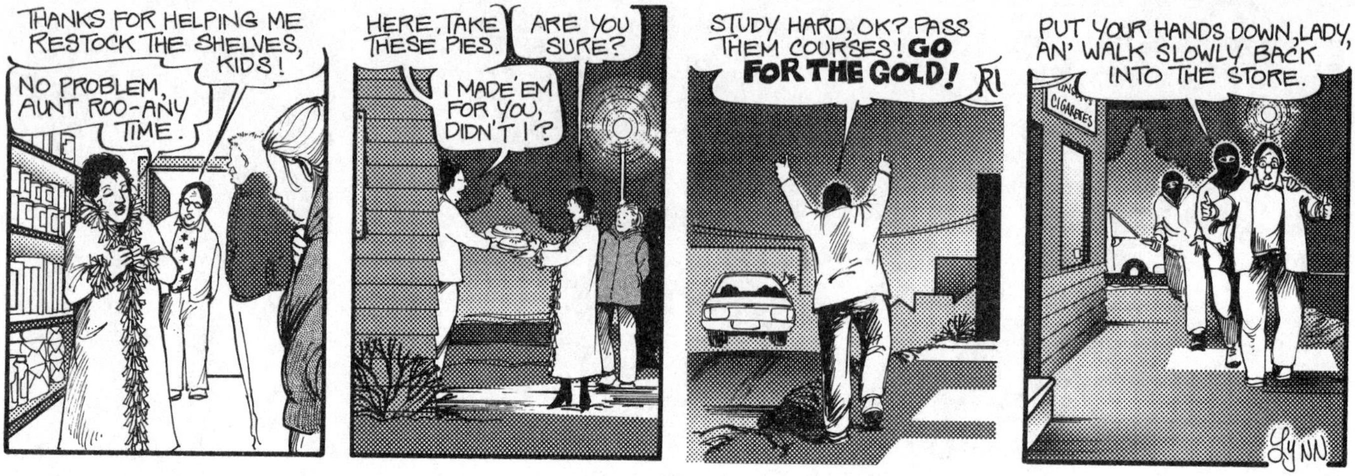
THANKS FOR HELPING ME RESTOCK THE SHELVES, KIDS!
NO PROBLEM, AUNT ROO-ANY TIME.
HERE, TAKE THESE PIES.
ARE YOU SURE?
I MADE 'EM FOR YOU, DIDN'T I?
STUDY HARD, OK? PASS THEM COURSES! GO FOR THE GOLD!
PUT YOUR HANDS DOWN, LADY, AN' WALK SLOWLY BACK INTO THE STORE.
CIGARETTES
LYNN

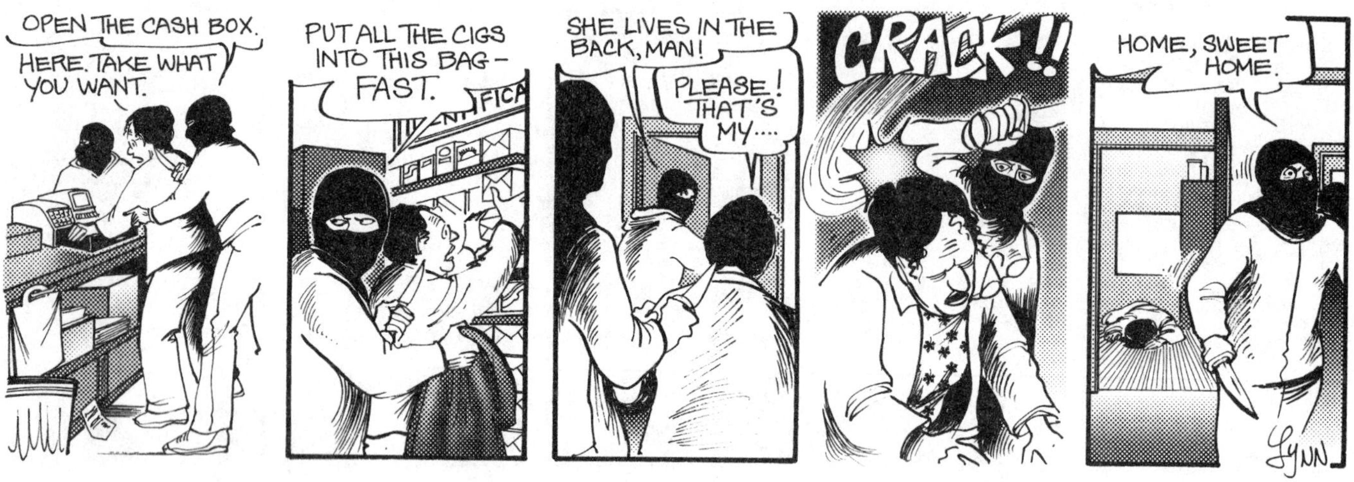
OPEN THE CASH BOX.
HERE. TAKE WHAT YOU WANT.
PUT ALL THE CIGS INTO THIS BAG - FAST.
SHE LIVES IN THE BACK, MAN!
PLEASE! THAT'S MY....
CRACK!!
HOME, SWEET HOME.
LYNN

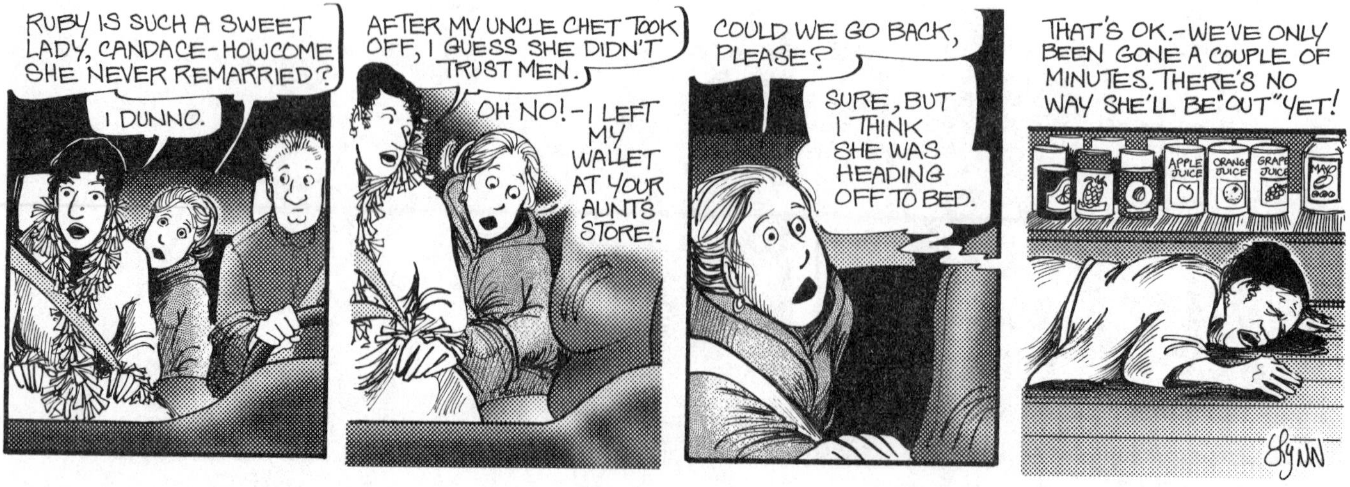
RUBY IS SUCH A SWEET LADY, CANDACE-HOWCOME SHE NEVER REMARRIED?
I DUNNO.
AFTER MY UNCLE CHET TOOK OFF, I GUESS SHE DIDN'T TRUST MEN.
OH NO! - I LEFT MY WALLET AT YOUR AUNT'S STORE!
COULD WE GO BACK, PLEASE?
SURE, BUT I THINK SHE WAS HEADING OFF TO BED.
THAT'S OK. - WE'VE ONLY BEEN GONE A COUPLE OF MINUTES. THERE'S NO WAY SHE'LL BE "OUT" YET!
APPLE JUICE
ORANGE JUICE
GRAPE JUICE
MAYO
LYNN

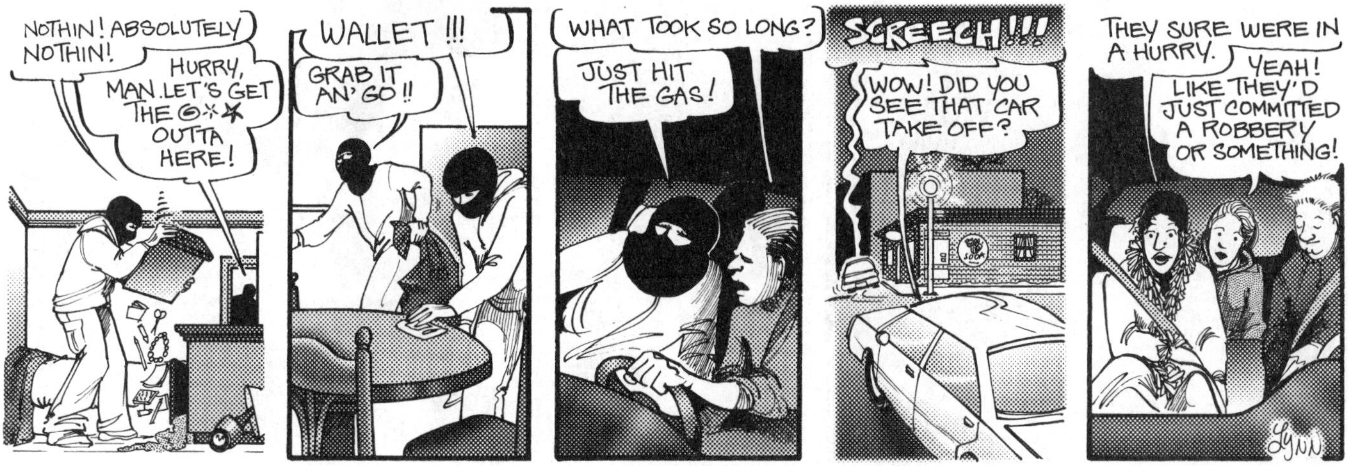
NOTHIN! ABSOLUTELY NOTHIN!
HURRY, MAN. LET'S GET THE @*☆ OUTTA HERE!
WALLET !!!
GRAB IT AN' GO !!
WHAT TOOK SO LONG?
JUST HIT THE GAS!
SCREECH!!!
WOW! DID YOU SEE THAT CAR TAKE OFF?
THEY SURE WERE IN A HURRY.
YEAH! LIKE THEY'D JUST COMMITTED A ROBBERY OR SOMETHING!
Lynn

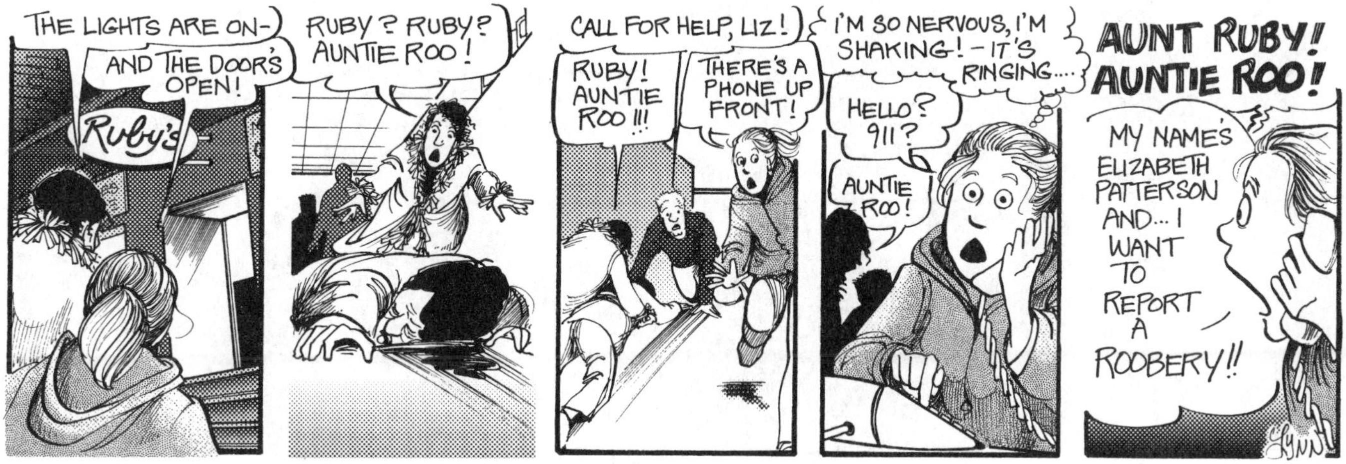
THE LIGHTS ARE ON-
AND THE DOOR'S OPEN!
Ruby's
RUBY? RUBY? AUNTIE ROO!
CALL FOR HELP, LIZ!
RUBY! AUNTIE ROO!!!
THERE'S A PHONE UP FRONT!
I'M SO NERVOUS, I'M SHAKING! - IT'S RINGING....
HELLO? 911?
AUNTIE ROO!
AUNT RUBY! AUNTIE ROO!
MY NAME'S ELIZABETH PATTERSON AND... I WANT TO REPORT A ROOBERY!!
Lynn

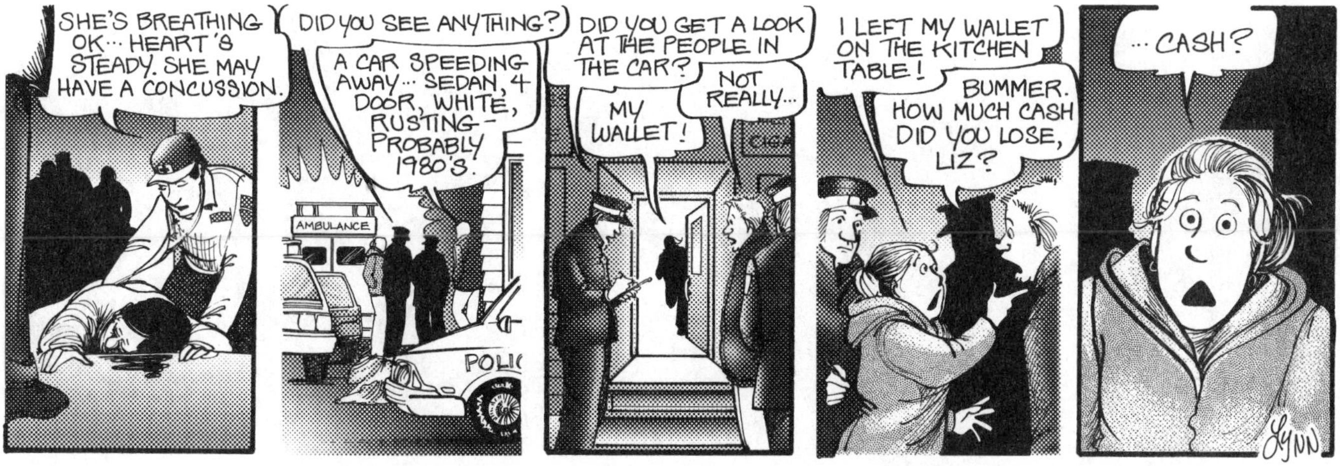
SHE'S BREATHING OK... HEART'S STEADY. SHE MAY HAVE A CONCUSSION.
DID YOU SEE ANYTHING?
A CAR SPEEDING AWAY... SEDAN, 4 DOOR, WHITE, RUSTING- PROBABLY 1980'S.
AMBULANCE
POLIC
DID YOU GET A LOOK AT THE PEOPLE IN THE CAR?
NOT REALLY...
MY WALLET!
CIGA
I LEFT MY WALLET ON THE KITCHEN TABLE!
BUMMER. HOW MUCH CASH DID YOU LOSE, LIZ?
...CASH?
Lynn

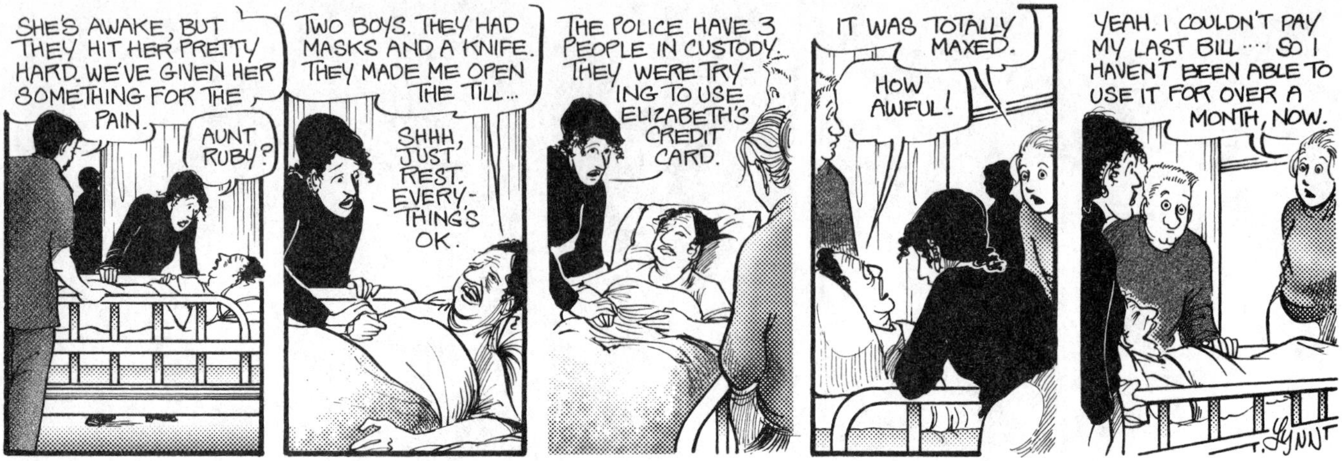
SHE'S AWAKE, BUT THEY HIT HER PRETTY HARD. WE'VE GIVEN HER SOMETHING FOR THE PAIN.
AUNT RUBY?
TWO BOYS. THEY HAD MASKS AND A KNIFE. THEY MADE ME OPEN THE TILL...
SHHH, JUST REST. EVERY-THING'S OK.
THE POLICE HAVE 3 PEOPLE IN CUSTODY. THEY WERE TRY-ING TO USE ELIZABETH'S CREDIT CARD.
IT WAS TOTALLY MAXED.
HOW AWFUL!
YEAH. I COULDN'T PAY MY LAST BILL.... SO I HAVEN'T BEEN ABLE TO USE IT FOR OVER A MONTH, NOW.

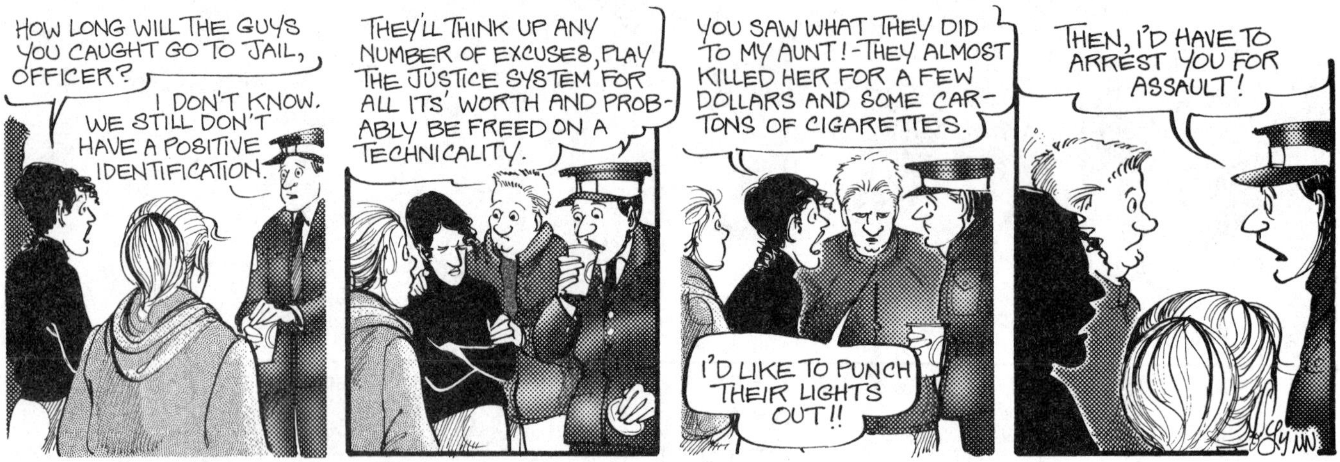
HOW LONG WILL THE GUYS YOU CAUGHT GO TO JAIL, OFFICER?
I DON'T KNOW. WE STILL DON'T HAVE A POSITIVE IDENTIFICATION.
THEY'LL THINK UP ANY NUMBER OF EXCUSES, PLAY THE JUSTICE SYSTEM FOR ALL ITS' WORTH AND PROB-ABLY BE FREED ON A TECHNICALITY.
YOU SAW WHAT THEY DID TO MY AUNT! -THEY ALMOST KILLED HER FOR A FEW DOLLARS AND SOME CAR-TONS OF CIGARETTES.
I'D LIKE TO PUNCH THEIR LIGHTS OUT!!
THEN, I'D HAVE TO ARREST YOU FOR ASSAULT!

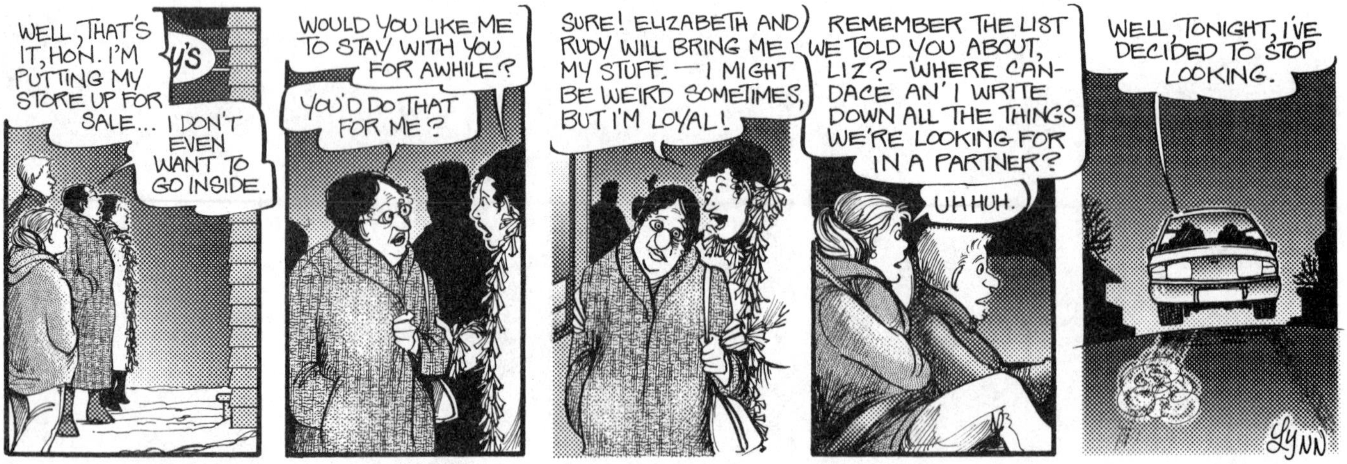
WELL, THAT'S IT, HON. I'M PUTTING MY STORE UP FOR SALE...
I DON'T EVEN WANT TO GO INSIDE.
WOULD YOU LIKE ME TO STAY WITH YOU FOR AWHILE?
YOU'D DO THAT FOR ME?
SURE! ELIZABETH AND RUDY WILL BRING ME MY STUFF. — I MIGHT BE WEIRD SOMETIMES, BUT I'M LOYAL!
REMEMBER THE LIST WE TOLD YOU ABOUT, LIZ? -WHERE CAN-DACE AN' I WRITE DOWN ALL THE THINGS WE'RE LOOKING FOR IN A PARTNER?
UH HUH.
WELL, TONIGHT, I'VE DECIDED TO STOP LOOKING.

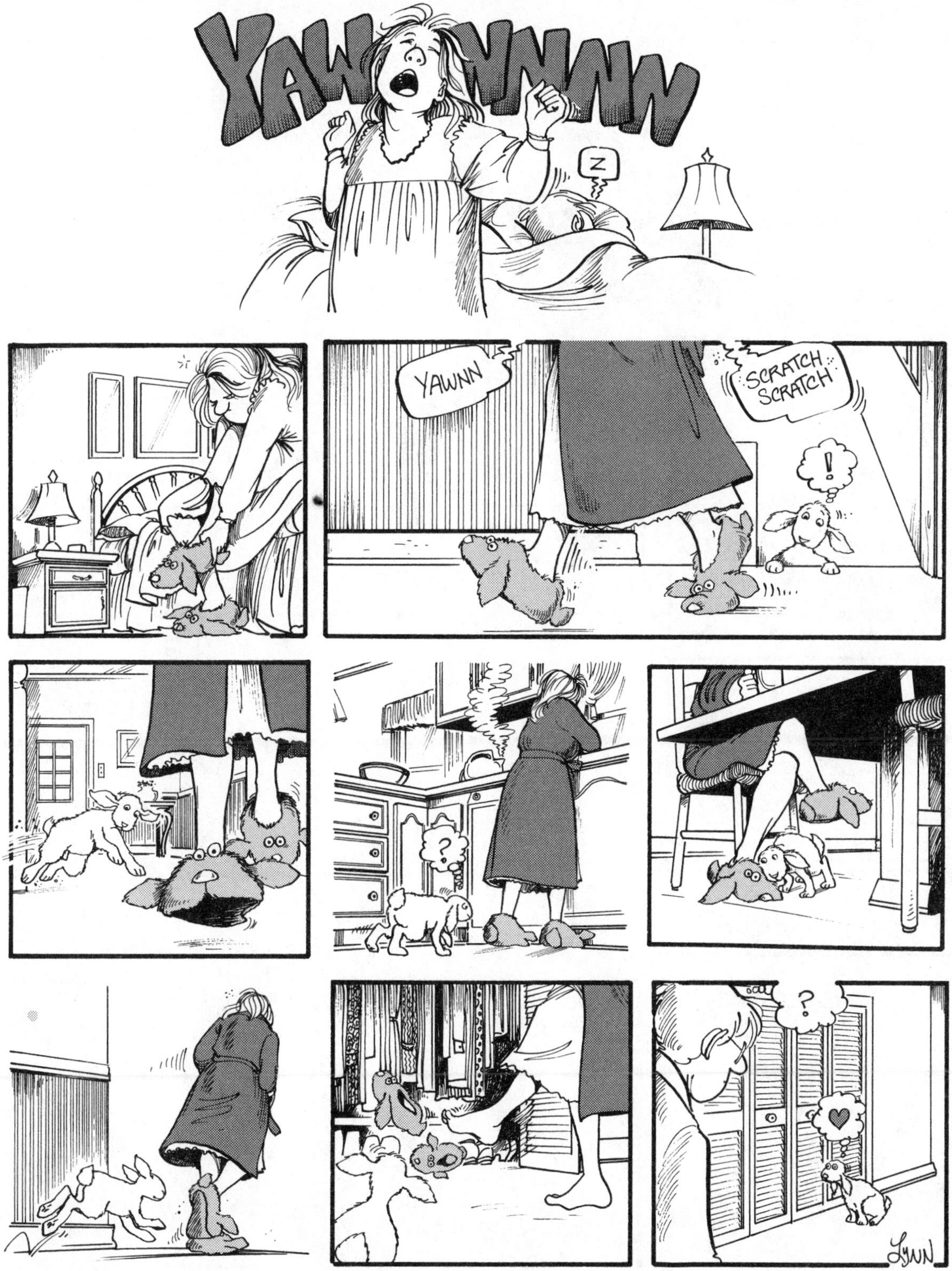
YAWNNNNN
Z
YAWNN
SCRATCH SCRATCH
!
?
?
LYNN

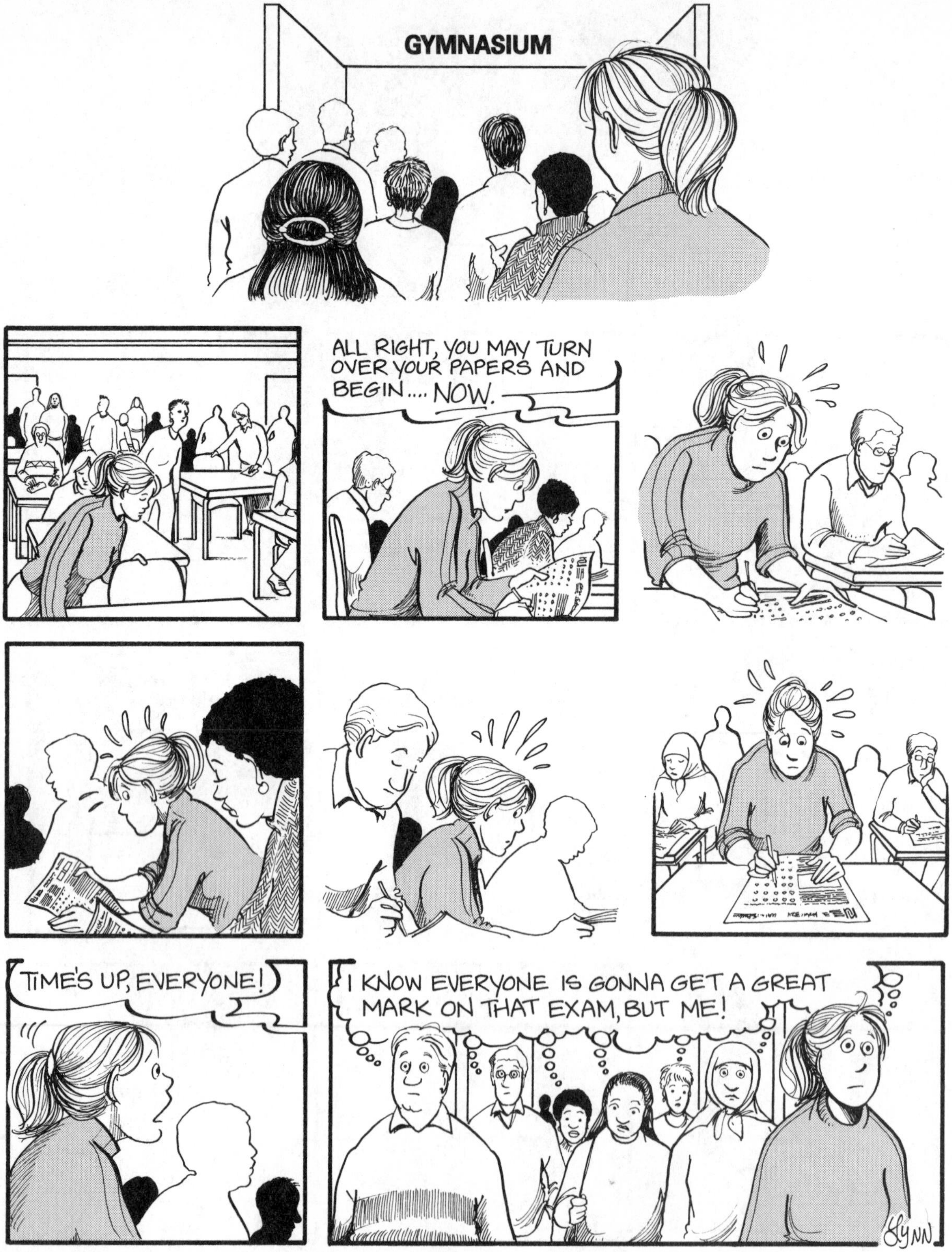
GYMNASIUM
ALL RIGHT, YOU MAY TURN OVER YOUR PAPERS AND BEGIN.... NOW.
TIME'S UP, EVERYONE!
I KNOW EVERYONE IS GONNA GET A GREAT MARK ON THAT EXAM, BUT ME!
LYNN

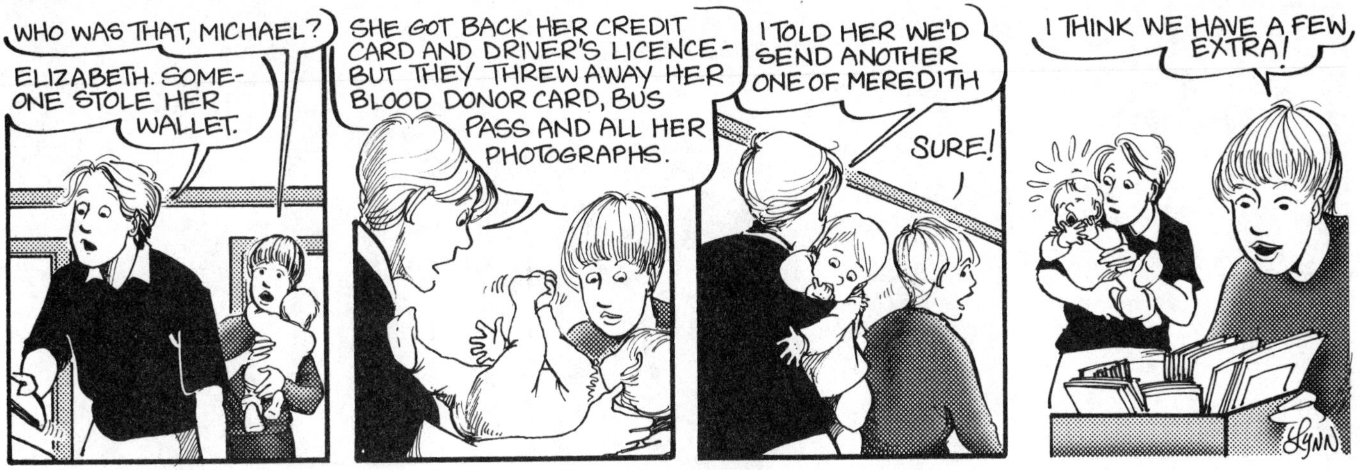
WHO WAS THAT, MICHAEL?
ELIZABETH. SOMEONE STOLE HER WALLET.
SHE GOT BACK HER CREDIT CARD AND DRIVER'S LICENCE- BUT THEY THREW AWAY HER BLOOD DONOR CARD, BUS PASS AND ALL HER PHOTOGRAPHS.
I TOLD HER WE'D SEND ANOTHER ONE OF MEREDITH
SURE!
I THINK WE HAVE A FEW EXTRA!
LYNN

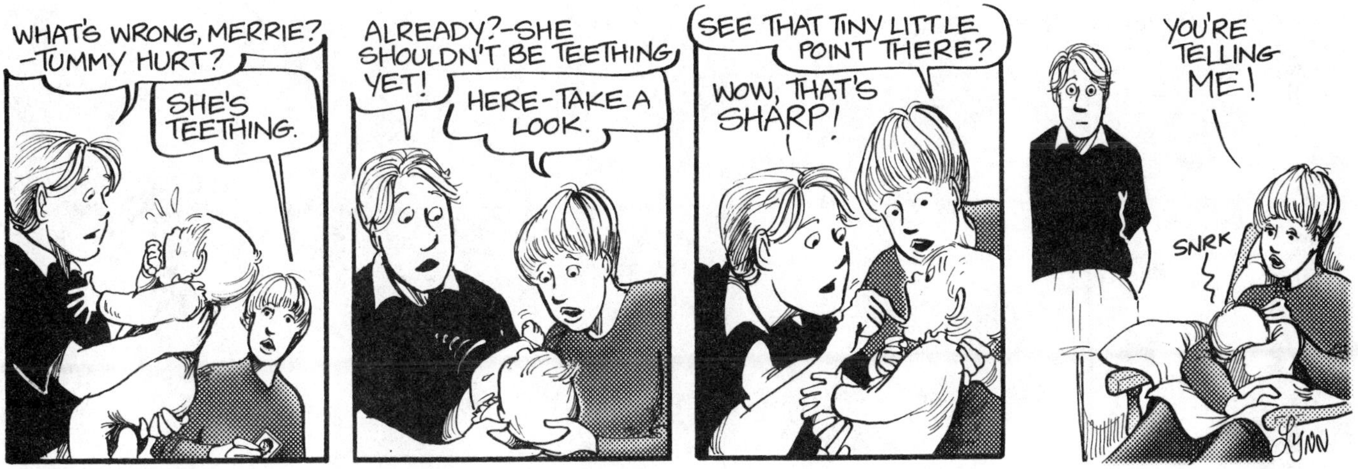
WHAT'S WRONG, MERRIE? -TUMMY HURT?
SHE'S TEETHING.
ALREADY?-SHE SHOULDN'T BE TEETHING YET!
HERE-TAKE A LOOK.
SEE THAT TINY LITTLE POINT THERE?
WOW, THAT'S SHARP!
YOU'RE TELLING ME!
SNRK
LYNN

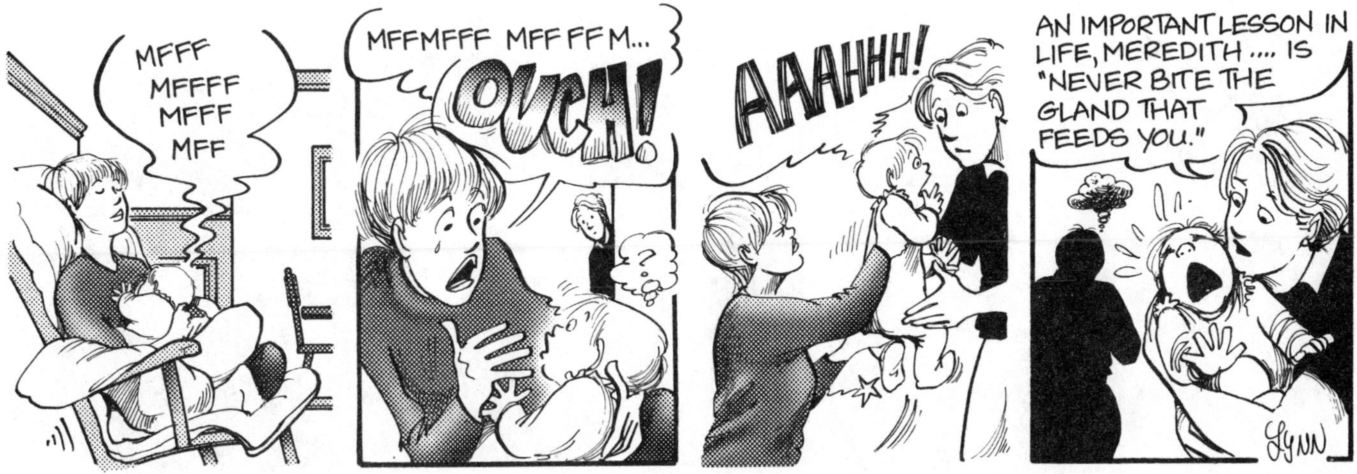
MFFF MFFFF MFFF MFF
MFFMFFF MFF FFM...
OUCH!
AAAHHH!
AN IMPORTANT LESSON IN LIFE, MEREDITH .... IS "NEVER BITE THE GLAND THAT FEEDS YOU."
LYNN

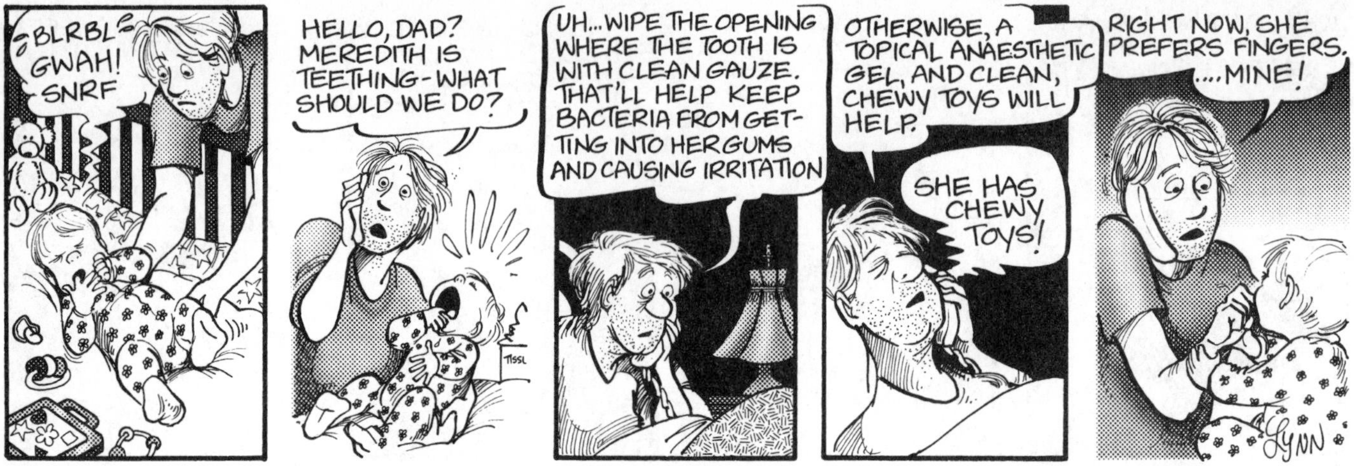
BLRBL GWAH! SNRF
HELLO, DAD? MEREDITH IS TEETHING - WHAT SHOULD WE DO?
UH... WIPE THE OPENING WHERE THE TOOTH IS WITH CLEAN GAUZE. THAT'LL HELP KEEP BACTERIA FROM GETTING INTO HER GUMS AND CAUSING IRRITATION
OTHERWISE, A TOPICAL ANAESTHETIC GEL, AND CLEAN, CHEWY TOYS WILL HELP.
SHE HAS CHEWY TOYS!
RIGHT NOW, SHE PREFERS FINGERS. ....MINE!
LYNN

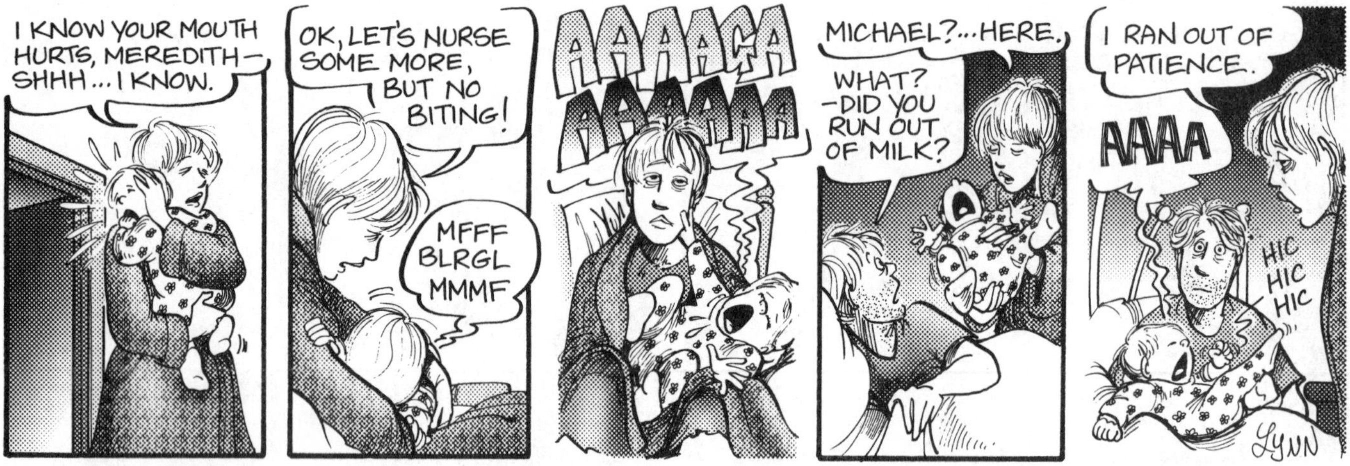
I KNOW YOUR MOUTH HURTS, MEREDITH — SHHH... I KNOW.
OK, LET'S NURSE SOME MORE, BUT NO BITING!
MFFF BLRGL MMMF
AAAAGA AAAAAA
MICHAEL?... HERE.
WHAT? -DID YOU RUN OUT OF MILK?
I RAN OUT OF PATIENCE.
AAAA
HIC HIC HIC
LYNN

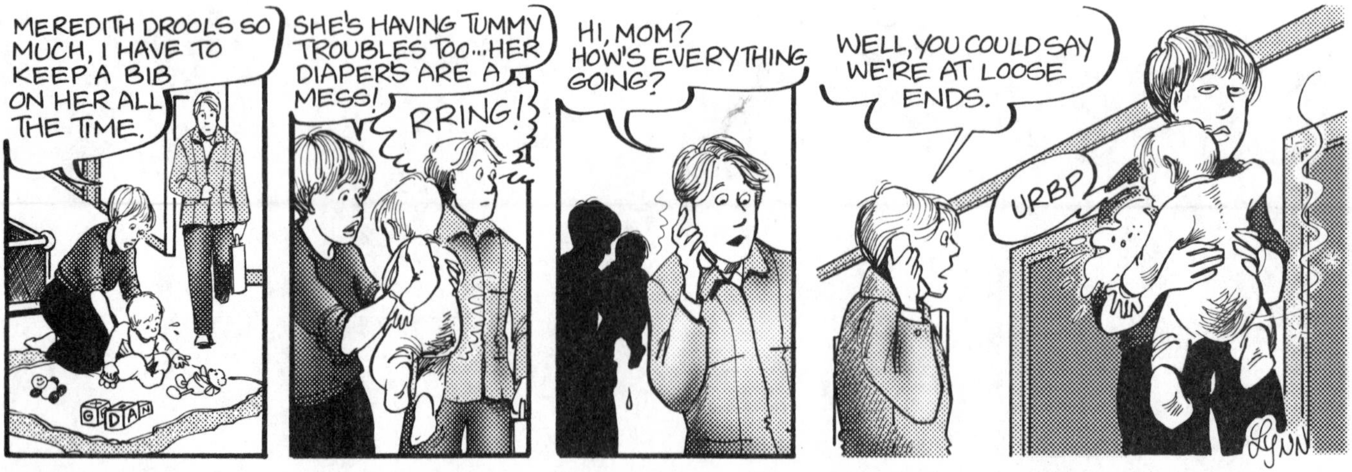
MEREDITH DROOLS SO MUCH, I HAVE TO KEEP A BIB ON HER ALL THE TIME.
SHE'S HAVING TUMMY TROUBLES TOO... HER DIAPERS ARE A MESS!
RRING!
HI, MOM? HOW'S EVERYTHING GOING?
WELL, YOU COULD SAY WE'RE AT LOOSE ENDS.
URBP
LYNN

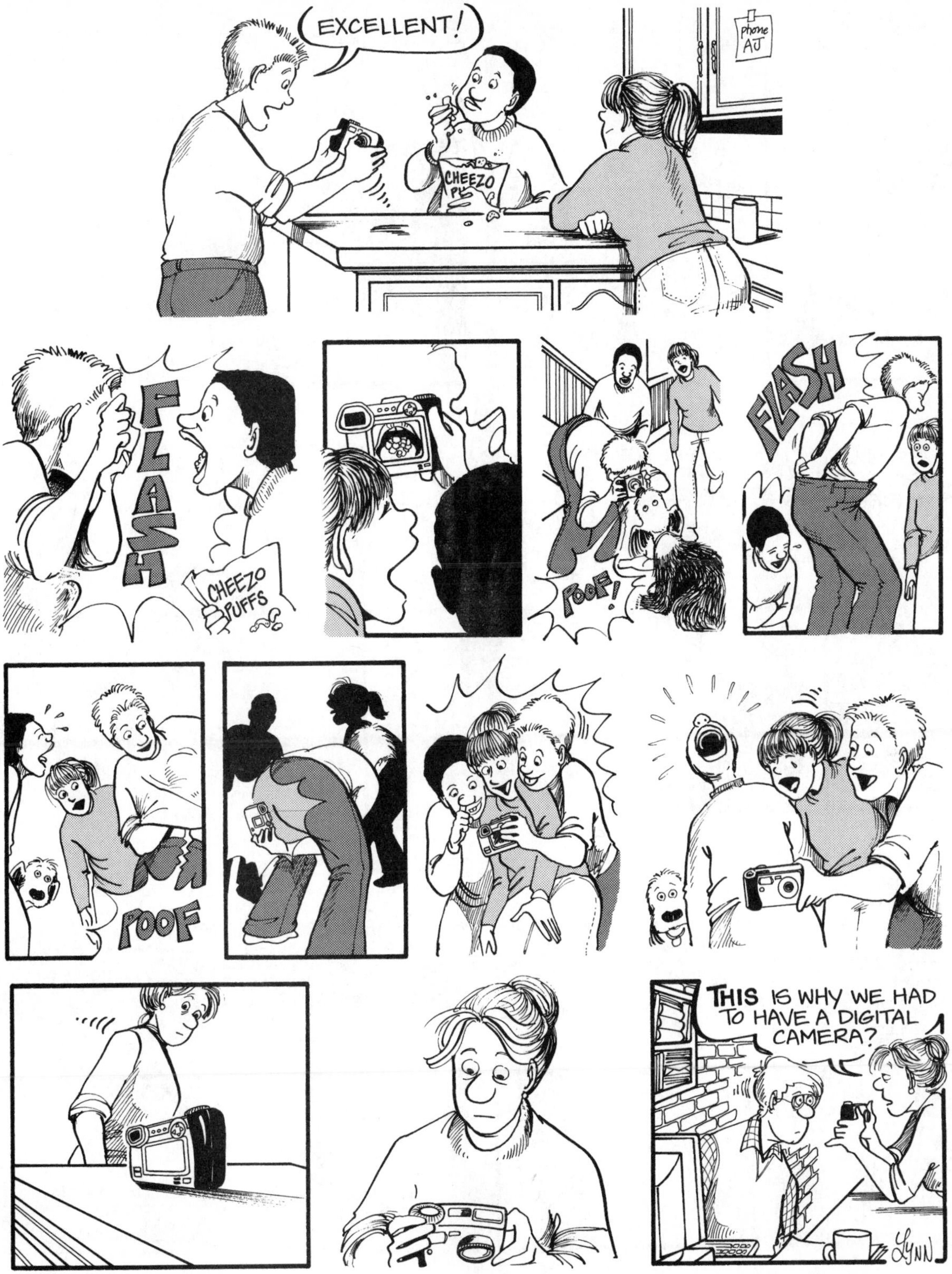
EXCELLENT!
phone AJ
CHEEZO PUFFS
FLASH
CHEEZO PUFFS
POOF!
FLASH
POOF
THIS IS WHY WE HAD TO HAVE A DIGITAL CAMERA?
LYNN

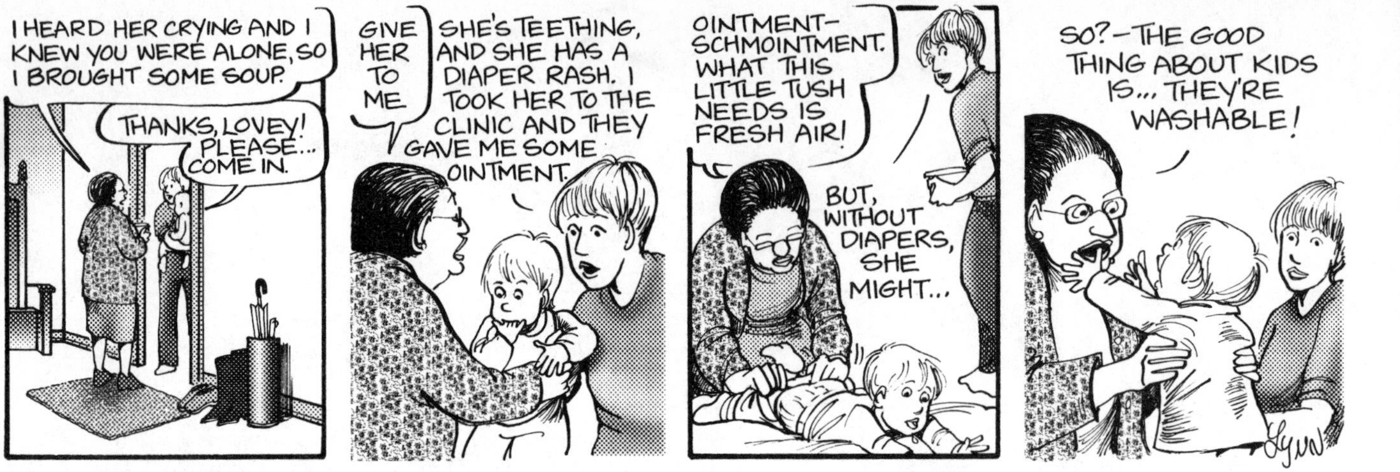
I HEARD HER CRYING AND I KNEW YOU WERE ALONE, SO I BROUGHT SOME SOUP.
THANKS, LOVEY! PLEASE... COME IN.
GIVE HER TO ME
SHE'S TEETHING, AND SHE HAS A DIAPER RASH. I TOOK HER TO THE CLINIC AND THEY GAVE ME SOME OINTMENT.
OINTMENT-SCHMOINTMENT. WHAT THIS LITTLE TUSH NEEDS IS FRESH AIR!
BUT, WITHOUT DIAPERS, SHE MIGHT...
SO?–THE GOOD THING ABOUT KIDS IS..., THEY'RE WASHABLE!
LYNN

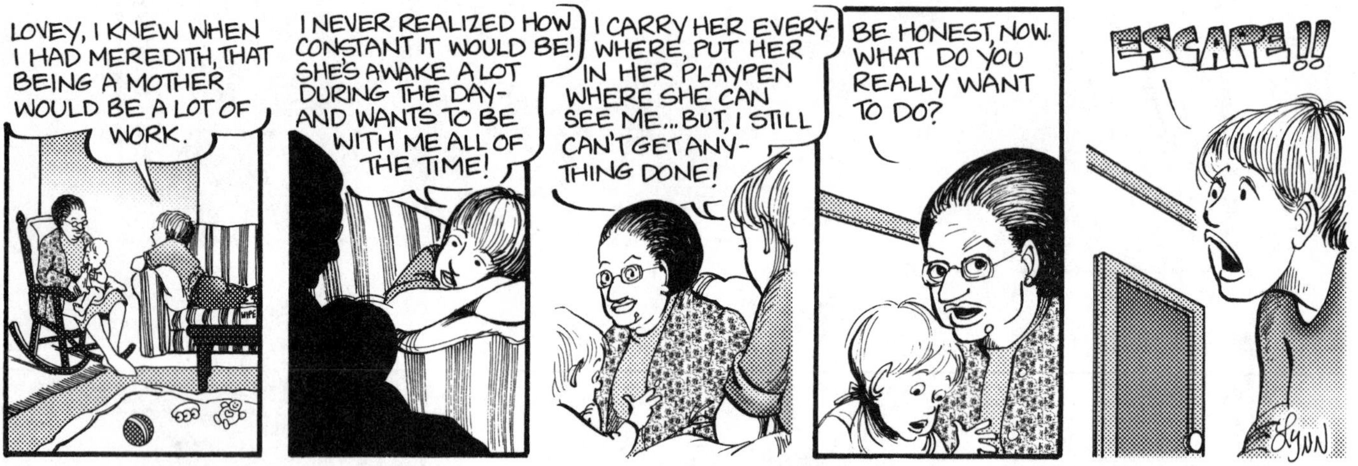
LOVEY, I KNEW WHEN I HAD MEREDITH, THAT BEING A MOTHER WOULD BE A LOT OF WORK.
I NEVER REALIZED HOW CONSTANT IT WOULD BE! SHE'S AWAKE A LOT DURING THE DAY- AND WANTS TO BE WITH ME ALL OF THE TIME!
I CARRY HER EVERY-WHERE, PUT HER IN HER PLAYPEN WHERE SHE CAN SEE ME... BUT, I STILL CAN'T GET ANY-THING DONE!
BE HONEST, NOW. WHAT DO YOU REALLY WANT TO DO?
ESCAPE!!
LYNN

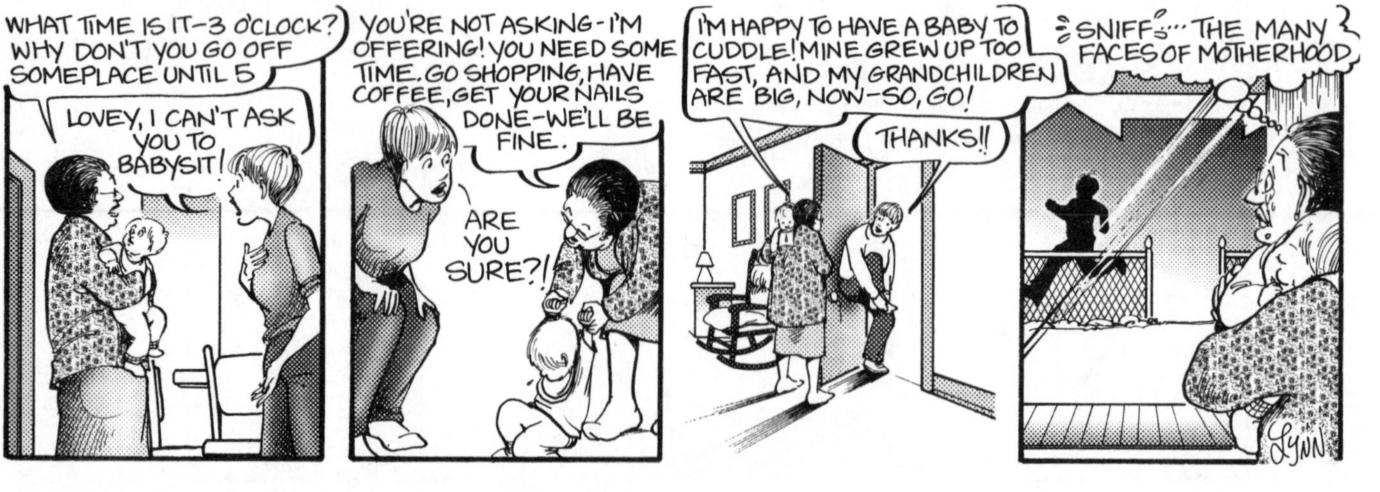
WHAT TIME IS IT–3 O'CLOCK? WHY DON'T YOU GO OFF SOMEPLACE UNTIL 5
LOVEY, I CAN'T ASK YOU TO BABYSIT!
YOU'RE NOT ASKING-I'M OFFERING! YOU NEED SOME TIME. GO SHOPPING, HAVE COFFEE, GET YOUR NAILS DONE–WE'LL BE FINE.
ARE YOU SURE?!
I'M HAPPY TO HAVE A BABY TO CUDDLE! MINE GREW UP TOO FAST, AND MY GRANDCHILDREN ARE BIG, NOW–SO, GO!
THANKS!!
SNIFF... THE MANY FACES OF MOTHERHOOD
LYNN

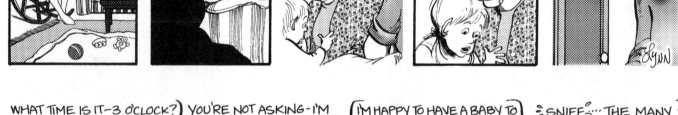

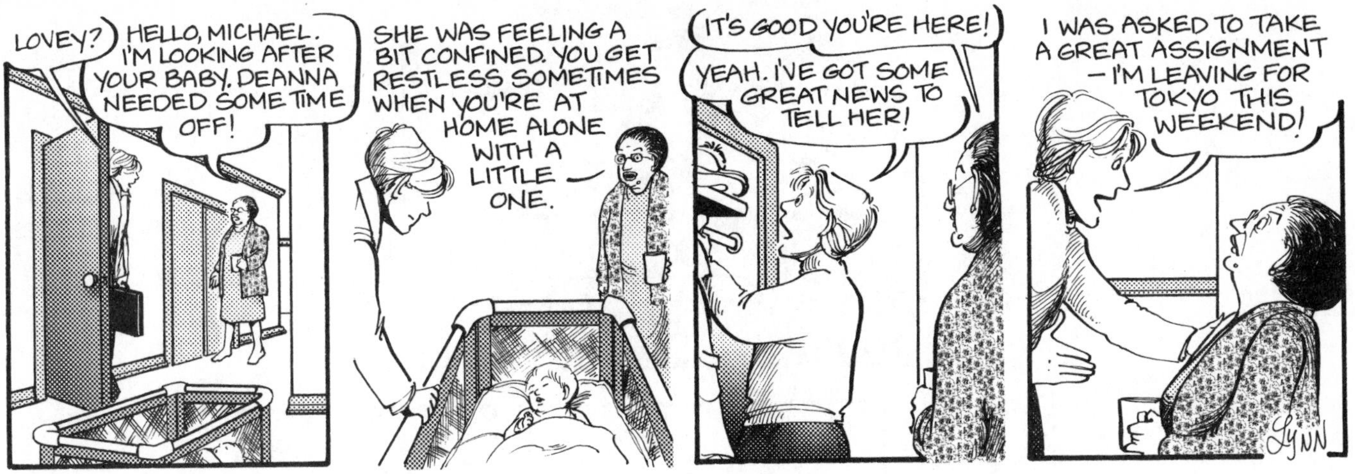
LOVEY?
HELLO, MICHAEL. I'M LOOKING AFTER YOUR BABY. DEANNA NEEDED SOME TIME OFF!
SHE WAS FEELING A BIT CONFINED. YOU GET RESTLESS SOMETIMES WHEN YOU'RE AT HOME ALONE WITH A LITTLE ONE.
IT'S GOOD YOU'RE HERE!
YEAH. I'VE GOT SOME GREAT NEWS TO TELL HER!
I WAS ASKED TO TAKE A GREAT ASSIGNMENT – I'M LEAVING FOR TOKYO THIS WEEKEND!
LYNN

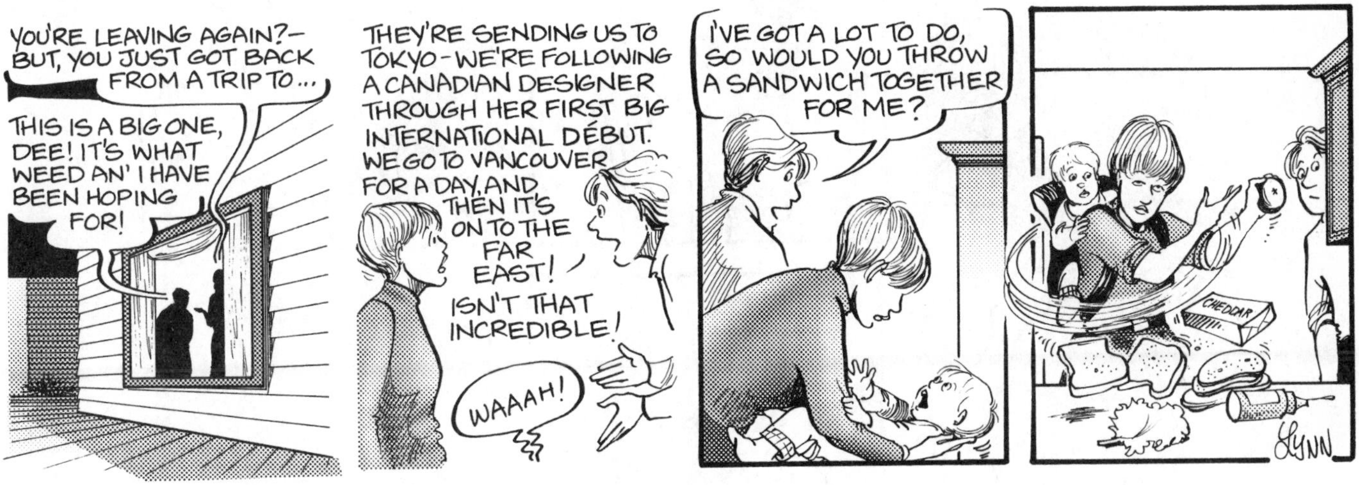
YOU'RE LEAVING AGAIN?– BUT, YOU JUST GOT BACK FROM A TRIP TO...
THIS IS A BIG ONE, DEE! IT'S WHAT WEED AN' I HAVE BEEN HOPING FOR!
THEY'RE SENDING US TO TOKYO - WE'RE FOLLOWING A CANADIAN DESIGNER THROUGH HER FIRST BIG INTERNATIONAL DÉBUT. WE GO TO VANCOUVER FOR A DAY, AND THEN IT'S ON TO THE FAR EAST!
ISN'T THAT INCREDIBLE!
WAAAH!
I'VE GOT A LOT TO DO, SO WOULD YOU THROW A SANDWICH TOGETHER FOR ME?
CHEDDAR
LYNN

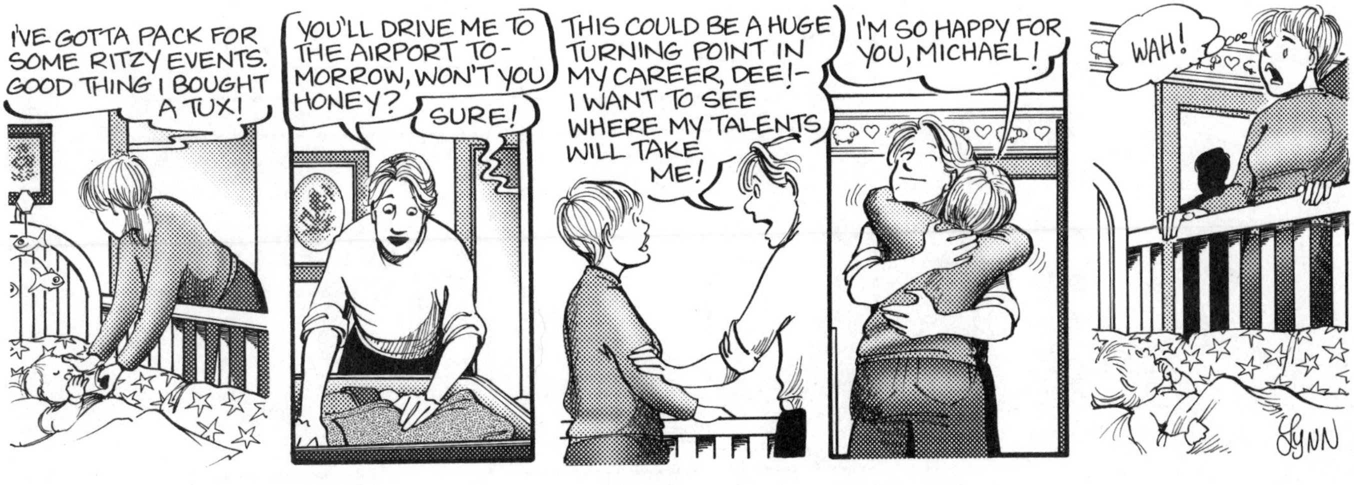
I'VE GOTTA PACK FOR SOME RITZY EVENTS. GOOD THING I BOUGHT A TUX!
YOU'LL DRIVE ME TO THE AIRPORT TO-MORROW, WON'T YOU HONEY?
SURE!
THIS COULD BE A HUGE TURNING POINT IN MY CAREER, DEE!– I WANT TO SEE WHERE MY TALENTS WILL TAKE ME!
I'M SO HAPPY FOR YOU, MICHAEL!
WAH!
LYNN

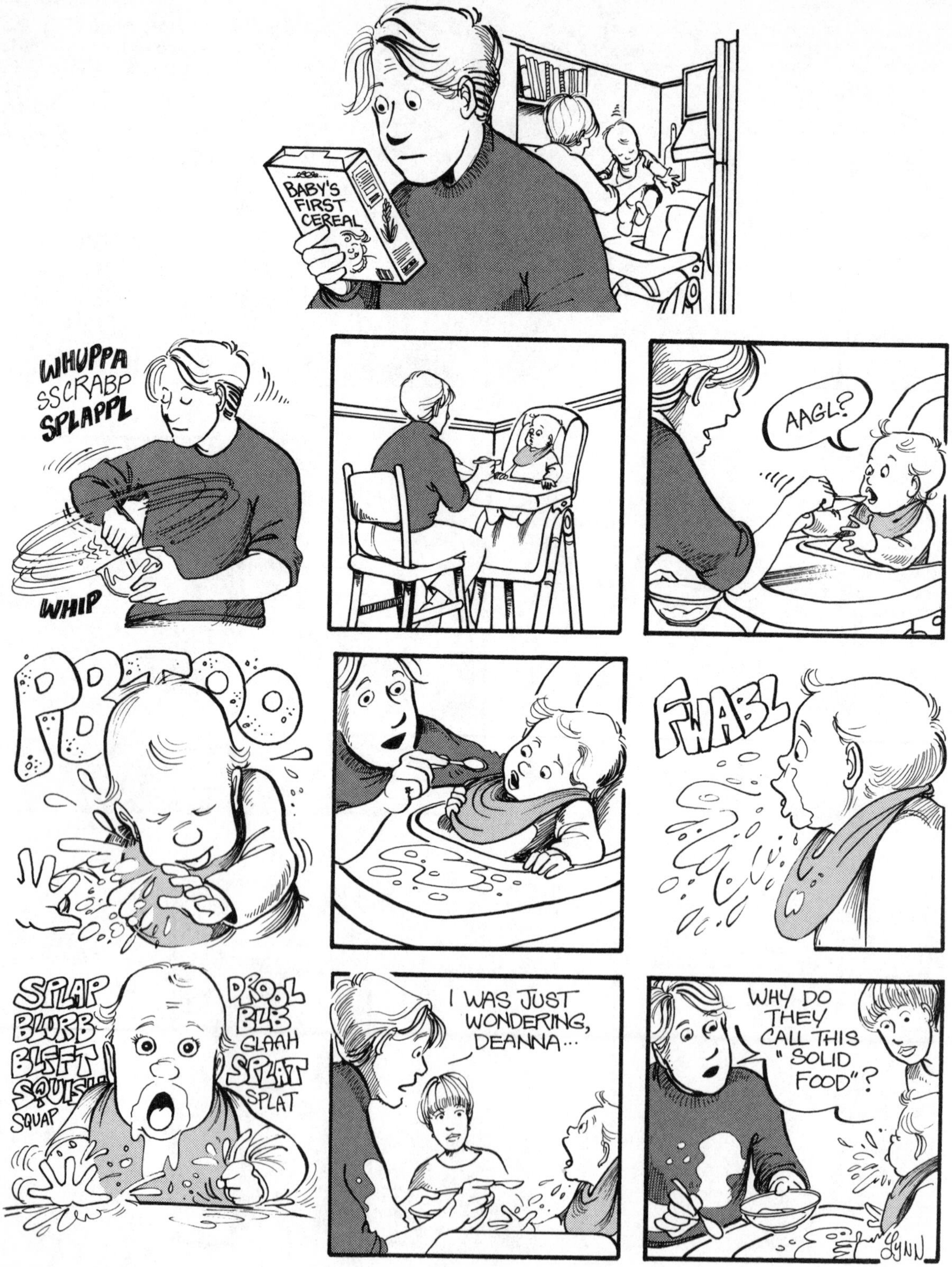
BABY'S FIRST CEREAL
WHUPPA
SSCRABP
SPLAPPL
WHIP
AAGL?
FWABL
SPLAP
BLURB
BLFFT
SQUAP
DROOL
BLB
GLAAH
SPLAT
SPLAT
I WAS JUST WONDERING, DEANNA...
WHY DO THEY CALL THIS "SOLID FOOD"?
LYNN

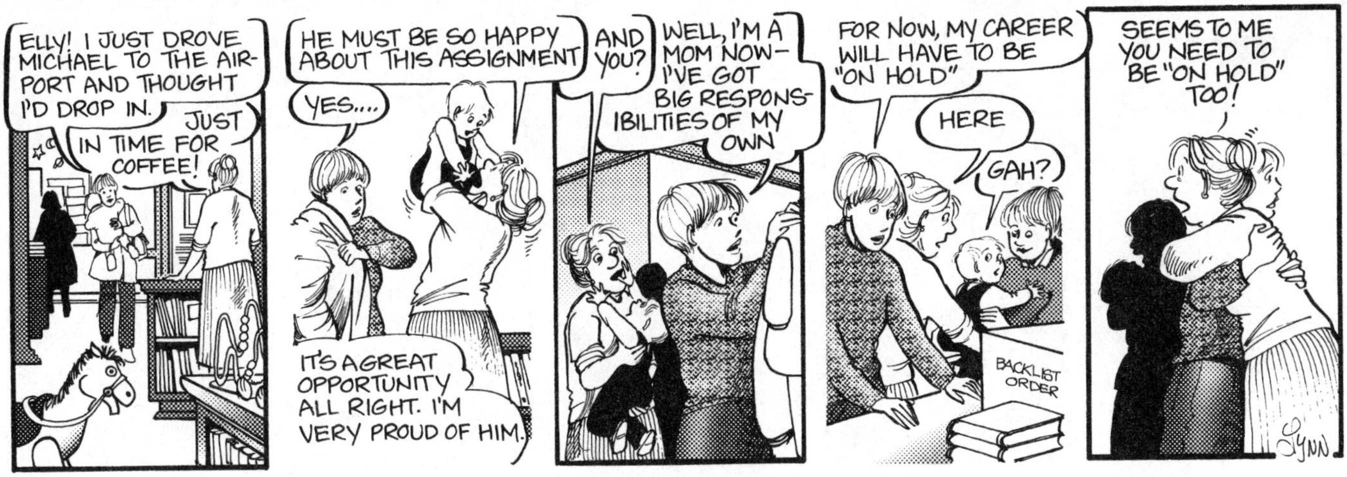
ELLY! I JUST DROVE MICHAEL TO THE AIR-PORT AND THOUGHT I'D DROP IN.
JUST IN TIME FOR COFFEE!
HE MUST BE SO HAPPY ABOUT THIS ASSIGNMENT
YES....
IT'S A GREAT OPPORTUNITY ALL RIGHT. I'M VERY PROUD OF HIM.
AND YOU?
WELL, I'M A MOM NOW– I'VE GOT BIG RESPONS-IBILITIES OF MY OWN
FOR NOW, MY CAREER WILL HAVE TO BE "ON HOLD"
HERE
GAH?
BACKLIST ORDER
SEEMS TO ME YOU NEED TO BE "ON HOLD" TOO!
LYNN

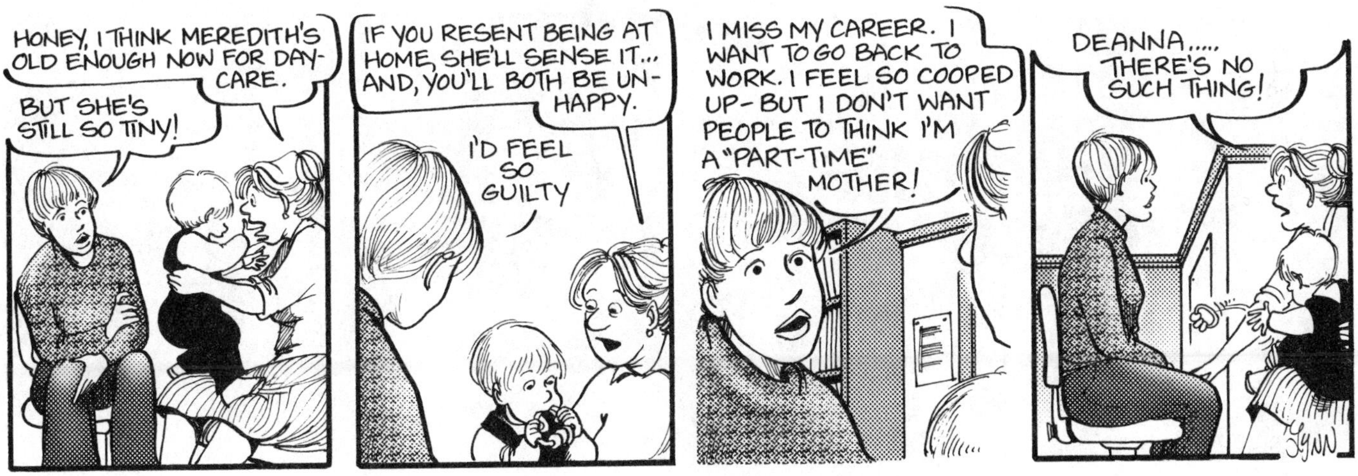
HONEY, I THINK MEREDITH'S OLD ENOUGH NOW FOR DAY-CARE.
BUT SHE'S STILL SO TINY!
IF YOU RESENT BEING AT HOME, SHE'LL SENSE IT... AND, YOU'LL BOTH BE UN-HAPPY.
I'D FEEL SO GUILTY
I MISS MY CAREER. I WANT TO GO BACK TO WORK. I FEEL SO COOPED UP– BUT I DON'T WANT PEOPLE TO THINK I'M A "PART-TIME" MOTHER!
DEANNA..... THERE'S NO SUCH THING!
LYNN

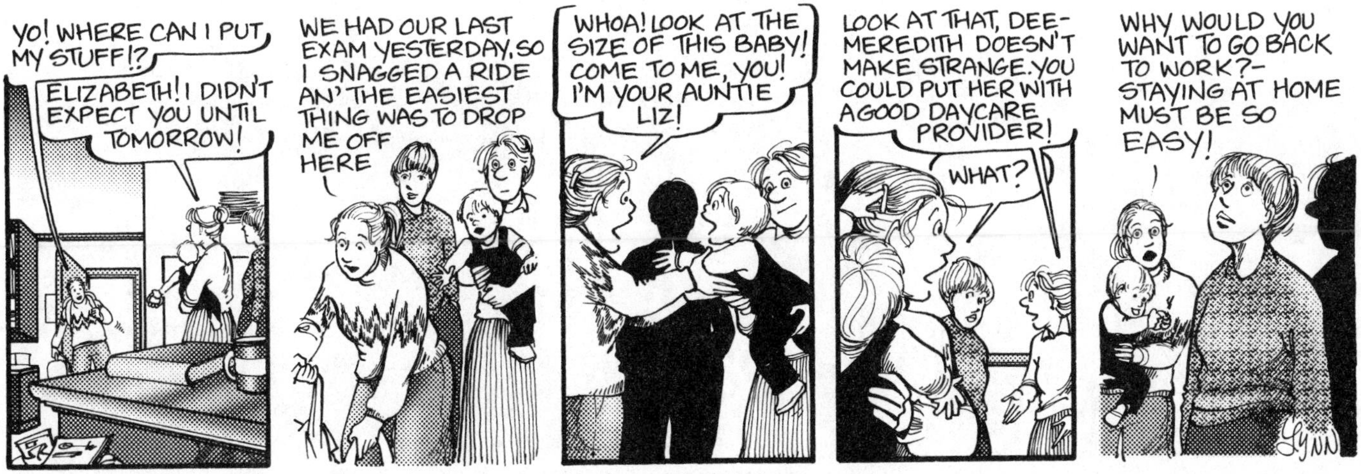
YO! WHERE CAN I PUT MY STUFF!?
ELIZABETH! I DIDN'T EXPECT YOU UNTIL TOMORROW!
WE HAD OUR LAST EXAM YESTERDAY, SO I SNAGGED A RIDE AN' THE EASIEST THING WAS TO DROP ME OFF HERE
WHOA! LOOK AT THE SIZE OF THIS BABY! COME TO ME, YOU! I'M YOUR AUNTIE LIZ!
LOOK AT THAT, DEE– MEREDITH DOESN'T MAKE STRANGE. YOU COULD PUT HER WITH A GOOD DAYCARE PROVIDER!
WHAT?
WHY WOULD YOU WANT TO GO BACK TO WORK?– STAYING AT HOME MUST BE SO EASY!
LYNN

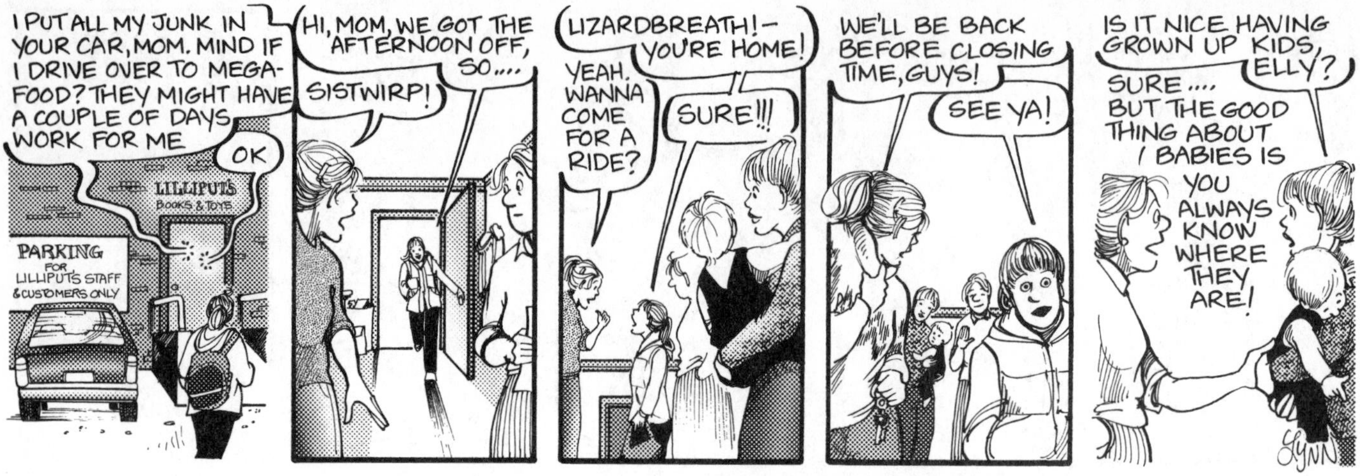
I PUT ALL MY JUNK IN YOUR CAR, MOM. MIND IF I DRIVE OVER TO MEGA-FOOD? THEY MIGHT HAVE A COUPLE OF DAYS WORK FOR ME
OK
LILLIPUTS BOOKS & TOYS
PARKING FOR LILLIPUTS STAFF & CUSTOMERS ONLY
HI, MOM, WE GOT THE AFTERNOON OFF, SO....
SISTWIRP!
LIZARDBREATH! — YOU'RE HOME!
YEAH. WANNA COME FOR A RIDE?
SURE!!!
WE'LL BE BACK BEFORE CLOSING TIME, GUYS!
SEE YA!
IS IT NICE HAVING GROWN UP KIDS, ELLY?
SURE.... BUT THE GOOD THING ABOUT BABIES IS YOU ALWAYS KNOW WHERE THEY ARE!
LYNN

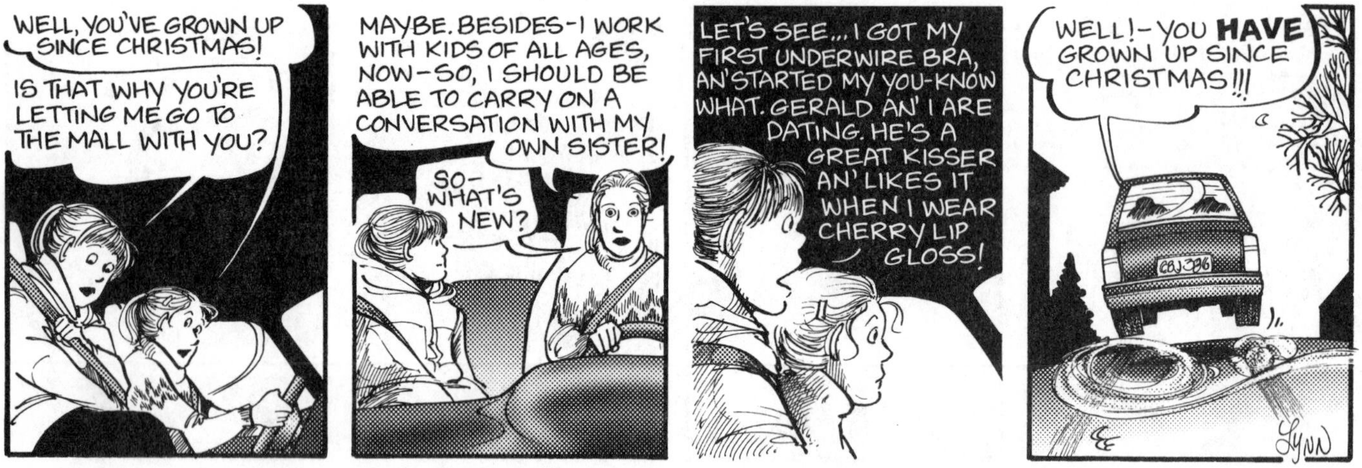
WELL, YOU'VE GROWN UP SINCE CHRISTMAS!
IS THAT WHY YOU'RE LETTING ME GO TO THE MALL WITH YOU?
MAYBE. BESIDES — I WORK WITH KIDS OF ALL AGES, NOW — SO, I SHOULD BE ABLE TO CARRY ON A CONVERSATION WITH MY OWN SISTER!
SO— WHAT'S NEW?
LET'S SEE... I GOT MY FIRST UNDERWIRE BRA, AN' STARTED MY YOU-KNOW WHAT. GERALD AN' I ARE DATING. HE'S A GREAT KISSER AN' LIKES IT WHEN I WEAR CHERRY LIP GLOSS!
WELL! — YOU HAVE GROWN UP SINCE CHRISTMAS!!!
LYNN

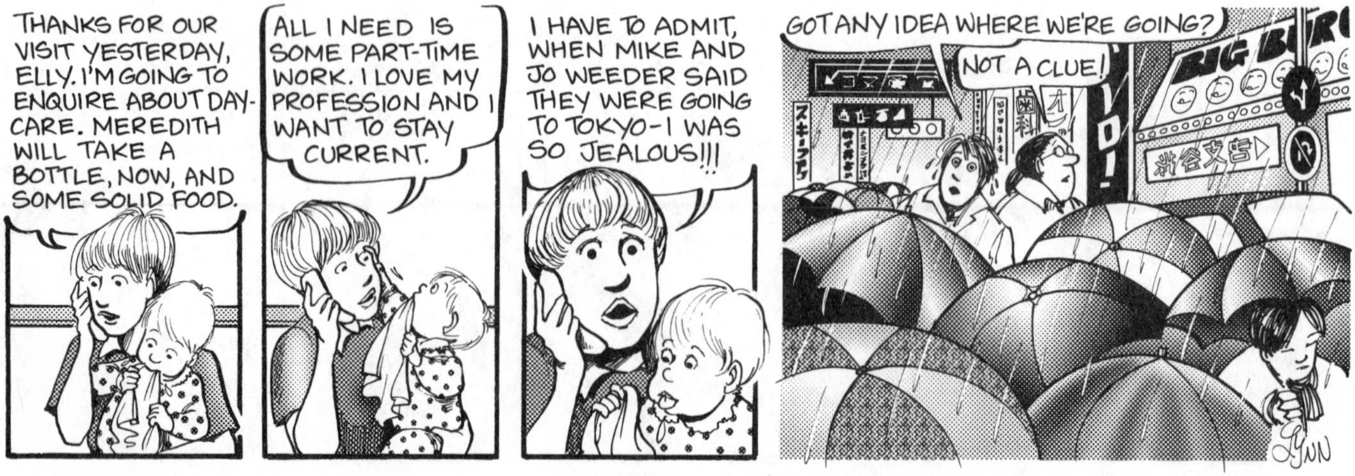
THANKS FOR OUR VISIT YESTERDAY, ELLY. I'M GOING TO ENQUIRE ABOUT DAY-CARE. MEREDITH WILL TAKE A BOTTLE, NOW, AND SOME SOLID FOOD.
ALL I NEED IS SOME PART-TIME WORK. I LOVE MY PROFESSION AND I WANT TO STAY CURRENT.
I HAVE TO ADMIT, WHEN MIKE AND JO WEEDER SAID THEY WERE GOING TO TOKYO — I WAS SO JEALOUS!!!
GOT ANY IDEA WHERE WE'RE GOING?
NOT A CLUE!
LYNN

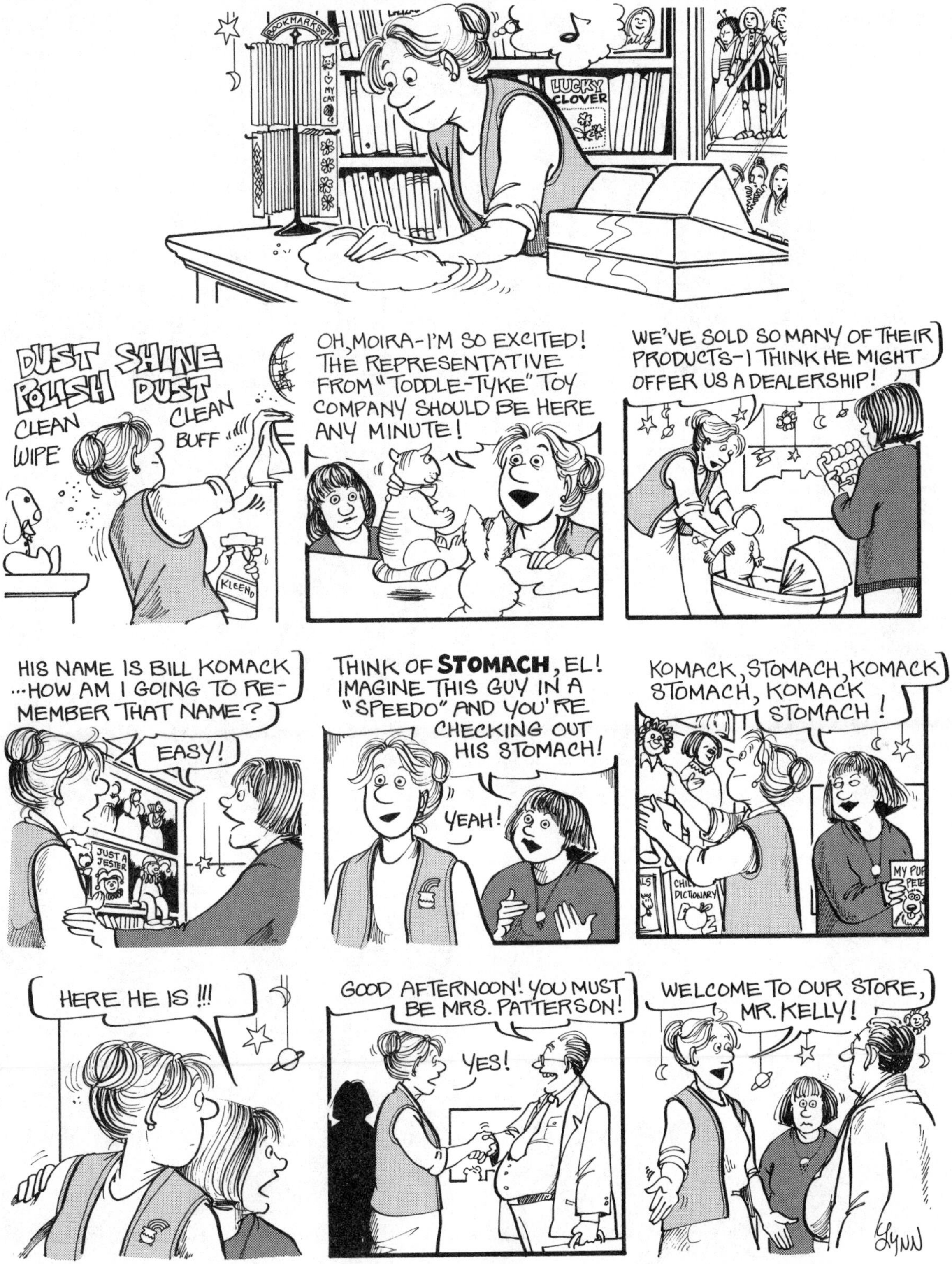
BOOKMARKS
I ♥ MY CAT
LUCKY CLOVER
DUST SHINE POLISH DUST
CLEAN WIPE CLEAN BUFF
KLEENO
OH, MOIRA- I'M SO EXCITED! THE REPRESENTATIVE FROM "TODDLE-TYKE" TOY COMPANY SHOULD BE HERE ANY MINUTE!
WE'VE SOLD SO MANY OF THEIR PRODUCTS- I THINK HE MIGHT OFFER US A DEALERSHIP!
HIS NAME IS BILL KOMACK ...HOW AM I GOING TO RE-MEMBER THAT NAME?
EASY!
JUST A JESTER
THINK OF STOMACH, EL! IMAGINE THIS GUY IN A "SPEEDO" AND YOU'RE CHECKING OUT HIS STOMACH!
YEAH!
KOMACK, STOMACH, KOMACK STOMACH, KOMACK STOMACH!
DICTIONARY
HERE HE IS!!!
GOOD AFTERNOON! YOU MUST BE MRS. PATTERSON!
YES!
WELCOME TO OUR STORE, MR. KELLY!
LYNN

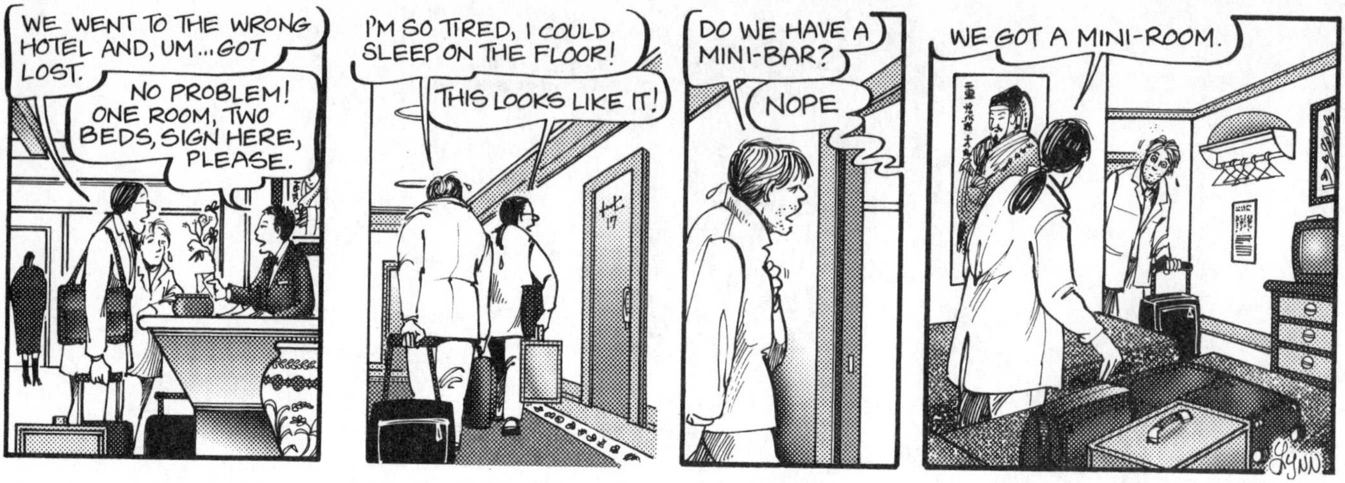
WE WENT TO THE WRONG HOTEL AND, UM...GOT LOST.
NO PROBLEM! ONE ROOM, TWO BEDS, SIGN HERE, PLEASE.
I'M SO TIRED, I COULD SLEEP ON THE FLOOR!
THIS LOOKS LIKE IT!
DO WE HAVE A MINI-BAR?
NOPE
WE GOT A MINI-ROOM.

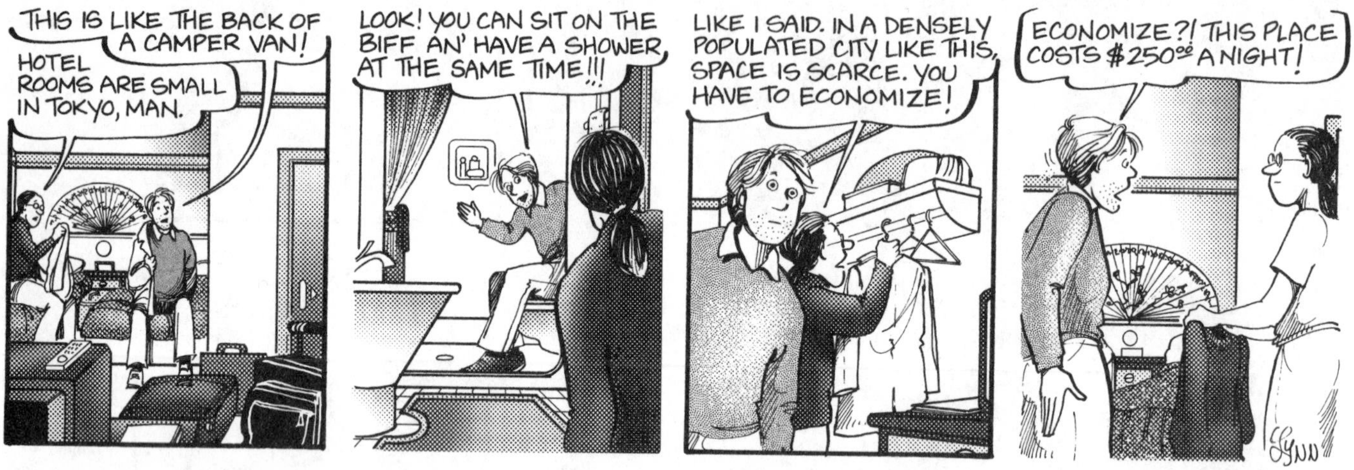
THIS IS LIKE THE BACK OF A CAMPER VAN!
HOTEL ROOMS ARE SMALL IN TOKYO, MAN.
LOOK! YOU CAN SIT ON THE BIFF AN' HAVE A SHOWER AT THE SAME TIME!!!
LIKE I SAID. IN A DENSELY POPULATED CITY LIKE THIS, SPACE IS SCARCE. YOU HAVE TO ECONOMIZE!
ECONOMIZE?! THIS PLACE COSTS $250.00 A NIGHT!

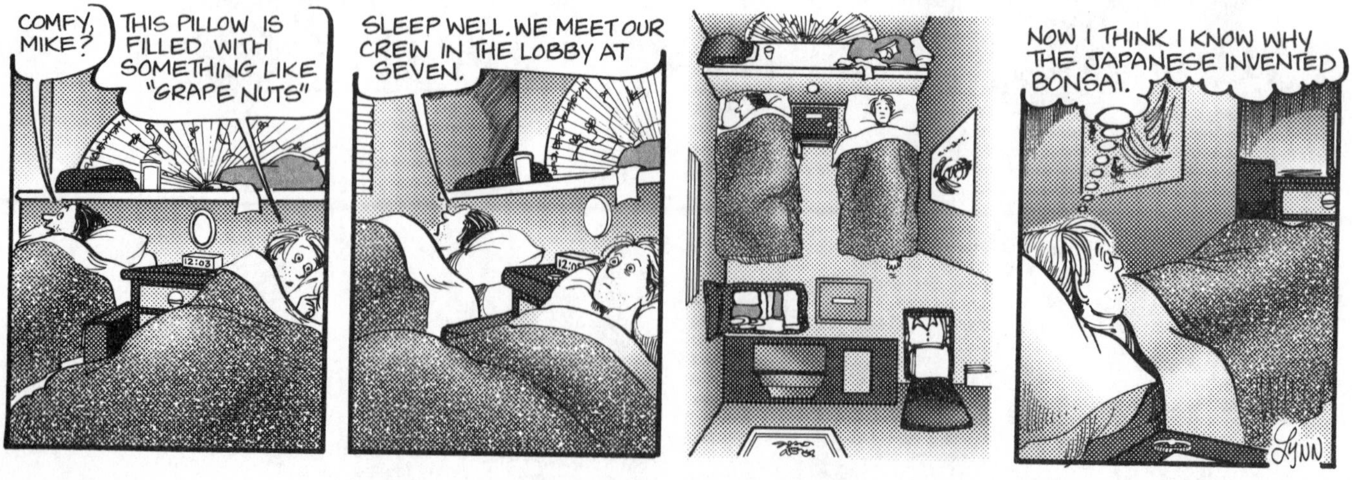
COMFY, MIKE?
THIS PILLOW IS FILLED WITH SOMETHING LIKE "GRAPE NUTS"
SLEEP WELL. WE MEET OUR CREW IN THE LOBBY AT SEVEN.
NOW I THINK I KNOW WHY THE JAPANESE INVENTED BONSAI.

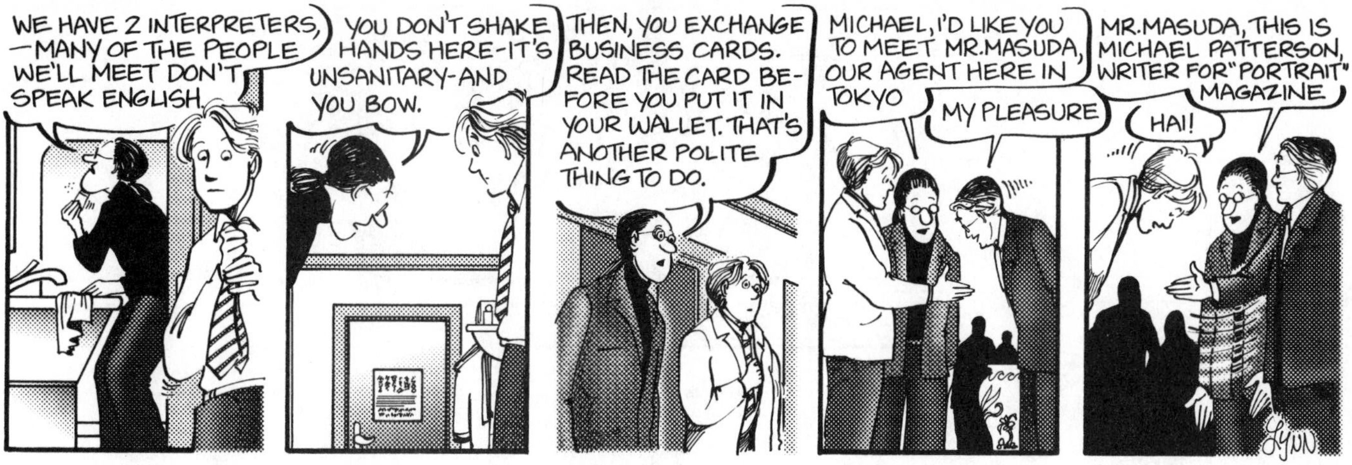
WE HAVE 2 INTERPRETERS, —MANY OF THE PEOPLE WE'LL MEET DON'T SPEAK ENGLISH.
YOU DON'T SHAKE HANDS HERE-IT'S UNSANITARY-AND YOU BOW.
THEN, YOU EXCHANGE BUSINESS CARDS. READ THE CARD BEFORE YOU PUT IT IN YOUR WALLET. THAT'S ANOTHER POLITE THING TO DO.
MICHAEL, I'D LIKE YOU TO MEET MR. MASUDA, OUR AGENT HERE IN TOKYO
MY PLEASURE
MR. MASUDA, THIS IS MICHAEL PATTERSON, WRITER FOR "PORTRAIT" MAGAZINE
HAI!
LYNN

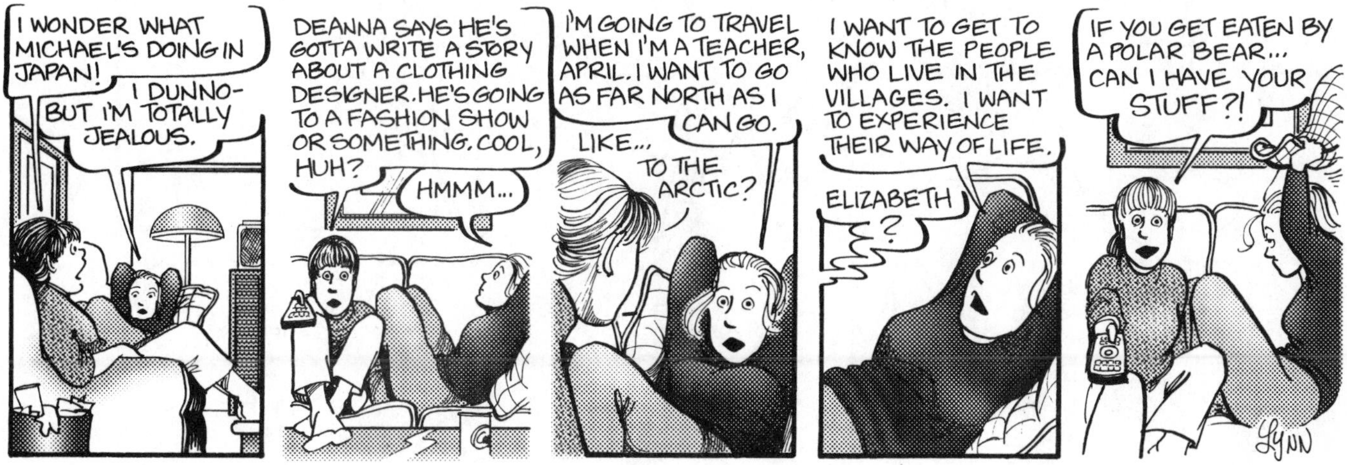
I WONDER WHAT MICHAEL'S DOING IN JAPAN!
I DUNNO-BUT I'M TOTALLY JEALOUS.
DEANNA SAYS HE'S GOTTA WRITE A STORY ABOUT A CLOTHING DESIGNER. HE'S GOING TO A FASHION SHOW OR SOMETHING. COOL, HUH?
HMMM...
I'M GOING TO TRAVEL WHEN I'M A TEACHER, APRIL. I WANT TO GO AS FAR NORTH AS I CAN GO.
LIKE... TO THE ARCTIC?
I WANT TO GET TO KNOW THE PEOPLE WHO LIVE IN THE VILLAGES. I WANT TO EXPERIENCE THEIR WAY OF LIFE.
ELIZABETH?
IF YOU GET EATEN BY A POLAR BEAR... CAN I HAVE YOUR STUFF?!
LYNN

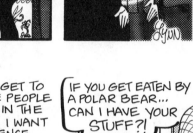

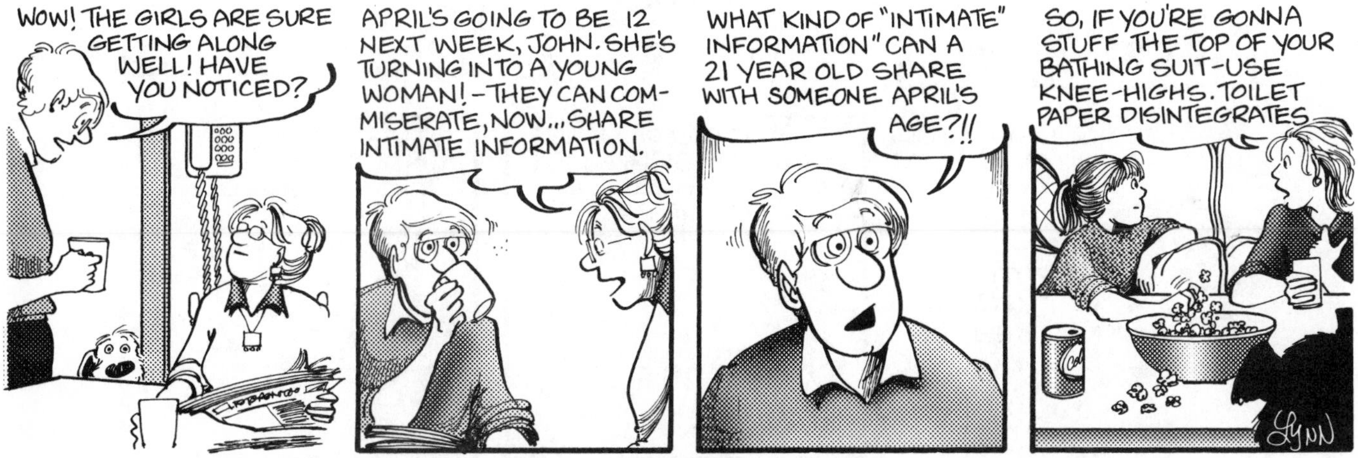
WOW! THE GIRLS ARE SURE GETTING ALONG WELL! HAVE YOU NOTICED?
APRIL'S GOING TO BE 12 NEXT WEEK, JOHN. SHE'S TURNING INTO A YOUNG WOMAN! -THEY CAN COMMISERATE, NOW... SHARE INTIMATE INFORMATION.
WHAT KIND OF "INTIMATE INFORMATION" CAN A 21 YEAR OLD SHARE WITH SOMEONE APRIL'S AGE?!!
SO, IF YOU'RE GONNA STUFF THE TOP OF YOUR BATHING SUIT-USE KNEE-HIGHS. TOILET PAPER DISINTEGRATES.
LYNN

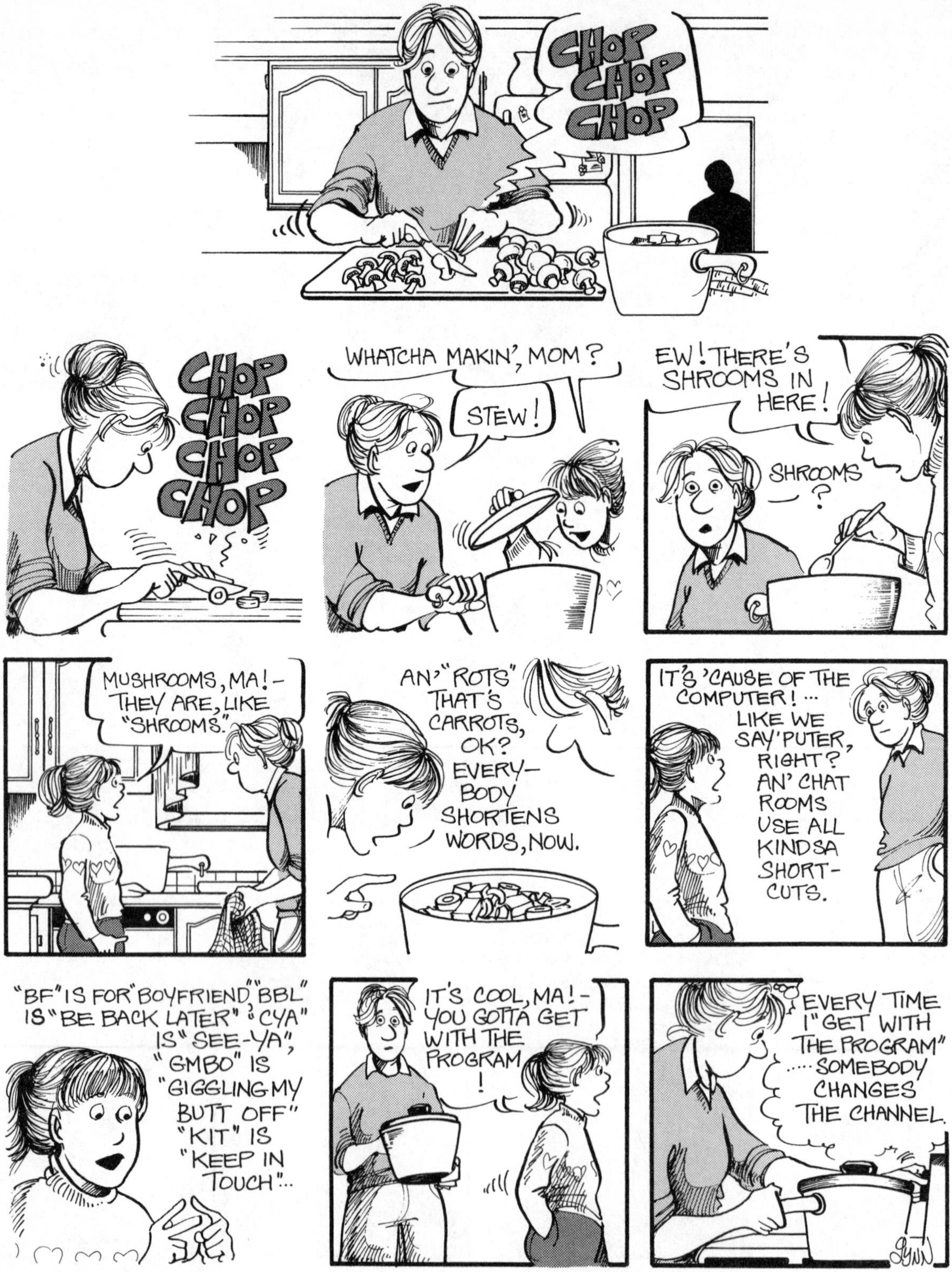
CHOP CHOP CHOP
CHOP CHOP CHOP CHOP
WHATCHA MAKIN', MOM?
STEW!
EW! THERE'S SHROOMS IN HERE!
SHROOMS —?
MUSHROOMS, MA! - THEY ARE, LIKE "SHROOMS."
AN' "ROTS" THAT'S CARROTS, OK? EVERY-BODY SHORTENS WORDS, NOW.
IT'S 'CAUSE OF THE COMPUTER!... LIKE WE SAY 'PUTER, RIGHT? AN' CHAT ROOMS USE ALL KINDSA SHORT-CUTS.
"BF" IS FOR "BOYFRIEND," "BBL" IS "BE BACK LATER" & "CYA" IS "SEE-YA", "GMBO" IS "GIGGLING MY BUTT OFF" "KIT" IS "KEEP IN TOUCH"...
IT'S COOL, MA! - YOU GOTTA GET WITH THE PROGRAM!
EVERY TIME I "GET WITH THE PROGRAM" .... SOMEBODY CHANGES THE CHANNEL.
LYNN

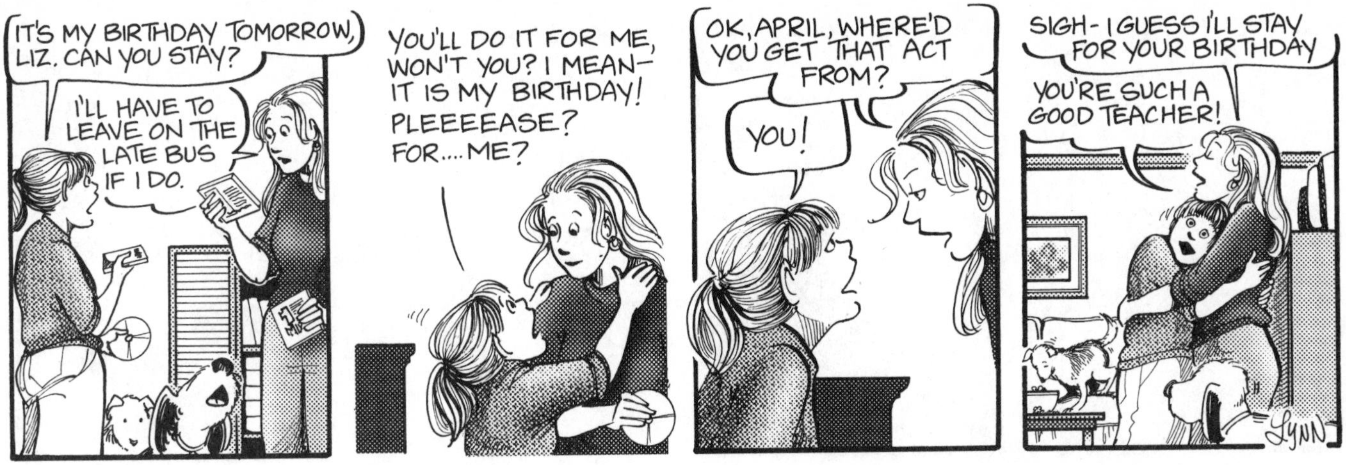
IT'S MY BIRTHDAY TOMORROW, LIZ. CAN YOU STAY?
I'LL HAVE TO LEAVE ON THE LATE BUS IF I DO.
YOU'LL DO IT FOR ME, WON'T YOU? I MEAN– IT IS MY BIRTHDAY! PLEEEEASE? FOR.... ME?
OK, APRIL, WHERE'D YOU GET THAT ACT FROM?
YOU!
SIGH- I GUESS I'LL STAY FOR YOUR BIRTHDAY
YOU'RE SUCH A GOOD TEACHER!
LYNN

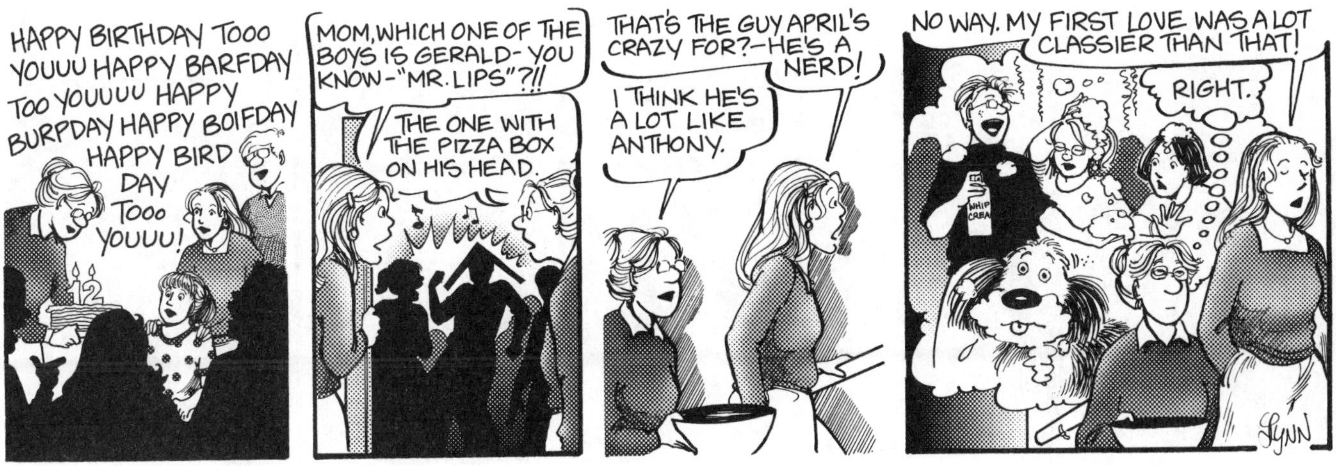
HAPPY BIRTHDAY TOOO YOUUU HAPPY BARFDAY TOO YOUUUU HAPPY BURPDAY HAPPY BOIFDAY HAPPY BIRD DAY TOOO YOUUU!
12
MOM, WHICH ONE OF THE BOYS IS GERALD- YOU KNOW-"MR. LIPS"?!!
THE ONE WITH THE PIZZA BOX ON HIS HEAD.
THAT'S THE GUY APRIL'S CRAZY FOR?–HE'S A NERD!
I THINK HE'S A LOT LIKE ANTHONY.
NO WAY. MY FIRST LOVE WAS A LOT CLASSIER THAN THAT!
RIGHT.
WHIP CREA
LYNN

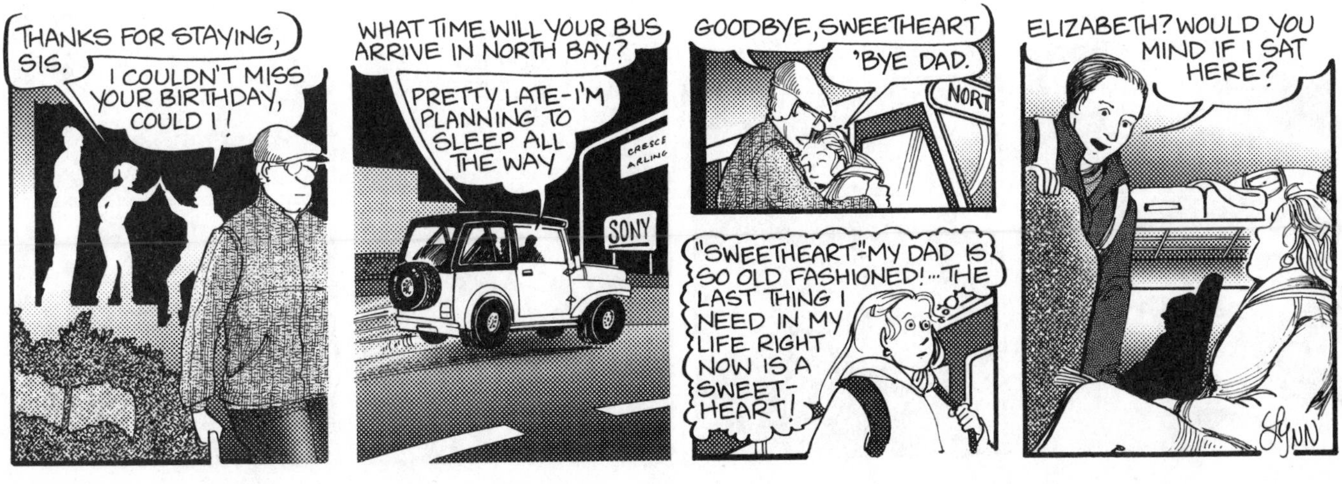
THANKS FOR STAYING, SIS.
I COULDN'T MISS YOUR BIRTHDAY, COULD I!
WHAT TIME WILL YOUR BUS ARRIVE IN NORTH BAY?
PRETTY LATE-I'M PLANNING TO SLEEP ALL THE WAY
SONY
GOODBYE, SWEETHEART
'BYE DAD.
NORT
"SWEETHEART"-MY DAD IS SO OLD FASHIONED!... THE LAST THING I NEED IN MY LIFE RIGHT NOW IS A SWEET-HEART!
ELIZABETH? WOULD YOU MIND IF I SAT HERE?
LYNN

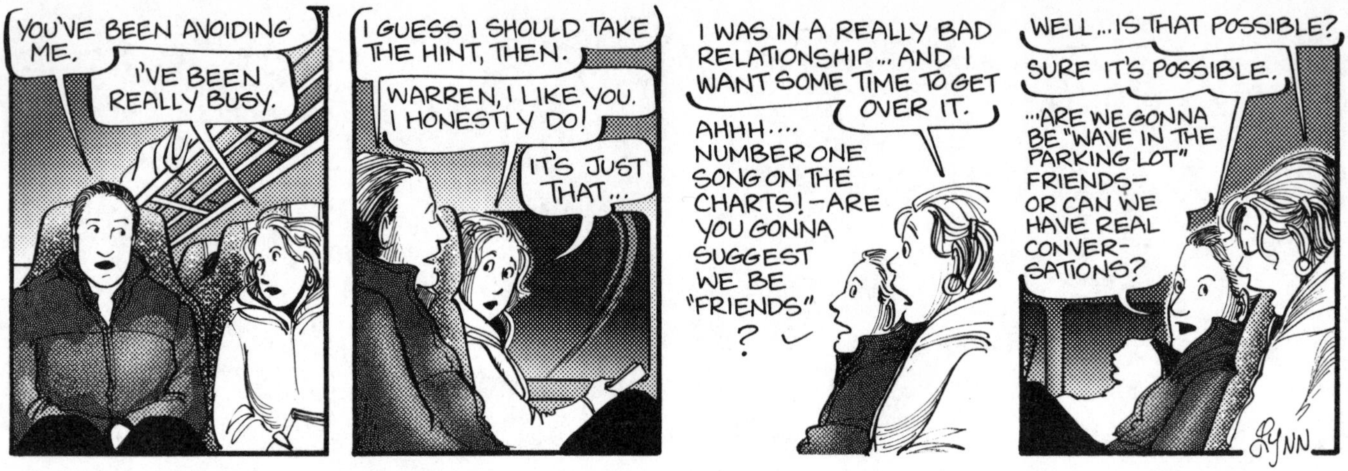
YOU'VE BEEN AVOIDING ME.
I'VE BEEN REALLY BUSY.
I GUESS I SHOULD TAKE THE HINT, THEN.
WARREN, I LIKE YOU. I HONESTLY DO!
IT'S JUST THAT...
I WAS IN A REALLY BAD RELATIONSHIP... AND I WANT SOME TIME TO GET OVER IT.
AHHH.... NUMBER ONE SONG ON THE CHARTS! –ARE YOU GONNA SUGGEST WE BE "FRIENDS"
WELL... IS THAT POSSIBLE?
SURE IT'S POSSIBLE.
...ARE WE GONNA BE "WAVE IN THE PARKING LOT" FRIENDS– OR CAN WE HAVE REAL CONVER-SATIONS?
LYNN

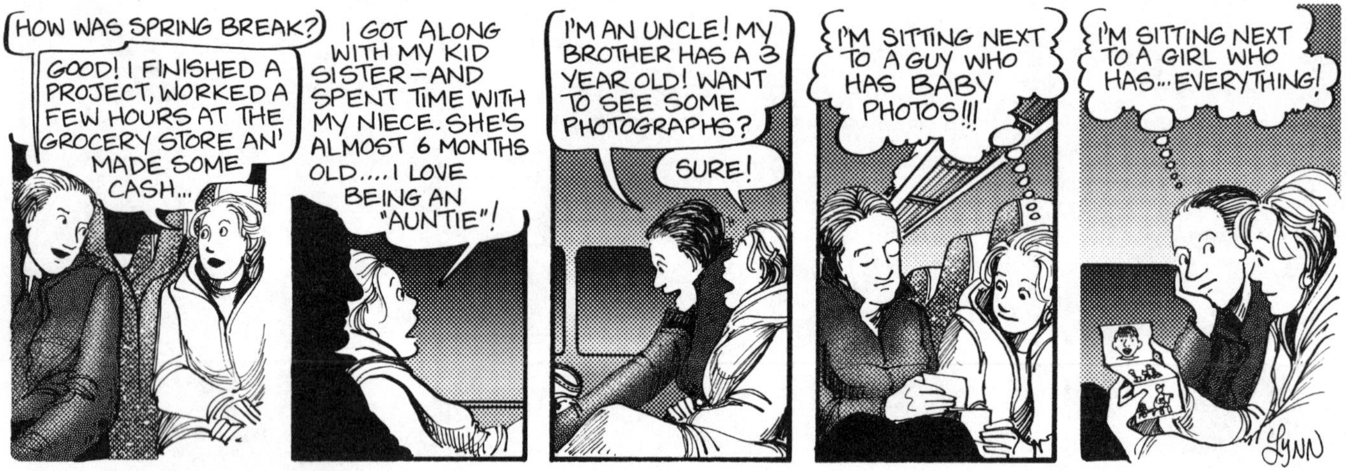
HOW WAS SPRING BREAK?
GOOD! I FINISHED A PROJECT, WORKED A FEW HOURS AT THE GROCERY STORE AN' MADE SOME CASH...
I GOT ALONG WITH MY KID SISTER–AND SPENT TIME WITH MY NIECE. SHE'S ALMOST 6 MONTHS OLD.... I LOVE BEING AN "AUNTIE"!
I'M AN UNCLE! MY BROTHER HAS A 3 YEAR OLD! WANT TO SEE SOME PHOTOGRAPHS?
SURE!
I'M SITTING NEXT TO A GUY WHO HAS BABY PHOTOS!!!
I'M SITTING NEXT TO A GIRL WHO HAS... EVERYTHING!
LYNN

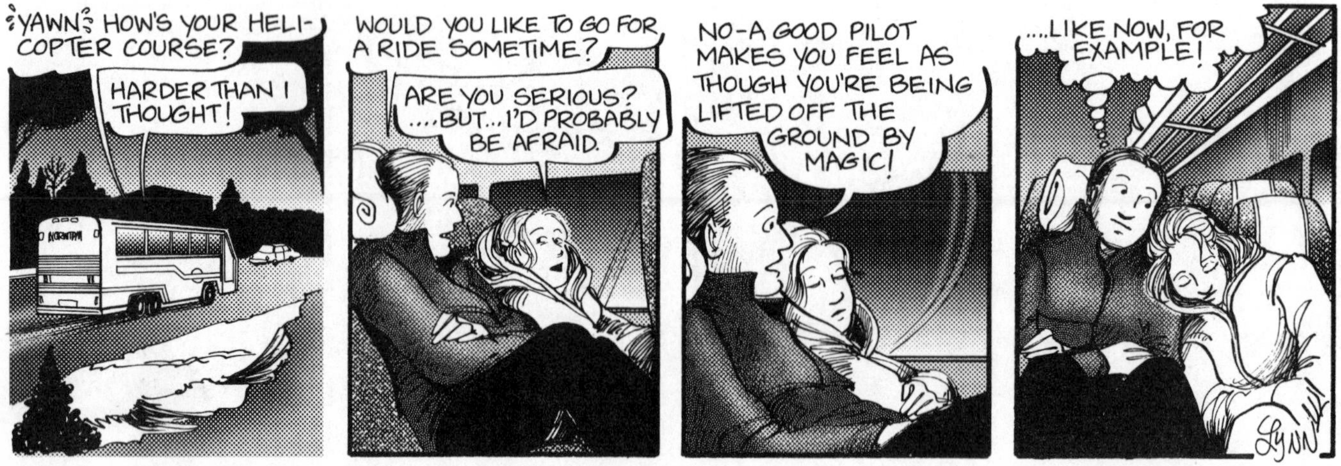
YAWN HOW'S YOUR HELI-COPTER COURSE?
HARDER THAN I THOUGHT!
WOULD YOU LIKE TO GO FOR A RIDE SOMETIME?
ARE YOU SERIOUS? ....BUT... I'D PROBABLY BE AFRAID.
NO–A GOOD PILOT MAKES YOU FEEL AS THOUGH YOU'RE BEING LIFTED OFF THE GROUND BY MAGIC!
....LIKE NOW, FOR EXAMPLE!
LYNN

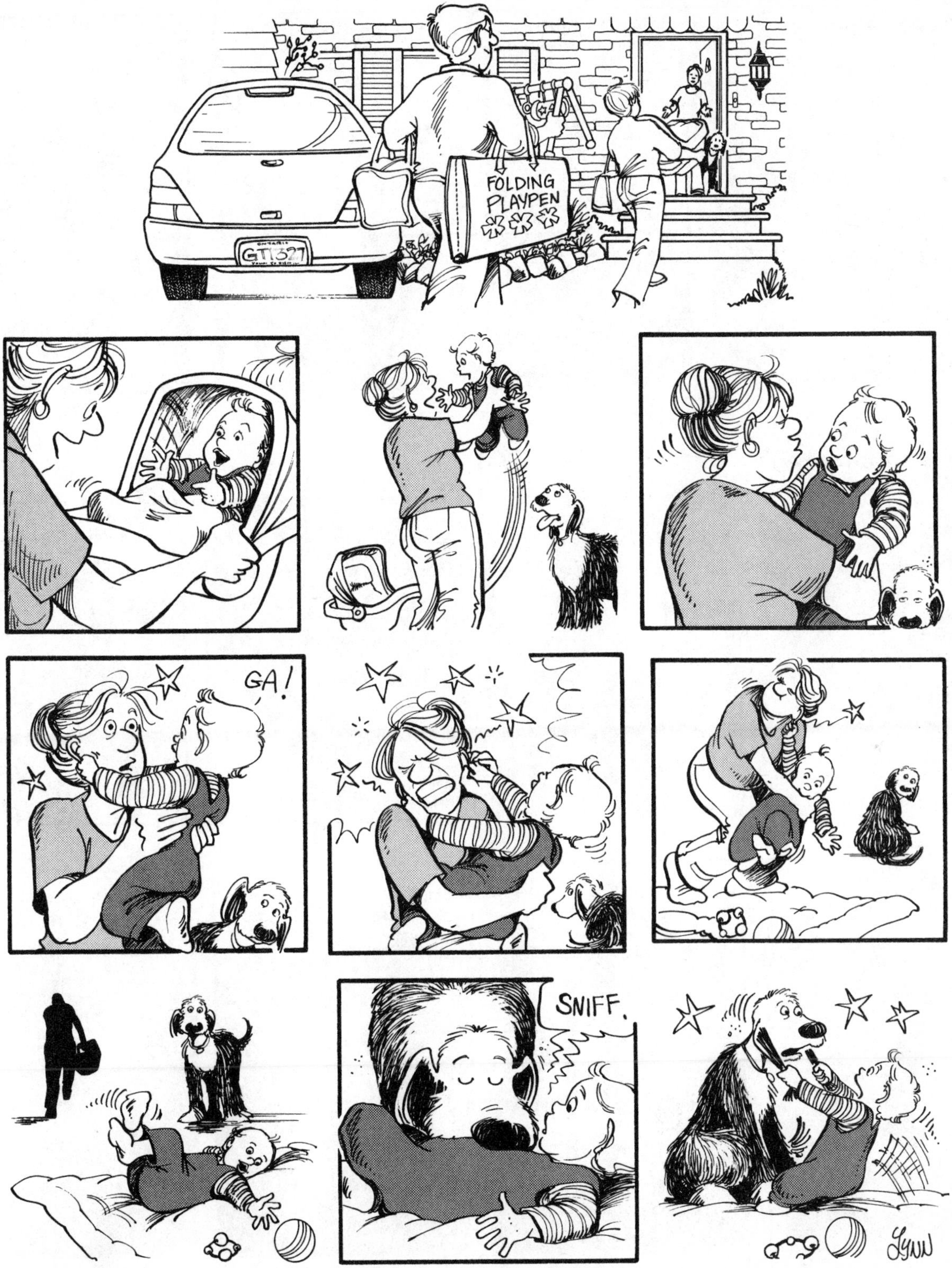
FOLDING
PLAYPEN
GA!
SNIFF.
LYNN

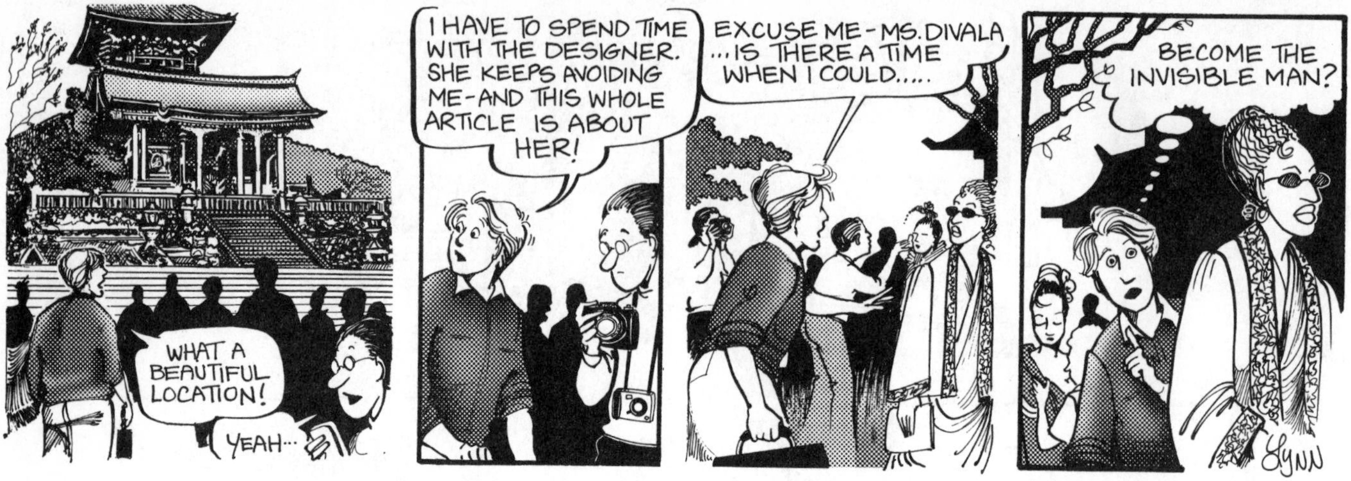
WHAT A BEAUTIFUL LOCATION!
YEAH...
I HAVE TO SPEND TIME WITH THE DESIGNER. SHE KEEPS AVOIDING ME-AND THIS WHOLE ARTICLE IS ABOUT HER!
EXCUSE ME-MS. DIVALA ...IS THERE A TIME WHEN I COULD.....
BECOME THE INVISIBLE MAN?
LYNN

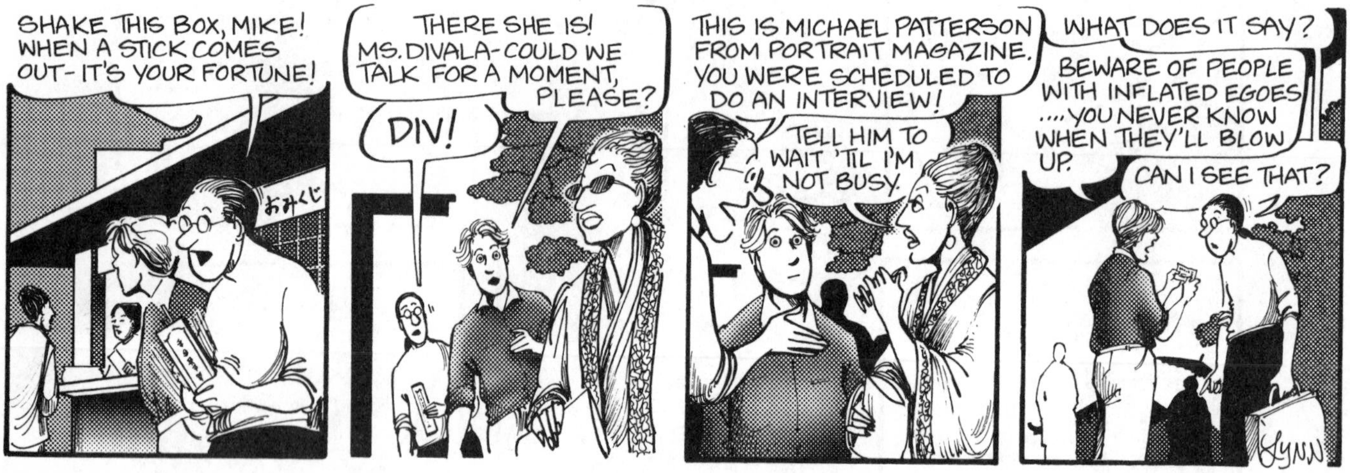
SHAKE THIS BOX, MIKE! WHEN A STICK COMES OUT-IT'S YOUR FORTUNE!
おみくじ
THERE SHE IS! MS. DIVALA-COULD WE TALK FOR A MOMENT, PLEASE?
DIV!
THIS IS MICHAEL PATTERSON FROM PORTRAIT MAGAZINE. YOU WERE SCHEDULED TO DO AN INTERVIEW!
TELL HIM TO WAIT 'TIL I'M NOT BUSY.
WHAT DOES IT SAY?
BEWARE OF PEOPLE WITH INFLATED EGOES ....YOU NEVER KNOW WHEN THEY'LL BLOW UP.
CAN I SEE THAT?
LYNN

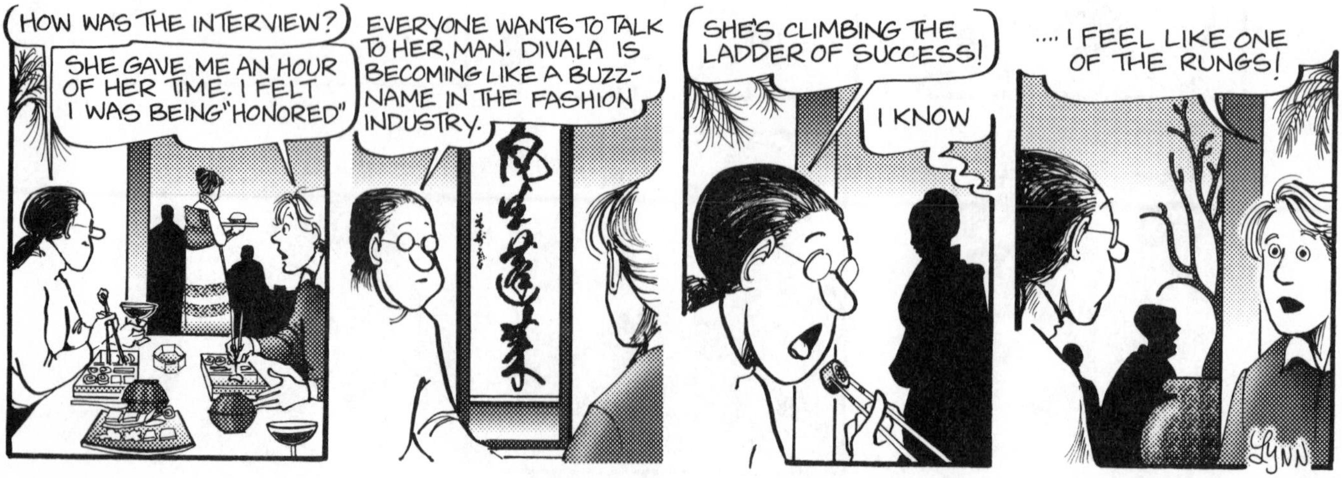
HOW WAS THE INTERVIEW?
SHE GAVE ME AN HOUR OF HER TIME. I FELT I WAS BEING "HONORED"
EVERYONE WANTS TO TALK TO HER, MAN. DIVALA IS BECOMING LIKE A BUZZ-NAME IN THE FASHION INDUSTRY.
SHE'S CLIMBING THE LADDER OF SUCCESS!
I KNOW
.... I FEEL LIKE ONE OF THE RUNGS!
LYNN

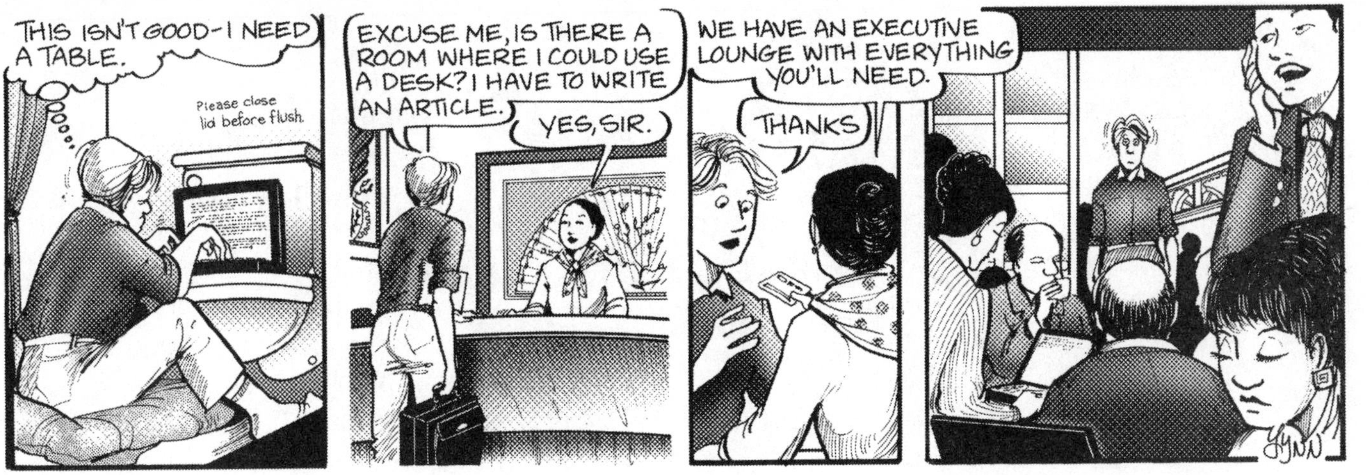
THIS ISN'T GOOD- I NEED A TABLE.
Please close lid before flush.
EXCUSE ME, IS THERE A ROOM WHERE I COULD USE A DESK? I HAVE TO WRITE AN ARTICLE.
YES, SIR.
WE HAVE AN EXECUTIVE LOUNGE WITH EVERYTHING YOU'LL NEED.
THANKS
LYNN

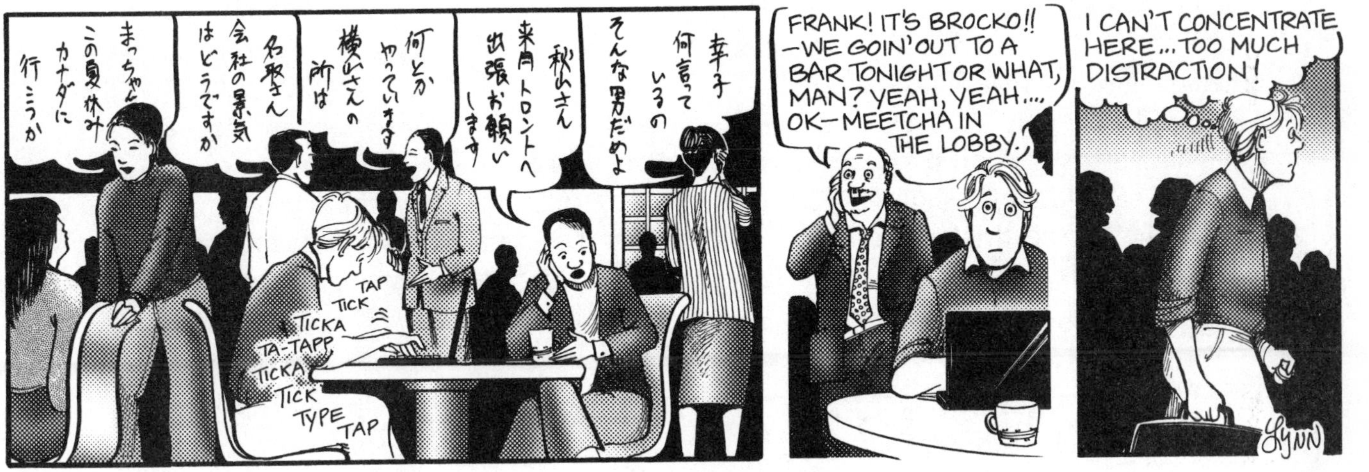
まっちゃん この夏休み カナダに 行こうか
名取さん 会社の景気 はどうですか
何とか やっています 横山さんの 所は
秋山さん 来月トロントへ 出張お願い します
幸子 何言っているの そんな男だめよ
TAP TICK TICKA TA-TAPP TICKA TICK TYPE TAP
FRANK! IT'S BROCKO!! -WE GOIN' OUT TO A BAR TONIGHT OR WHAT, MAN? YEAH, YEAH..., OK-MEETCHA IN THE LOBBY.
I CAN'T CONCENTRATE HERE... TOO MUCH DISTRACTION!
LYNN

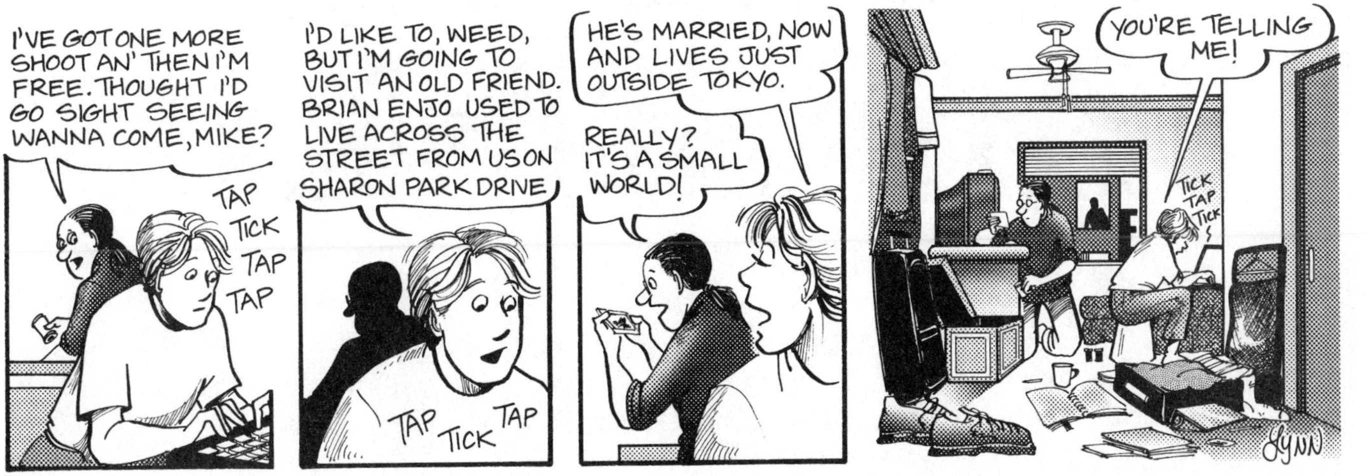
I'VE GOT ONE MORE SHOOT AN' THEN I'M FREE. THOUGHT I'D GO SIGHT SEEING WANNA COME, MIKE?
TAP TICK TAP TAP
I'D LIKE TO, WEED, BUT I'M GOING TO VISIT AN OLD FRIEND. BRIAN ENJO USED TO LIVE ACROSS THE STREET FROM US ON SHARON PARK DRIVE
TAP TICK TAP
HE'S MARRIED, NOW AND LIVES JUST OUTSIDE TOKYO.
REALLY? IT'S A SMALL WORLD!
YOU'RE TELLING ME!
TICK TAP TICK
LYNN

When Mike and Weed went to Japan, I wanted to make signs and language authentic. Japanese characters were found in pictures of Tokyo, worked into the comic art, and readers were pleased. "Usually," they said, "North American cartoonists just scribble something that looks like Japanese, and you took the time to use real words!" This was wonderful feedback. We also had the help of our friend Masahiro Nagasawa, chef and owner of the Kabuki House, a fine restaurant in North Bay, Ontario.

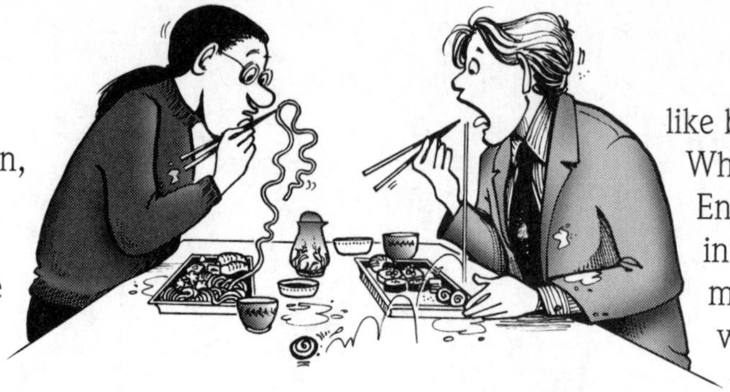

I drew an illustration showing Michael in a busy hotel executive lounge, able to concentrate on his work because the foreign language being spoken around him was like background music. When a man speaks English, he's suddenly interrupted and needs a more private space to work! I wanted real dialogue coming from the Japanese people surrounding Mike and I asked Masahiro to make up something fun to read. He was pleased to do so, and with the ease of a scribe, he wrote on the original art, the characters you see here! We've given you the translation, and Sachiko is his daughter! Some of his friends are also mentioned and had a great laugh when they saw their names in the paper.

This collaboration was so much fun. This is what makes research worth doing, and this is what helps to make these situations come alive for myself and others.

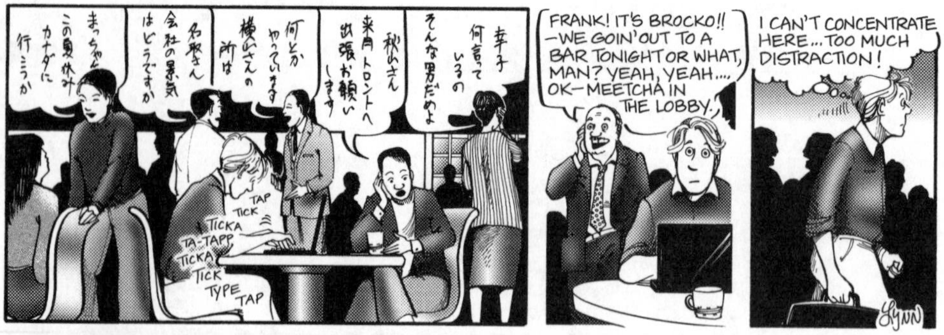
まっちゃん この夏休み カナダに 行こうか
名取さん 会社の景気 はどうですか
何とか やっています 横山さんの 所は
秋山さん 来月トロントへ 出張お願い します
幸子 何言って いるの そんな男だめよ
TAP
TICK
TICKA
TA-TAPP
TICKA
TICK
TYPE
TAP
FRANK! IT'S BROCKO!! —WE GOIN' OUT TO A BAR TONIGHT OR WHAT, MAN? YEAH, YEAH.... OK—MEETCHA IN THE LOBBY.
I CAN'T CONCENTRATE HERE... TOO MUCH DISTRACTION!
LYNN

LEFT TO RIGHT:

"Machan, let's go to Canada this summer."
"Natori, how's business?"
"We're surviving, Mr. Yokoyama. How about your business?"
"Mr. Akiyama—I want you to go to Toronto next month for business."
"Sachiko, what are you talking about? Forget that good-for-nothing guy!"

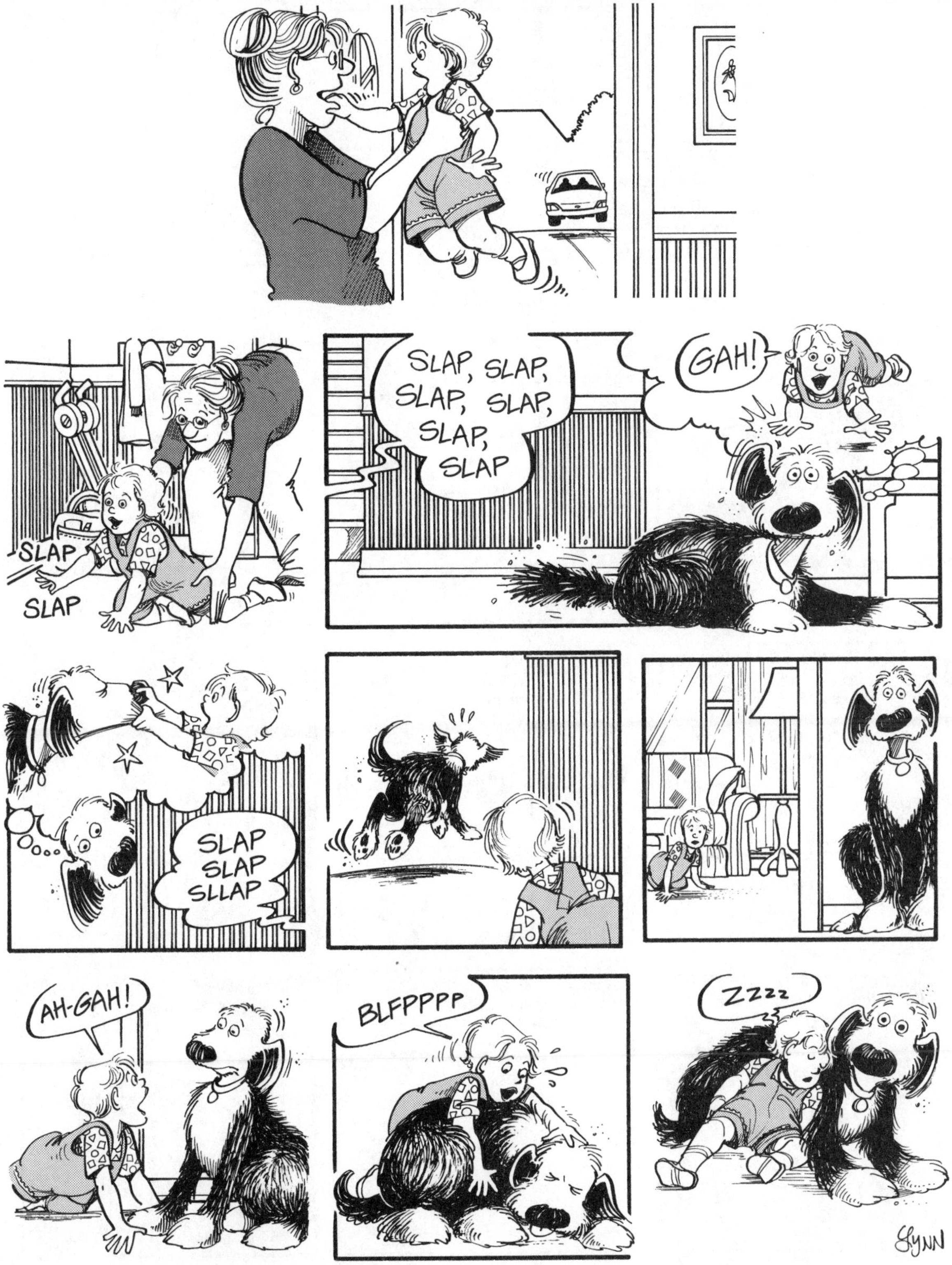
SLAP
SLAP
SLAP, SLAP, SLAP, SLAP, SLAP, SLAP
GAH!
SLAP SLAP SLLAP
AH-GAH!
BLFPPPP
Zzzz
LYNN

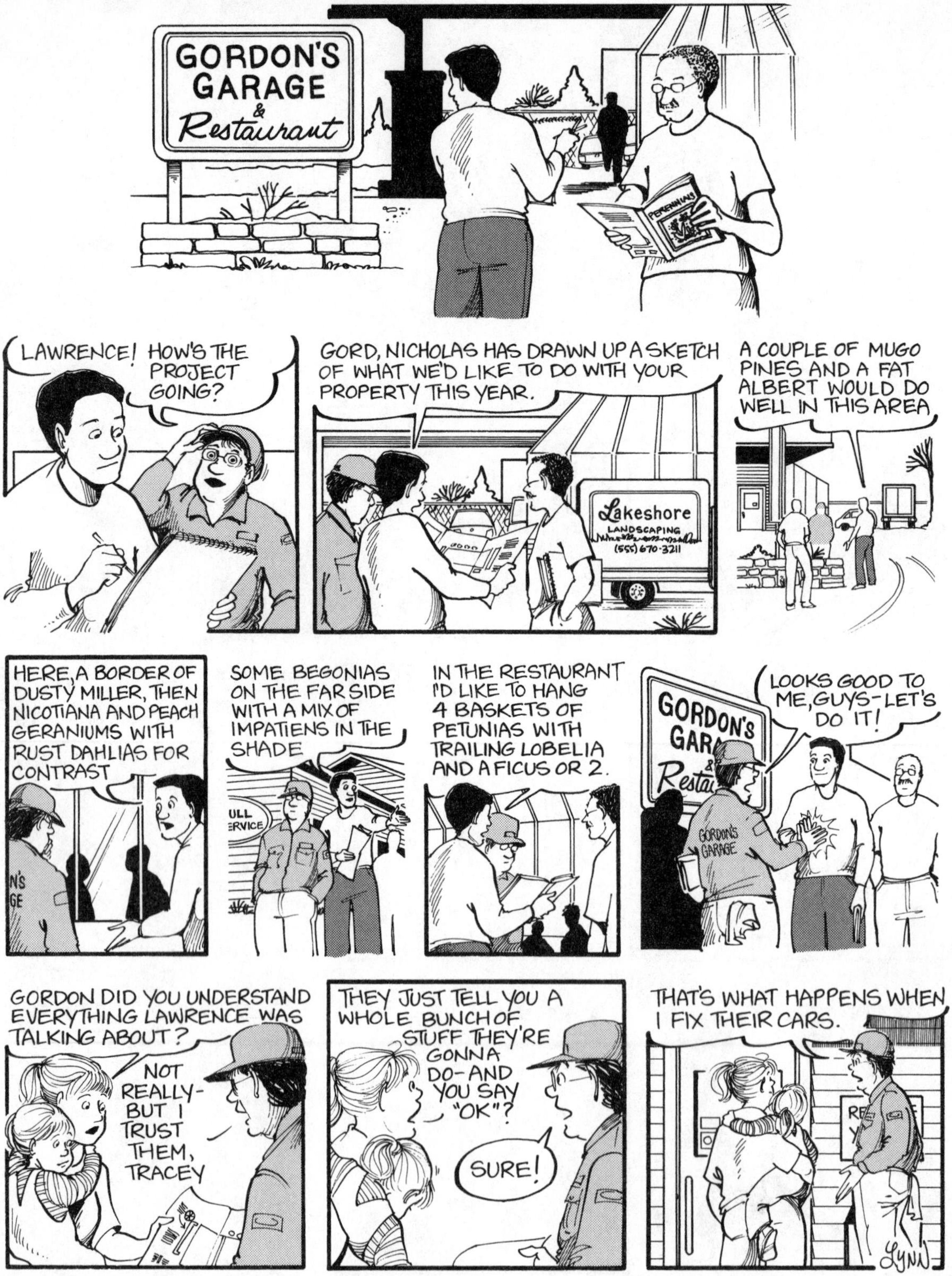
GORDON'S GARAGE & Restaurant
PERENNIALS
LAWRENCE! HOW'S THE PROJECT GOING?
GORD, NICHOLAS HAS DRAWN UP A SKETCH OF WHAT WE'D LIKE TO DO WITH YOUR PROPERTY THIS YEAR.
Lakeshore LANDSCAPING (555) 670-3211
A COUPLE OF MUGO PINES AND A FAT ALBERT WOULD DO WELL IN THIS AREA
HERE, A BORDER OF DUSTY MILLER, THEN NICOTIANA AND PEACH GERANIUMS WITH RUST DAHLIAS FOR CONTRAST
SOME BEGONIAS ON THE FAR SIDE WITH A MIX OF IMPATIENS IN THE SHADE
IN THE RESTAURANT I'D LIKE TO HANG 4 BASKETS OF PETUNIAS WITH TRAILING LOBELIA AND A FICUS OR 2.
LOOKS GOOD TO ME, GUYS - LET'S DO IT!
GORDON'S GARAGE
GORDON DID YOU UNDERSTAND EVERYTHING LAWRENCE WAS TALKING ABOUT?
NOT REALLY - BUT I TRUST THEM, TRACEY
THEY JUST TELL YOU A WHOLE BUNCH OF STUFF THEY'RE GONNA DO - AND YOU SAY "OK"?
SURE!
THAT'S WHAT HAPPENS WHEN I FIX THEIR CARS.
LYNN

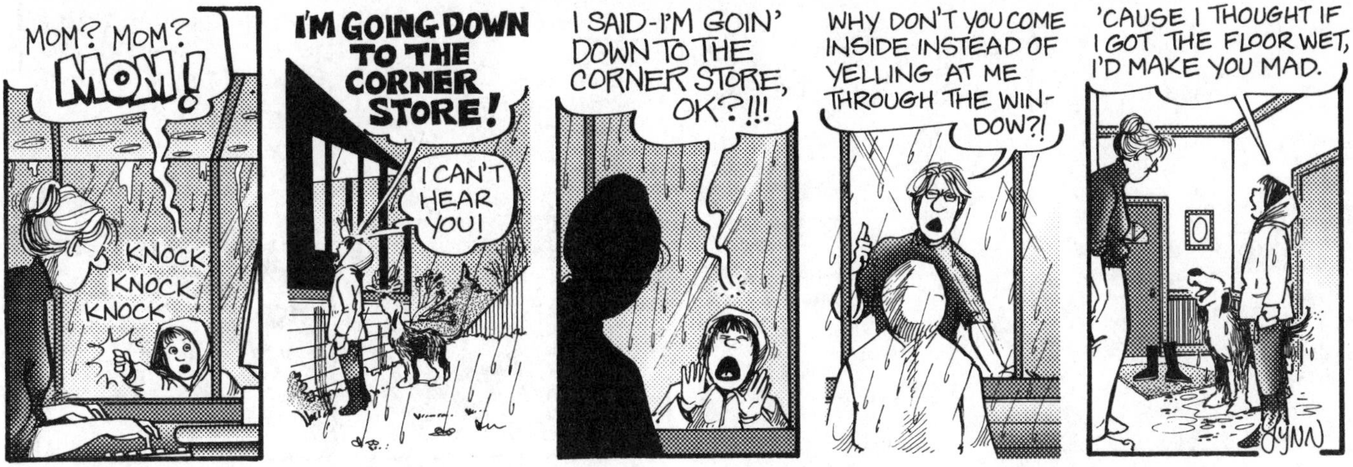
MOM? MOM? MOM!
KNOCK KNOCK KNOCK
I'M GOING DOWN TO THE CORNER STORE!
I CAN'T HEAR YOU!
I SAID-I'M GOIN' DOWN TO THE CORNER STORE, OK?!!!
WHY DON'T YOU COME INSIDE INSTEAD OF YELLING AT ME THROUGH THE WIN-DOW?!
'CAUSE I THOUGHT IF I GOT THE FLOOR WET, I'D MAKE YOU MAD.
LYNN

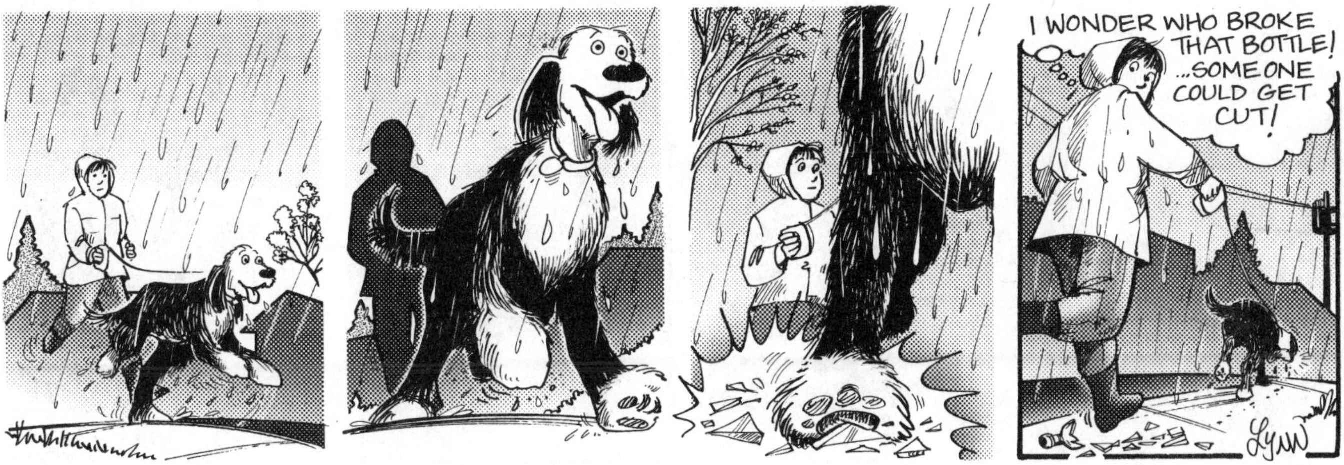
I WONDER WHO BROKE THAT BOTTLE! ...SOME ONE COULD GET CUT!
LYNN

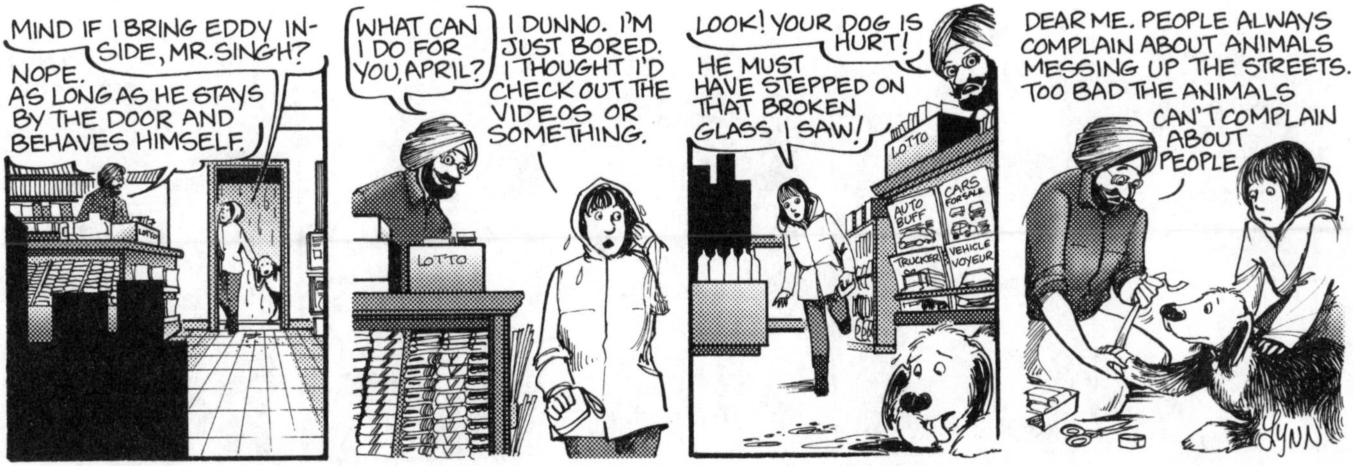
MIND IF I BRING EDDY IN-SIDE, MR. SINGH?
NOPE. AS LONG AS HE STAYS BY THE DOOR AND BEHAVES HIMSELF.
LOTTO
WHAT CAN I DO FOR YOU, APRIL?
I DUNNO. I'M JUST BORED. I THOUGHT I'D CHECK OUT THE VIDEOS OR SOMETHING.
LOTTO
LOOK! YOUR DOG IS HURT!
HE MUST HAVE STEPPED ON THAT BROKEN GLASS I SAW!
LOTTO
AUTO BUFF
CARS FOR SALE
TRUCKER
VEHICLE VOYEUR
DEAR ME. PEOPLE ALWAYS COMPLAIN ABOUT ANIMALS MESSING UP THE STREETS. TOO BAD THE ANIMALS CAN'T COMPLAIN ABOUT PEOPLE
LYNN

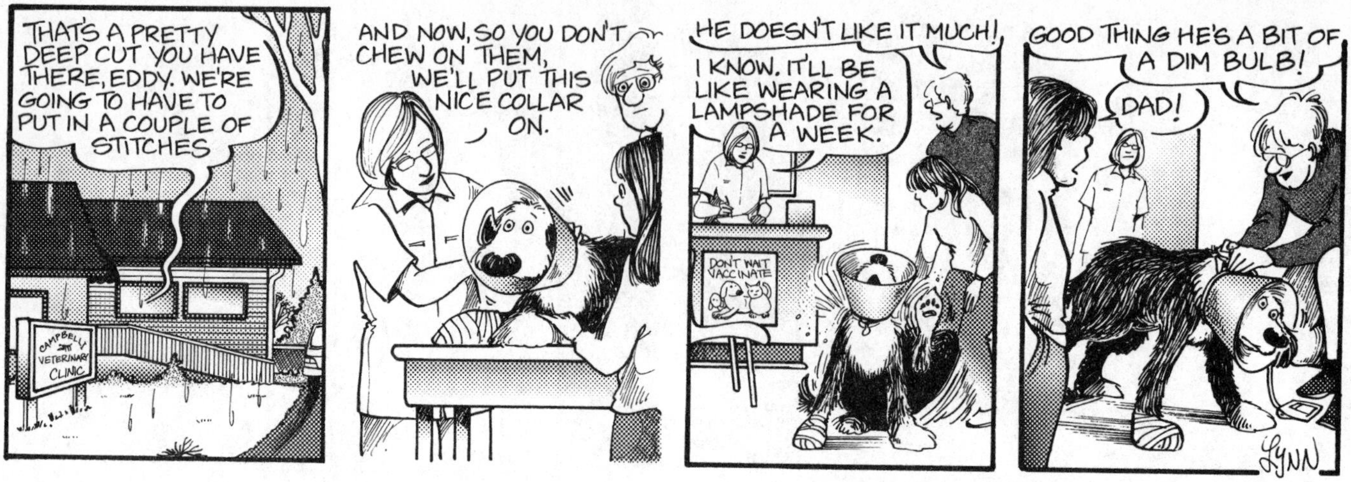
THAT'S A PRETTY DEEP CUT YOU HAVE THERE, EDDY. WE'RE GOING TO HAVE TO PUT IN A COUPLE OF STITCHES
CAMPBELL VETERINARY CLINIC
AND NOW, SO YOU DON'T CHEW ON THEM,
WE'LL PUT THIS NICE COLLAR ON.
HE DOESN'T LIKE IT MUCH!
I KNOW. IT'LL BE LIKE WEARING A LAMPSHADE FOR A WEEK.
DON'T WAIT VACCINATE
GOOD THING HE'S A BIT OF A DIM BULB!
DAD!
LYNN

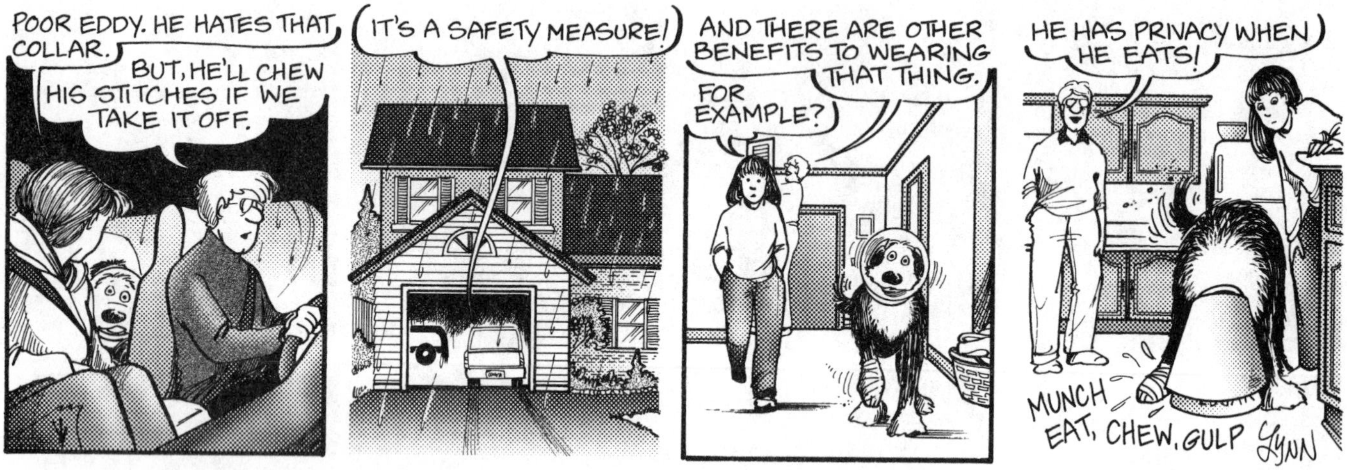
POOR EDDY. HE HATES THAT COLLAR.
BUT, HE'LL CHEW HIS STITCHES IF WE TAKE IT OFF.
IT'S A SAFETY MEASURE!
AND THERE ARE OTHER BENEFITS TO WEARING THAT THING.
FOR EXAMPLE?
HE HAS PRIVACY WHEN HE EATS!
MUNCH
EAT, CHEW, GULP
LYNN

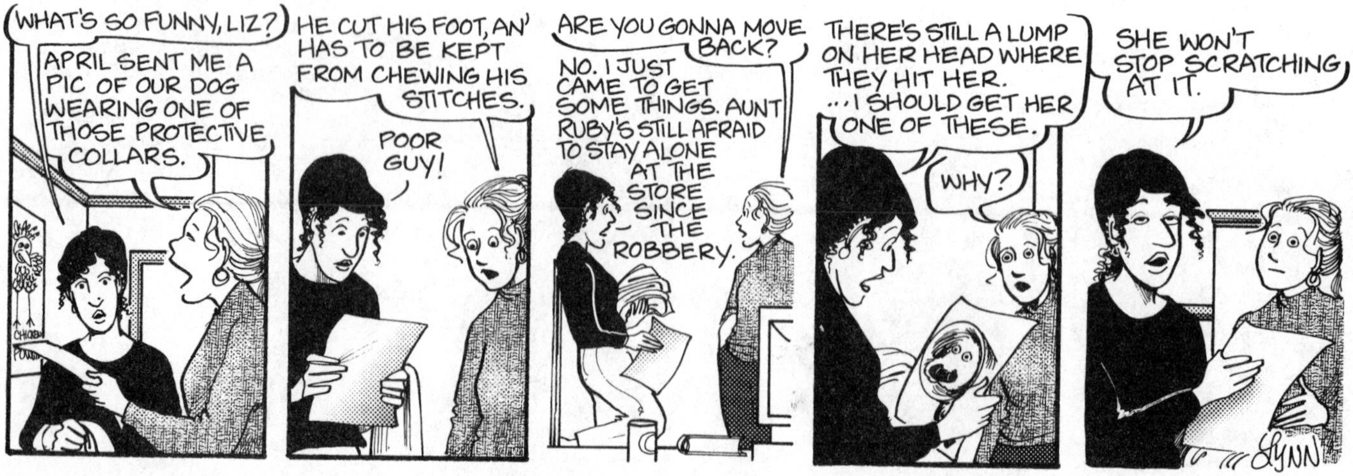
WHAT'S SO FUNNY, LIZ?
APRIL SENT ME A PIC OF OUR DOG WEARING ONE OF THOSE PROTECTIVE COLLARS.
HE CUT HIS FOOT, AN' HAS TO BE KEPT FROM CHEWING HIS STITCHES.
POOR GUY!
ARE YOU GONNA MOVE BACK?
NO. I JUST CAME TO GET SOME THINGS. AUNT RUBY'S STILL AFRAID TO STAY ALONE AT THE STORE SINCE THE ROBBERY.
THERE'S STILL A LUMP ON HER HEAD WHERE THEY HIT HER.
...I SHOULD GET HER ONE OF THESE.
WHY?
SHE WON'T STOP SCRATCHING AT IT.
LYNN

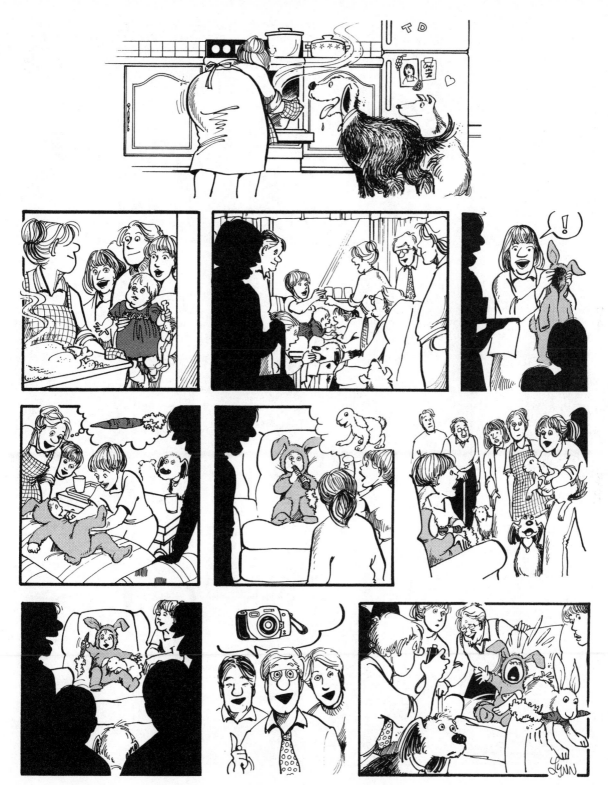

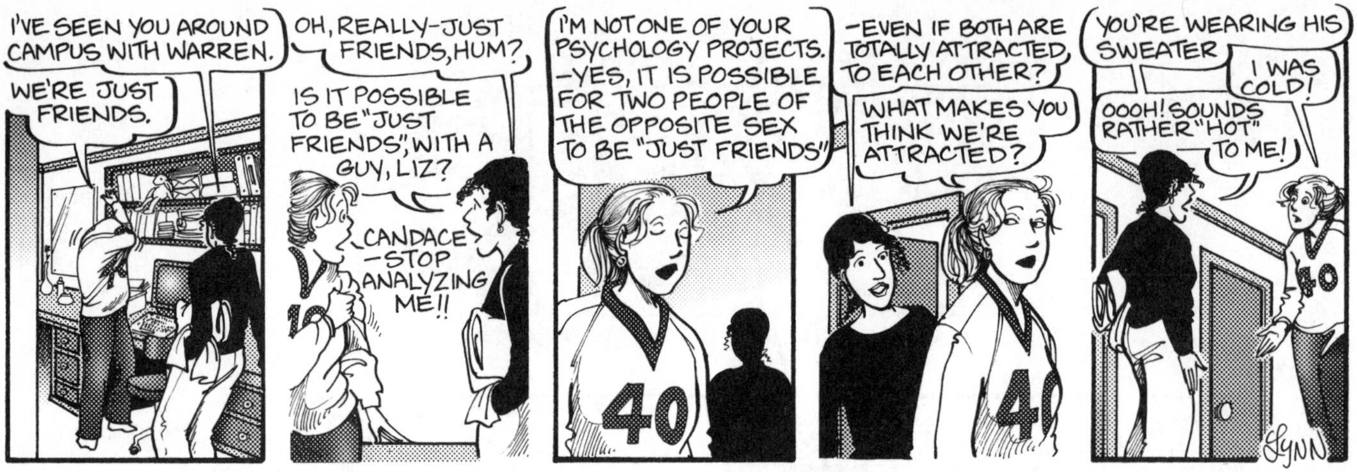
I'VE SEEN YOU AROUND CAMPUS WITH WARREN.
WE'RE JUST FRIENDS.
OH, REALLY–JUST FRIENDS, HUM?
IS IT POSSIBLE TO BE "JUST FRIENDS", WITH A GUY, LIZ?
CANDACE –STOP ANALYZING ME!!
I'M NOT ONE OF YOUR PSYCHOLOGY PROJECTS. –YES, IT IS POSSIBLE FOR TWO PEOPLE OF THE OPPOSITE SEX TO BE "JUST FRIENDS"
–EVEN IF BOTH ARE TOTALLY ATTRACTED TO EACH OTHER?
WHAT MAKES YOU THINK WE'RE ATTRACTED?
YOU'RE WEARING HIS SWEATER
I WAS COLD!
OOOH! SOUNDS RATHER "HOT" TO ME!
LYNN

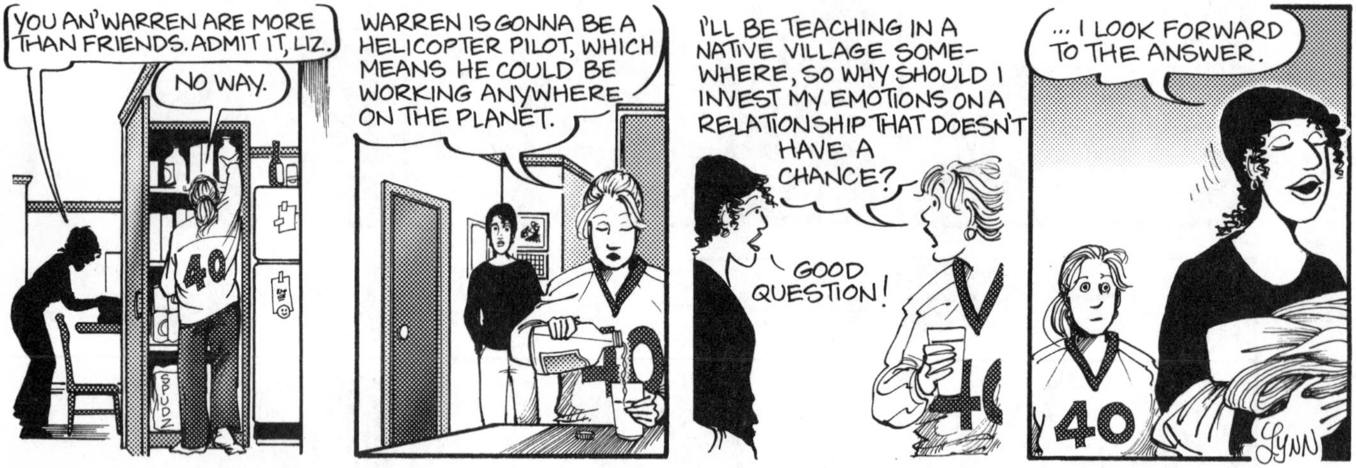
YOU AN' WARREN ARE MORE THAN FRIENDS. ADMIT IT, LIZ.
NO WAY.
WARREN IS GONNA BE A HELICOPTER PILOT, WHICH MEANS HE COULD BE WORKING ANYWHERE ON THE PLANET.
I'LL BE TEACHING IN A NATIVE VILLAGE SOMEWHERE, SO WHY SHOULD I INVEST MY EMOTIONS ON A RELATIONSHIP THAT DOESN'T HAVE A CHANCE?
GOOD QUESTION!
... I LOOK FORWARD TO THE ANSWER.
LYNN

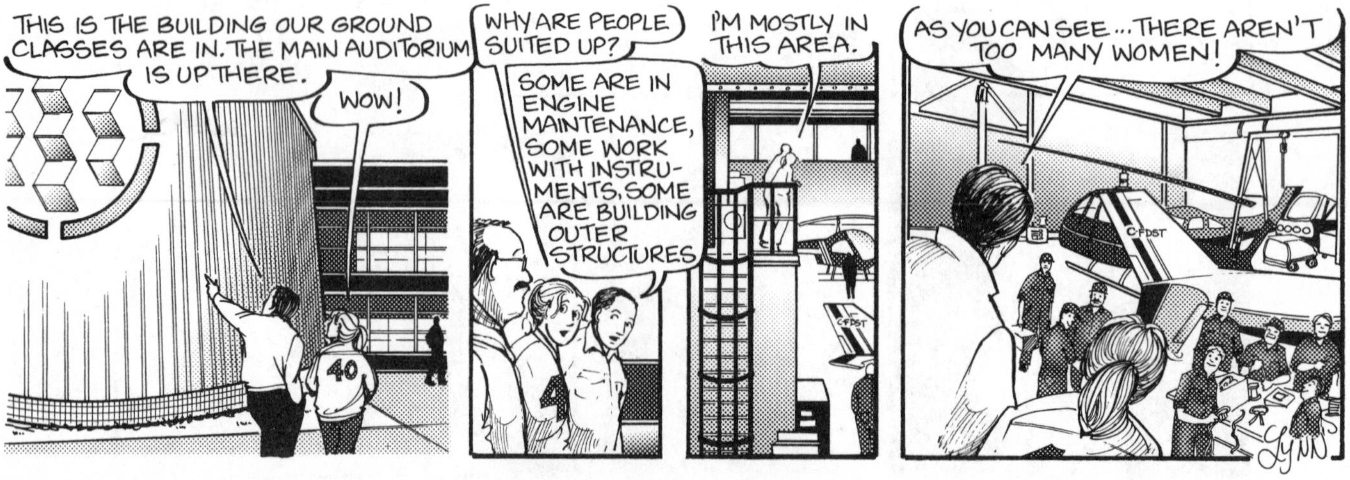
THIS IS THE BUILDING OUR GROUND CLASSES ARE IN. THE MAIN AUDITORIUM IS UP THERE.
WOW!
WHY ARE PEOPLE SUITED UP?
SOME ARE IN ENGINE MAINTENANCE, SOME WORK WITH INSTRUMENTS, SOME ARE BUILDING OUTER STRUCTURES
I'M MOSTLY IN THIS AREA.
AS YOU CAN SEE... THERE AREN'T TOO MANY WOMEN!
LYNN

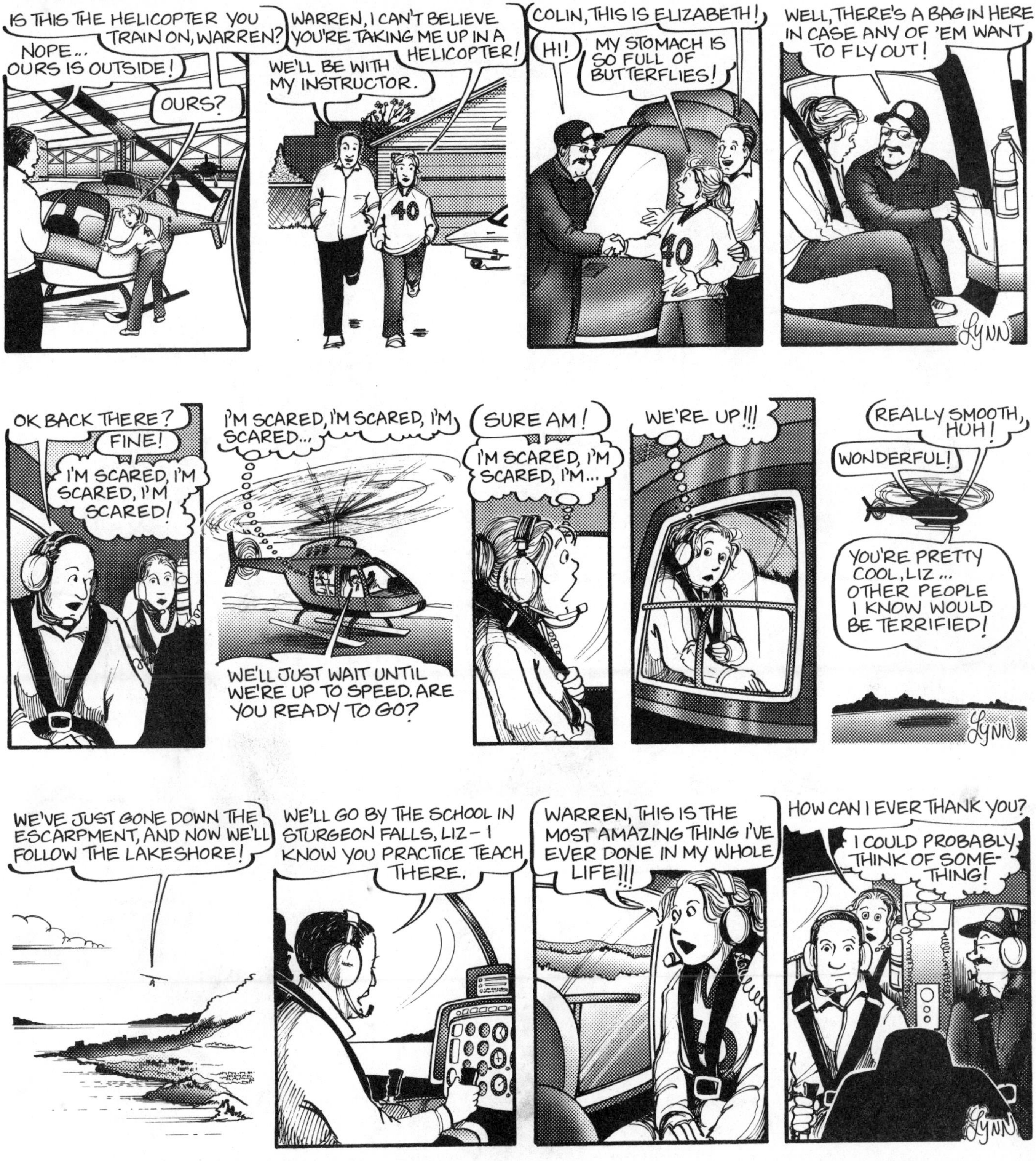
IS THIS THE HELICOPTER YOU TRAIN ON, WARREN?
NOPE... OURS IS OUTSIDE!
OURS?
WARREN, I CAN'T BELIEVE YOU'RE TAKING ME UP IN A HELICOPTER!
WE'LL BE WITH MY INSTRUCTOR.
COLIN, THIS IS ELIZABETH!
HI!
MY STOMACH IS SO FULL OF BUTTERFLIES!
WELL, THERE'S A BAG IN HERE IN CASE ANY OF 'EM WANT TO FLY OUT!
LYNN
OK BACK THERE?
FINE!
I'M SCARED, I'M SCARED, I'M SCARED!
I'M SCARED, I'M SCARED, I'M SCARED...
WE'LL JUST WAIT UNTIL WE'RE UP TO SPEED. ARE YOU READY TO GO?
SURE AM!
I'M SCARED, I'M SCARED, I'M...
WE'RE UP!!!
REALLY SMOOTH, HUH!
WONDERFUL!
YOU'RE PRETTY COOL, LIZ... OTHER PEOPLE I KNOW WOULD BE TERRIFIED!
LYNN
WE'VE JUST GONE DOWN THE ESCARPMENT, AND NOW WE'LL FOLLOW THE LAKESHORE!
WE'LL GO BY THE SCHOOL IN STURGEON FALLS, LIZ– I KNOW YOU PRACTICE TEACH THERE.
WARREN, THIS IS THE MOST AMAZING THING I'VE EVER DONE IN MY WHOLE LIFE!!!
HOW CAN I EVER THANK YOU?
I COULD PROBABLY THINK OF SOMETHING!
LYNN

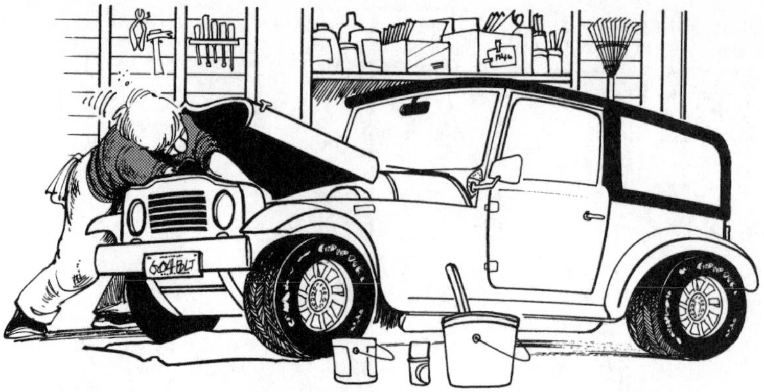
604 BLT

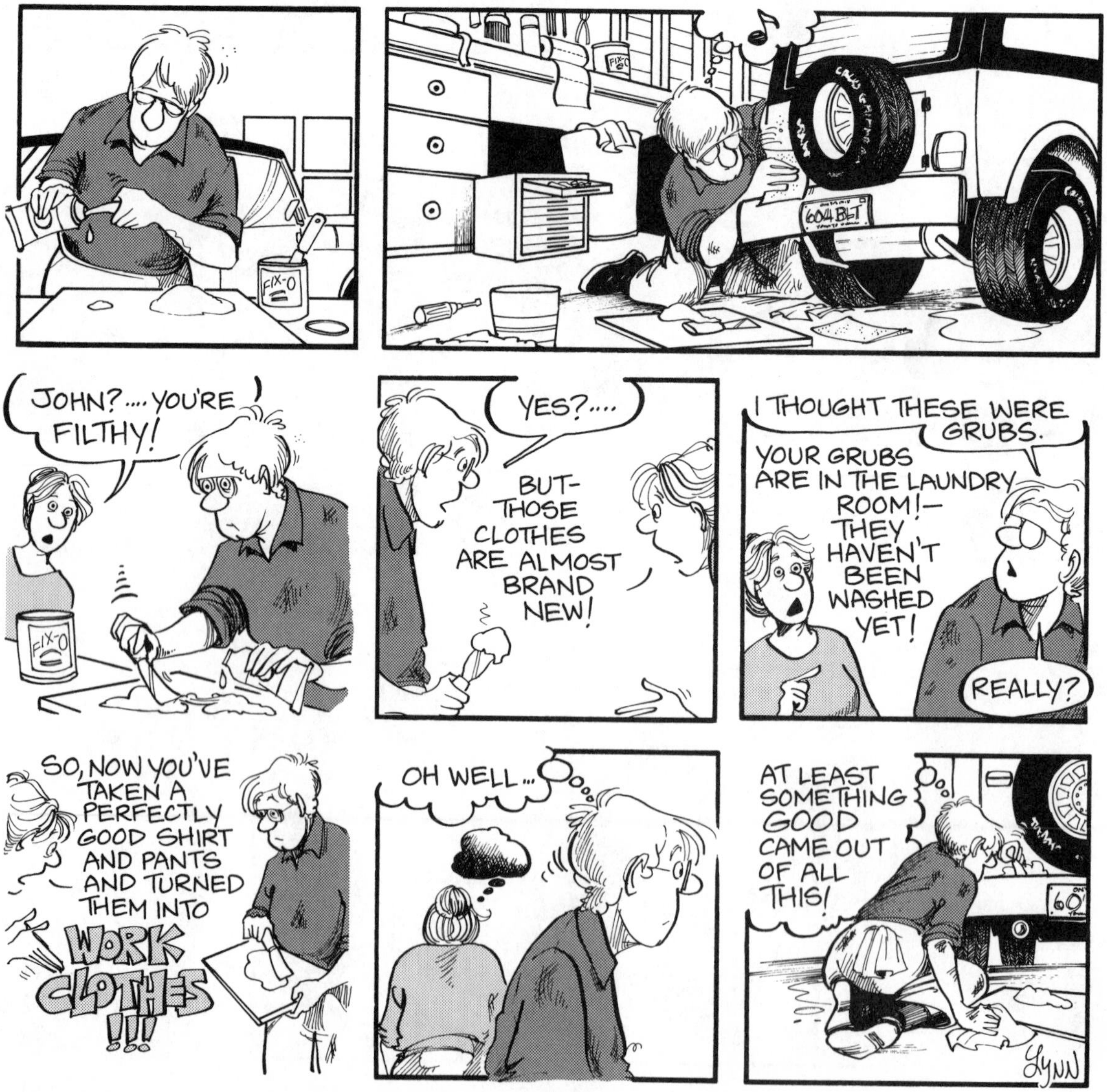
FIX-O
604 BLT
JOHN?.... YOU'RE FILTHY!
YES?....
BUT- THOSE CLOTHES ARE ALMOST BRAND NEW!
I THOUGHT THESE WERE GRUBS.
YOUR GRUBS ARE IN THE LAUNDRY ROOM!— THEY HAVEN'T BEEN WASHED YET!
REALLY?
SO, NOW YOU'VE TAKEN A PERFECTLY GOOD SHIRT AND PANTS AND TURNED THEM INTO WORK CLOTHES !!!
OH WELL...
AT LEAST SOMETHING GOOD CAME OUT OF ALL THIS!
LYNN

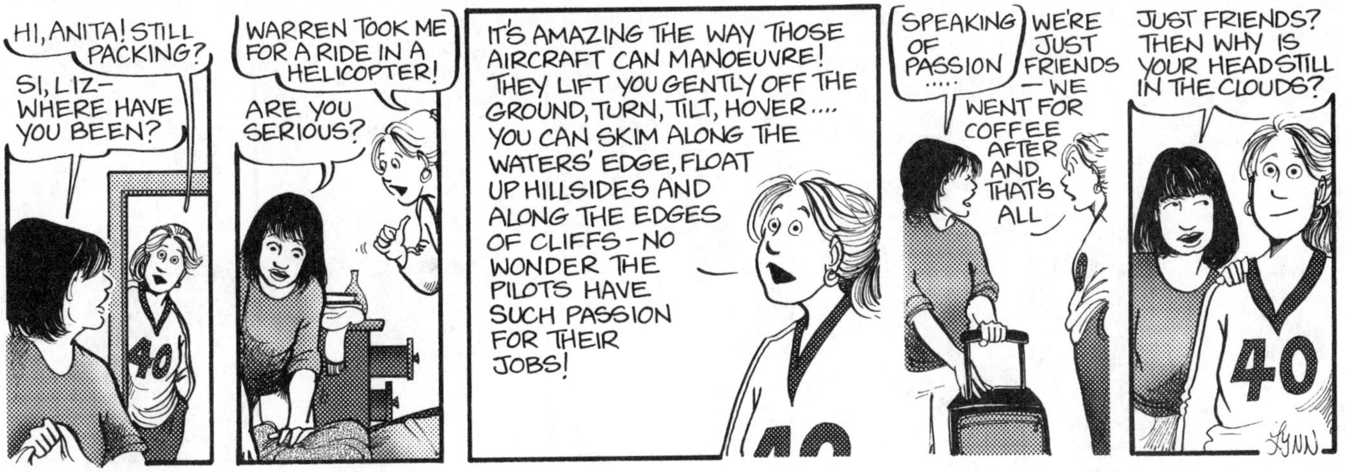
HI, ANITA! STILL PACKING?
SI, LIZ- WHERE HAVE YOU BEEN?
WARREN TOOK ME FOR A RIDE IN A HELICOPTER!
ARE YOU SERIOUS?
IT'S AMAZING THE WAY THOSE AIRCRAFT CAN MANOEUVRE! THEY LIFT YOU GENTLY OFF THE GROUND, TURN, TILT, HOVER.... YOU CAN SKIM ALONG THE WATERS' EDGE, FLOAT UP HILLSIDES AND ALONG THE EDGES OF CLIFFS - NO WONDER THE PILOTS HAVE SUCH PASSION FOR THEIR JOBS!
SPEAKING OF PASSION .....
WE'RE JUST FRIENDS — WE WENT FOR COFFEE AFTER AND THAT'S ALL
JUST FRIENDS? THEN WHY IS YOUR HEAD STILL IN THE CLOUDS?
LYNN

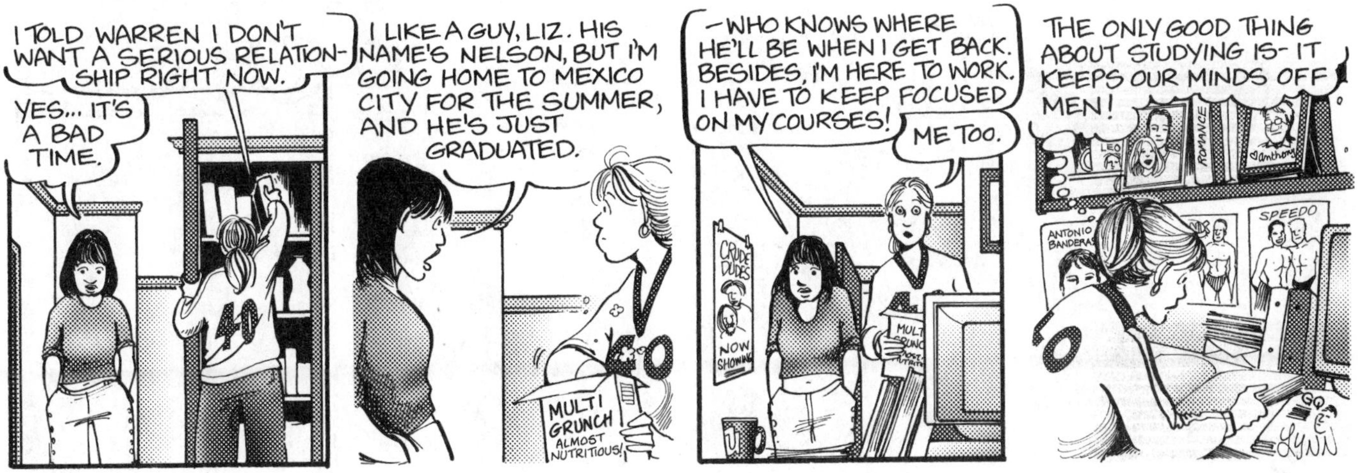
I TOLD WARREN I DON'T WANT A SERIOUS RELATIONSHIP RIGHT NOW.
YES... IT'S A BAD TIME.
I LIKE A GUY, LIZ. HIS NAME'S NELSON, BUT I'M GOING HOME TO MEXICO CITY FOR THE SUMMER, AND HE'S JUST GRADUATED.
MULTI GRUNCH ALMOST NUTRITIOUS!
—WHO KNOWS WHERE HE'LL BE WHEN I GET BACK. BESIDES, I'M HERE TO WORK. I HAVE TO KEEP FOCUSED ON MY COURSES!
ME TOO.
CRUDE DUDES
NOW SHOWING
THE ONLY GOOD THING ABOUT STUDYING IS- IT KEEPS OUR MINDS OFF MEN!
LEO
ROMANCE
anthony
ANTONIO BANDERAS
SPEEDO
LYNN

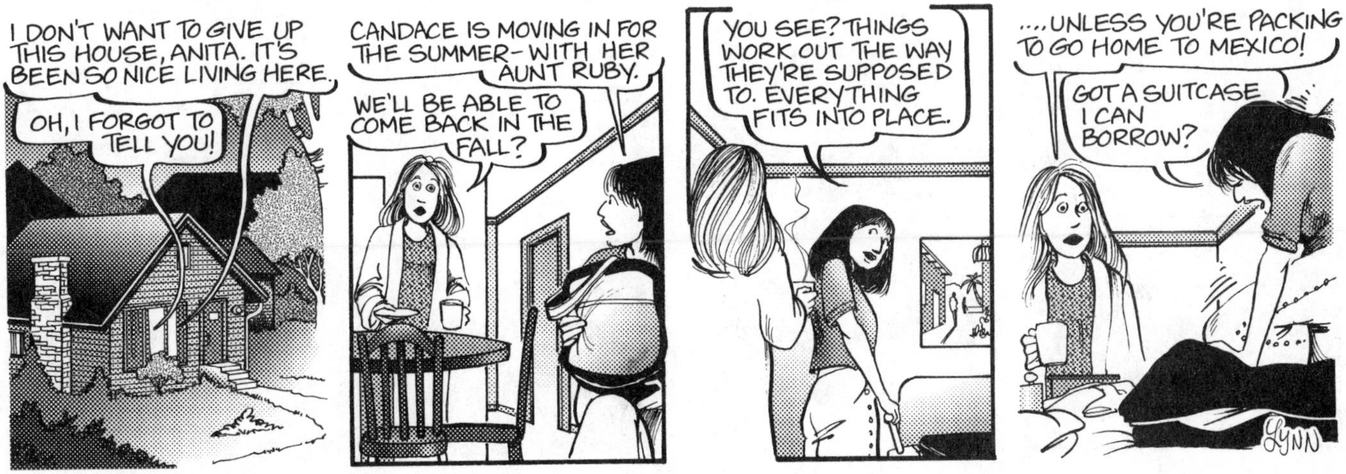
I DON'T WANT TO GIVE UP THIS HOUSE, ANITA. IT'S BEEN SO NICE LIVING HERE.
OH, I FORGOT TO TELL YOU!
CANDACE IS MOVING IN FOR THE SUMMER- WITH HER AUNT RUBY.
WE'LL BE ABLE TO COME BACK IN THE FALL?
YOU SEE? THINGS WORK OUT THE WAY THEY'RE SUPPOSED TO. EVERYTHING FITS INTO PLACE.
....UNLESS YOU'RE PACKING TO GO HOME TO MEXICO!
GOT A SUITCASE I CAN BORROW?
LYNN

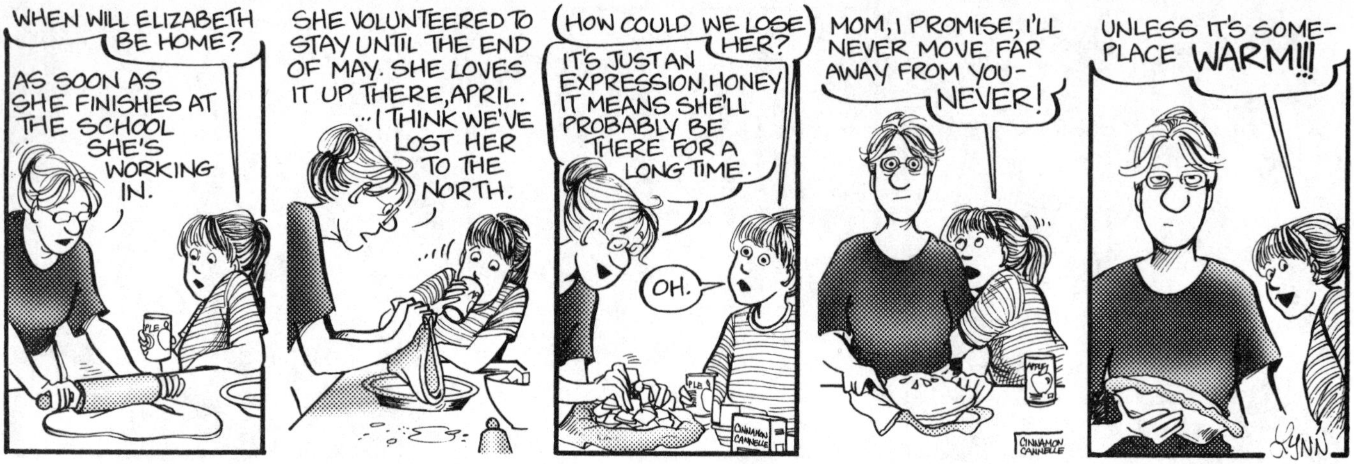
WHEN WILL ELIZABETH BE HOME?
AS SOON AS SHE FINISHES AT THE SCHOOL SHE'S WORKING IN.
SHE VOLUNTEERED TO STAY UNTIL THE END OF MAY. SHE LOVES IT UP THERE, APRIL.
...I THINK WE'VE LOST HER TO THE NORTH.
HOW COULD WE LOSE HER?
IT'S JUST AN EXPRESSION, HONEY IT MEANS SHE'LL PROBABLY BE THERE FOR A LONG TIME.
OH.
CINNAMON CANNELLE
MOM, I PROMISE, I'LL NEVER MOVE FAR AWAY FROM YOU- NEVER!
CINNAMON CANNELLE
UNLESS IT'S SOME-PLACE WARM!!!
LYNN

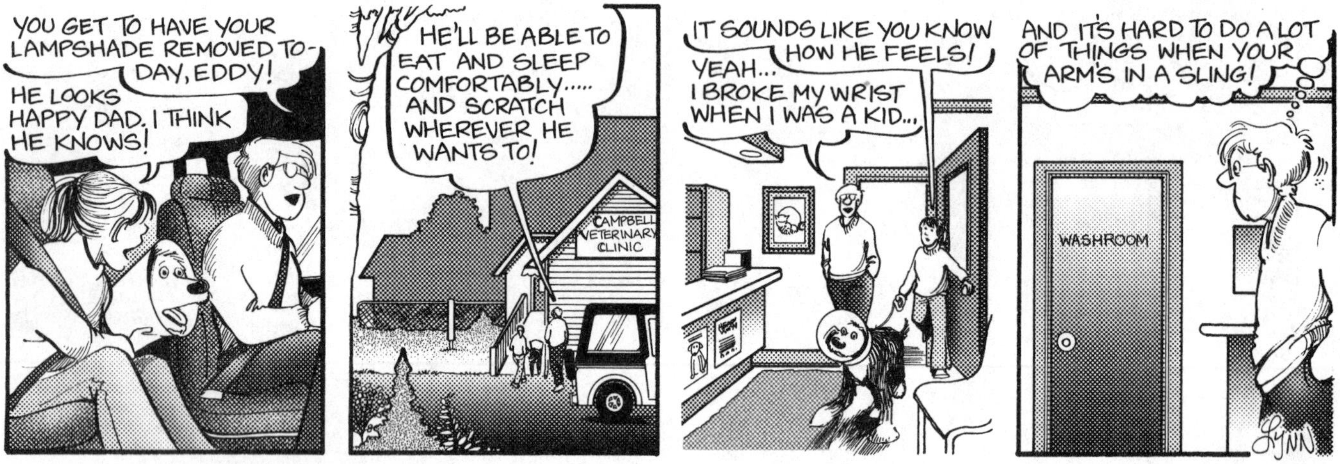
YOU GET TO HAVE YOUR LAMPSHADE REMOVED TO-DAY, EDDY!
HE LOOKS HAPPY DAD. I THINK HE KNOWS!
HE'LL BE ABLE TO EAT AND SLEEP COMFORTABLY..... AND SCRATCH WHEREVER HE WANTS TO!
CAMPBELL VETERINARY CLINIC
IT SOUNDS LIKE YOU KNOW HOW HE FEELS!
YEAH... I BROKE MY WRIST WHEN I WAS A KID...
AND IT'S HARD TO DO A LOT OF THINGS WHEN YOUR ARM'S IN A SLING!
WASHROOM
LYNN

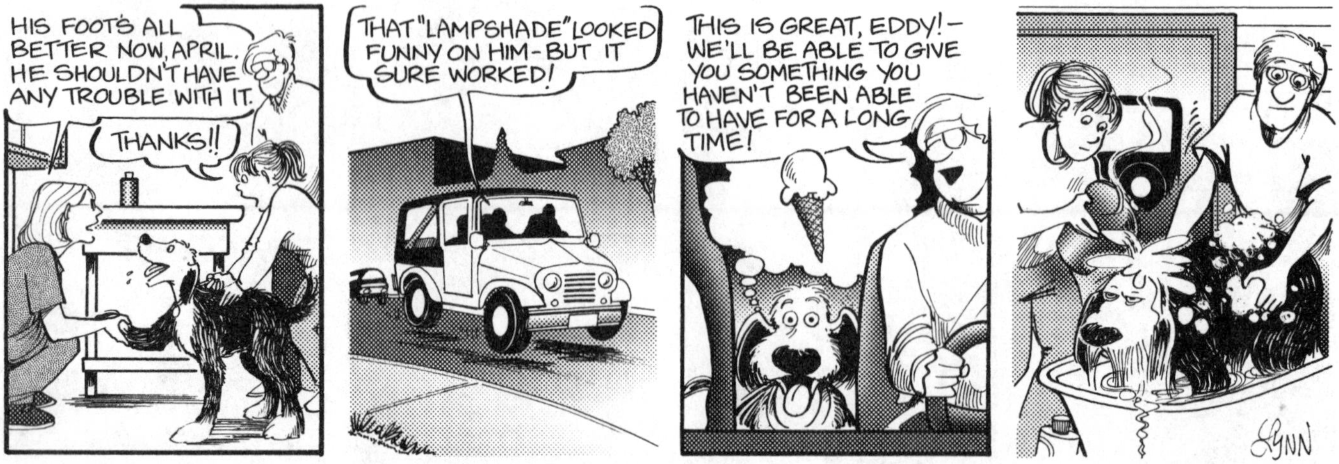
HIS FOOT'S ALL BETTER NOW, APRIL. HE SHOULDN'T HAVE ANY TROUBLE WITH IT.
THANKS!!
THAT "LAMPSHADE" LOOKED FUNNY ON HIM- BUT IT SURE WORKED!
THIS IS GREAT, EDDY!- WE'LL BE ABLE TO GIVE YOU SOMETHING YOU HAVEN'T BEEN ABLE TO HAVE FOR A LONG TIME!
LYNN

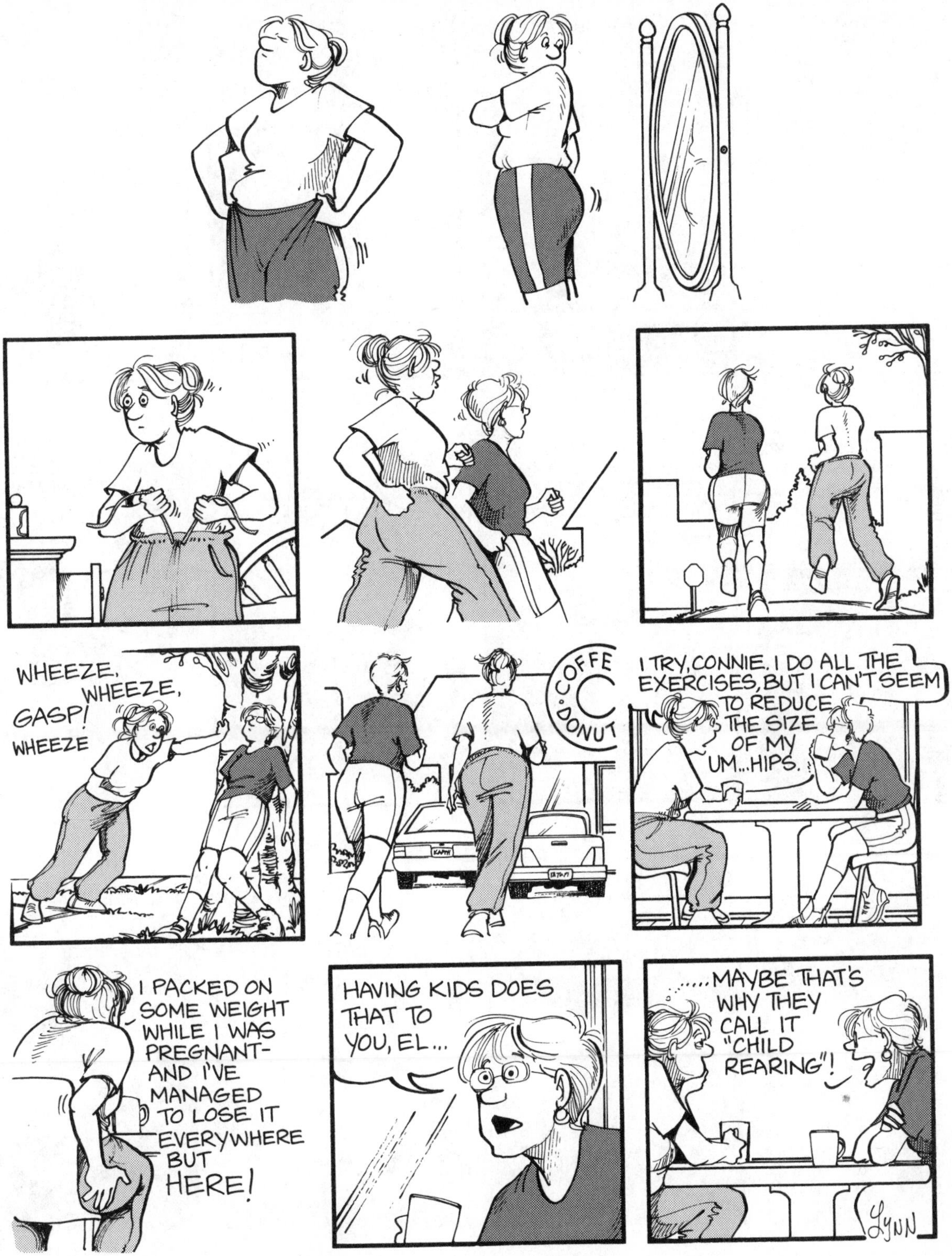

WHEEZE, WHEEZE, GASP! WHEEZE
COFFE
DONUT
I TRY, CONNIE. I DO ALL THE EXERCISES, BUT I CAN'T SEEM TO REDUCE THE SIZE OF MY UM...HIPS.
I PACKED ON SOME WEIGHT WHILE I WAS PREGNANT- AND I'VE MANAGED TO LOSE IT EVERYWHERE BUT HERE!
HAVING KIDS DOES THAT TO YOU, EL...
.....MAYBE THAT'S WHY THEY CALL IT "CHILD REARING"!
LYNN

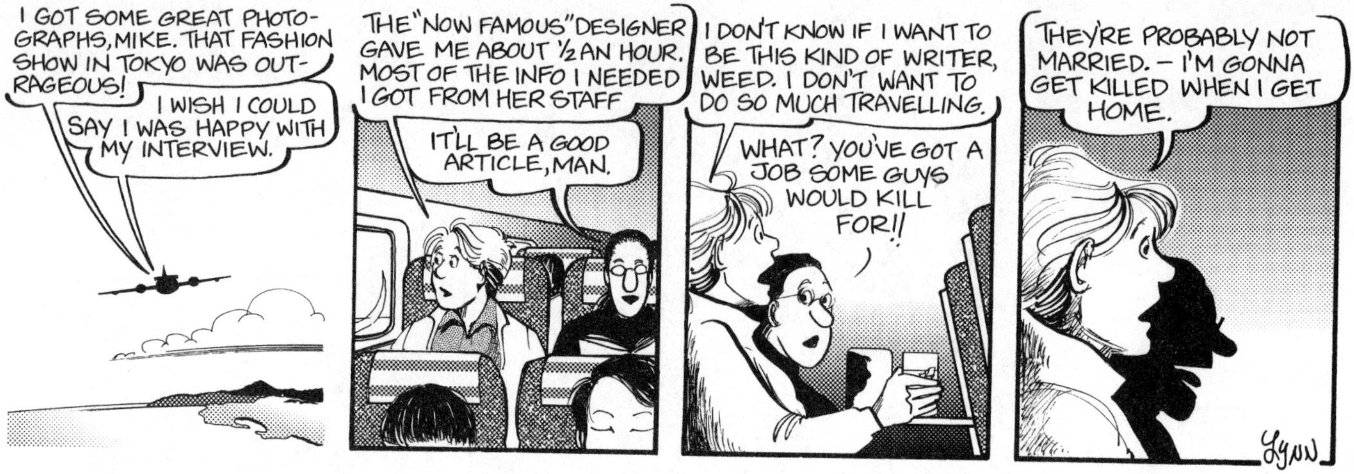
I GOT SOME GREAT PHOTOGRAPHS, MIKE. THAT FASHION SHOW IN TOKYO WAS OUTRAGEOUS!
I WISH I COULD SAY I WAS HAPPY WITH MY INTERVIEW.
THE "NOW FAMOUS" DESIGNER GAVE ME ABOUT ½ AN HOUR. MOST OF THE INFO I NEEDED I GOT FROM HER STAFF
IT'LL BE A GOOD ARTICLE, MAN.
I DON'T KNOW IF I WANT TO BE THIS KIND OF WRITER, WEED. I DON'T WANT TO DO SO MUCH TRAVELLING.
WHAT? YOU'VE GOT A JOB SOME GUYS WOULD KILL FOR!!
THEY'RE PROBABLY NOT MARRIED. – I'M GONNA GET KILLED WHEN I GET HOME.
LYNN

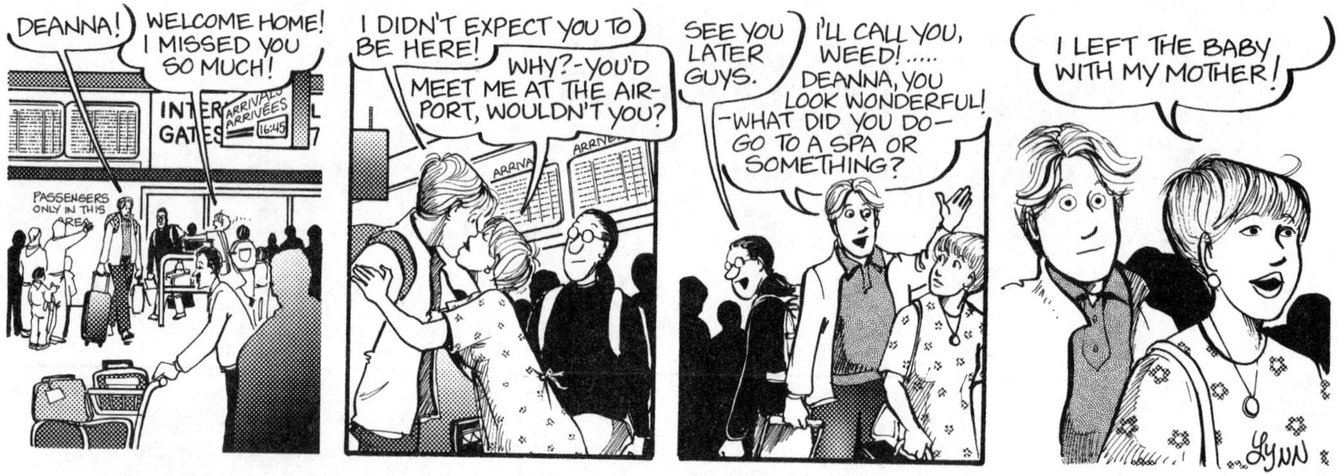
DEANNA!
WELCOME HOME! I MISSED YOU SO MUCH!
INTER GATES
ARRIVALS ARRIVÉES 16:45
PASSENGERS ONLY IN THIS AREA
I DIDN'T EXPECT YOU TO BE HERE!
WHY?-YOU'D MEET ME AT THE AIRPORT, WOULDN'T YOU?
SEE YOU LATER GUYS.
I'LL CALL YOU, WEED!..... DEANNA, YOU LOOK WONDERFUL! -WHAT DID YOU DO-GO TO A SPA OR SOMETHING?
I LEFT THE BABY WITH MY MOTHER!
LYNN

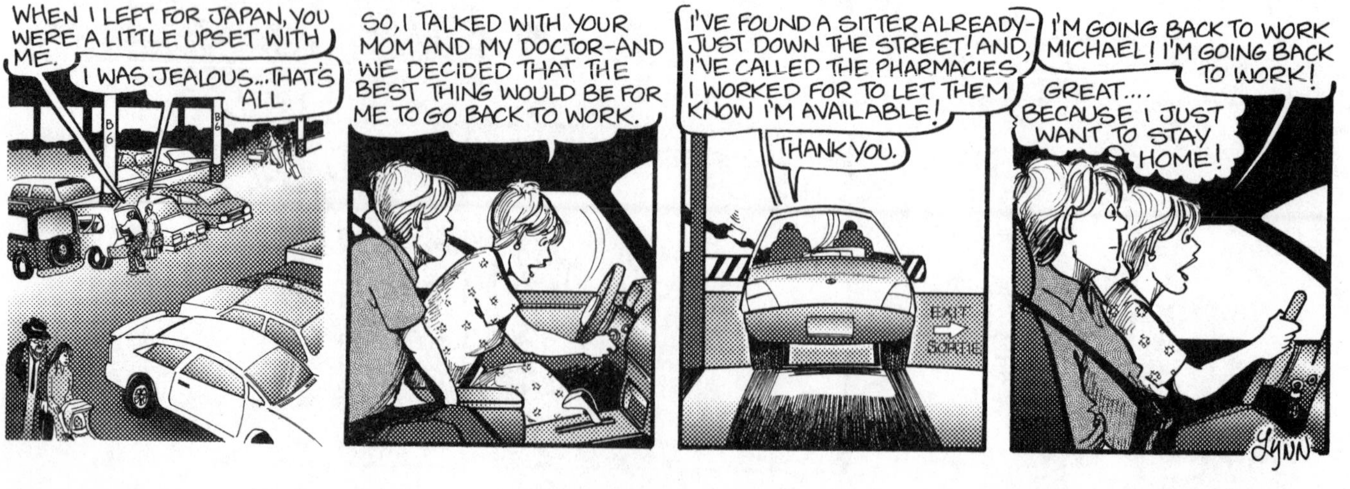
WHEN I LEFT FOR JAPAN, YOU WERE A LITTLE UPSET WITH ME.
I WAS JEALOUS...THAT'S ALL.
SO, I TALKED WITH YOUR MOM AND MY DOCTOR-AND WE DECIDED THAT THE BEST THING WOULD BE FOR ME TO GO BACK TO WORK.
I'VE FOUND A SITTER ALREADY-JUST DOWN THE STREET! AND, I'VE CALLED THE PHARMACIES I WORKED FOR TO LET THEM KNOW I'M AVAILABLE!
THANK YOU.
EXIT SORTIE
I'M GOING BACK TO WORK MICHAEL! I'M GOING BACK TO WORK!
GREAT.... BECAUSE I JUST WANT TO STAY HOME!
LYNN

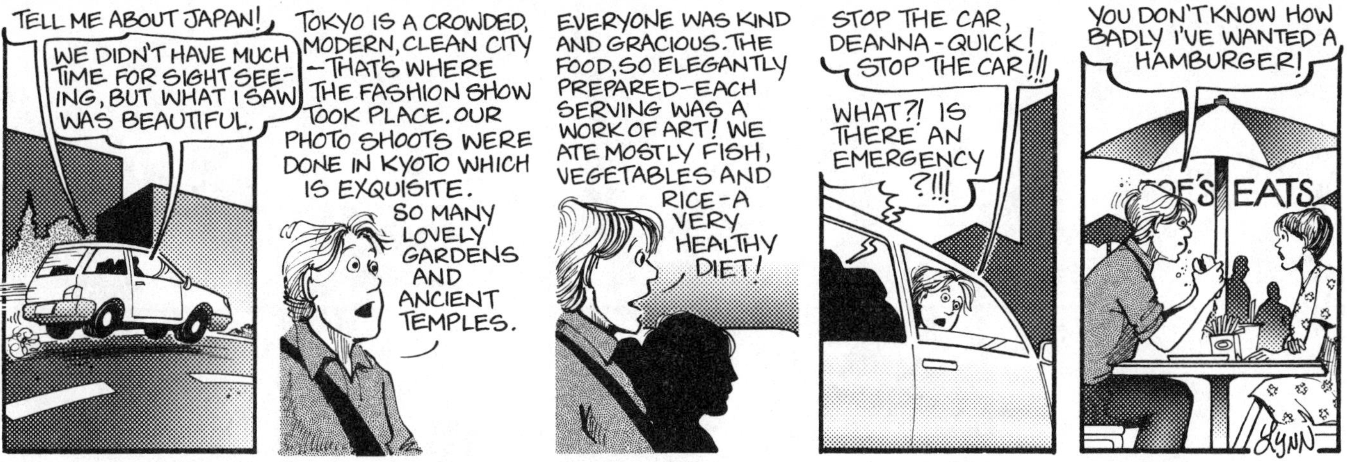
TELL ME ABOUT JAPAN!
WE DIDN'T HAVE MUCH TIME FOR SIGHT SEEING, BUT WHAT I SAW WAS BEAUTIFUL.
TOKYO IS A CROWDED, MODERN, CLEAN CITY — THAT'S WHERE THE FASHION SHOW TOOK PLACE. OUR PHOTO SHOOTS WERE DONE IN KYOTO WHICH IS EXQUISITE.
SO MANY LOVELY GARDENS AND ANCIENT TEMPLES.
EVERYONE WAS KIND AND GRACIOUS. THE FOOD, SO ELEGANTLY PREPARED—EACH SERVING WAS A WORK OF ART! WE ATE MOSTLY FISH, VEGETABLES AND RICE—A VERY HEALTHY DIET!
STOP THE CAR, DEANNA - QUICK! STOP THE CAR!!!
WHAT?! IS THERE AN EMERGENCY ?!!!
YOU DON'T KNOW HOW BADLY I'VE WANTED A HAMBURGER!
JOE'S EATS
LYNN

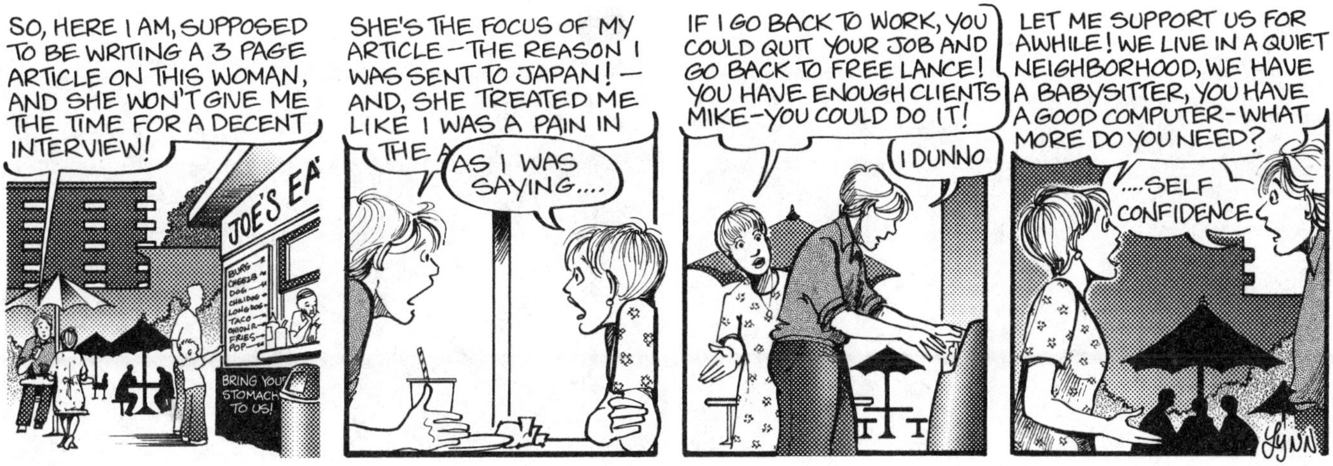
SO, HERE I AM, SUPPOSED TO BE WRITING A 3 PAGE ARTICLE ON THIS WOMAN, AND SHE WON'T GIVE ME THE TIME FOR A DECENT INTERVIEW!
JOE'S EA
BRING YOUR STOMACH TO US!
SHE'S THE FOCUS OF MY ARTICLE — THE REASON I WAS SENT TO JAPAN! — AND, SHE TREATED ME LIKE I WAS A PAIN IN THE A
AS I WAS SAYING....
IF I GO BACK TO WORK, YOU COULD QUIT YOUR JOB AND GO BACK TO FREE LANCE! YOU HAVE ENOUGH CLIENTS MIKE—YOU COULD DO IT!
I DUNNO
LET ME SUPPORT US FOR AWHILE! WE LIVE IN A QUIET NEIGHBORHOOD, WE HAVE A BABYSITTER, YOU HAVE A GOOD COMPUTER—WHAT MORE DO YOU NEED?
....SELF CONFIDENCE
LYNN

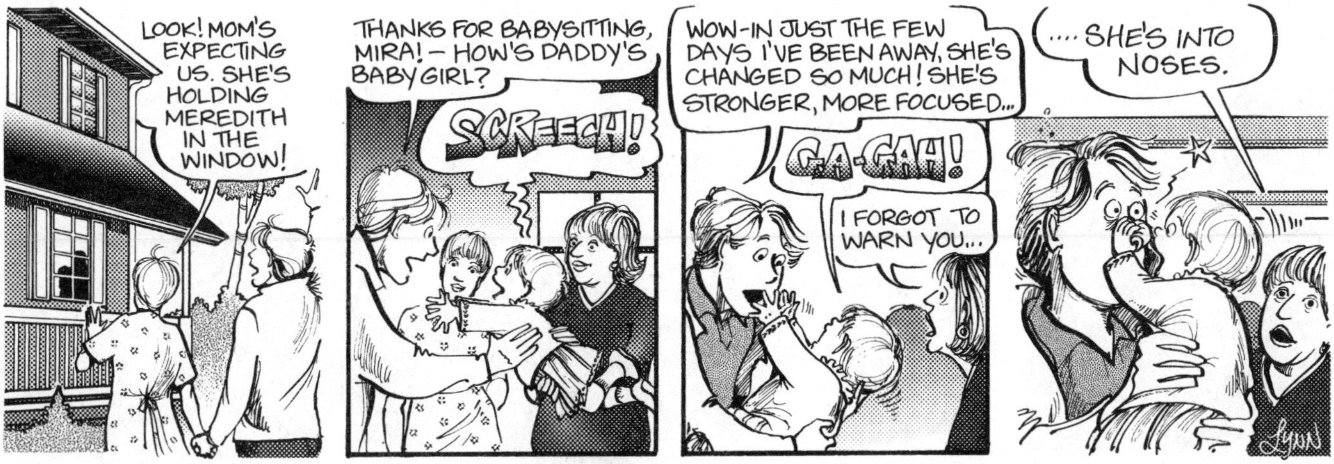
LOOK! MOM'S EXPECTING US. SHE'S HOLDING MEREDITH IN THE WINDOW!
THANKS FOR BABYSITTING, MIRA! — HOW'S DADDY'S BABY GIRL?
SCREECH!
WOW—IN JUST THE FEW DAYS I'VE BEEN AWAY, SHE'S CHANGED SO MUCH! SHE'S STRONGER, MORE FOCUSED...
GA-GAH!
I FORGOT TO WARN YOU...
.... SHE'S INTO NOSES.
LYNN

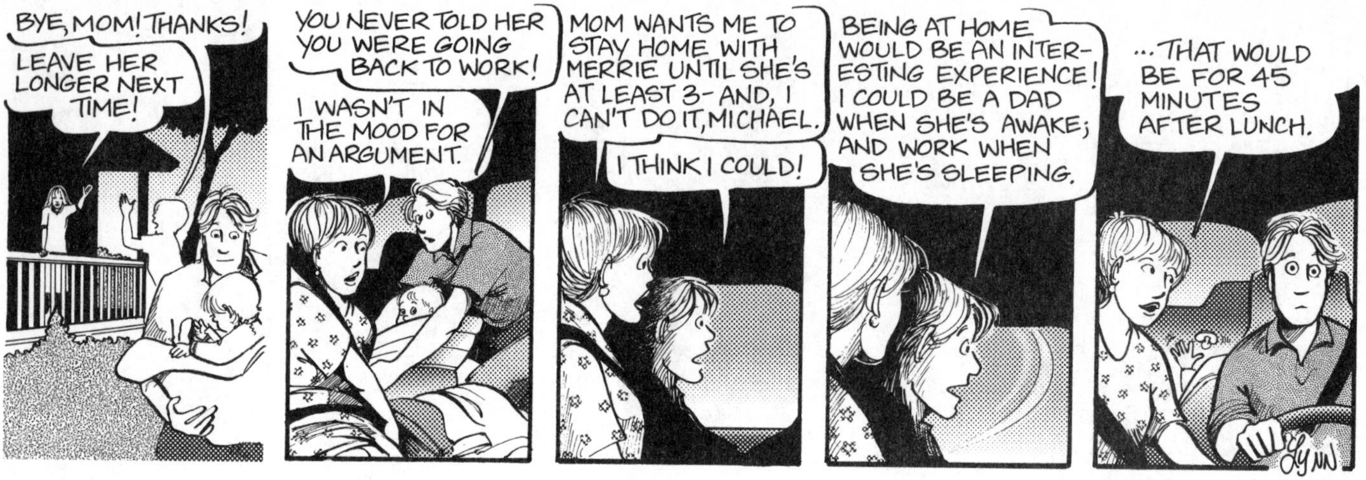
BYE, MOM! THANKS!
LEAVE HER LONGER NEXT TIME!
YOU NEVER TOLD HER YOU WERE GOING BACK TO WORK!
I WASN'T IN THE MOOD FOR AN ARGUMENT.
MOM WANTS ME TO STAY HOME WITH MERRIE UNTIL SHE'S AT LEAST 3- AND, I CAN'T DO IT, MICHAEL.
I THINK I COULD!
BEING AT HOME WOULD BE AN INTERESTING EXPERIENCE! I COULD BE A DAD WHEN SHE'S AWAKE; AND WORK WHEN SHE'S SLEEPING.
...THAT WOULD BE FOR 45 MINUTES AFTER LUNCH.
LYNN

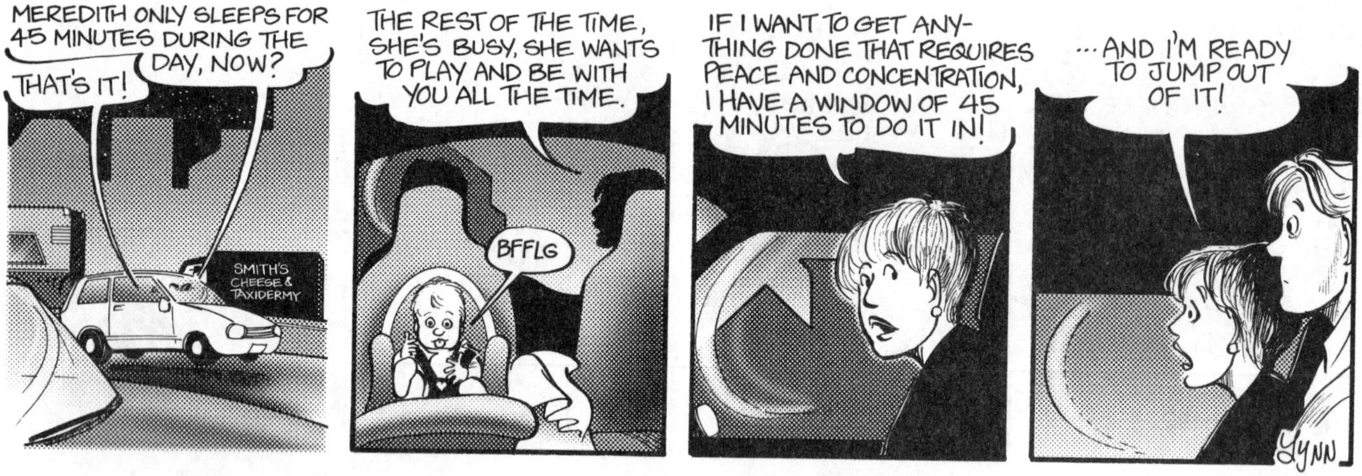
MEREDITH ONLY SLEEPS FOR 45 MINUTES DURING THE DAY, NOW?
THAT'S IT!
SMITH'S CHEESE & TAXIDERMY
THE REST OF THE TIME, SHE'S BUSY, SHE WANTS TO PLAY AND BE WITH YOU ALL THE TIME.
BFFLG
IF I WANT TO GET ANYTHING DONE THAT REQUIRES PEACE AND CONCENTRATION, I HAVE A WINDOW OF 45 MINUTES TO DO IT IN!
...AND I'M READY TO JUMP OUT OF IT!
LYNN

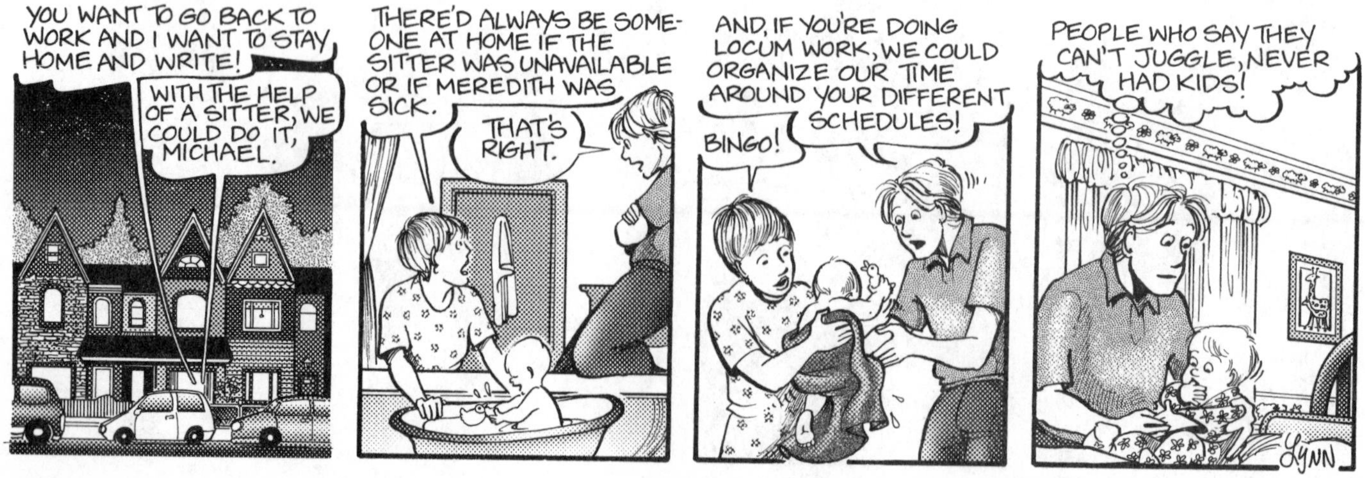
YOU WANT TO GO BACK TO WORK AND I WANT TO STAY HOME AND WRITE!
WITH THE HELP OF A SITTER, WE COULD DO IT, MICHAEL.
THERE'D ALWAYS BE SOMEONE AT HOME IF THE SITTER WAS UNAVAILABLE OR IF MEREDITH WAS SICK.
THAT'S RIGHT.
AND, IF YOU'RE DOING LOCUM WORK, WE COULD ORGANIZE OUR TIME AROUND YOUR DIFFERENT SCHEDULES!
BINGO!
PEOPLE WHO SAY THEY CAN'T JUGGLE, NEVER HAD KIDS!
LYNN

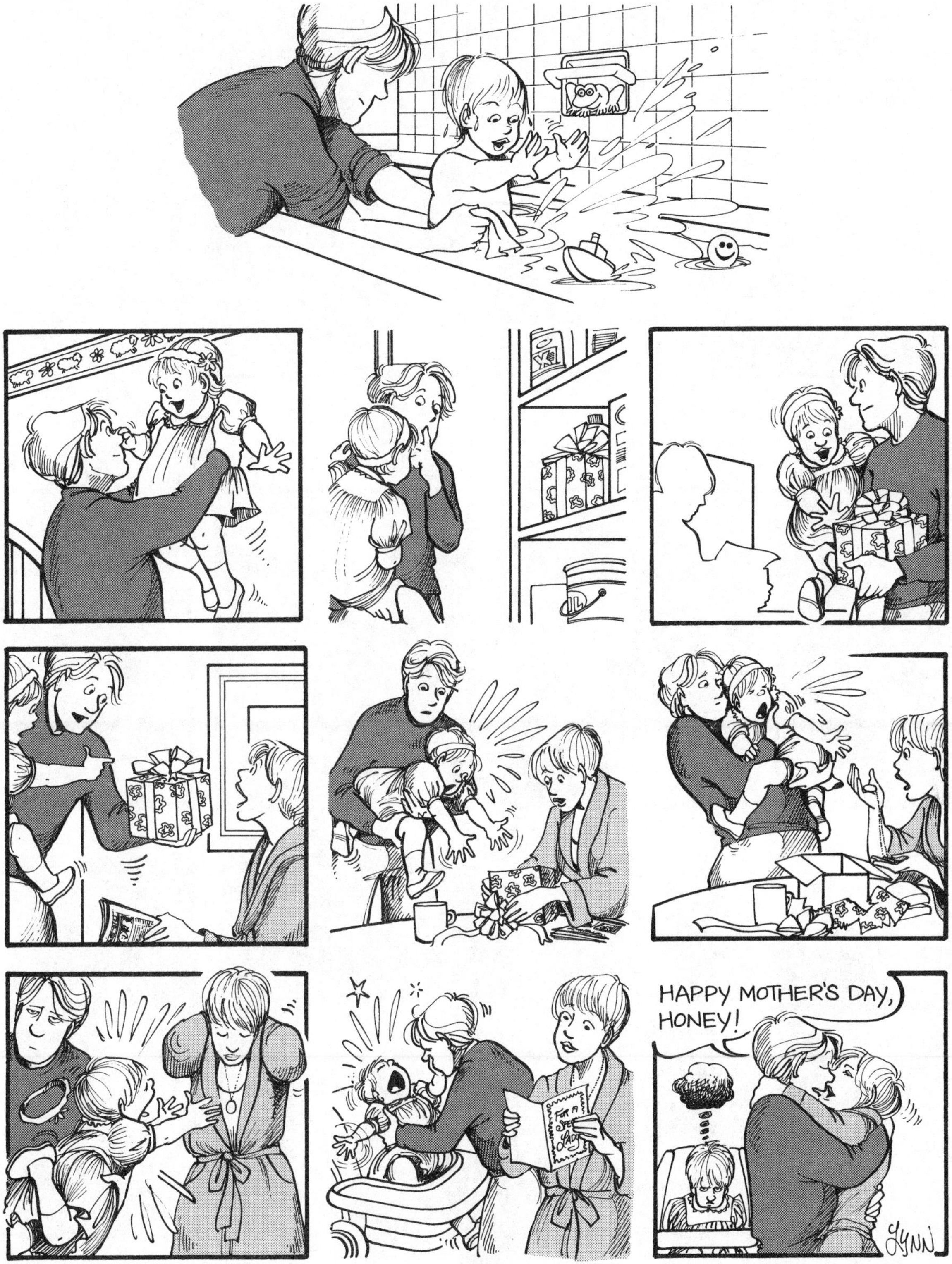
HAPPY MOTHER'S DAY,
HONEY!

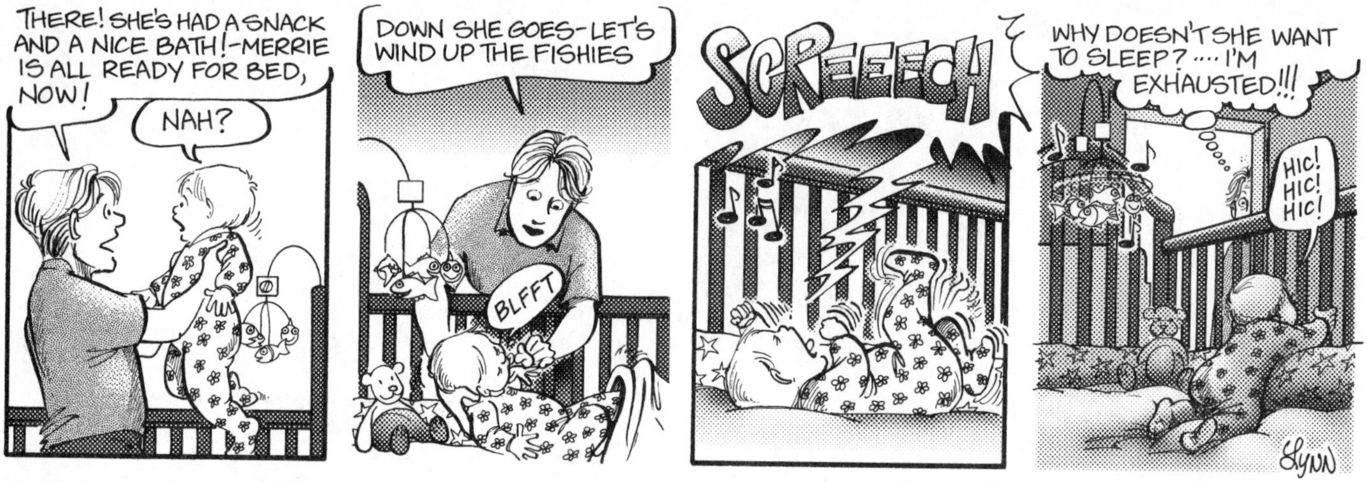
THERE! SHE'S HAD A SNACK AND A NICE BATH!-MERRIE IS ALL READY FOR BED, NOW!
NAH?
DOWN SHE GOES-LET'S WIND UP THE FISHIES
BLFFT
SCREEECH
WHY DOESN'T SHE WANT TO SLEEP? .... I'M EXHAUSTED!!!
HIC! HIC! HIC!
LYNN

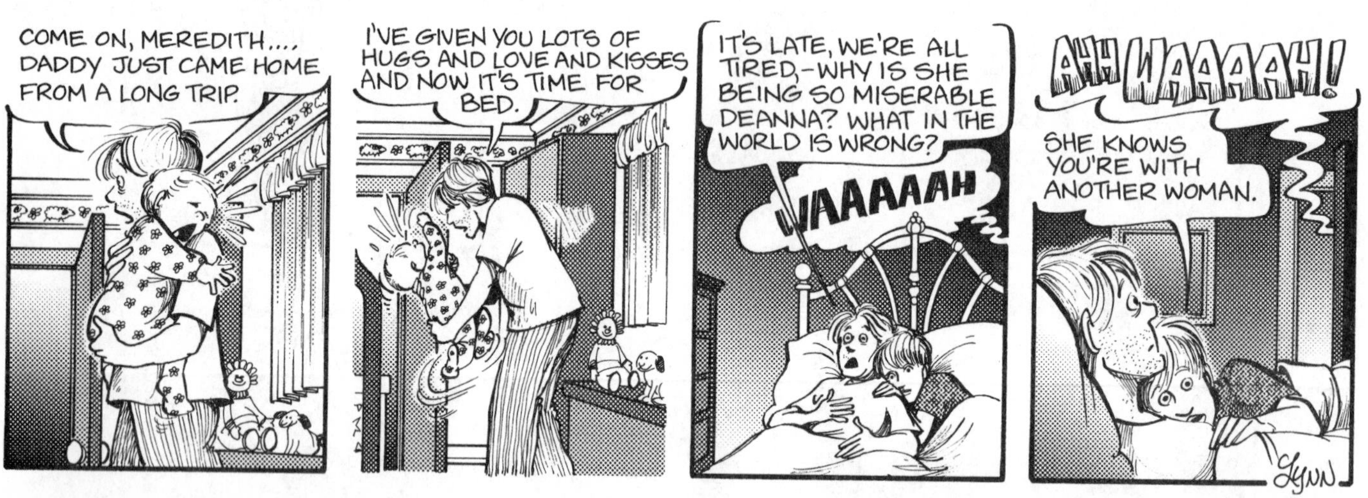
COME ON, MEREDITH...., DADDY JUST CAME HOME FROM A LONG TRIP.
I'VE GIVEN YOU LOTS OF HUGS AND LOVE AND KISSES AND NOW IT'S TIME FOR BED.
IT'S LATE, WE'RE ALL TIRED,-WHY IS SHE BEING SO MISERABLE DEANNA? WHAT IN THE WORLD IS WRONG?
WAAAAAH
AHH WAAAAAH!
SHE KNOWS YOU'RE WITH ANOTHER WOMAN.
LYNN

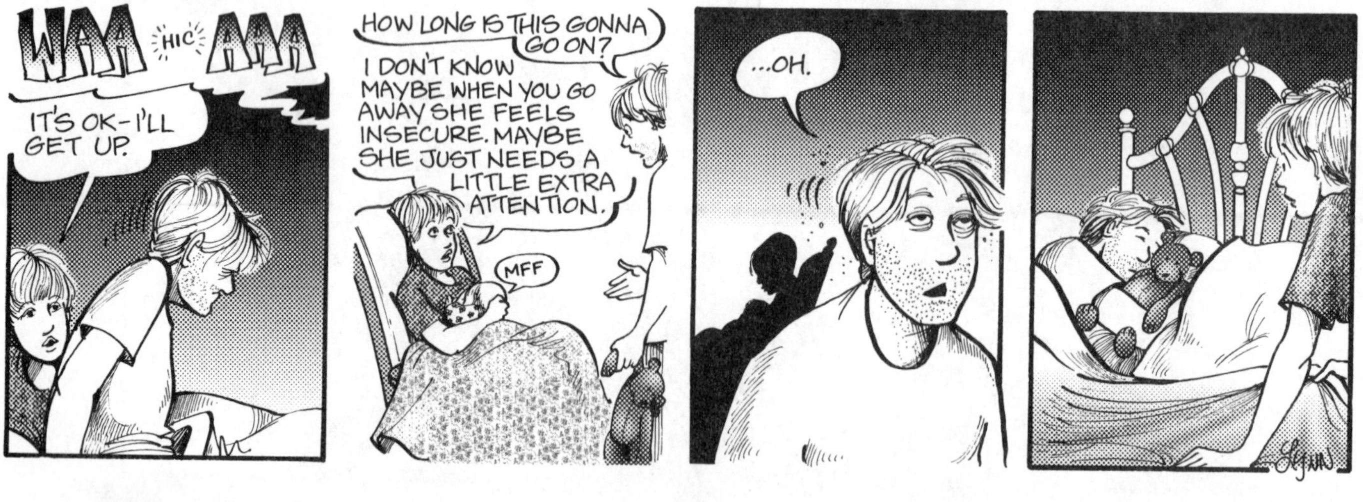
WAA HIC AAA
IT'S OK-I'LL GET UP.
HOW LONG IS THIS GONNA GO ON?
I DON'T KNOW MAYBE WHEN YOU GO AWAY SHE FEELS INSECURE. MAYBE SHE JUST NEEDS A LITTLE EXTRA ATTENTION.
MFF
...OH.
LYNN

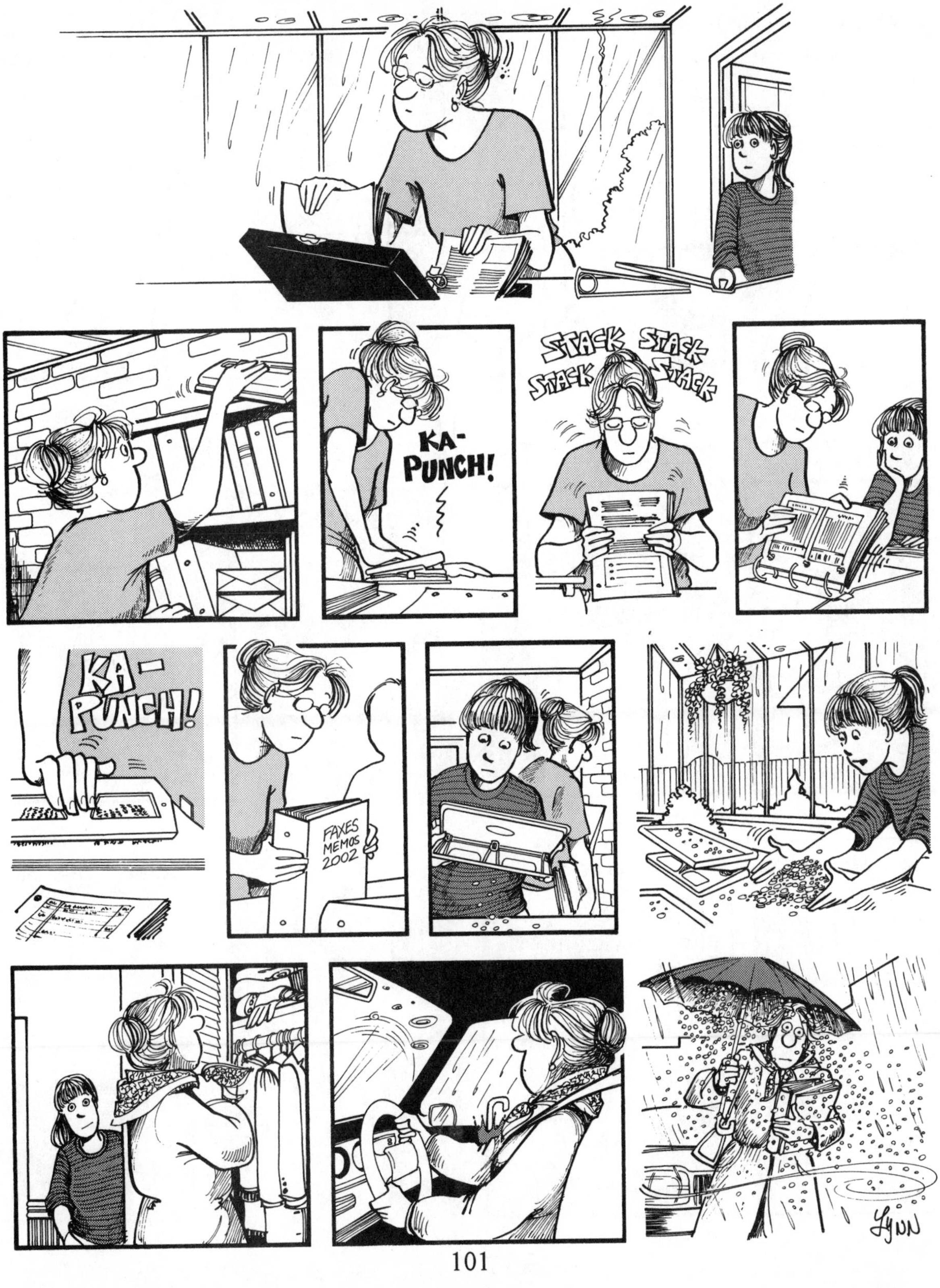
KA-
PUNCH!
STACK STACK
STACK STACK
KA-
PUNCH!
FAXES
MEMOS
2002
LYNN

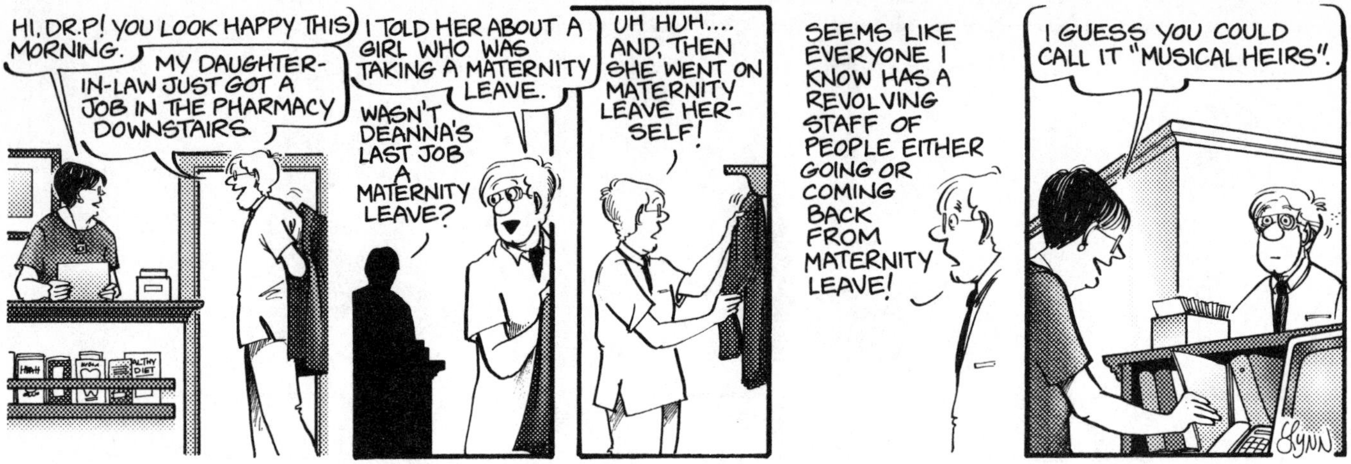
HI, DR.P! YOU LOOK HAPPY THIS MORNING.
MY DAUGHTER-IN-LAW JUST GOT A JOB IN THE PHARMACY DOWNSTAIRS.
I TOLD HER ABOUT A GIRL WHO WAS TAKING A MATERNITY LEAVE.
WASN'T DEANNA'S LAST JOB A MATERNITY LEAVE?
UH HUH.... AND, THEN SHE WENT ON MATERNITY LEAVE HER-SELF!
SEEMS LIKE EVERYONE I KNOW HAS A REVOLVING STAFF OF PEOPLE EITHER GOING OR COMING BACK FROM MATERNITY LEAVE!
I GUESS YOU COULD CALL IT "MUSICAL HEIRS".
LYNN

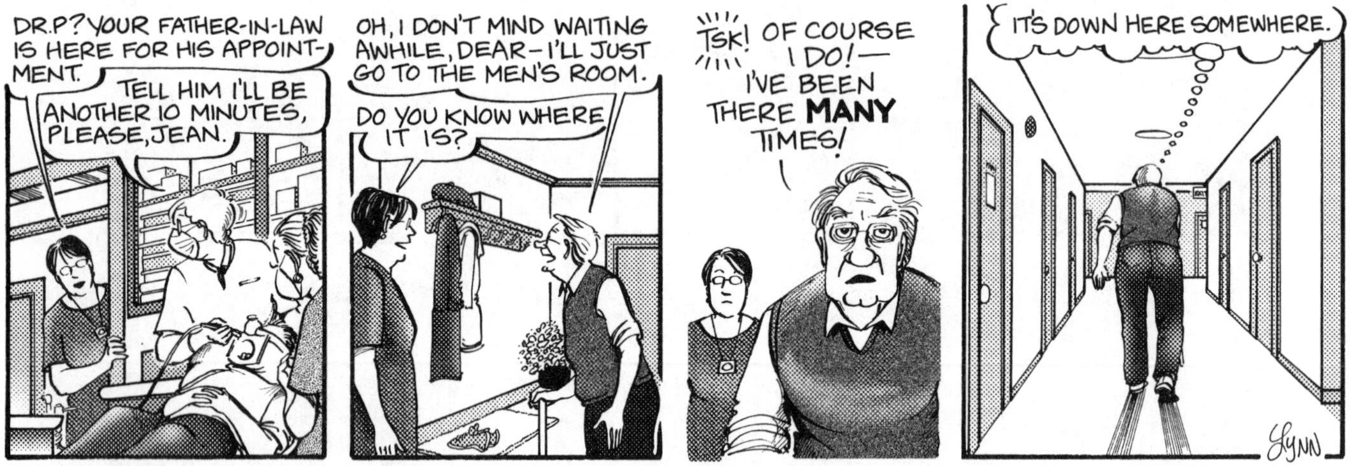
DR.P? YOUR FATHER-IN-LAW IS HERE FOR HIS APPOINT-MENT.
TELL HIM I'LL BE ANOTHER 10 MINUTES, PLEASE, JEAN.
OH, I DON'T MIND WAITING AWHILE, DEAR– I'LL JUST GO TO THE MEN'S ROOM.
DO YOU KNOW WHERE IT IS?
TSK!
OF COURSE I DO!— I'VE BEEN THERE **MANY** TIMES!
IT'S DOWN HERE SOMEWHERE.
LYNN

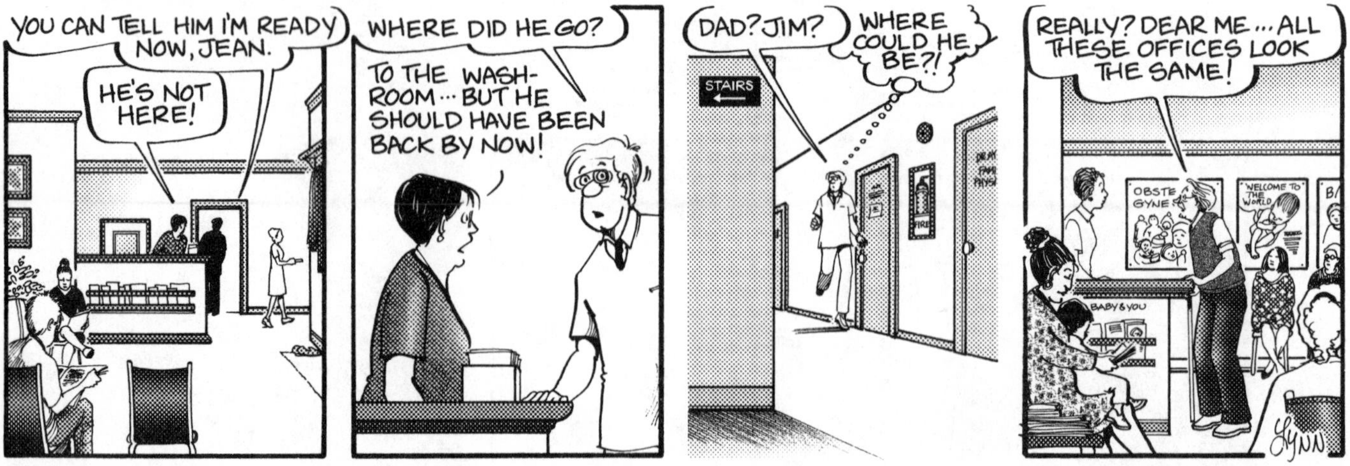
YOU CAN TELL HIM I'M READY NOW, JEAN.
HE'S NOT HERE!
WHERE DID HE GO?
TO THE WASH-ROOM ... BUT HE SHOULD HAVE BEEN BACK BY NOW!
DAD? JIM?
WHERE COULD HE BE?!
STAIRS
REALLY? DEAR ME ... ALL THESE OFFICES LOOK THE SAME!
LYNN

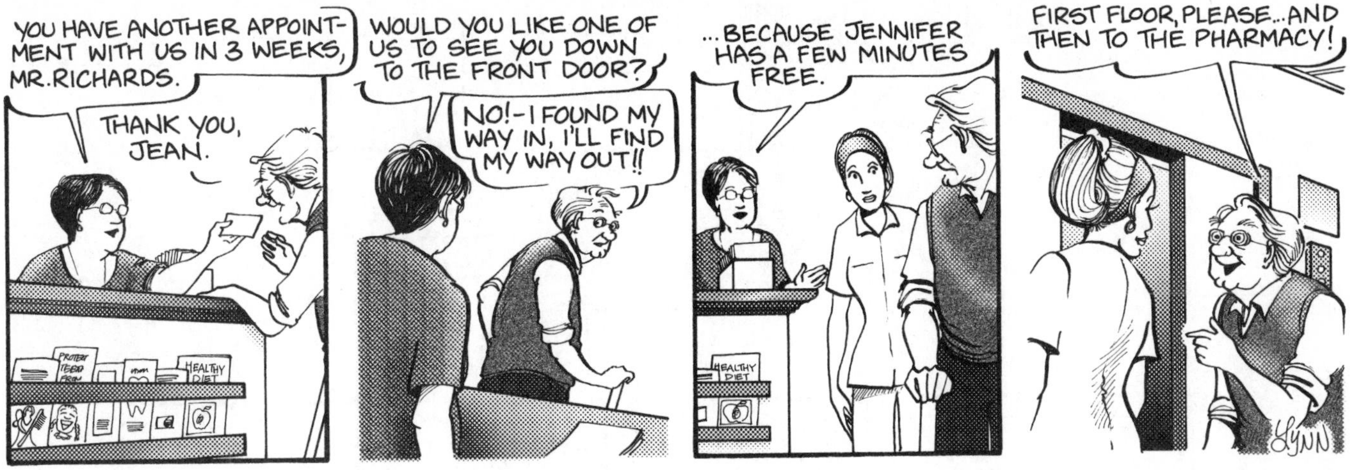
YOU HAVE ANOTHER APPOINT-MENT WITH US IN 3 WEEKS, MR. RICHARDS.
THANK YOU, JEAN.
WOULD YOU LIKE ONE OF US TO SEE YOU DOWN TO THE FRONT DOOR?
NO!-I FOUND MY WAY IN, I'LL FIND MY WAY OUT!!
...BECAUSE JENNIFER HAS A FEW MINUTES FREE.
HEALTHY DIET
FIRST FLOOR, PLEASE...AND THEN TO THE PHARMACY!
LYNN

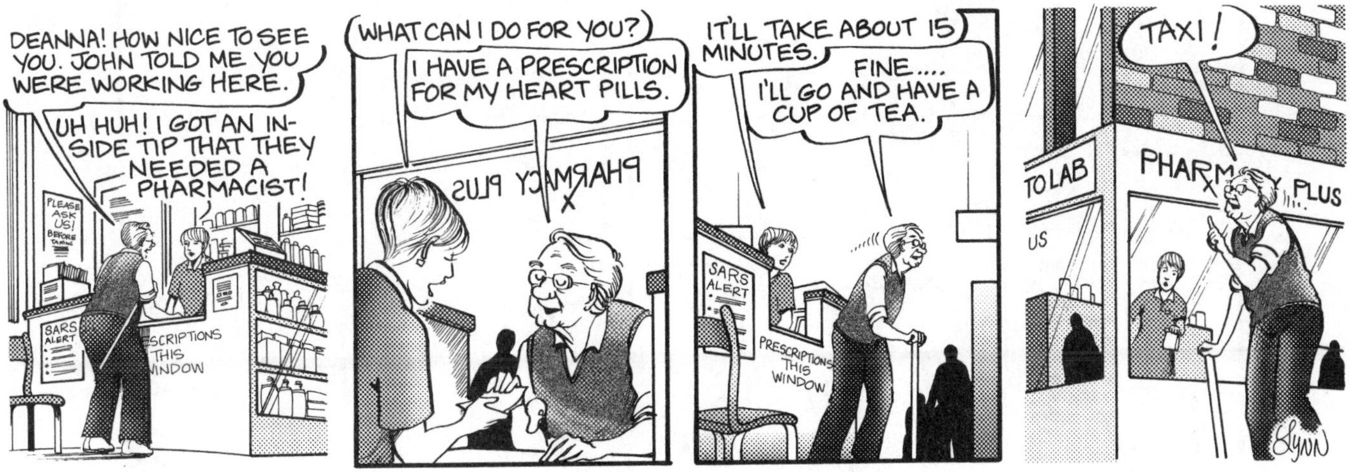
DEANNA! HOW NICE TO SEE YOU. JOHN TOLD ME YOU WERE WORKING HERE.
UH HUH! I GOT AN IN-SIDE TIP THAT THEY NEEDED A PHARMACIST!
SARS ALERT
PRESCRIPTIONS THIS WINDOW
WHAT CAN I DO FOR YOU?
I HAVE A PRESCRIPTION FOR MY HEART PILLS.
PHARMACY PLUS
IT'LL TAKE ABOUT 15 MINUTES.
FINE.... I'LL GO AND HAVE A CUP OF TEA.
SARS ALERT
PRESCRIPTIONS THIS WINDOW
TAXI!
TO LAB
PHARM PLUS
LYNN

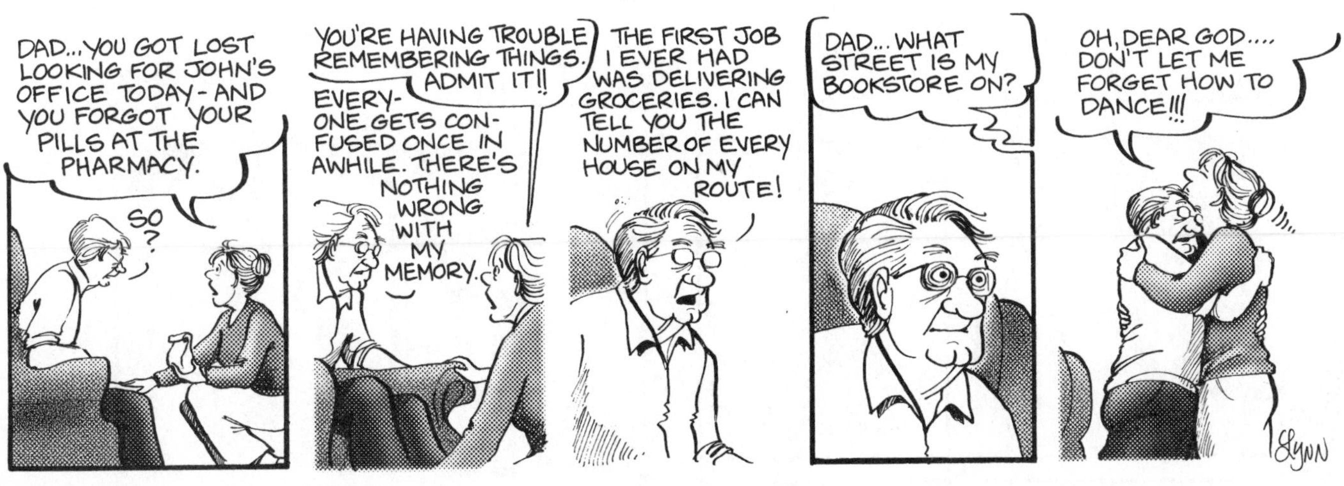
DAD...YOU GOT LOST LOOKING FOR JOHN'S OFFICE TODAY - AND YOU FORGOT YOUR PILLS AT THE PHARMACY.
SO?
YOU'RE HAVING TROUBLE REMEMBERING THINGS. ADMIT IT!!
EVERY-ONE GETS CON-FUSED ONCE IN AWHILE. THERE'S NOTHING WRONG WITH MY MEMORY.
THE FIRST JOB I EVER HAD WAS DELIVERING GROCERIES. I CAN TELL YOU THE NUMBER OF EVERY HOUSE ON MY ROUTE!
DAD... WHAT STREET IS MY BOOKSTORE ON?
OH, DEAR GOD.... DON'T LET ME FORGET HOW TO DANCE!!!
LYNN

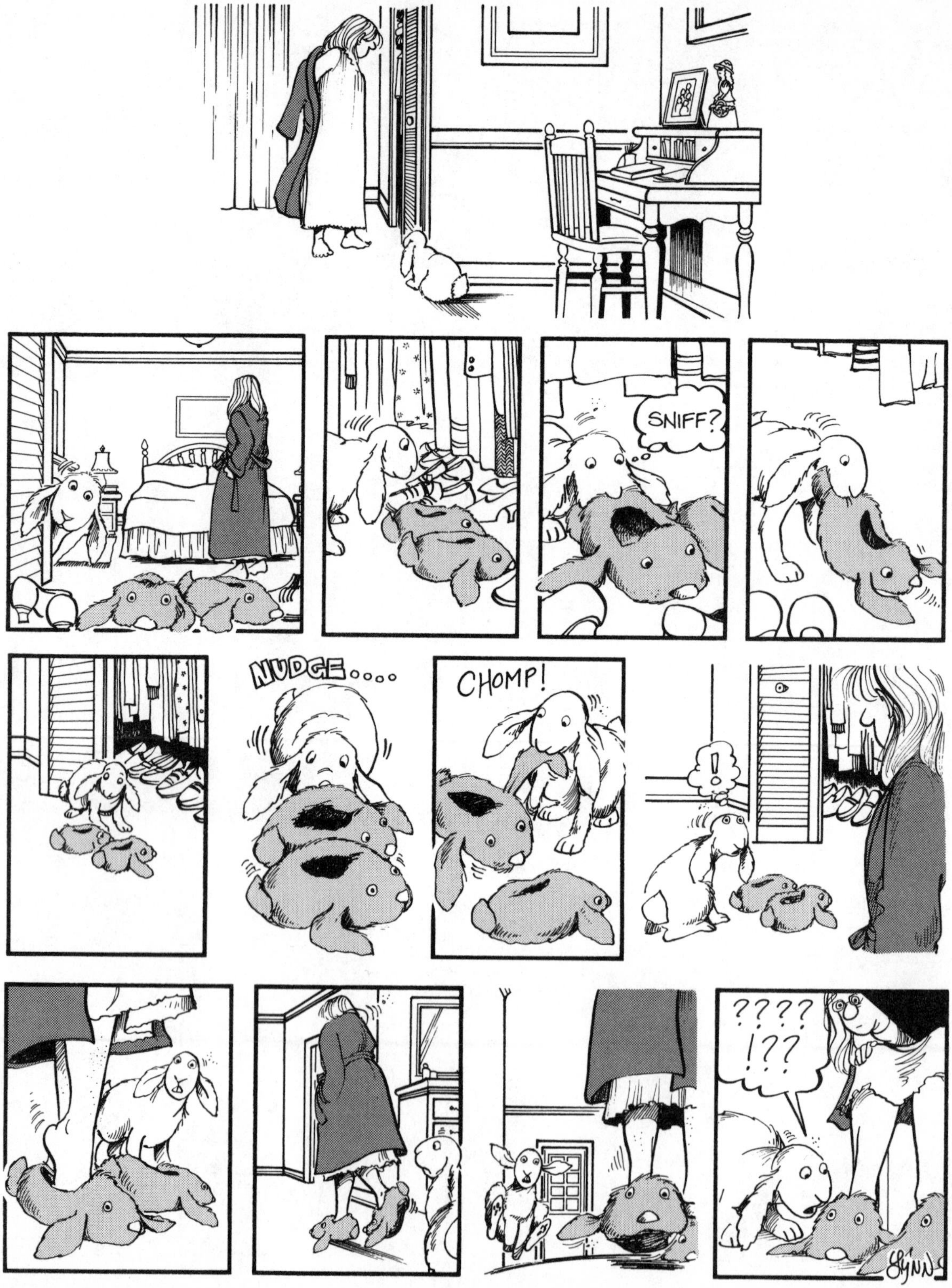
SNIFF?
NUDGE....
CHOMP!
!
????
!??
LYNN

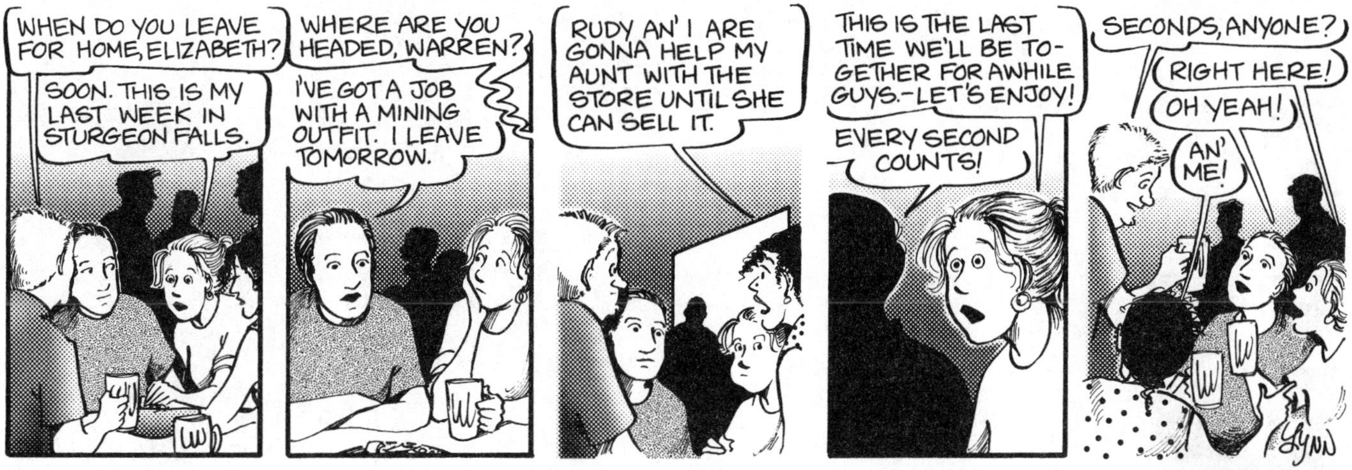
WHEN DO YOU LEAVE FOR HOME, ELIZABETH?
SOON. THIS IS MY LAST WEEK IN STURGEON FALLS.
WHERE ARE YOU HEADED, WARREN?
I'VE GOT A JOB WITH A MINING OUTFIT. I LEAVE TOMORROW.
RUDY AN' I ARE GONNA HELP MY AUNT WITH THE STORE UNTIL SHE CAN SELL IT.
THIS IS THE LAST TIME WE'LL BE TO-GETHER FOR AWHILE GUYS.-LET'S ENJOY!
EVERY SECOND COUNTS!
SECONDS, ANYONE?
RIGHT HERE!
OH YEAH!
AN' ME!
LYNN

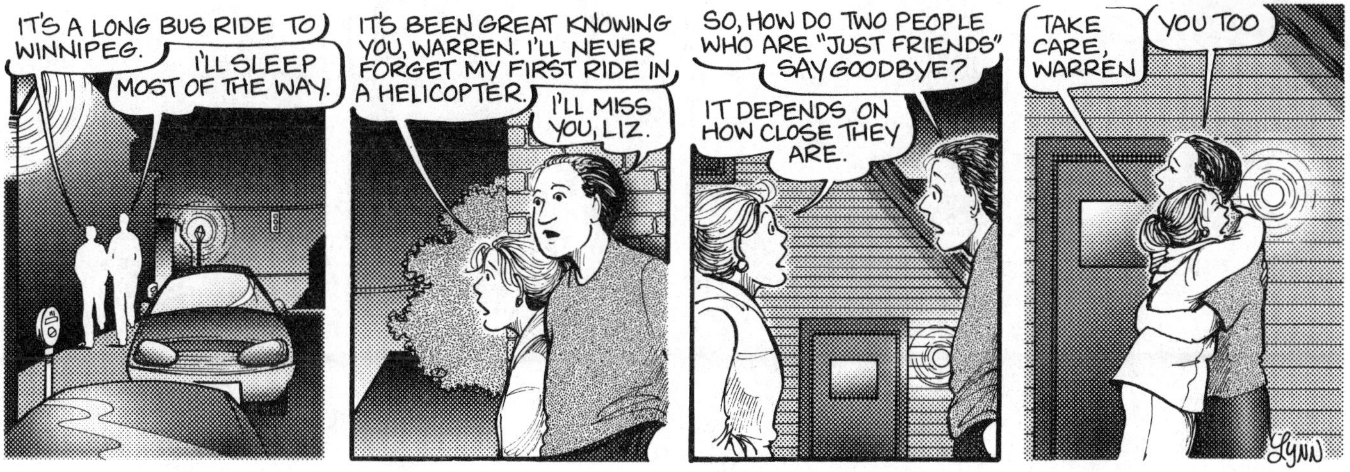
IT'S A LONG BUS RIDE TO WINNIPEG.
I'LL SLEEP MOST OF THE WAY.
IT'S BEEN GREAT KNOWING YOU, WARREN. I'LL NEVER FORGET MY FIRST RIDE IN A HELICOPTER.
I'LL MISS YOU, LIZ.
SO, HOW DO TWO PEOPLE WHO ARE "JUST FRIENDS" SAY GOODBYE?
IT DEPENDS ON HOW CLOSE THEY ARE.
TAKE CARE, WARREN
YOU TOO
LYNN

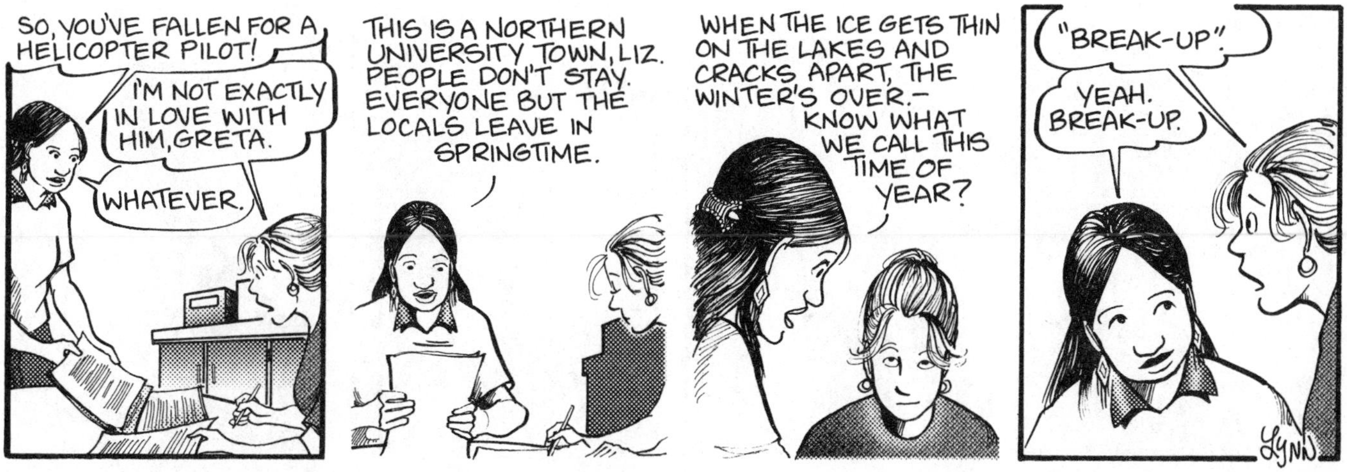
SO, YOU'VE FALLEN FOR A HELICOPTER PILOT!
I'M NOT EXACTLY IN LOVE WITH HIM, GRETA.
WHATEVER.
THIS IS A NORTHERN UNIVERSITY TOWN, LIZ. PEOPLE DON'T STAY. EVERYONE BUT THE LOCALS LEAVE IN SPRINGTIME.
WHEN THE ICE GETS THIN ON THE LAKES AND CRACKS APART, THE WINTER'S OVER.–
KNOW WHAT WE CALL THIS TIME OF YEAR?
"BREAK-UP".
YEAH. BREAK-UP.
LYNN

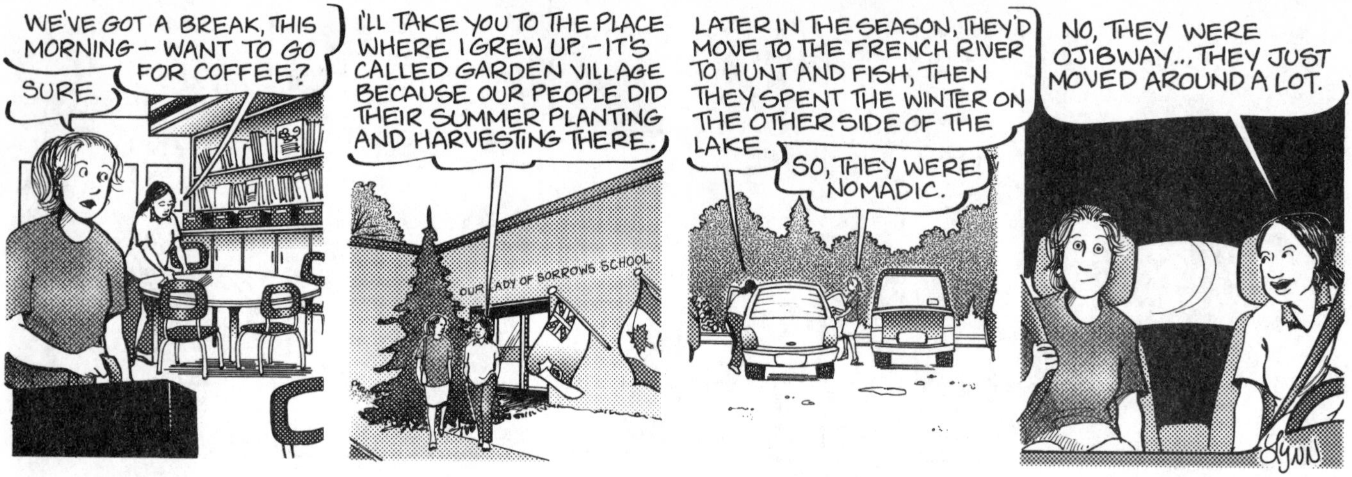
WE'VE GOT A BREAK, THIS MORNING – WANT TO GO FOR COFFEE?
SURE.
I'LL TAKE YOU TO THE PLACE WHERE I GREW UP. – IT'S CALLED GARDEN VILLAGE BECAUSE OUR PEOPLE DID THEIR SUMMER PLANTING AND HARVESTING THERE.
OUR LADY OF SORROWS SCHOOL
LATER IN THE SEASON, THEY'D MOVE TO THE FRENCH RIVER TO HUNT AND FISH, THEN THEY SPENT THE WINTER ON THE OTHER SIDE OF THE LAKE.
SO, THEY WERE NOMADIC.
NO, THEY WERE OJIBWAY... THEY JUST MOVED AROUND A LOT.
LYNN

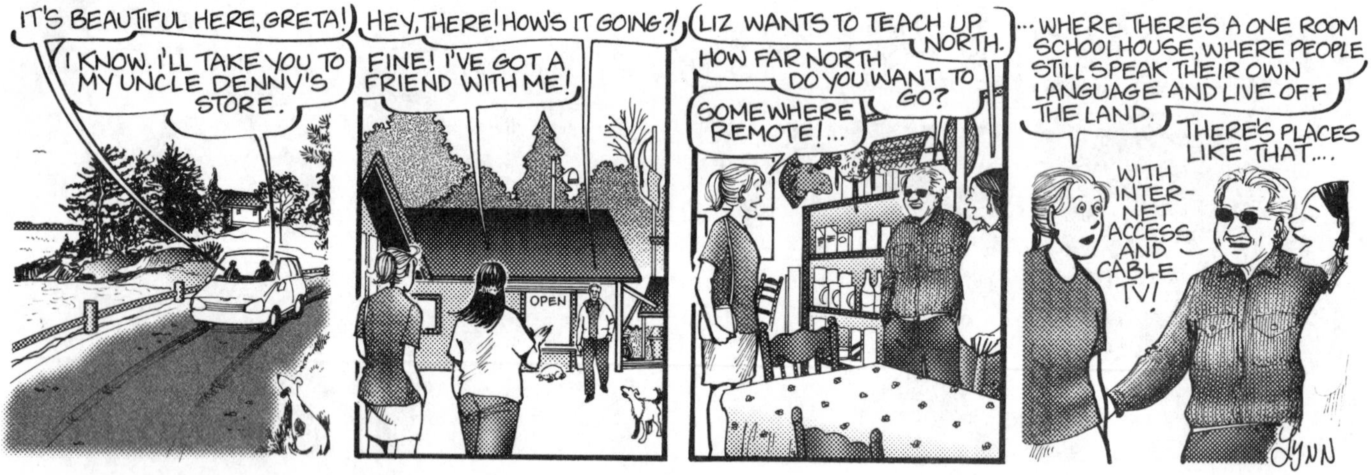
IT'S BEAUTIFUL HERE, GRETA!
I KNOW. I'LL TAKE YOU TO MY UNCLE DENNY'S STORE.
HEY, THERE! HOW'S IT GOING?!
FINE! I'VE GOT A FRIEND WITH ME!
OPEN
LIZ WANTS TO TEACH UP NORTH.
HOW FAR NORTH DO YOU WANT TO GO?
SOMEWHERE REMOTE!...
...WHERE THERE'S A ONE ROOM SCHOOLHOUSE, WHERE PEOPLE STILL SPEAK THEIR OWN LANGUAGE AND LIVE OFF THE LAND.
THERE'S PLACES LIKE THAT....
WITH INTERNET ACCESS AND CABLE TV!
LYNN

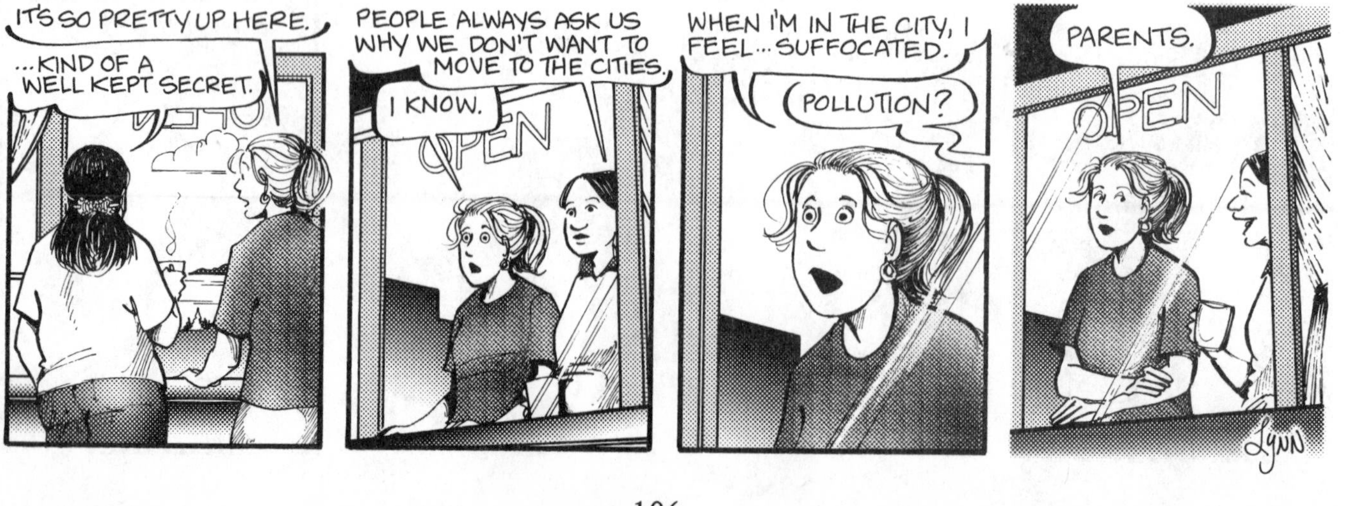
IT'S SO PRETTY UP HERE.
...KIND OF A WELL KEPT SECRET.
PEOPLE ALWAYS ASK US WHY WE DON'T WANT TO MOVE TO THE CITIES.
I KNOW.
OPEN
WHEN I'M IN THE CITY, I FEEL... SUFFOCATED.
POLLUTION?
PARENTS.
OPEN
LYNN

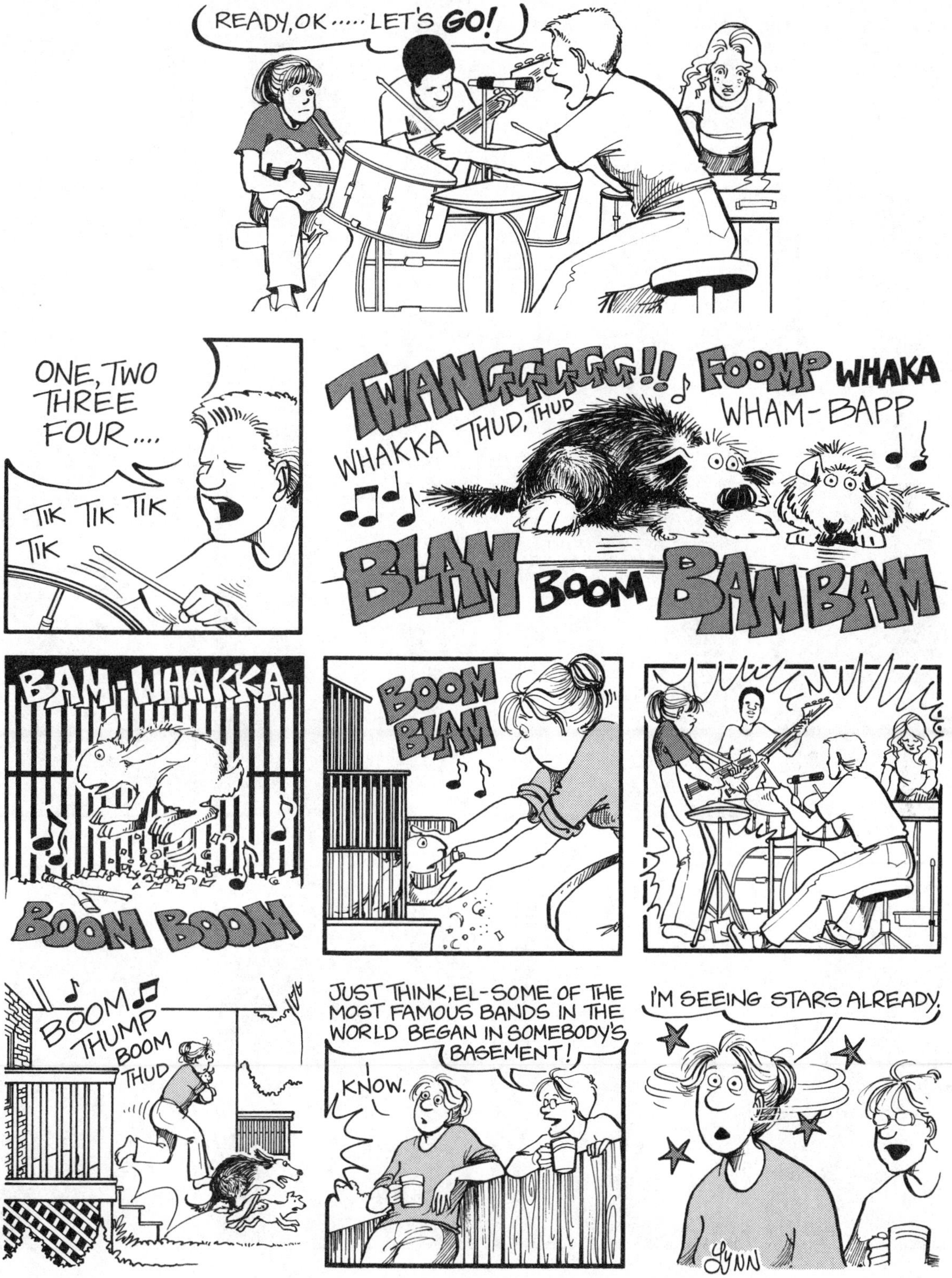
READY, OK..... LET'S GO!
ONE, TWO THREE FOUR....
TIK TIK TIK TIK
TWANGGGGG!! FOOMP WHAKA
WHAKKA THUD, THUD
WHAM-BAPP
BLAM BOOM BAMBAM
BAM-WHAKKA
BOOM BOOM
BOOM BLAM
BOOM THUMP BOOM THUD
JUST THINK, EL-SOME OF THE MOST FAMOUS BANDS IN THE WORLD BEGAN IN SOMEBODY'S BASEMENT!
I KNOW.
I'M SEEING STARS ALREADY.
LYNN

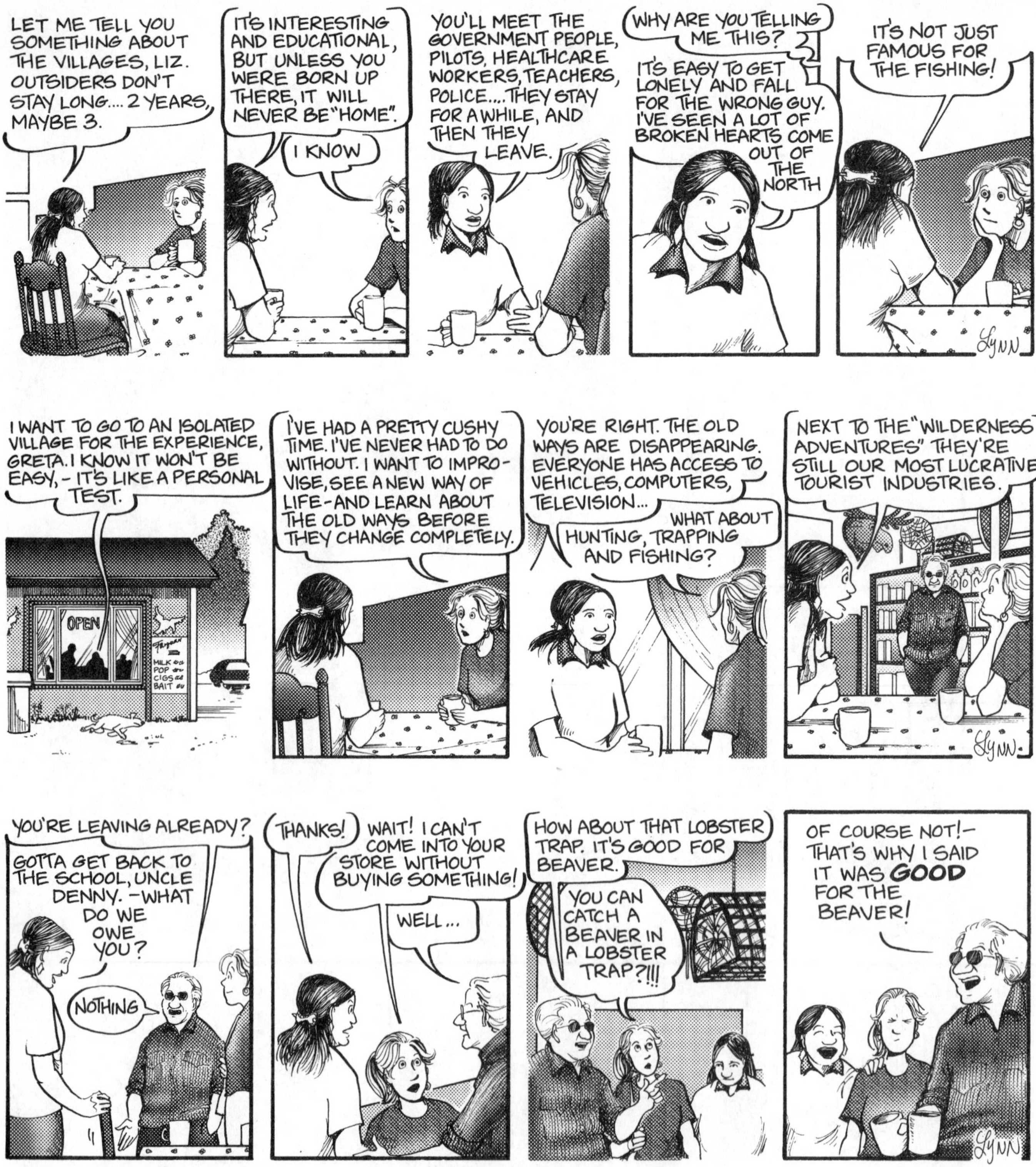
LET ME TELL YOU SOMETHING ABOUT THE VILLAGES, LIZ. OUTSIDERS DON'T STAY LONG.... 2 YEARS, MAYBE 3.
IT'S INTERESTING AND EDUCATIONAL, BUT UNLESS YOU WERE BORN UP THERE, IT WILL NEVER BE "HOME".
I KNOW
YOU'LL MEET THE GOVERNMENT PEOPLE, PILOTS, HEALTHCARE WORKERS, TEACHERS, POLICE.... THEY STAY FOR A WHILE, AND THEN THEY LEAVE.
WHY ARE YOU TELLING ME THIS?
IT'S EASY TO GET LONELY AND FALL FOR THE WRONG GUY. I'VE SEEN A LOT OF BROKEN HEARTS COME OUT OF THE NORTH
IT'S NOT JUST FAMOUS FOR THE FISHING!
LYNN
I WANT TO GO TO AN ISOLATED VILLAGE FOR THE EXPERIENCE, GRETA. I KNOW IT WON'T BE EASY, - IT'S LIKE A PERSONAL TEST.
OPEN
MILK
POP
CIGS
BAIT
I'VE HAD A PRETTY CUSHY TIME. I'VE NEVER HAD TO DO WITHOUT. I WANT TO IMPROVISE, SEE A NEW WAY OF LIFE - AND LEARN ABOUT THE OLD WAYS BEFORE THEY CHANGE COMPLETELY.
YOU'RE RIGHT. THE OLD WAYS ARE DISAPPEARING. EVERYONE HAS ACCESS TO VEHICLES, COMPUTERS, TELEVISION...
WHAT ABOUT HUNTING, TRAPPING AND FISHING?
NEXT TO THE "WILDERNESS ADVENTURES" THEY'RE STILL OUR MOST LUCRATIVE TOURIST INDUSTRIES.
LYNN
YOU'RE LEAVING ALREADY?
GOTTA GET BACK TO THE SCHOOL, UNCLE DENNY. - WHAT DO WE OWE YOU?
NOTHING
THANKS!
WAIT! I CAN'T COME INTO YOUR STORE WITHOUT BUYING SOMETHING!
WELL...
HOW ABOUT THAT LOBSTER TRAP. IT'S GOOD FOR BEAVER.
YOU CAN CATCH A BEAVER IN A LOBSTER TRAP?!!!
OF COURSE NOT! - THAT'S WHY I SAID IT WAS **GOOD** FOR THE BEAVER!
LYNN

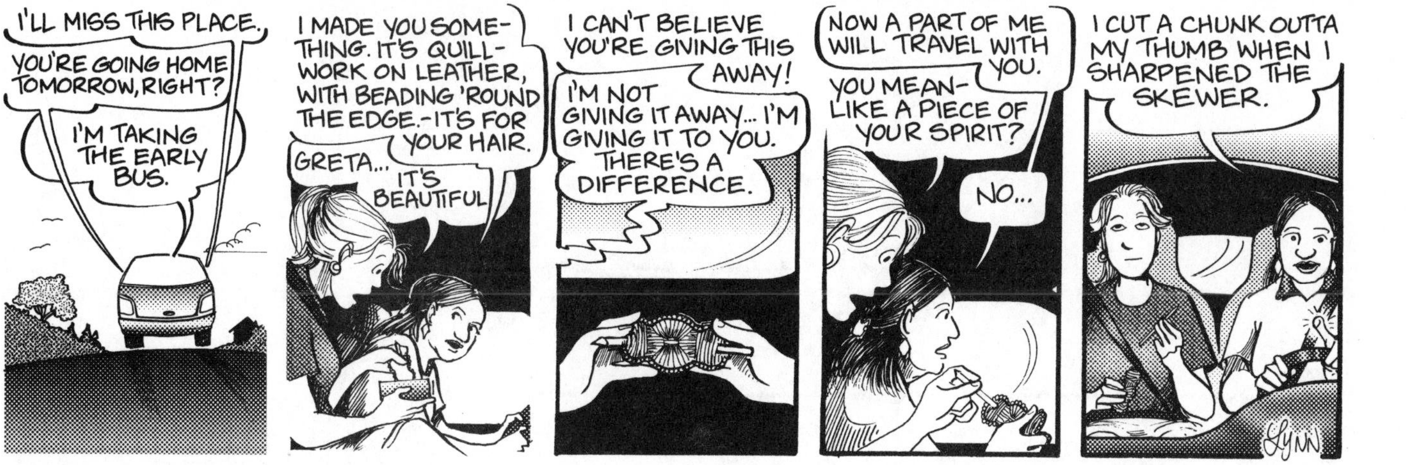
I'LL MISS THIS PLACE.
YOU'RE GOING HOME TOMORROW, RIGHT?
I'M TAKING THE EARLY BUS.
I MADE YOU SOMETHING. IT'S QUILL-WORK ON LEATHER, WITH BEADING 'ROUND THE EDGE.-IT'S FOR YOUR HAIR.
GRETA... IT'S BEAUTIFUL
I CAN'T BELIEVE YOU'RE GIVING THIS AWAY!
I'M NOT GIVING IT AWAY... I'M GIVING IT TO YOU. THERE'S A DIFFERENCE.
NOW A PART OF ME WILL TRAVEL WITH YOU.
YOU MEAN- LIKE A PIECE OF YOUR SPIRIT?
NO...
I CUT A CHUNK OUTTA MY THUMB WHEN I SHARPENED THE SKEWER.
LYNN

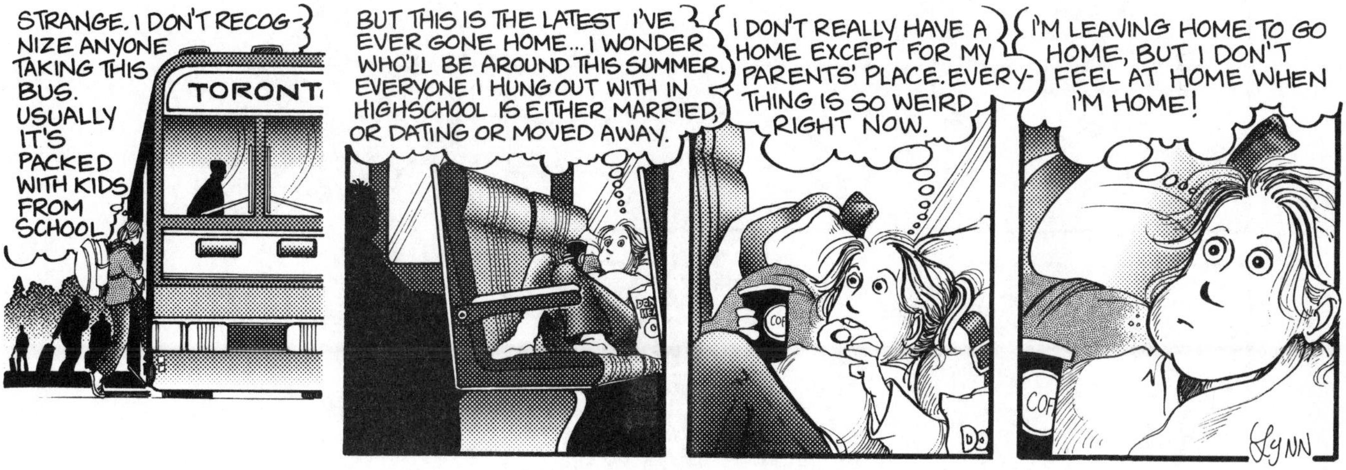
STRANGE. I DON'T RECOGNIZE ANYONE TAKING THIS BUS. USUALLY IT'S PACKED WITH KIDS FROM SCHOOL.
TORONT
BUT THIS IS THE LATEST I'VE EVER GONE HOME... I WONDER WHO'LL BE AROUND THIS SUMMER. EVERYONE I HUNG OUT WITH IN HIGHSCHOOL IS EITHER MARRIED, OR DATING OR MOVED AWAY.
I DON'T REALLY HAVE A HOME EXCEPT FOR MY PARENTS' PLACE. EVERYTHING IS SO WEIRD RIGHT NOW.
I'M LEAVING HOME TO GO HOME, BUT I DON'T FEEL AT HOME WHEN I'M HOME!
LYNN

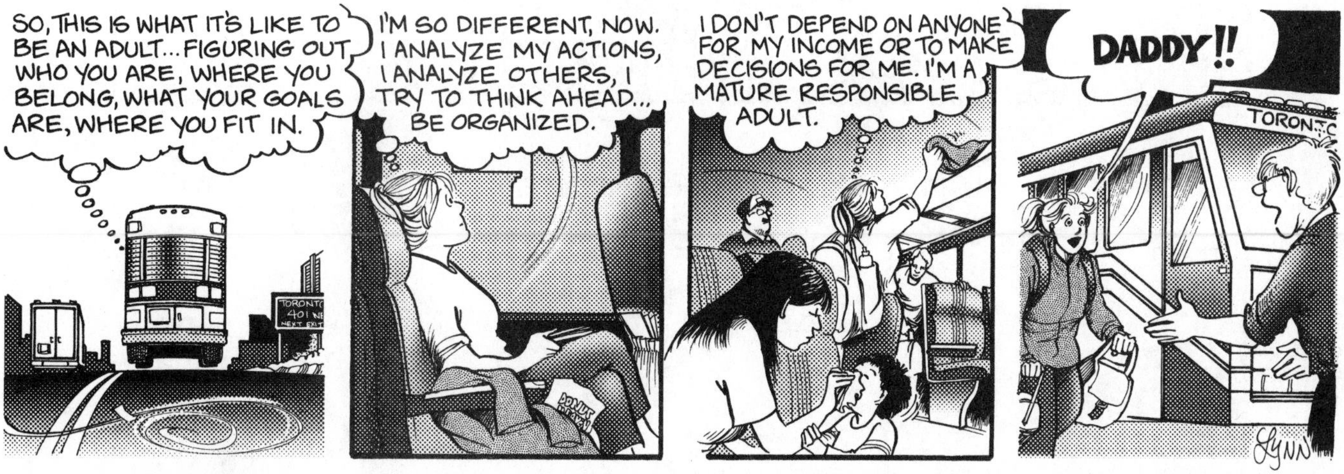
SO, THIS IS WHAT IT'S LIKE TO BE AN ADULT... FIGURING OUT WHO YOU ARE, WHERE YOU BELONG, WHAT YOUR GOALS ARE, WHERE YOU FIT IN.
I'M SO DIFFERENT, NOW. I ANALYZE MY ACTIONS, I ANALYZE OTHERS, I TRY TO THINK AHEAD... BE ORGANIZED.
I DON'T DEPEND ON ANYONE FOR MY INCOME OR TO MAKE DECISIONS FOR ME. I'M A MATURE RESPONSIBLE ADULT.
DADDY!!
TORONTO
LYNN

HEY, DEE-LOOK AT THIS!

THEY'VE ACTUALLY INVENTED A PET-WASHING MACHINE!

IT'S LIKE A CAR WASH!— YOU JUST PUT YOUR PET INSIDE AN' IT COMES OUT CLEAN!

WOW! BLOW-DRIED AN' EVERYTHING. THE PETS SEEM TO LIKE IT, TOO!

DID YOU GET A NUMBER?!!

BLAP! BLAP BLAPP

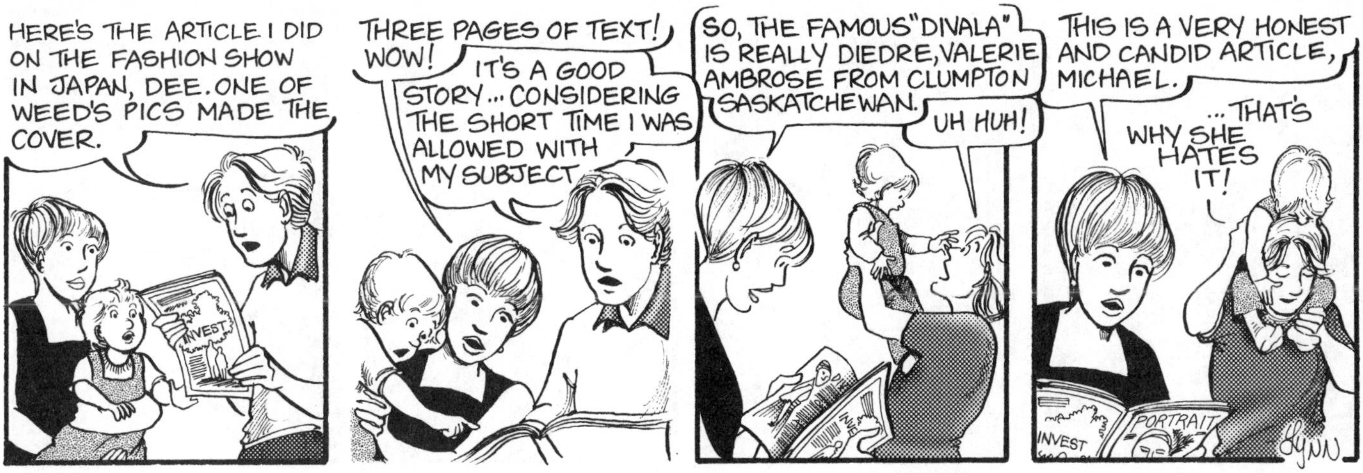
HERE'S THE ARTICLE I DID ON THE FASHION SHOW IN JAPAN, DEE. ONE OF WEED'S PICS MADE THE COVER.
INVEST
THREE PAGES OF TEXT! WOW!
IT'S A GOOD STORY... CONSIDERING THE SHORT TIME I WAS ALLOWED WITH MY SUBJECT.
SO, THE FAMOUS "DIVALA" IS REALLY DIEDRE, VALERIE AMBROSE FROM CLUMPTON SASKATCHEWAN.
UH HUH!
THIS IS A VERY HONEST AND CANDID ARTICLE, MICHAEL.
...THAT'S WHY SHE HATES IT!
INVEST
PORTRAIT
LYNN

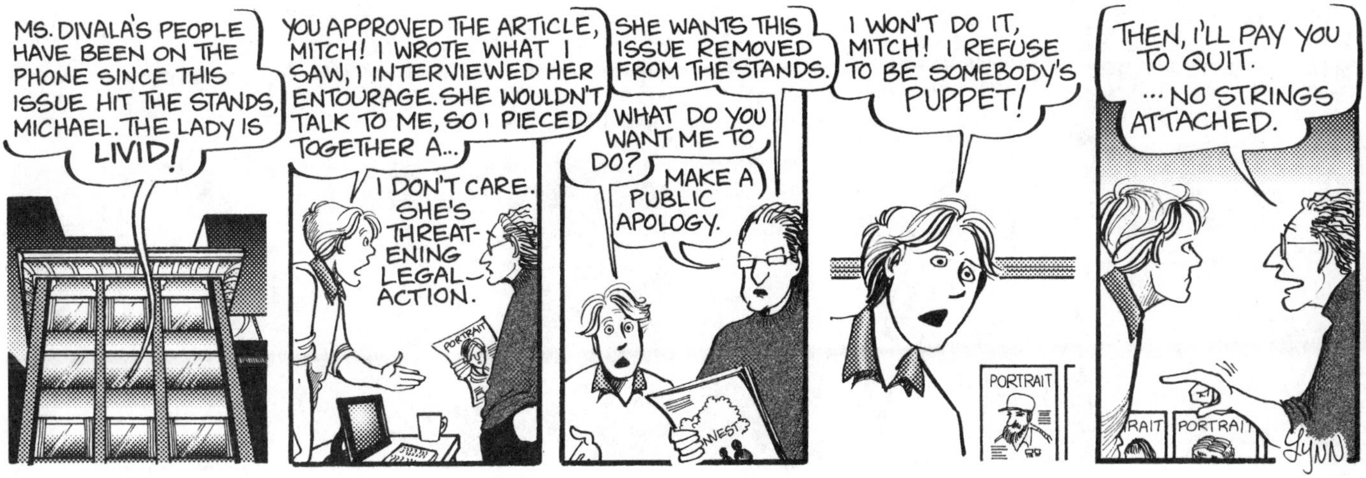
MS. DIVALA'S PEOPLE HAVE BEEN ON THE PHONE SINCE THIS ISSUE HIT THE STANDS, MICHAEL. THE LADY IS LIVID!
YOU APPROVED THE ARTICLE, MITCH! I WROTE WHAT I SAW, I INTERVIEWED HER ENTOURAGE. SHE WOULDN'T TALK TO ME, SO I PIECED TOGETHER A...
I DON'T CARE. SHE'S THREATENING LEGAL ACTION.
PORTRAIT
SHE WANTS THIS ISSUE REMOVED FROM THE STANDS.
WHAT DO YOU WANT ME TO DO?
MAKE A PUBLIC APOLOGY.
INVEST
I WON'T DO IT, MITCH! I REFUSE TO BE SOMEBODY'S PUPPET!
PORTRAIT
THEN, I'LL PAY YOU TO QUIT.
...NO STRINGS ATTACHED.
PORTRAIT
LYNN

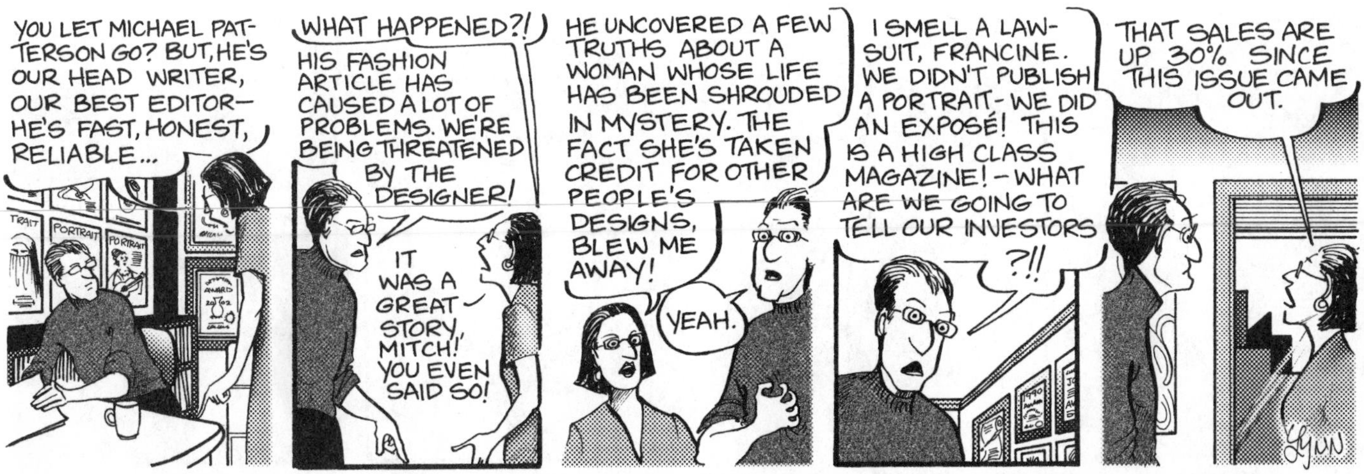
YOU LET MICHAEL PATTERSON GO? BUT, HE'S OUR HEAD WRITER, OUR BEST EDITOR— HE'S FAST, HONEST, RELIABLE...
PORTRAIT
AWARD
WHAT HAPPENED?!
HIS FASHION ARTICLE HAS CAUSED A LOT OF PROBLEMS. WE'RE BEING THREATENED BY THE DESIGNER!
IT WAS A GREAT STORY, MITCH! YOU EVEN SAID SO!
HE UNCOVERED A FEW TRUTHS ABOUT A WOMAN WHOSE LIFE HAS BEEN SHROUDED IN MYSTERY. THE FACT SHE'S TAKEN CREDIT FOR OTHER PEOPLE'S DESIGNS, BLEW ME AWAY!
YEAH.
I SMELL A LAWSUIT, FRANCINE. WE DIDN'T PUBLISH A PORTRAIT- WE DID AN EXPOSÉ! THIS IS A HIGH CLASS MAGAZINE! — WHAT ARE WE GOING TO TELL OUR INVESTORS ?!!
THAT SALES ARE UP 30% SINCE THIS ISSUE CAME OUT.
LYNN

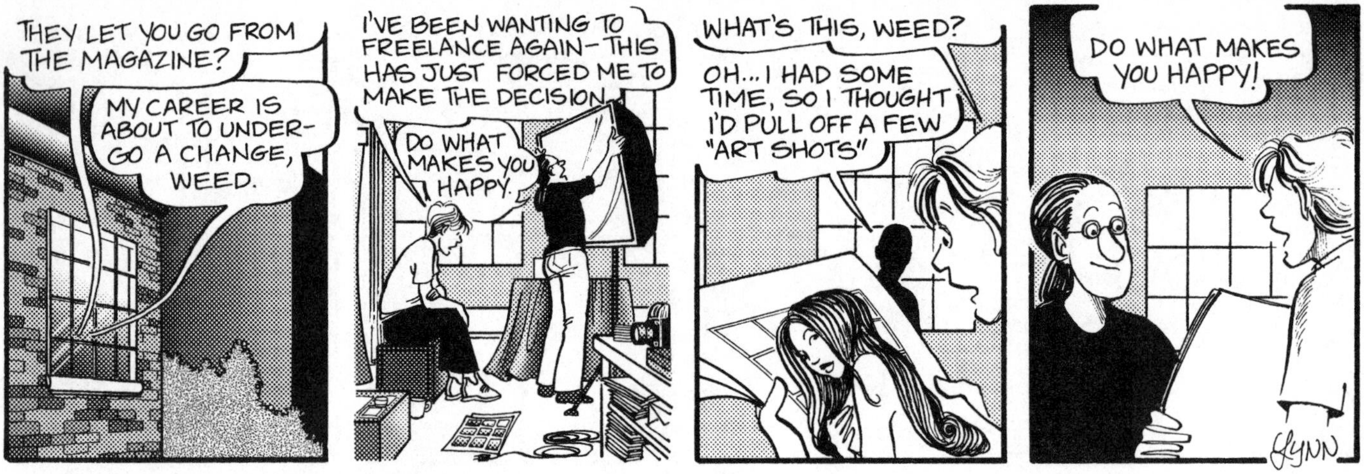
THEY LET YOU GO FROM THE MAGAZINE?
MY CAREER IS ABOUT TO UNDER-GO A CHANGE, WEED.
I'VE BEEN WANTING TO FREELANCE AGAIN– THIS HAS JUST FORCED ME TO MAKE THE DECISION.
DO WHAT MAKES YOU HAPPY.
WHAT'S THIS, WEED?
OH... I HAD SOME TIME, SO I THOUGHT I'D PULL OFF A FEW "ART SHOTS"
DO WHAT MAKES YOU HAPPY!
LYNN

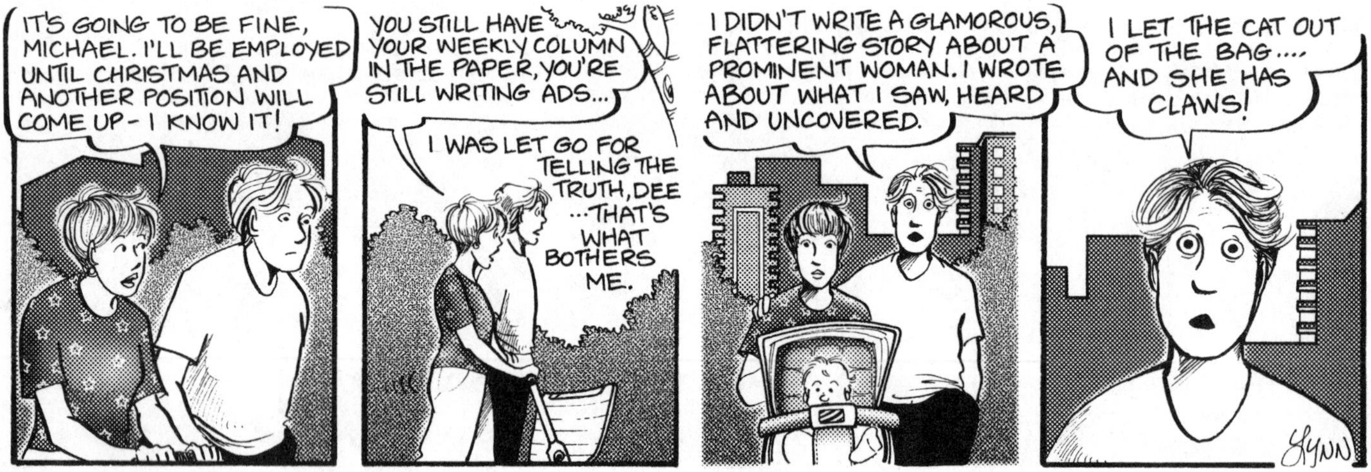
IT'S GOING TO BE FINE, MICHAEL. I'LL BE EMPLOYED UNTIL CHRISTMAS AND ANOTHER POSITION WILL COME UP– I KNOW IT!
YOU STILL HAVE YOUR WEEKLY COLUMN IN THE PAPER, YOU'RE STILL WRITING ADS...
I WAS LET GO FOR TELLING THE TRUTH, DEE ...THAT'S WHAT BOTHERS ME.
I DIDN'T WRITE A GLAMOROUS, FLATTERING STORY ABOUT A PROMINENT WOMAN. I WROTE ABOUT WHAT I SAW, HEARD AND UNCOVERED.
I LET THE CAT OUT OF THE BAG.... AND SHE HAS CLAWS!
LYNN

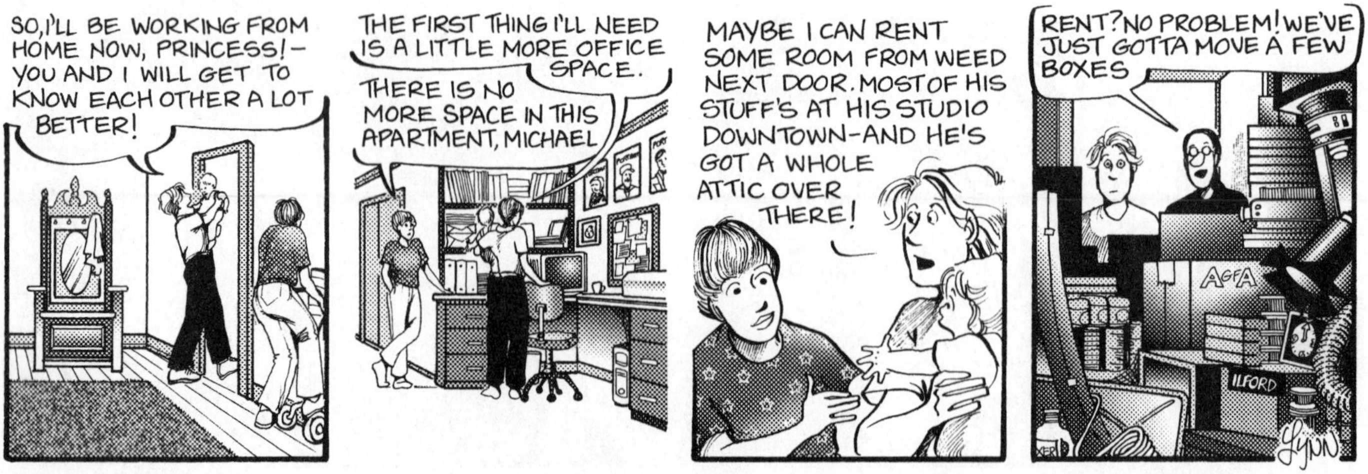
SO, I'LL BE WORKING FROM HOME NOW, PRINCESS!– YOU AND I WILL GET TO KNOW EACH OTHER A LOT BETTER!
THE FIRST THING I'LL NEED IS A LITTLE MORE OFFICE SPACE.
THERE IS NO MORE SPACE IN THIS APARTMENT, MICHAEL
MAYBE I CAN RENT SOME ROOM FROM WEED NEXT DOOR. MOST OF HIS STUFF'S AT HIS STUDIO DOWNTOWN– AND HE'S GOT A WHOLE ATTIC OVER THERE!
RENT? NO PROBLEM! WE'VE JUST GOTTA MOVE A FEW BOXES
AGFA
ILFORD
LYNN

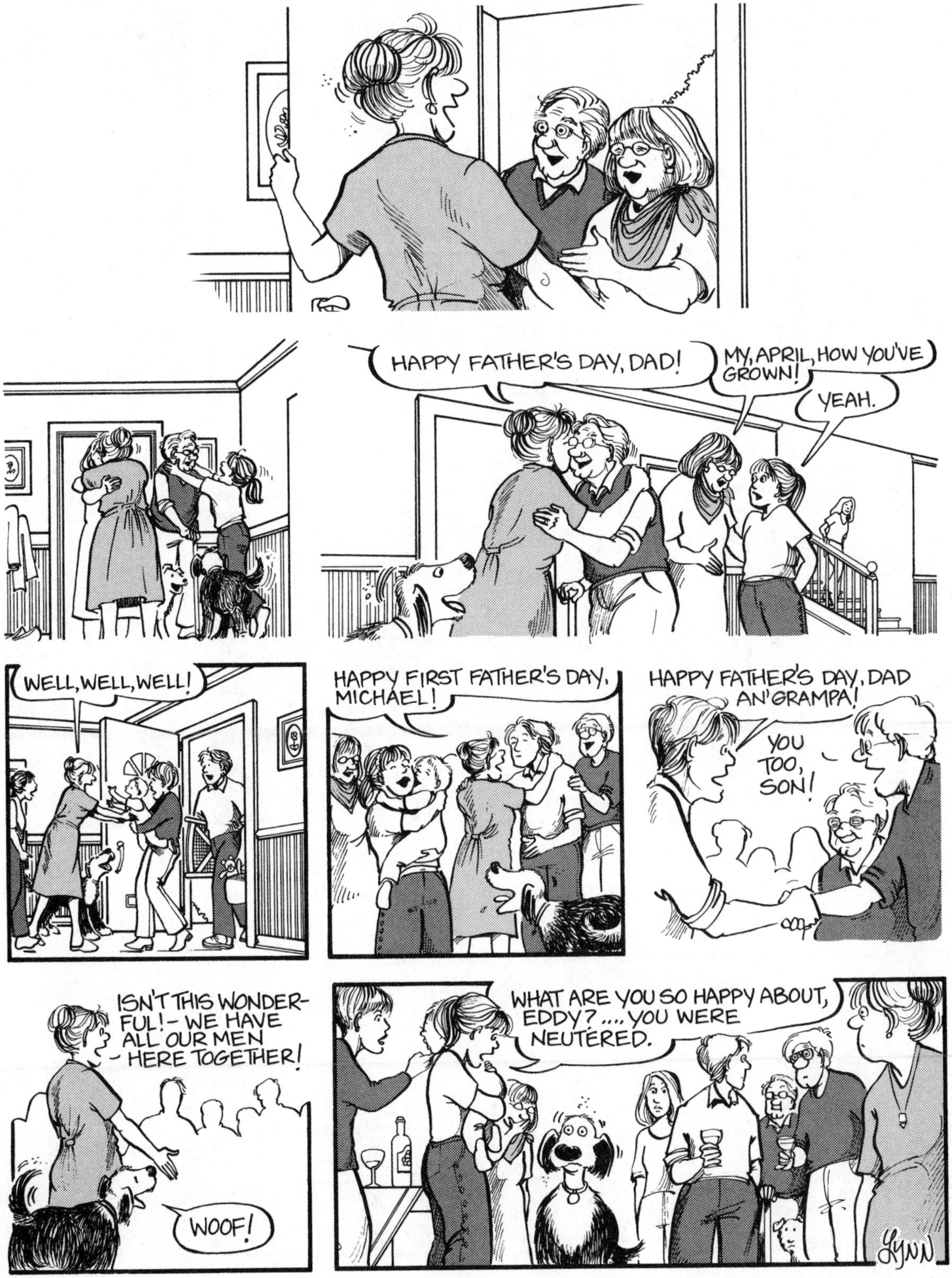
HAPPY FATHER'S DAY, DAD!
MY, APRIL, HOW YOU'VE GROWN!
YEAH.
WELL, WELL, WELL!
HAPPY FIRST FATHER'S DAY, MICHAEL!
HAPPY FATHER'S DAY, DAD AN' GRAMPA!
YOU TOO, SON!
ISN'T THIS WONDERFUL! - WE HAVE ALL OUR MEN HERE TOGETHER!
WOOF!
WHAT ARE YOU SO HAPPY ABOUT, EDDY? .... YOU WERE NEUTERED.
LYNN

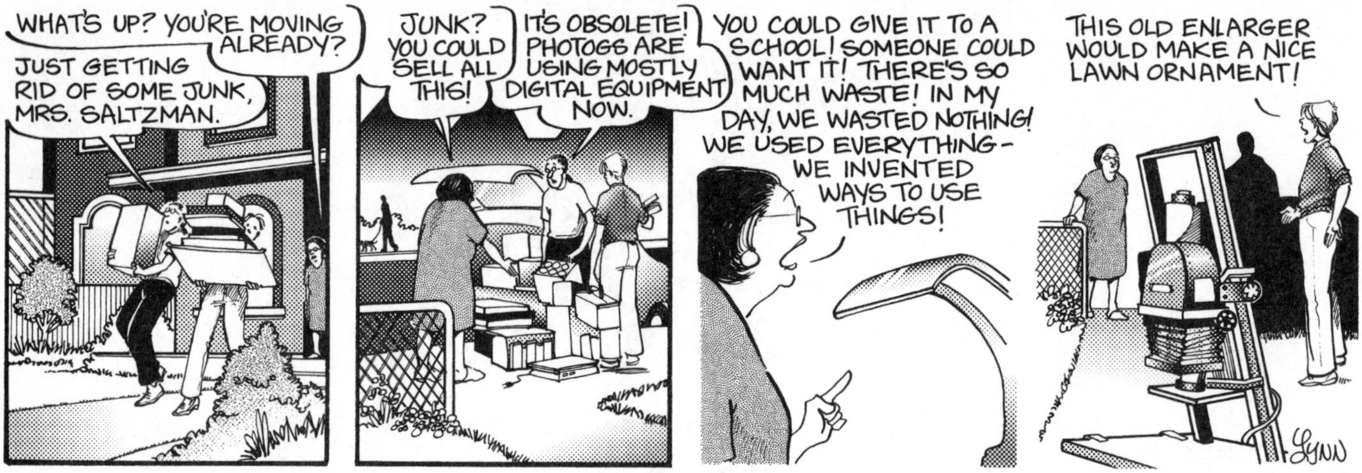
WHAT'S UP? YOU'RE MOVING ALREADY?
JUST GETTING RID OF SOME JUNK, MRS. SALTZMAN.
JUNK? YOU COULD SELL ALL THIS!
IT'S OBSOLETE! PHOTOGS ARE USING MOSTLY DIGITAL EQUIPMENT NOW.
YOU COULD GIVE IT TO A SCHOOL! SOMEONE COULD WANT IT! THERE'S SO MUCH WASTE! IN MY DAY, WE WASTED NOTHING! WE USED EVERYTHING- WE INVENTED WAYS TO USE THINGS!
THIS OLD ENLARGER WOULD MAKE A NICE LAWN ORNAMENT!
LYNN

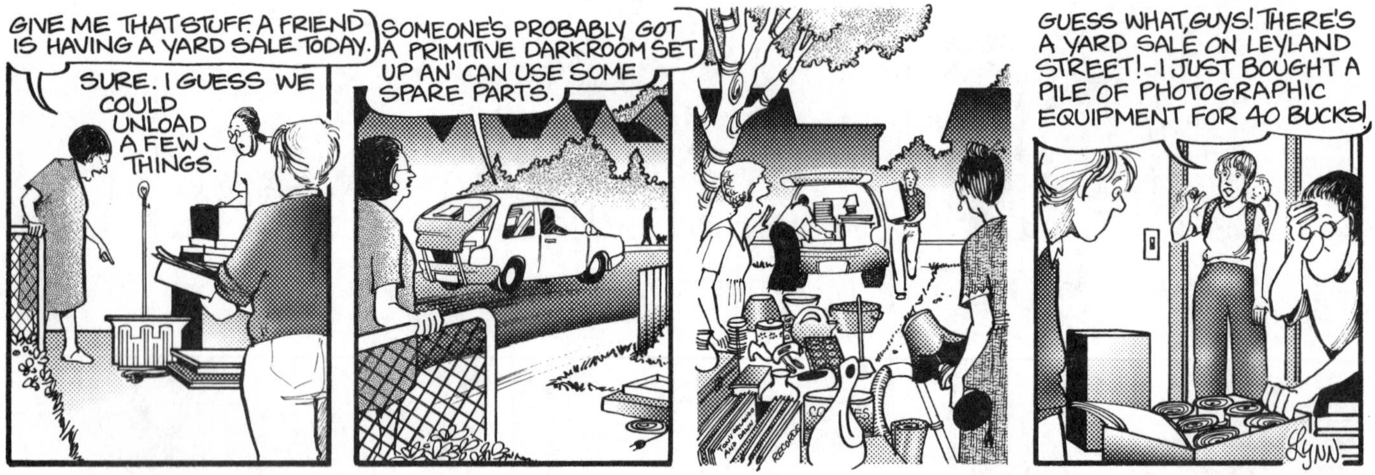
GIVE ME THAT STUFF. A FRIEND IS HAVING A YARD SALE TODAY.
SURE. I GUESS WE COULD UNLOAD A FEW THINGS.
SOMEONE'S PROBABLY GOT A PRIMITIVE DARKROOM SET UP AN' CAN USE SOME SPARE PARTS.
GUESS WHAT, GUYS! THERE'S A YARD SALE ON LEYLAND STREET!-I JUST BOUGHT A PILE OF PHOTOGRAPHIC EQUIPMENT FOR 40 BUCKS!
LYNN

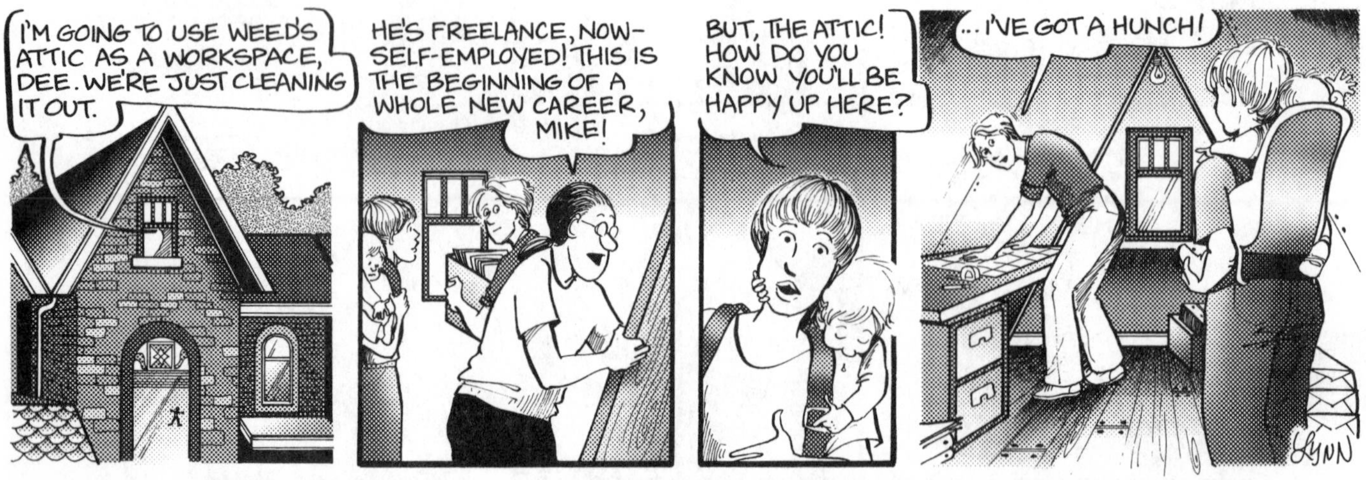
I'M GOING TO USE WEED'S ATTIC AS A WORKSPACE, DEE. WE'RE JUST CLEANING IT OUT.
HE'S FREELANCE, NOW- SELF-EMPLOYED! THIS IS THE BEGINNING OF A WHOLE NEW CAREER, MIKE!
BUT, THE ATTIC! HOW DO YOU KNOW YOU'LL BE HAPPY UP HERE?
... I'VE GOT A HUNCH!
LYNN

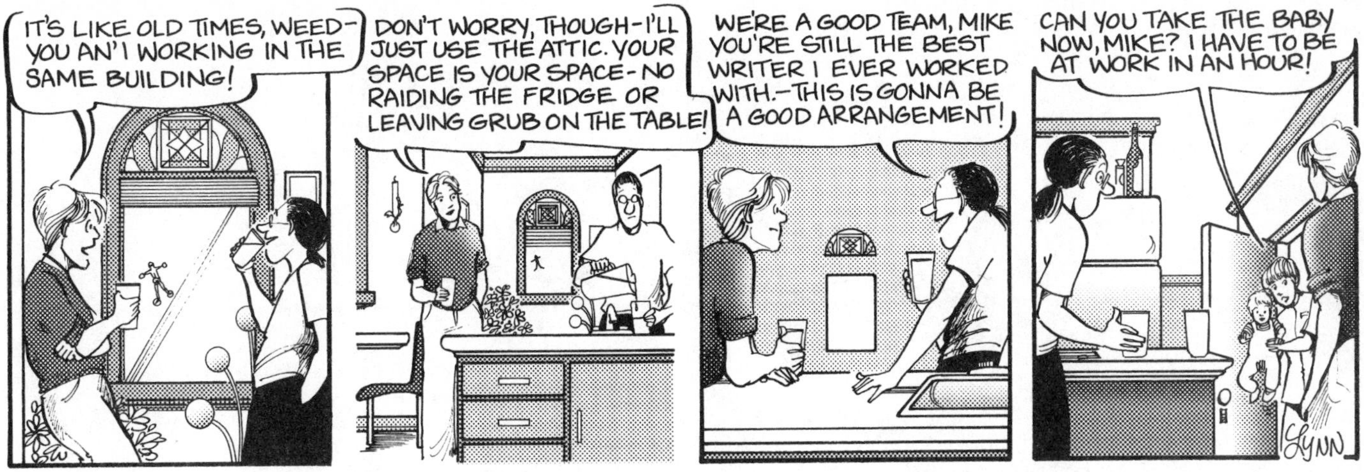
IT'S LIKE OLD TIMES, WEED- YOU AN' I WORKING IN THE SAME BUILDING!
DON'T WORRY, THOUGH - I'LL JUST USE THE ATTIC. YOUR SPACE IS YOUR SPACE - NO RAIDING THE FRIDGE OR LEAVING GRUB ON THE TABLE!
WE'RE A GOOD TEAM, MIKE YOU'RE STILL THE BEST WRITER I EVER WORKED WITH.- THIS IS GONNA BE A GOOD ARRANGEMENT!
CAN YOU TAKE THE BABY NOW, MIKE? I HAVE TO BE AT WORK IN AN HOUR!
LYNN

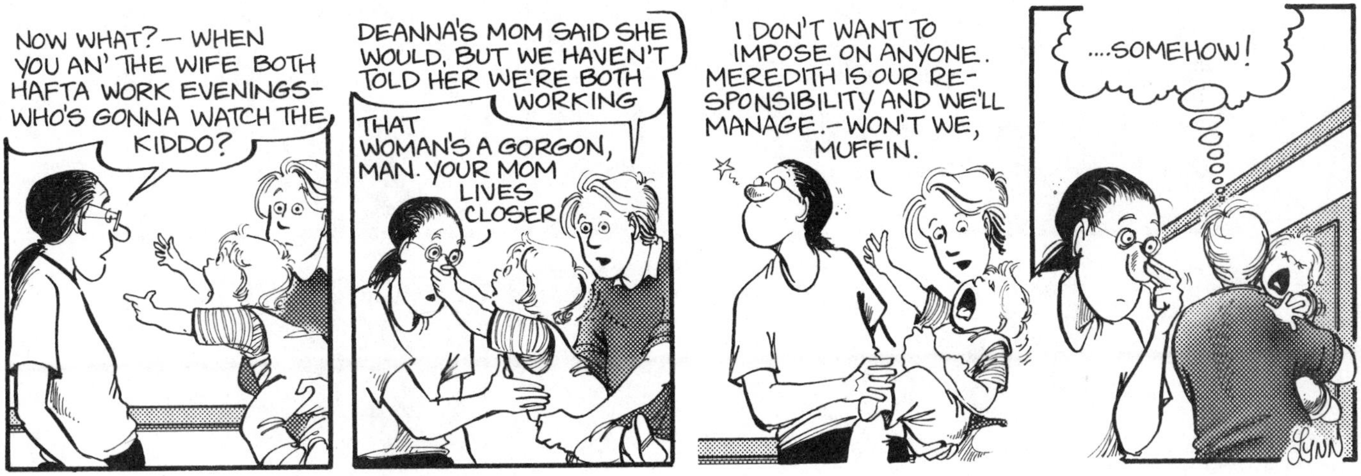
NOW WHAT?— WHEN YOU AN' THE WIFE BOTH HAFTA WORK EVENINGS- WHO'S GONNA WATCH THE KIDDO?
DEANNA'S MOM SAID SHE WOULD, BUT WE HAVEN'T TOLD HER WE'RE BOTH WORKING
THAT WOMAN'S A GORGON, MAN. YOUR MOM LIVES CLOSER
I DON'T WANT TO IMPOSE ON ANYONE. MEREDITH IS OUR RESPONSIBILITY AND WE'LL MANAGE.- WON'T WE, MUFFIN.
....SOMEHOW!
LYNN

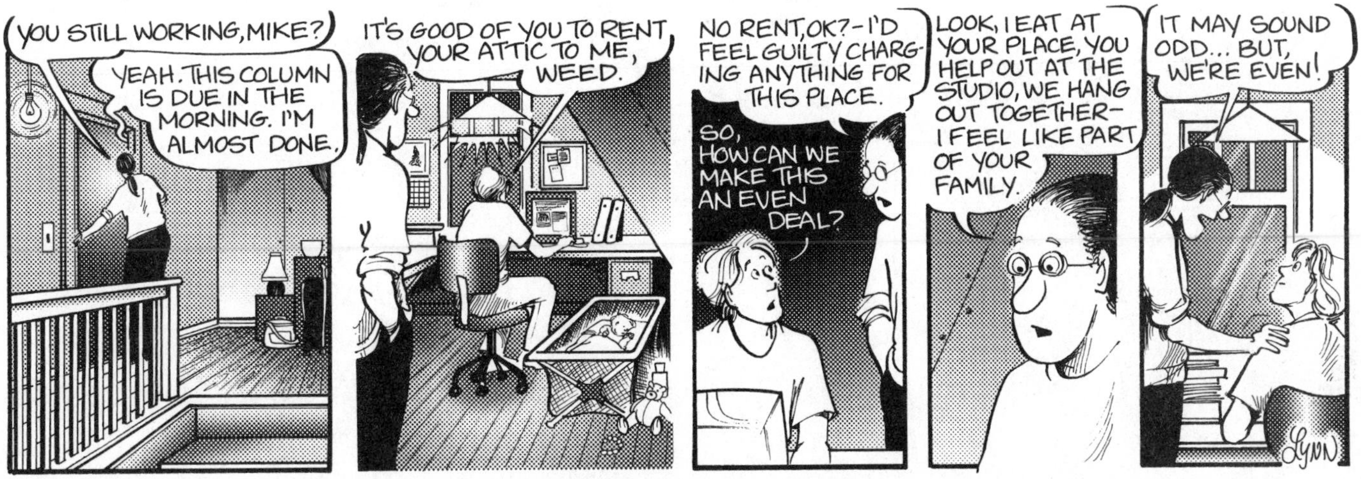
YOU STILL WORKING, MIKE?
YEAH. THIS COLUMN IS DUE IN THE MORNING. I'M ALMOST DONE.
IT'S GOOD OF YOU TO RENT YOUR ATTIC TO ME, WEED.
NO RENT, OK? - I'D FEEL GUILTY CHARGING ANYTHING FOR THIS PLACE.
SO, HOW CAN WE MAKE THIS AN EVEN DEAL?
LOOK, I EAT AT YOUR PLACE, YOU HELP OUT AT THE STUDIO, WE HANG OUT TOGETHER- I FEEL LIKE PART OF YOUR FAMILY.
IT MAY SOUND ODD... BUT, WE'RE EVEN!
LYNN

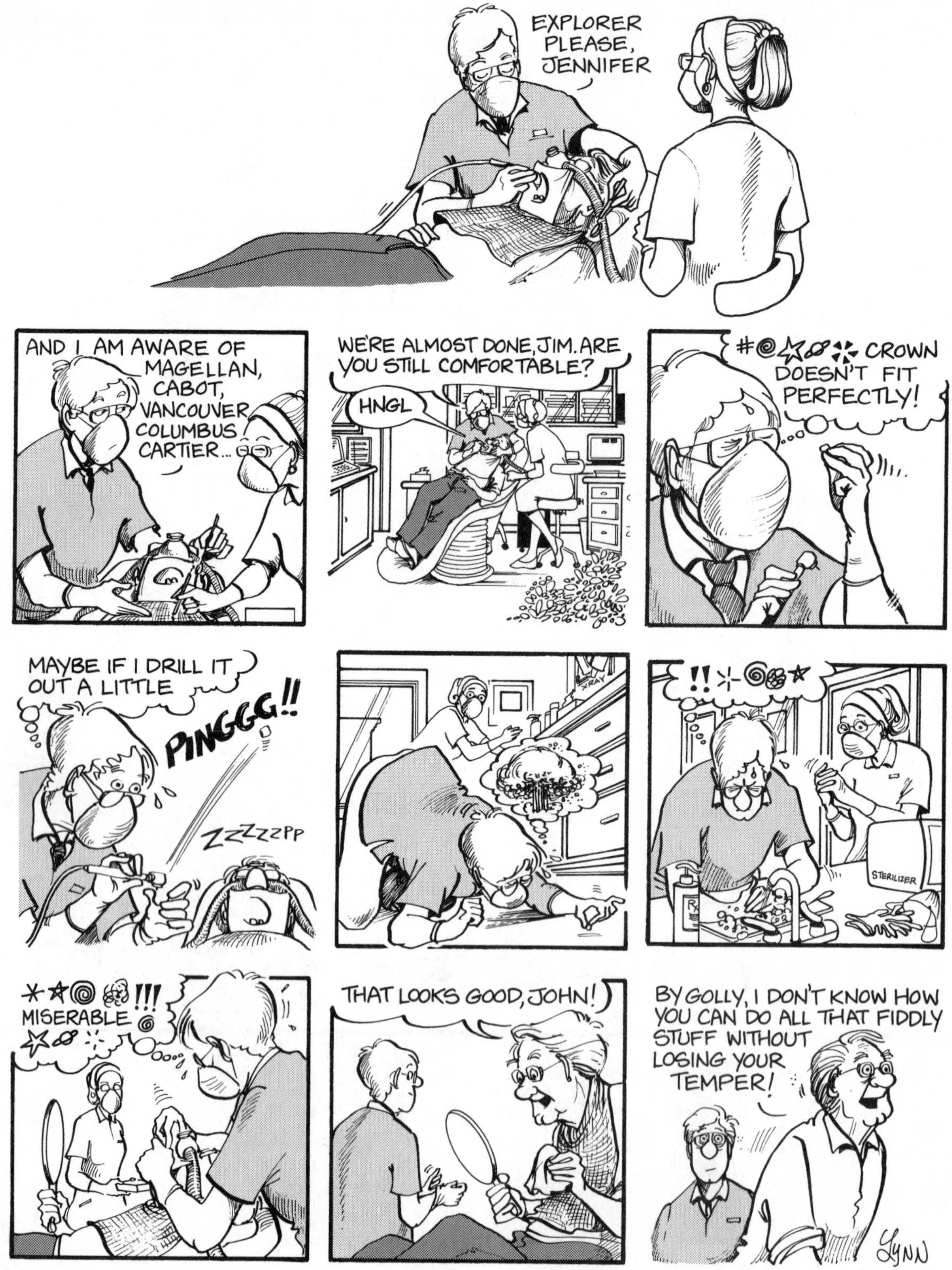
EXPLORER PLEASE, JENNIFER
AND I AM AWARE OF MAGELLAN, CABOT, VANCOUVER COLUMBUS CARTIER...
WE'RE ALMOST DONE, JIM. ARE YOU STILL COMFORTABLE?
HNGL
CROWN DOESN'T FIT PERFECTLY!
MAYBE IF I DRILL IT OUT A LITTLE
PINGGG!!
ZZZZZPP
XRAY
!!
STERILIZER
!!!
MISERABLE
THAT LOOKS GOOD, JOHN!
BY GOLLY, I DON'T KNOW HOW YOU CAN DO ALL THAT FIDDLY STUFF WITHOUT LOSING YOUR TEMPER!
LYNN

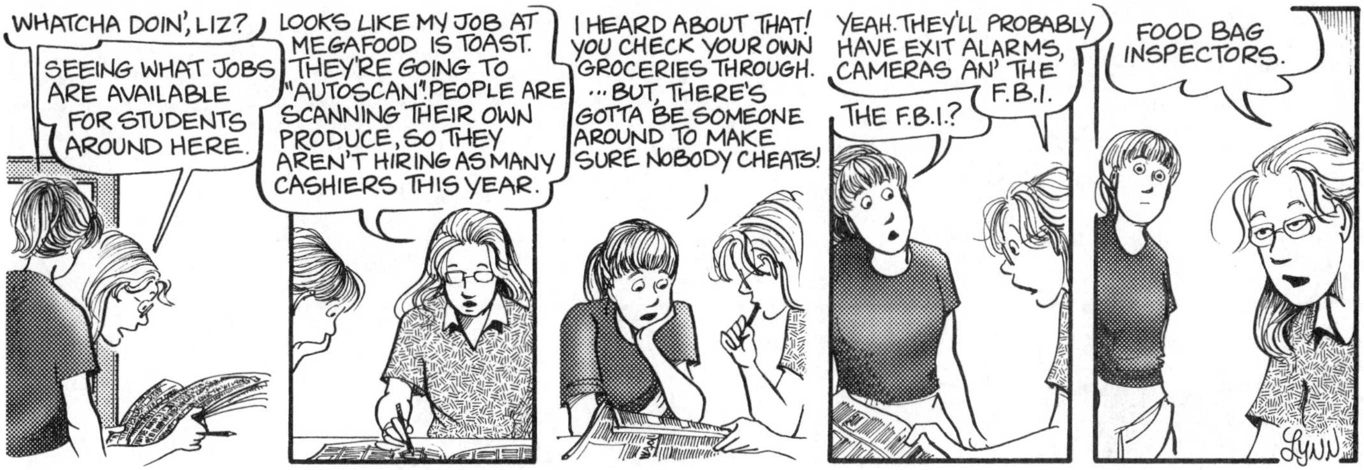
WHATCHA DOIN', LIZ?
SEEING WHAT JOBS ARE AVAILABLE FOR STUDENTS AROUND HERE.
LOOKS LIKE MY JOB AT MEGAFOOD IS TOAST. THEY'RE GOING TO "AUTOSCAN". PEOPLE ARE SCANNING THEIR OWN PRODUCE, SO THEY AREN'T HIRING AS MANY CASHIERS THIS YEAR.
I HEARD ABOUT THAT! YOU CHECK YOUR OWN GROCERIES THROUGH. ...BUT, THERE'S GOTTA BE SOMEONE AROUND TO MAKE SURE NOBODY CHEATS!
YEAH. THEY'LL PROBABLY HAVE EXIT ALARMS, CAMERAS AN' THE F.B.I.
THE F.B.I.?
FOOD BAG INSPECTORS.
LYNN

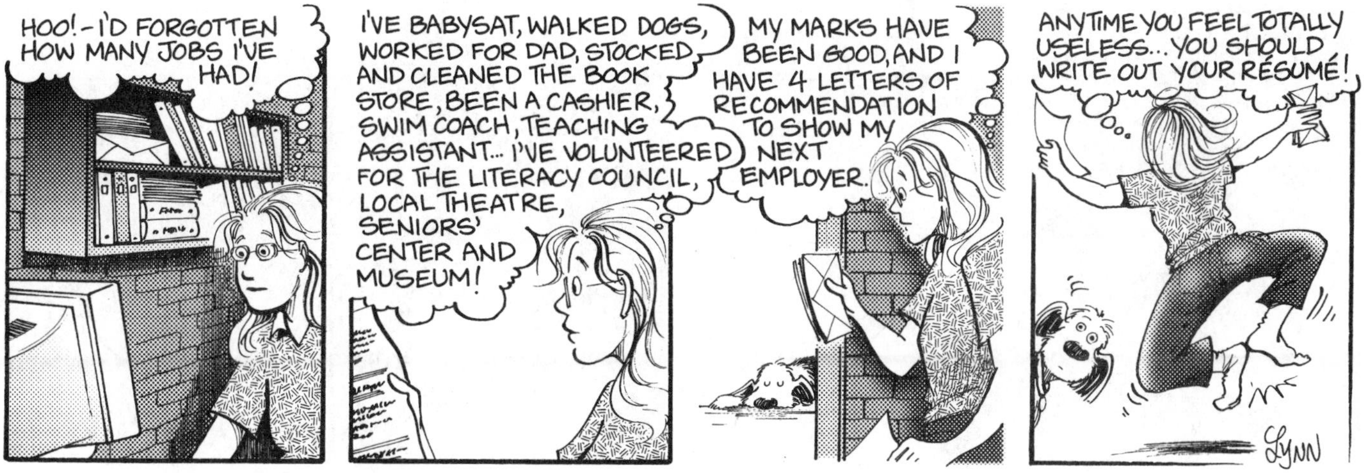
HOO! - I'D FORGOTTEN HOW MANY JOBS I'VE HAD!
I'VE BABYSAT, WALKED DOGS, WORKED FOR DAD, STOCKED AND CLEANED THE BOOK STORE, BEEN A CASHIER, SWIM COACH, TEACHING ASSISTANT... I'VE VOLUNTEERED FOR THE LITERACY COUNCIL, LOCAL THEATRE, SENIORS' CENTER AND MUSEUM!
MY MARKS HAVE BEEN GOOD, AND I HAVE 4 LETTERS OF RECOMMENDATION TO SHOW MY NEXT EMPLOYER.
ANYTIME YOU FEEL TOTALLY USELESS... YOU SHOULD WRITE OUT YOUR RÉSUMÉ!
LYNN

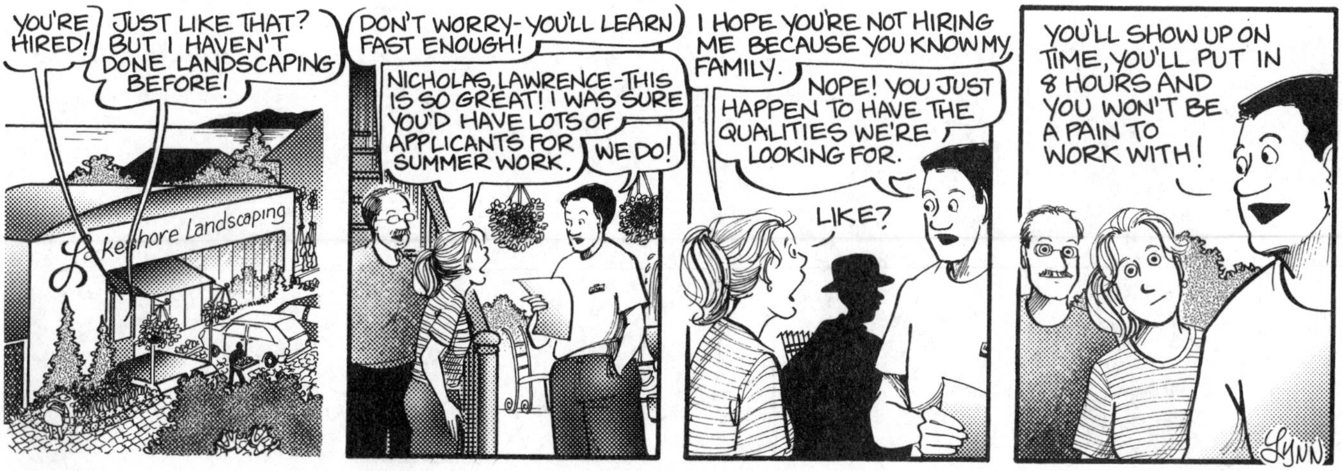
YOU'RE HIRED!
JUST LIKE THAT? BUT I HAVEN'T DONE LANDSCAPING BEFORE!
Lakeshore Landscaping
DON'T WORRY- YOU'LL LEARN FAST ENOUGH!
NICHOLAS, LAWRENCE-THIS IS SO GREAT! I WAS SURE YOU'D HAVE LOTS OF APPLICANTS FOR SUMMER WORK.
WE DO!
I HOPE YOU'RE NOT HIRING ME BECAUSE YOU KNOW MY FAMILY.
NOPE! YOU JUST HAPPEN TO HAVE THE QUALITIES WE'RE LOOKING FOR.
LIKE?
YOU'LL SHOW UP ON TIME, YOU'LL PUT IN 8 HOURS AND YOU WON'T BE A PAIN TO WORK WITH!
LYNN

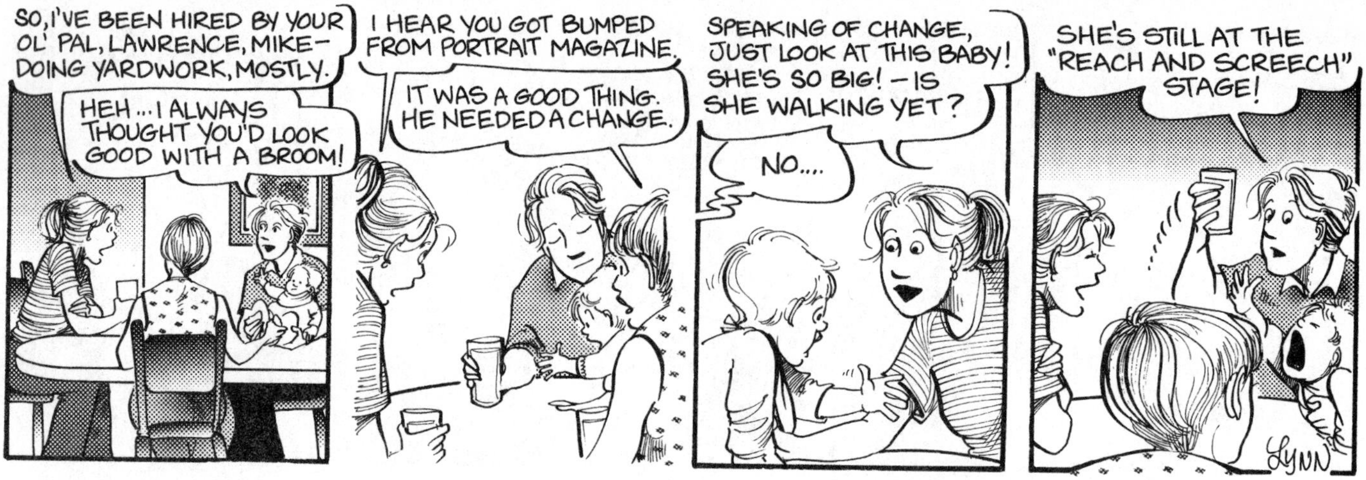
SO, I'VE BEEN HIRED BY YOUR OL' PAL, LAWRENCE, MIKE- DOING YARDWORK, MOSTLY.
HEH... I ALWAYS THOUGHT YOU'D LOOK GOOD WITH A BROOM!
I HEAR YOU GOT BUMPED FROM PORTRAIT MAGAZINE.
IT WAS A GOOD THING. HE NEEDED A CHANGE.
SPEAKING OF CHANGE, JUST LOOK AT THIS BABY! SHE'S SO BIG! - IS SHE WALKING YET?
NO....
SHE'S STILL AT THE "REACH AND SCREECH" STAGE!
LYNN

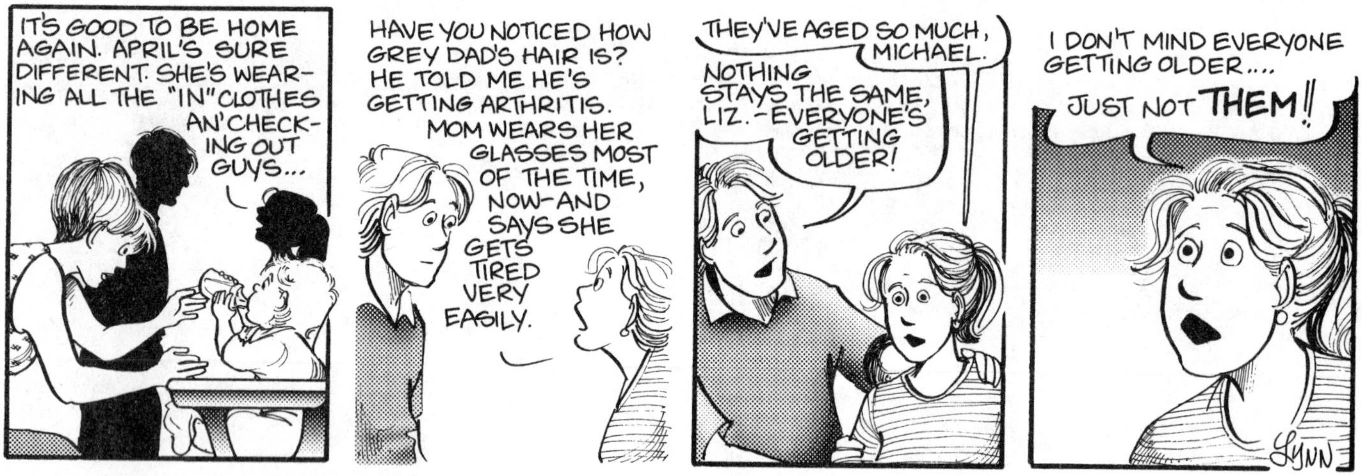
IT'S GOOD TO BE HOME AGAIN. APRIL'S SURE DIFFERENT. SHE'S WEARING ALL THE "IN" CLOTHES AN' CHECKING OUT GUYS...
HAVE YOU NOTICED HOW GREY DAD'S HAIR IS? HE TOLD ME HE'S GETTING ARTHRITIS.
MOM WEARS HER GLASSES MOST OF THE TIME, NOW- AND SAYS SHE GETS TIRED VERY EASILY.
THEY'VE AGED SO MUCH, MICHAEL.
NOTHING STAYS THE SAME, LIZ. - EVERYONE'S GETTING OLDER!
I DON'T MIND EVERYONE GETTING OLDER....
JUST NOT THEM!!
LYNN

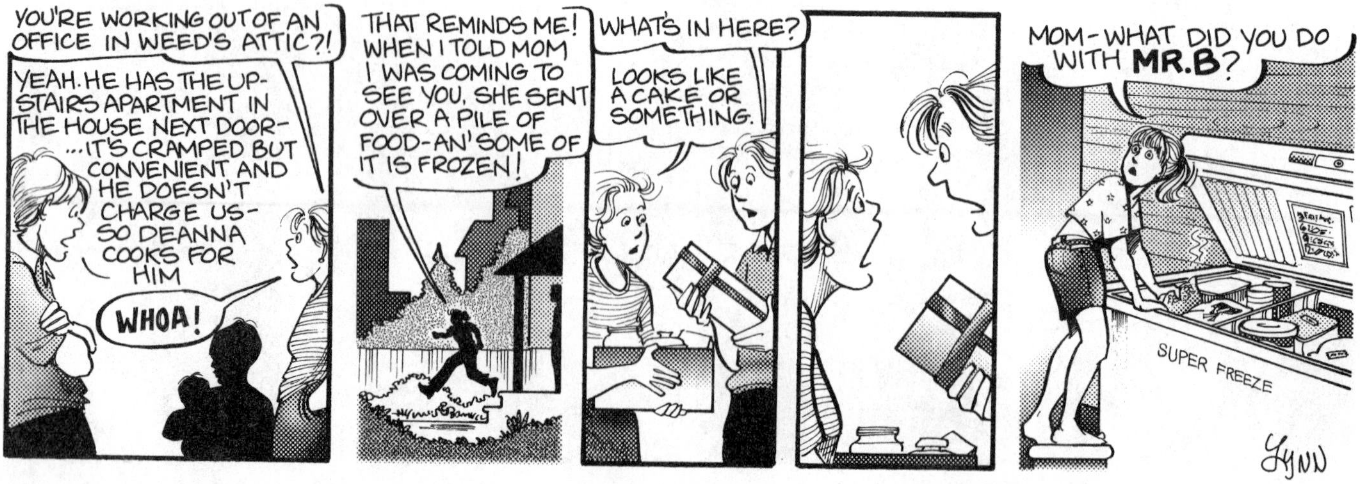
YOU'RE WORKING OUT OF AN OFFICE IN WEED'S ATTIC?!
YEAH. HE HAS THE UPSTAIRS APARTMENT IN THE HOUSE NEXT DOOR- ...IT'S CRAMPED BUT CONVENIENT AND HE DOESN'T CHARGE US- SO DEANNA COOKS FOR HIM
WHOA!
THAT REMINDS ME! WHEN I TOLD MOM I WAS COMING TO SEE YOU, SHE SENT OVER A PILE OF FOOD- AN' SOME OF IT IS FROZEN!
WHAT'S IN HERE?
LOOKS LIKE A CAKE OR SOMETHING.
MOM- WHAT DID YOU DO WITH MR. B?
SUPER FREEZE
LYNN

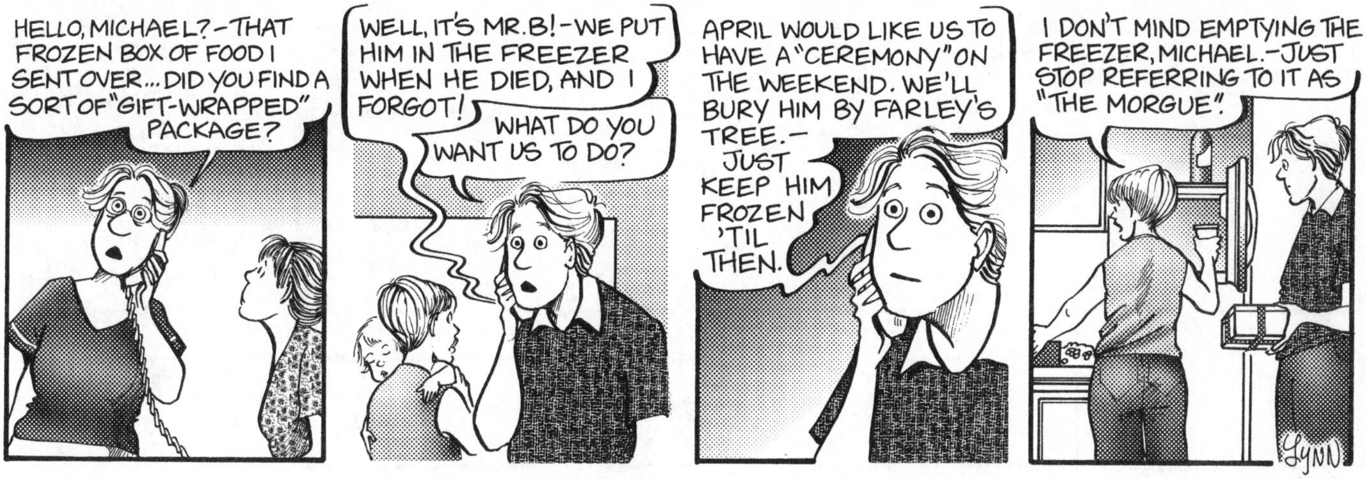
HELLO, MICHAEL? -THAT FROZEN BOX OF FOOD I SENT OVER... DID YOU FIND A SORT OF "GIFT-WRAPPED" PACKAGE?
WELL, IT'S MR. B! -WE PUT HIM IN THE FREEZER WHEN HE DIED, AND I FORGOT!
WHAT DO YOU WANT US TO DO?
APRIL WOULD LIKE US TO HAVE A "CEREMONY" ON THE WEEKEND. WE'LL BURY HIM BY FARLEY'S TREE. -JUST KEEP HIM FROZEN 'TIL THEN.
I DON'T MIND EMPTYING THE FREEZER, MICHAEL. -JUST STOP REFERRING TO IT AS "THE MORGUE".
LYNN

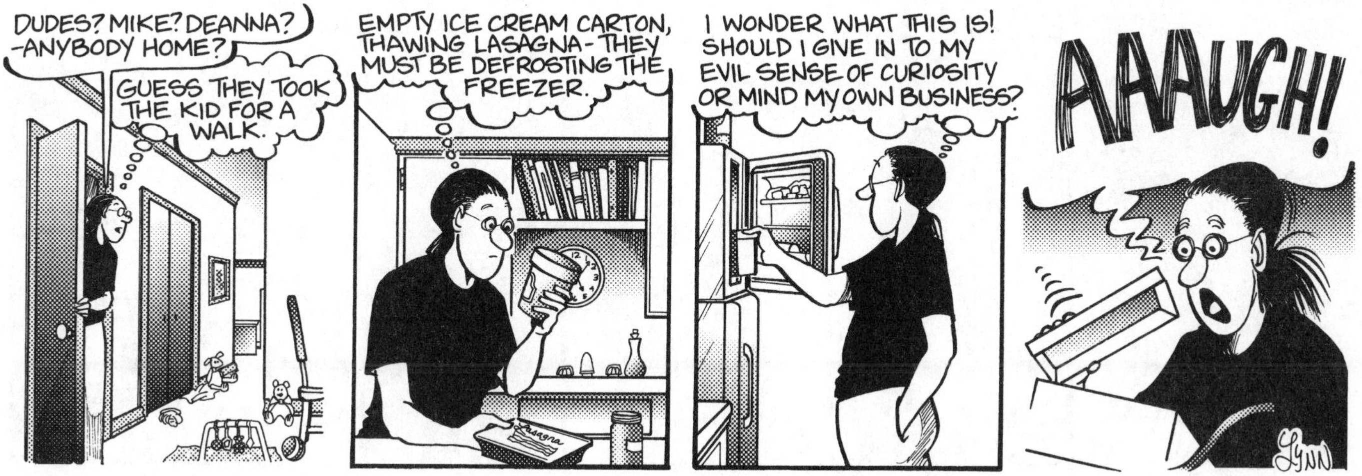
DUDES? MIKE? DEANNA? -ANYBODY HOME?
GUESS THEY TOOK THE KID FOR A WALK.
EMPTY ICE CREAM CARTON, THAWING LASAGNA- THEY MUST BE DEFROSTING THE FREEZER.
Lasagna
I WONDER WHAT THIS IS! SHOULD I GIVE IN TO MY EVIL SENSE OF CURIOSITY OR MIND MY OWN BUSINESS?
AAAUGH!
LYNN

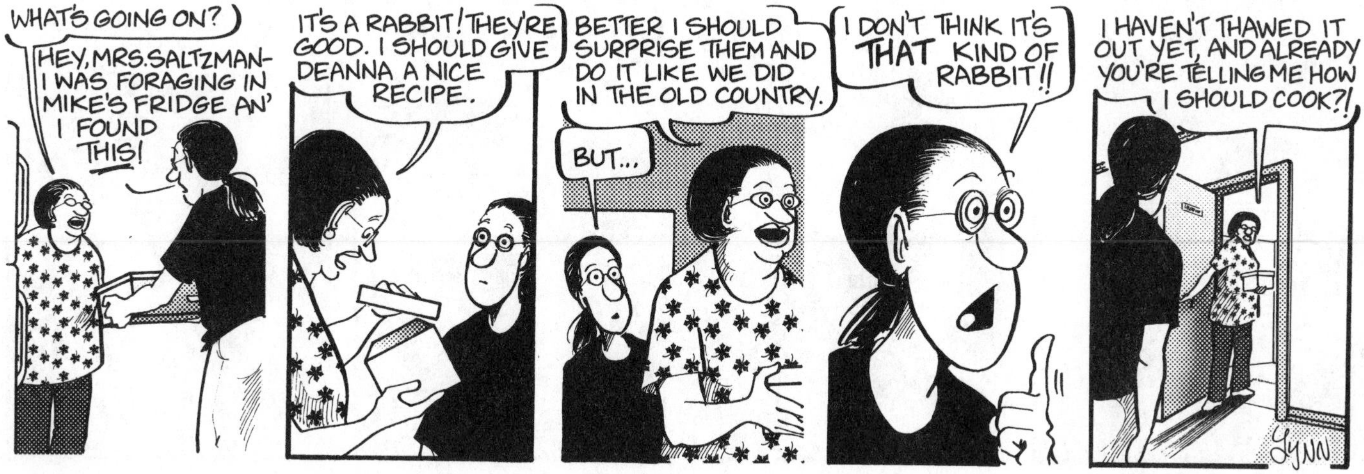
WHAT'S GOING ON?
HEY, MRS. SALTZMAN- I WAS FORAGING IN MIKE'S FRIDGE AN' I FOUND THIS!
IT'S A RABBIT! THEY'RE GOOD. I SHOULD GIVE DEANNA A NICE RECIPE.
BETTER I SHOULD SURPRISE THEM AND DO IT LIKE WE DID IN THE OLD COUNTRY.
BUT...
I DON'T THINK IT'S THAT KIND OF RABBIT!!
I HAVEN'T THAWED IT OUT YET, AND ALREADY YOU'RE TELLING ME HOW I SHOULD COOK?!
LYNN

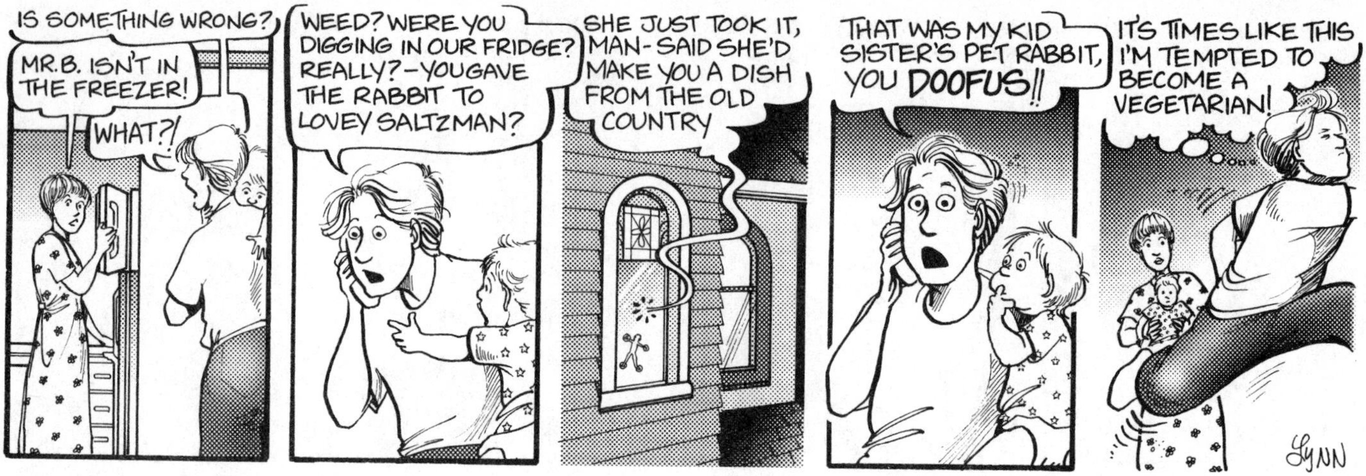
IS SOMETHING WRONG?
MR.B. ISN'T IN THE FREEZER!
WHAT?!
WEED? WERE YOU DIGGING IN OUR FRIDGE? REALLY?–YOU GAVE THE RABBIT TO LOVEY SALTZMAN?
SHE JUST TOOK IT, MAN- SAID SHE'D MAKE YOU A DISH FROM THE OLD COUNTRY
THAT WAS MY KID SISTER'S PET RABBIT, YOU DOOFUS!!
IT'S TIMES LIKE THIS I'M TEMPTED TO BECOME A VEGETARIAN!
LYNN

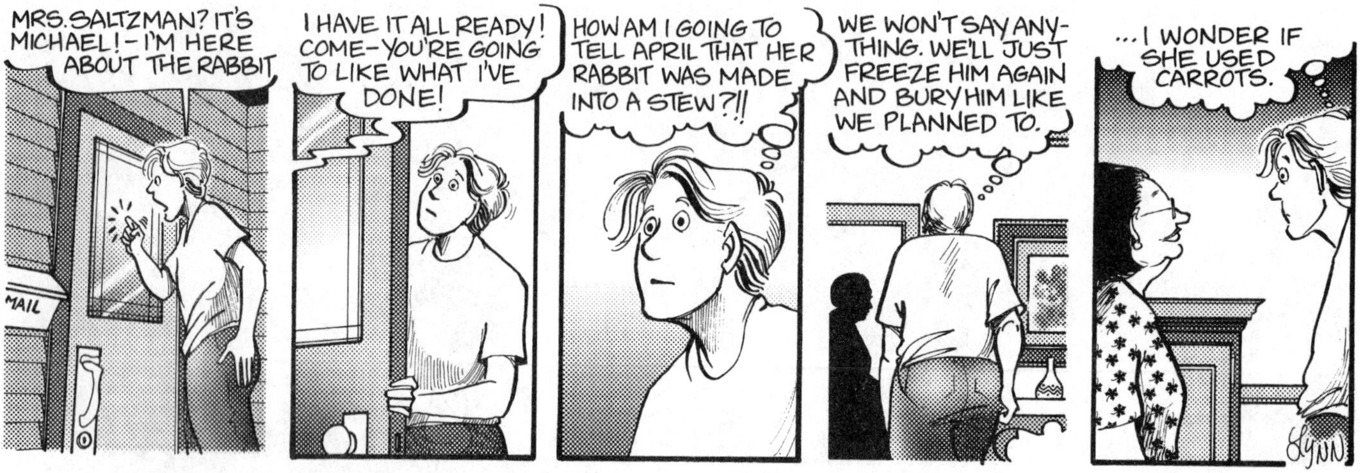
MRS. SALTZMAN? IT'S MICHAEL! - I'M HERE ABOUT THE RABBIT
MAIL
I HAVE IT ALL READY! COME- YOU'RE GOING TO LIKE WHAT I'VE DONE!
HOW AM I GOING TO TELL APRIL THAT HER RABBIT WAS MADE INTO A STEW?!!
WE WON'T SAY ANY-THING. WE'LL JUST FREEZE HIM AGAIN AND BURY HIM LIKE WE PLANNED TO.
...I WONDER IF SHE USED CARROTS.
LYNN

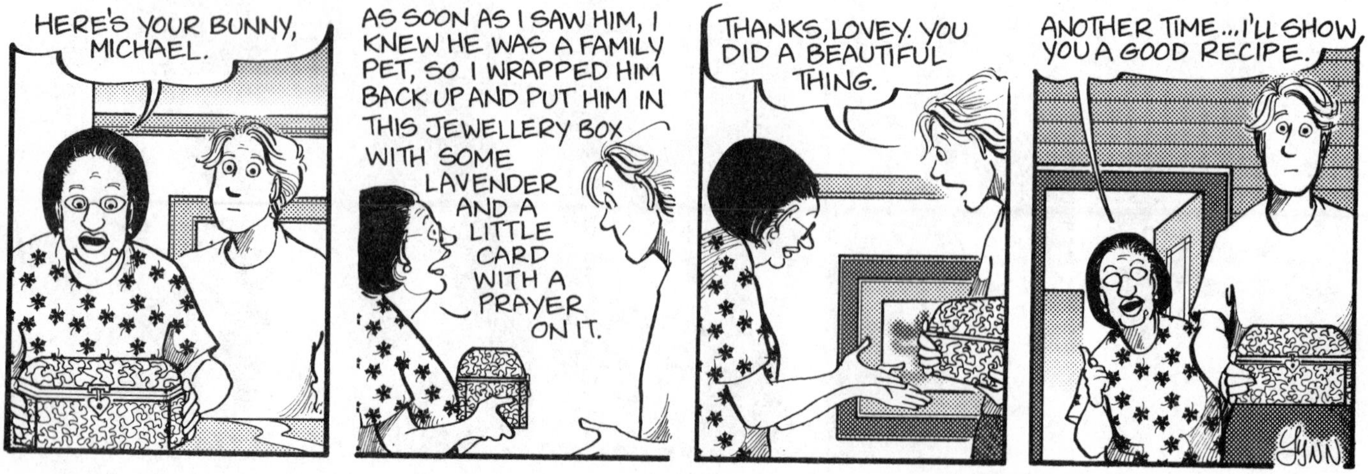
HERE'S YOUR BUNNY, MICHAEL.
AS SOON AS I SAW HIM, I KNEW HE WAS A FAMILY PET, SO I WRAPPED HIM BACK UP AND PUT HIM IN THIS JEWELLERY BOX WITH SOME LAVENDER AND A LITTLE CARD WITH A PRAYER ON IT.
THANKS, LOVEY. YOU DID A BEAUTIFUL THING.
ANOTHER TIME...I'LL SHOW YOU A GOOD RECIPE.
LYNN

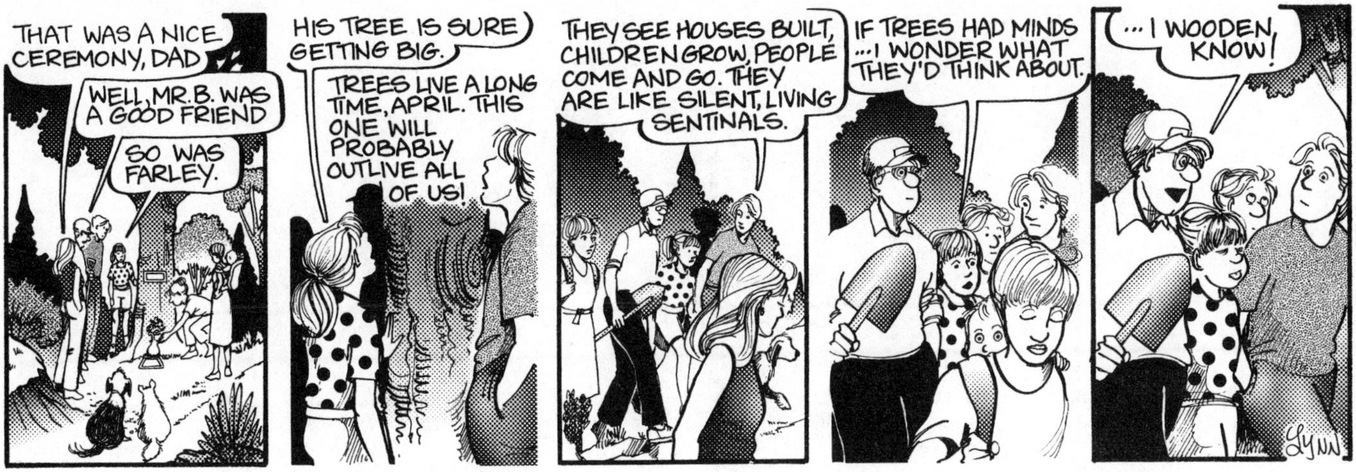
THAT WAS A NICE CEREMONY, DAD
WELL, MR. B. WAS A GOOD FRIEND
SO WAS FARLEY.
HIS TREE IS SURE GETTING BIG.
TREES LIVE A LONG TIME, APRIL. THIS ONE WILL PROBABLY OUTLIVE ALL OF US!
THEY SEE HOUSES BUILT, CHILDREN GROW, PEOPLE COME AND GO. THEY ARE LIKE SILENT, LIVING SENTINALS.
IF TREES HAD MINDS ...I WONDER WHAT THEY'D THINK ABOUT.
...I WOODEN, KNOW!
LYNN

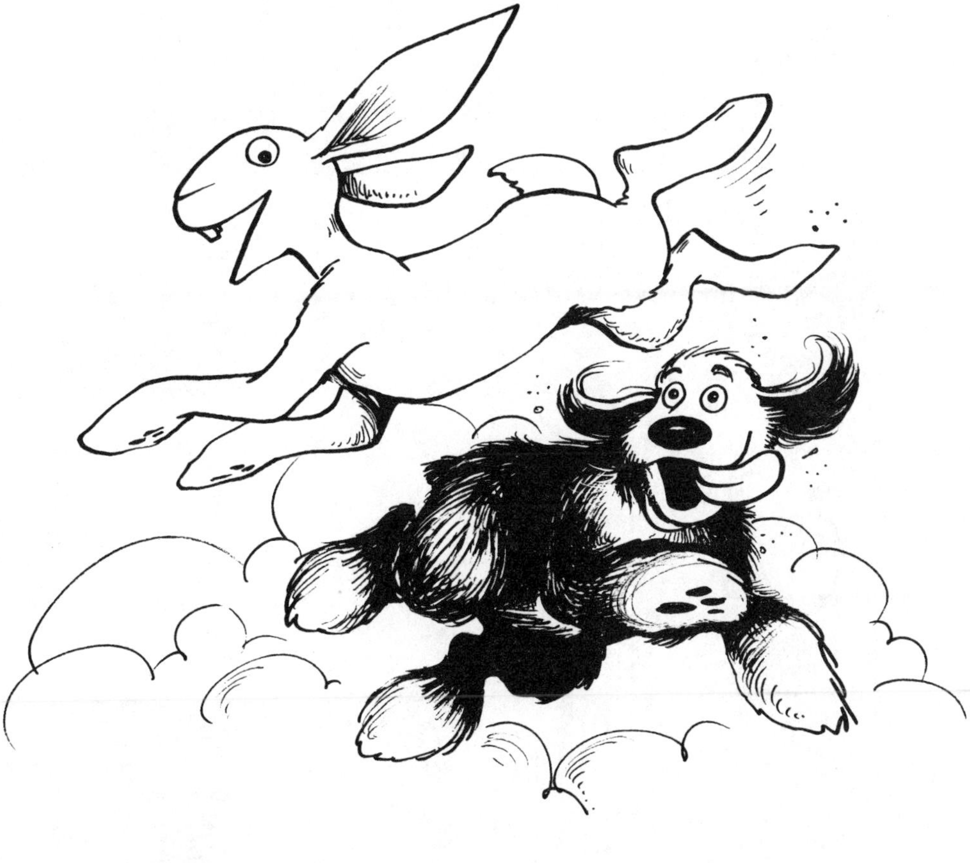

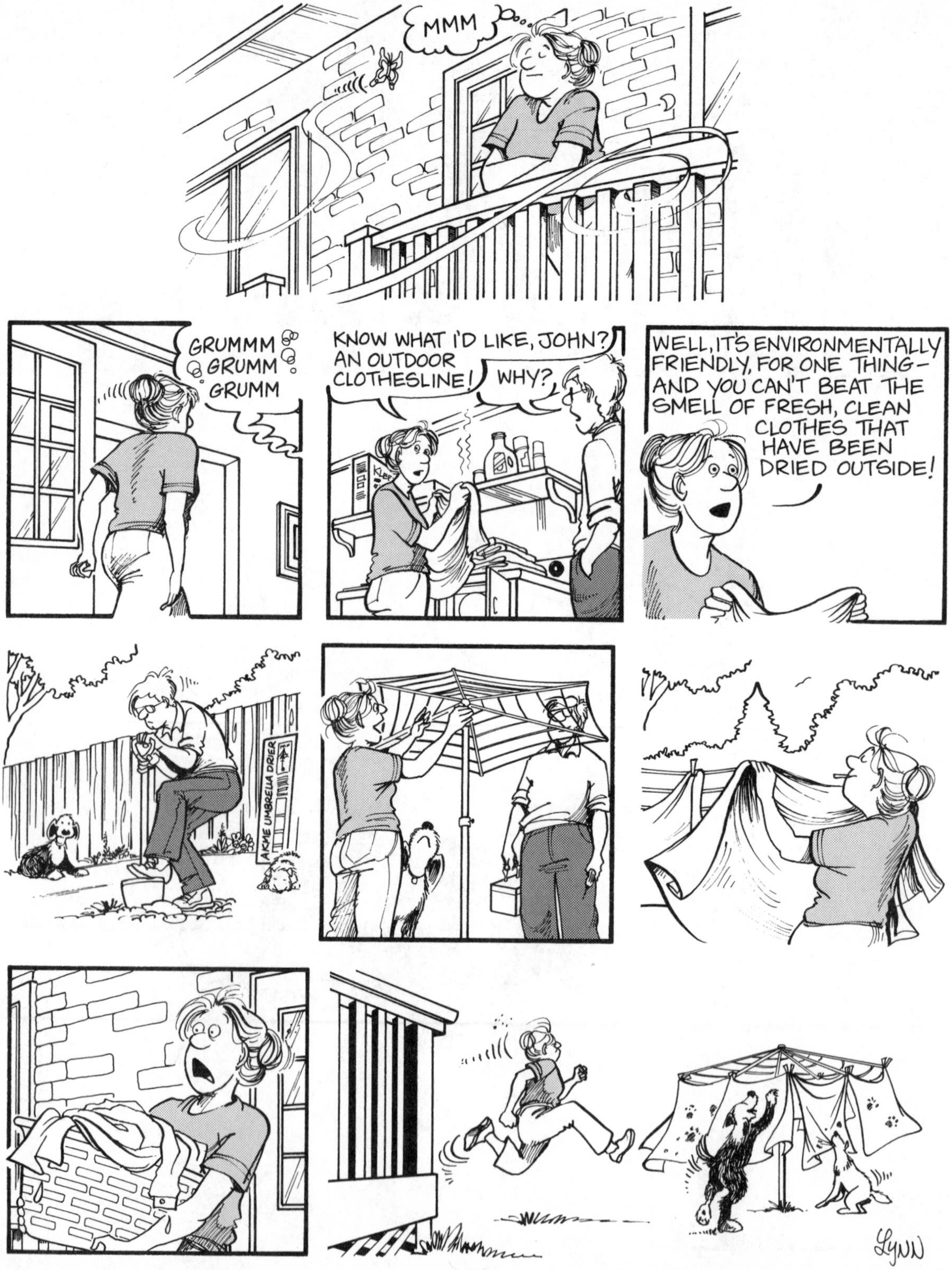
MMM
GRUMMM GRUMM GRUMM
KNOW WHAT I'D LIKE, JOHN? AN OUTDOOR CLOTHESLINE!
WHY?
WELL, IT'S ENVIRONMENTALLY FRIENDLY, FOR ONE THING- AND YOU CAN'T BEAT THE SMELL OF FRESH, CLEAN CLOTHES THAT HAVE BEEN DRIED OUTSIDE!
ACME UMBRELLA DRIER
LYNN

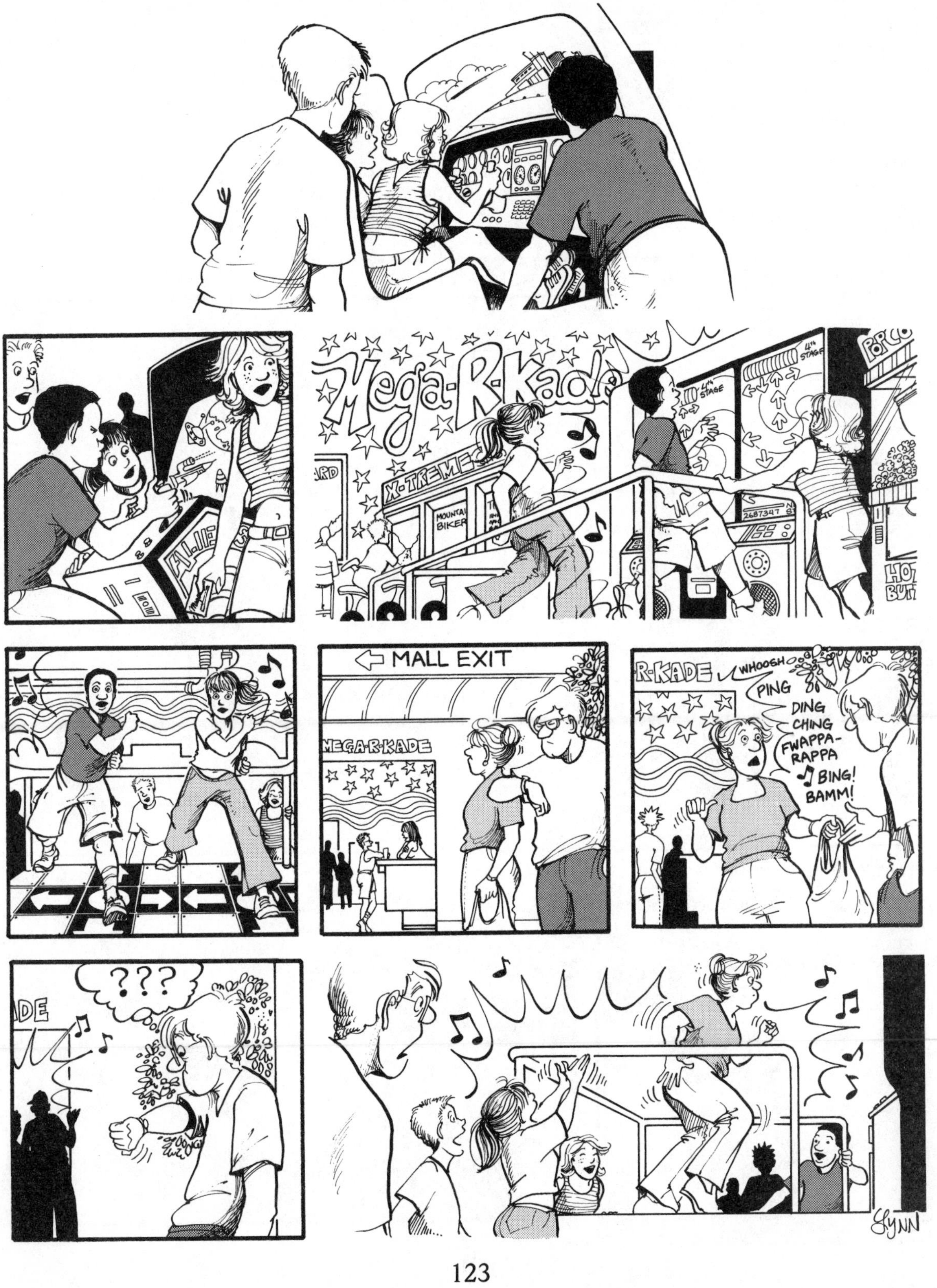
Mega-R-Kade
4th STAGE
X-TREME
MOUNTAIN BIKER
2687347
MALL EXIT
MEGA-R-KADE
R-KADE
WHOOSH
PING
DING
CHING
FWAPPA-RAPPA
BING!
BAMM!
???
LYNN

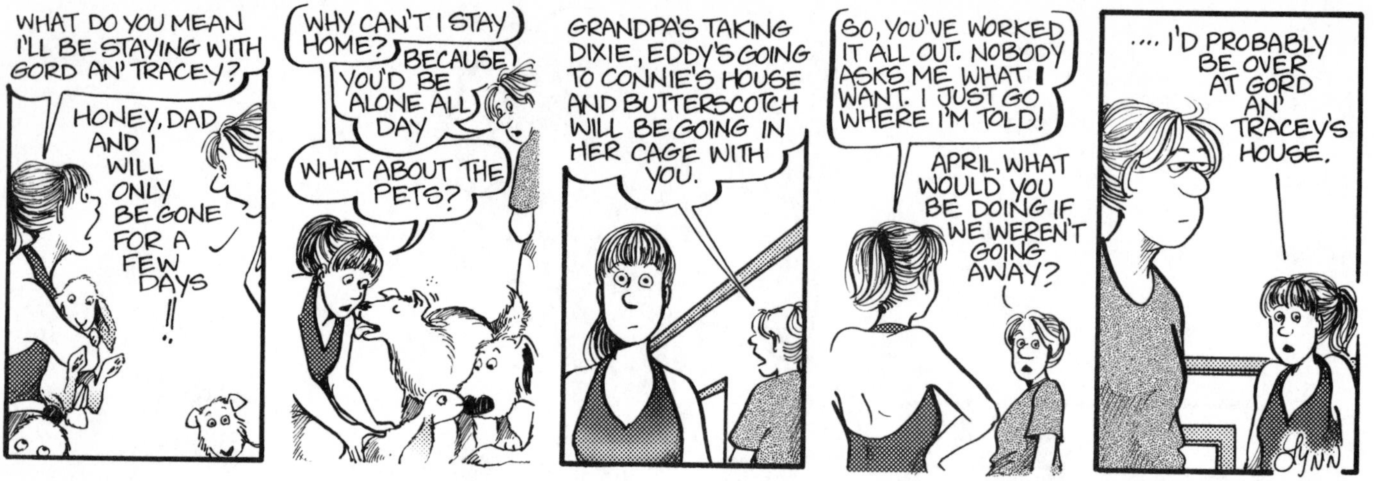
WHAT DO YOU MEAN I'LL BE STAYING WITH GORD AN' TRACEY?
HONEY, DAD AND I WILL ONLY BE GONE FOR A FEW DAYS !!
WHY CAN'T I STAY HOME?
BECAUSE YOU'D BE ALONE ALL DAY
WHAT ABOUT THE PETS?
GRANDPA'S TAKING DIXIE, EDDY'S GOING TO CONNIE'S HOUSE AND BUTTERSCOTCH WILL BE GOING IN HER CAGE WITH YOU.
SO, YOU'VE WORKED IT ALL OUT. NOBODY ASKS ME WHAT I WANT. I JUST GO WHERE I'M TOLD!
APRIL, WHAT WOULD YOU BE DOING IF WE WEREN'T GOING AWAY?
.... I'D PROBABLY BE OVER AT GORD AN' TRACEY'S HOUSE.
LYNN

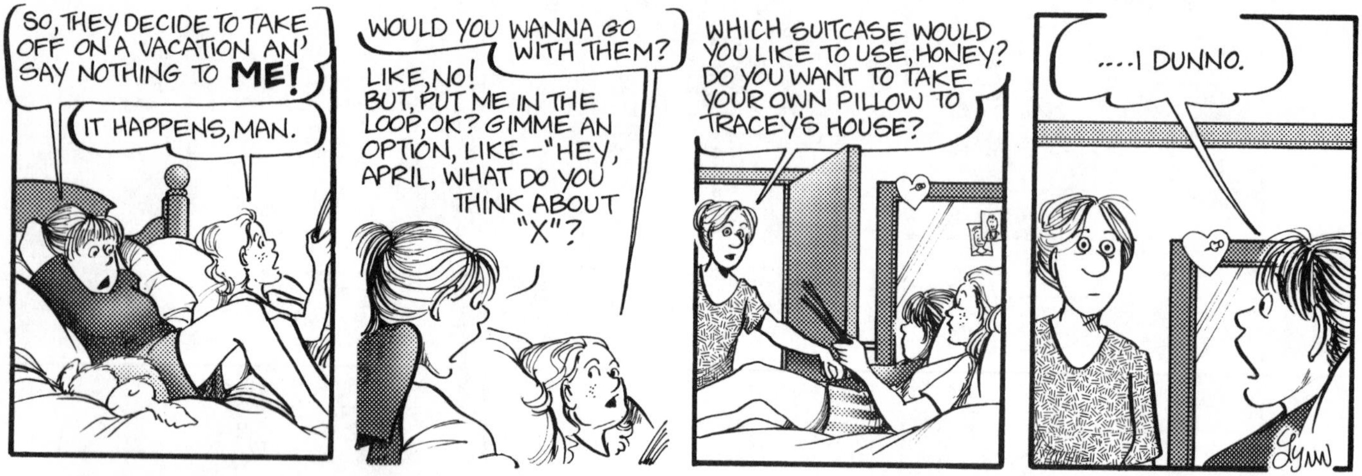
SO, THEY DECIDE TO TAKE OFF ON A VACATION AN' SAY NOTHING TO ME!
IT HAPPENS, MAN.
WOULD YOU WANNA GO WITH THEM?
LIKE, NO! BUT, PUT ME IN THE LOOP, OK? GIMME AN OPTION, LIKE—"HEY, APRIL, WHAT DO YOU THINK ABOUT "X"?
WHICH SUITCASE WOULD YOU LIKE TO USE, HONEY? DO YOU WANT TO TAKE YOUR OWN PILLOW TO TRACEY'S HOUSE?
....I DUNNO.
LYNN

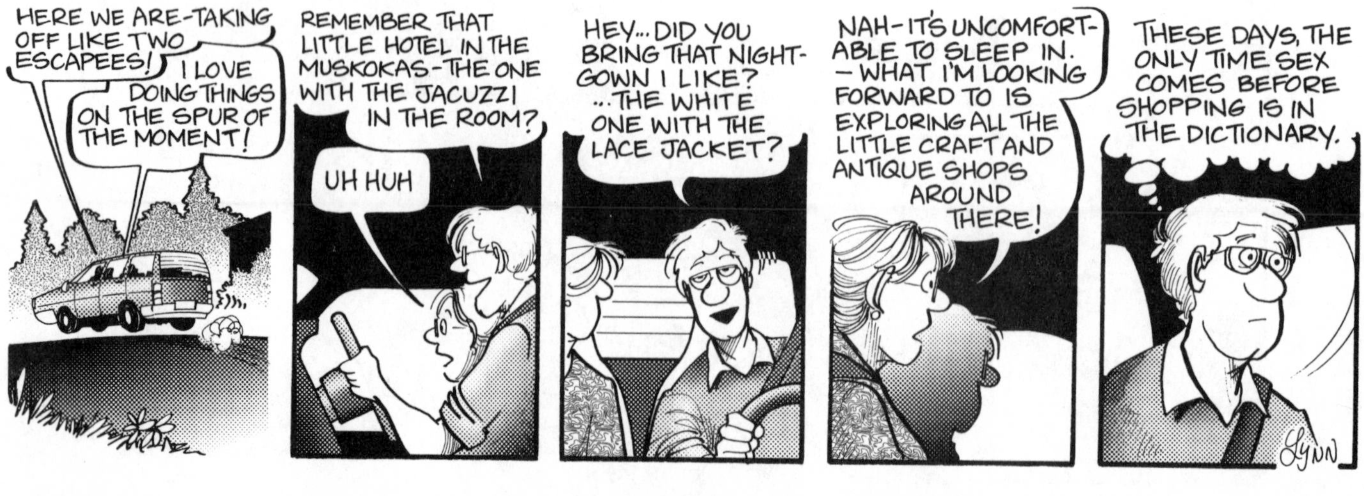
HERE WE ARE-TAKING OFF LIKE TWO ESCAPEES!
I LOVE DOING THINGS ON THE SPUR OF THE MOMENT!
REMEMBER THAT LITTLE HOTEL IN THE MUSKOKAS-THE ONE WITH THE JACUZZI IN THE ROOM?
UH HUH
HEY... DID YOU BRING THAT NIGHT-GOWN I LIKE? ...THE WHITE ONE WITH THE LACE JACKET?
NAH- IT'S UNCOMFORT-ABLE TO SLEEP IN. —WHAT I'M LOOKING FORWARD TO IS EXPLORING ALL THE LITTLE CRAFT AND ANTIQUE SHOPS AROUND THERE!
THESE DAYS, THE ONLY TIME SEX COMES BEFORE SHOPPING IS IN THE DICTIONARY.
LYNN

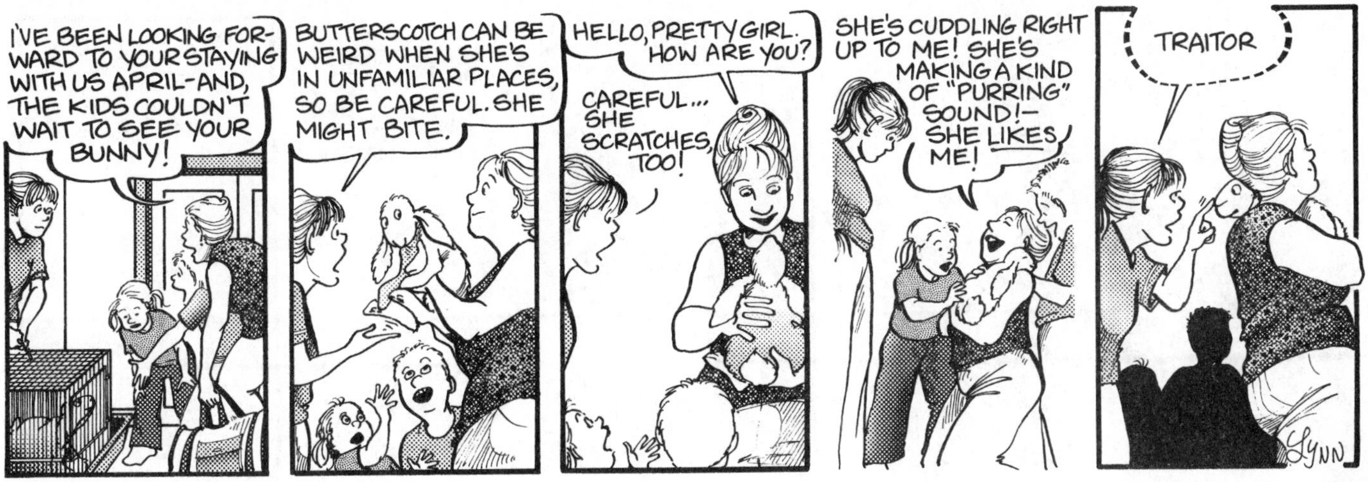
I'VE BEEN LOOKING FORWARD TO YOUR STAYING WITH US APRIL-AND, THE KIDS COULDN'T WAIT TO SEE YOUR BUNNY!
BUTTERSCOTCH CAN BE WEIRD WHEN SHE'S IN UNFAMILIAR PLACES, SO BE CAREFUL. SHE MIGHT BITE.
HELLO, PRETTY GIRL. HOW ARE YOU?
CAREFUL... SHE SCRATCHES, TOO!
SHE'S CUDDLING RIGHT UP TO ME! SHE'S MAKING A KIND OF "PURRING" SOUND!- SHE LIKES ME!
TRAITOR
LYNN

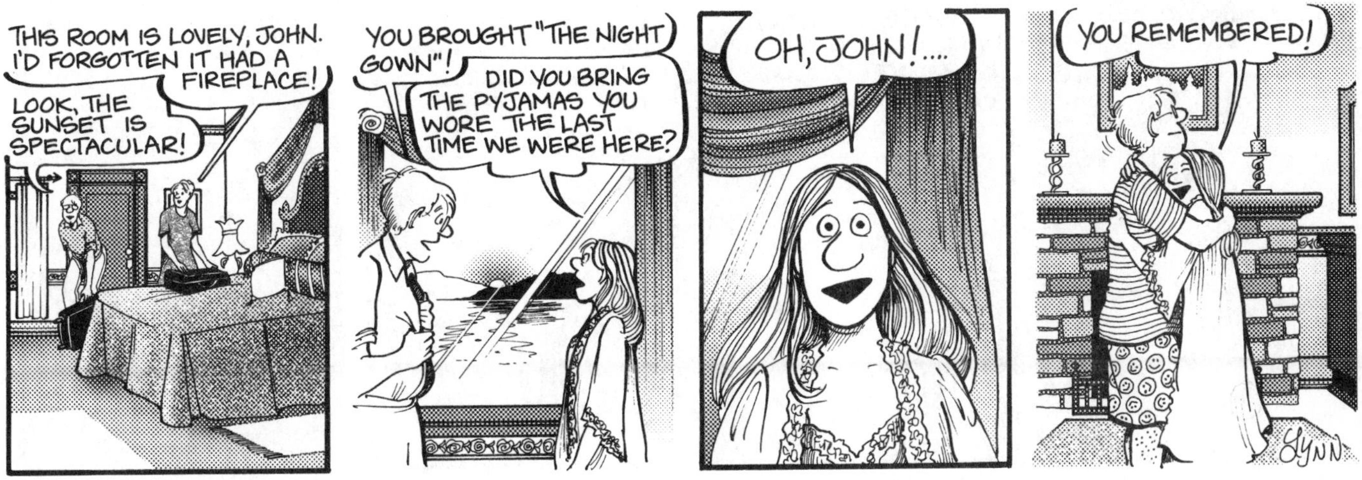
THIS ROOM IS LOVELY, JOHN. I'D FORGOTTEN IT HAD A FIREPLACE!
LOOK, THE SUNSET IS SPECTACULAR!
YOU BROUGHT "THE NIGHT GOWN"!
DID YOU BRING THE PYJAMAS YOU WORE THE LAST TIME WE WERE HERE?
OH, JOHN!....
YOU REMEMBERED!
LYNN

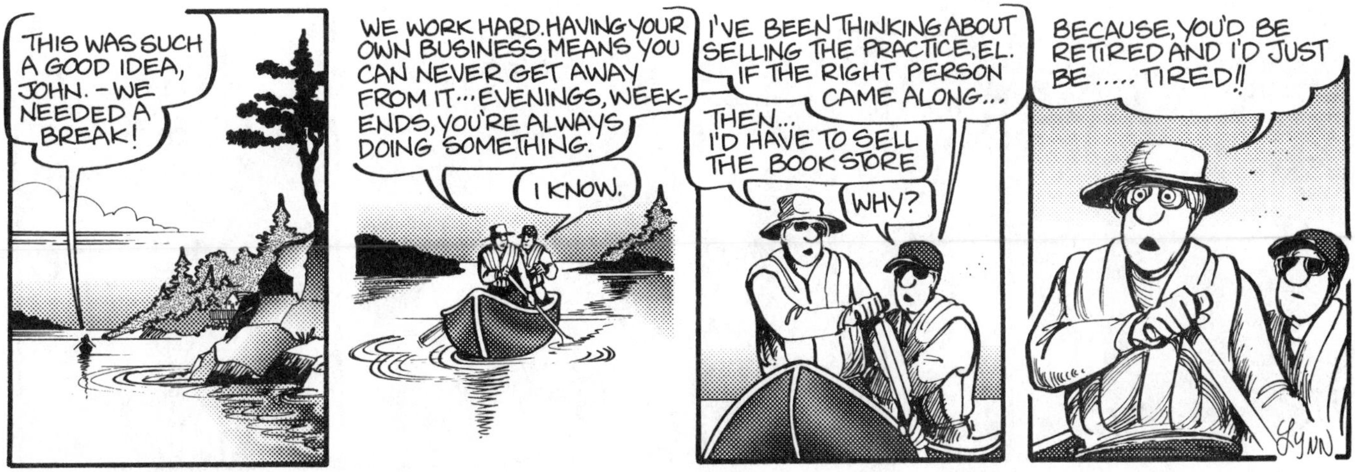
THIS WAS SUCH A GOOD IDEA, JOHN. - WE NEEDED A BREAK!
WE WORK HARD. HAVING YOUR OWN BUSINESS MEANS YOU CAN NEVER GET AWAY FROM IT... EVENINGS, WEEKENDS, YOU'RE ALWAYS DOING SOMETHING.
I KNOW.
I'VE BEEN THINKING ABOUT SELLING THE PRACTICE, EL. IF THE RIGHT PERSON CAME ALONG...
THEN... I'D HAVE TO SELL THE BOOK STORE
WHY?
BECAUSE, YOU'D BE RETIRED AND I'D JUST BE ..... TIRED!!
LYNN

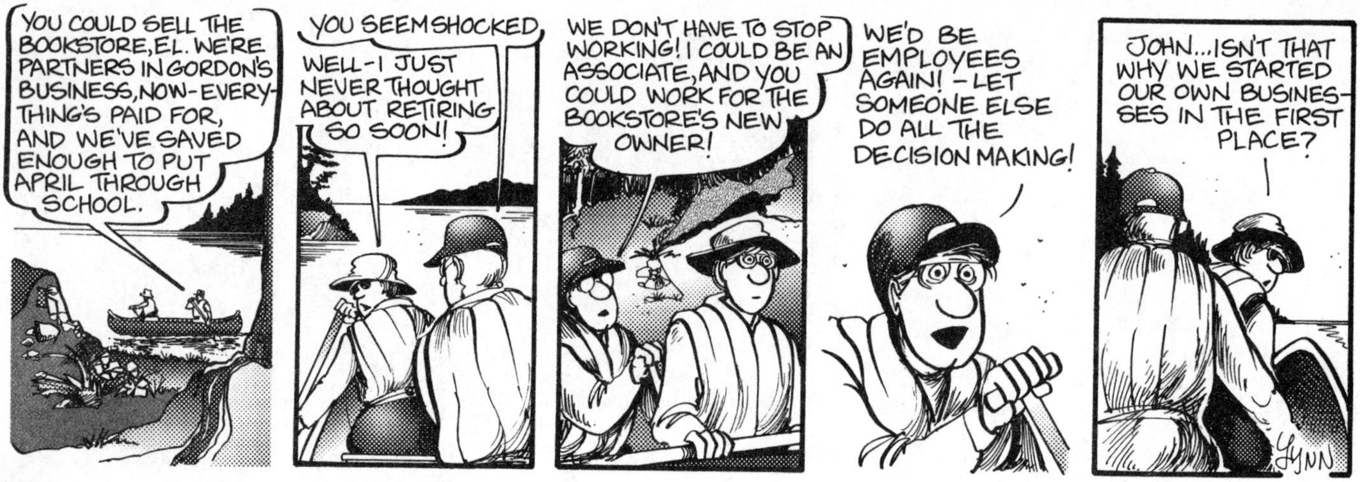
YOU COULD SELL THE BOOKSTORE, EL. WE'RE PARTNERS IN GORDON'S BUSINESS, NOW - EVERYTHING'S PAID FOR, AND WE'VE SAVED ENOUGH TO PUT APRIL THROUGH SCHOOL.
YOU SEEM SHOCKED.
WELL - I JUST NEVER THOUGHT ABOUT RETIRING SO SOON!
WE DON'T HAVE TO STOP WORKING! I COULD BE AN ASSOCIATE, AND YOU COULD WORK FOR THE BOOKSTORE'S NEW OWNER!
WE'D BE EMPLOYEES AGAIN! - LET SOMEONE ELSE DO ALL THE DECISION MAKING!
JOHN... ISN'T THAT WHY WE STARTED OUR OWN BUSINESSES IN THE FIRST PLACE?
LYNN

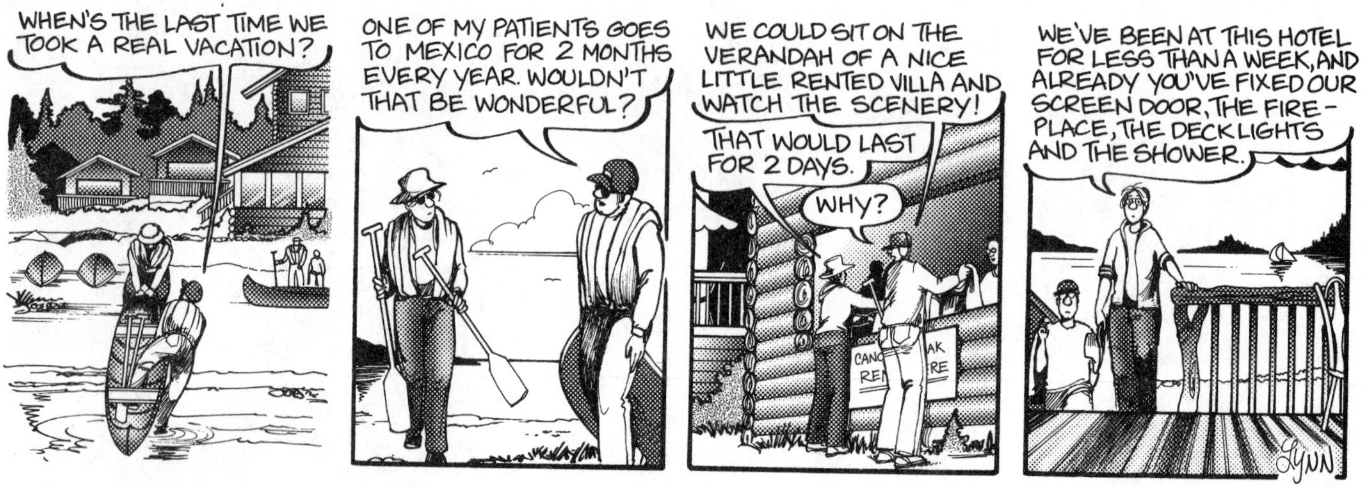
WHEN'S THE LAST TIME WE TOOK A REAL VACATION?
ONE OF MY PATIENTS GOES TO MEXICO FOR 2 MONTHS EVERY YEAR. WOULDN'T THAT BE WONDERFUL?
WE COULD SIT ON THE VERANDAH OF A NICE LITTLE RENTED VILLA AND WATCH THE SCENERY!
THAT WOULD LAST FOR 2 DAYS.
WHY?
WE'VE BEEN AT THIS HOTEL FOR LESS THAN A WEEK, AND ALREADY YOU'VE FIXED OUR SCREEN DOOR, THE FIREPLACE, THE DECK LIGHTS AND THE SHOWER.
LYNN

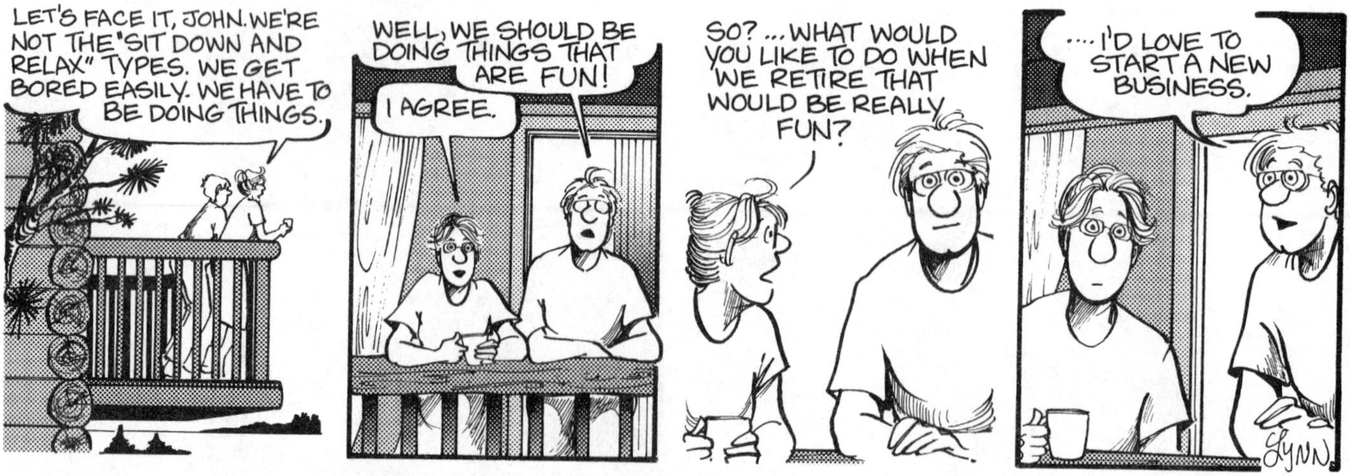
LET'S FACE IT, JOHN. WE'RE NOT THE "SIT DOWN AND RELAX" TYPES. WE GET BORED EASILY. WE HAVE TO BE DOING THINGS.
WELL, WE SHOULD BE DOING THINGS THAT ARE FUN!
I AGREE.
SO? ... WHAT WOULD YOU LIKE TO DO WHEN WE RETIRE THAT WOULD BE REALLY FUN?
.... I'D LOVE TO START A NEW BUSINESS.
LYNN

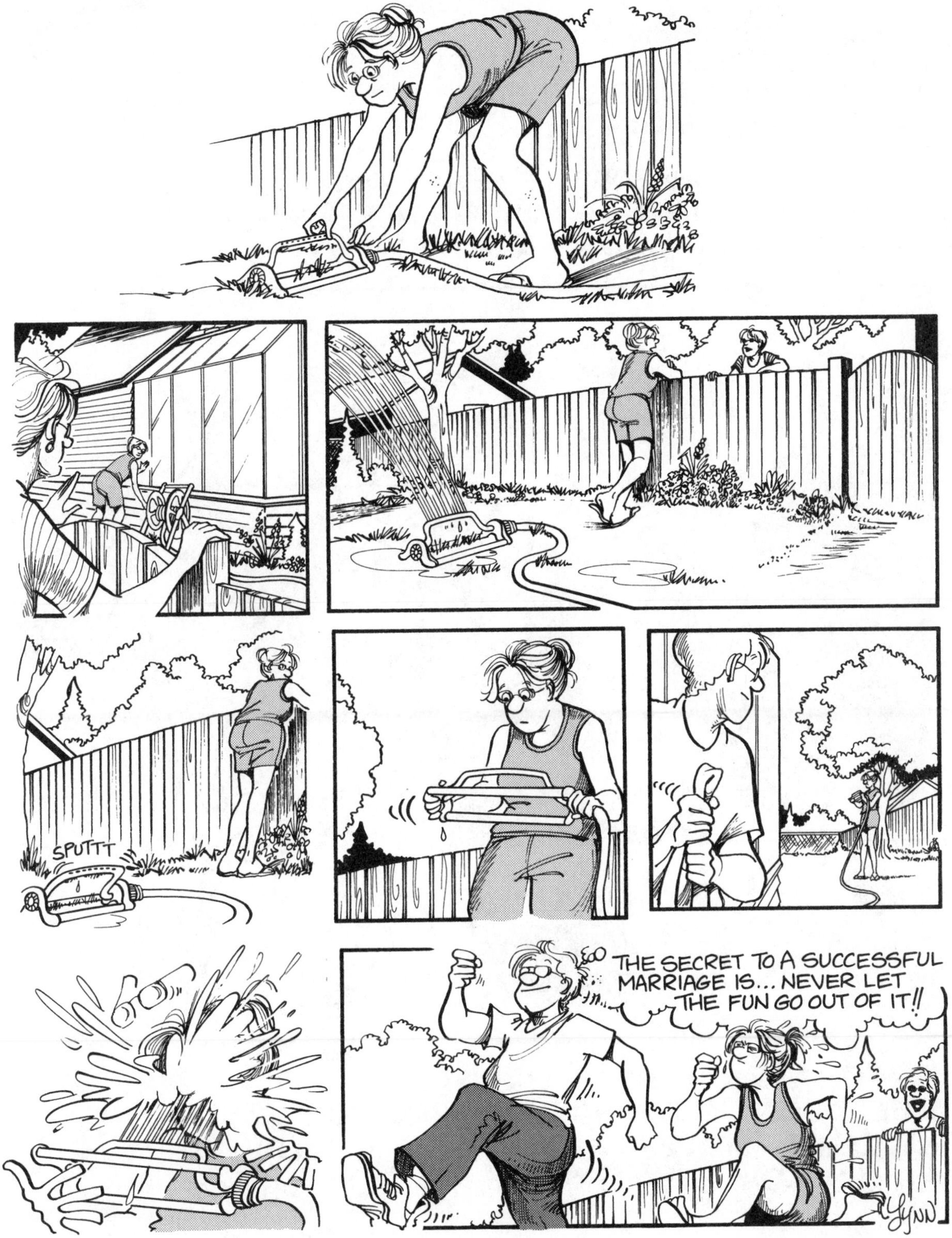
SPUTTT
THE SECRET TO A SUCCESSFUL MARRIAGE IS... NEVER LET THE FUN GO OUT OF IT!!
LYNN

SING, DARN-YA SING!
SING FER ALL YER WORTH IT!
EVEN IF THE WORDS FORGOT,
SING, DARN-YA SING.

I KNOW A MAN WHOSE LIFE WAS DOWN
HIS DOG, HE DIED - HIS WIFE LEFT TOWN
AN' ALL HE DID WAS PINE AND FROWN
NOW, SING DARN-YA SING!

DON'T MATTER IF YER YOUNG OR OLD
LIFE'S UPS AN' DOWNS, THEY WILL UNFOLD
YE CAN'T TURN BACK THE TIME, I'M TOLD
SO SING DARN-YA SINGGG!!

© LYNN 2004